The
Intentional
Teacher

Choosing the
Best Strategies
for Young Children's
Learning

Ann S. Epstein

Washington, DC

Ypsilanti, MI

naeyc®

National Association for the
Education of Young Children
1313 L Street NW, Suite 500
Washington, DC 20005-4101
202-232-8777 • 800-424-2460
www.naeyc.org

NAEYC Books

Chief Publishing Officer
Derry Koralek

Editor-in-Chief
Kathy Charner

Director of Creative Services
Edwin Malstrom

Managing Editor
Mary Jaffe

Senior Editor
Holly Bohart

Senior Graphic Designer
Malini Dominey

Associate Editor
Elizabeth Wegner

Editorial Assistant
Ryan Smith

Through its publications program, the National Association for the Education of Young Children (NAEYC) provides a forum for discussion of major issues and ideas in the early childhood field, with the hope of provoking thought and promoting professional growth. The views expressed or implied in this book are not necessarily those of the Association or its members.

A copublication of the National Association for the Education of Young Children and HighScope Press, a division of the HighScope Educational Research Foundation, 600 North River Street, Ypsilanti, MI, 48198-2898

Photo Credits

Cover photograph © NAEYC

Copyright © Ken Alswang: 129; Peggy Callaghan / © NAEYC: 36 (bottom left); Laura J. Colker: 125; Bob Ebbesen: 26, 33 (bottom), 38, 64, 93, 111, 115, 118, 119, 122, 160, 174; Sandra Lighter-Jones: 16; Julia Luckenbill: 5, 7, 32, 180; Elisabeth Nichols: 162; Karen Phillips: 37, 40, 51, 76, 80, 85, 95, 116, 145, 165, 185, 192, 205; Jude Keith Rose: 66, 168; Ellen Senisi: 23, 46, 49, 58, 71, 101, 105, 107, 136, 149, 154, 173, 184, 193, 213, 214, 221 (top and bottom), 223, 238; Kathy Sible: 86

Circular head shots:

Chapter 3: © Bob Ebbesen (child), © NAEYC (adult)
Chapter 4: © Ken Alswang (child), Susan Woog Wagner/© NAEYC (adult)
Chapter 5: © Ellen Senisi (child), © Ellen Senisi (adult)
Chapter 6: © Bob Ebbesen (child), © Ellen Senisi (adult)
Chapter 7: © Ellen Senisi (child), © Elisabeth Nichols (adult)
Chapter 8: © Ellen Senisi (child), © Ellen Senisi (adult)
Chapter 9: © Ellen Senisi (child), © Thinkstock (adult)
Chapter 10: © Bob Ebbesen (child), © Ellen Senisi (adult)

Credits

Cover design: Edwin Malstrom
Layout and production: Michael Brady Design
Consultant: Karen Nemeth
Copy editor: Stacey Reid
Indexer: Sherri Emmons

Library of Congress Control Number: 2014931261
ISBN: 978-1-938113-06-2
NAEYC Item 1120

About the Author

 Ann S. Epstein is the Senior Director of Curriculum Development at HighScope Educational Research Foundation in Ypsilanti, Michigan, where she has worked since 1975. Her areas of expertise include curriculum development, professional development, research and program evaluation, and child and program assessment. Dr. Epstein has published many books, articles, and curriculum manuals for professional and practitioner audiences in all areas of child development, including literacy, mathematics, social and emotional learning, social studies, and the creative arts. She is a consulting editor on several journals and has served as a member of numerous policy and program task forces. She has a PhD in Developmental Psychology from the University of Michigan and an MFA from Eastern Michigan University.

Acknowledgments

Writing a book as ambitious in purpose and wide ranging in scope as *The Intentional Teacher* entails the help and encouragement of many people. First and foremost, I want to thank Carol Copple, the former director of publications for NAEYC. A decade ago, as I groped my way toward defining the problem I took up in the first edition of this book and identifying a balanced solution, Carol and I engaged in lively discussions about the terms of the debate and how much we could push the field forward by honestly addressing our concerns and critics, as well as embracing the latest developments from research and practice. The first edition of *The Intentional Teacher* was consequently the most difficult but also the most rewarding book I had ever written. I owe that satisfaction to Carol's unflagging faith that I could do it and her support during the lengthy process of research, reflection, and creation.

The decision to write a second edition was so spontaneous and natural that it is impossible to say whether the idea originated with me or with NAEYC. It was gratifying that the first edition still inspired educators, and yet it was clear that it could continue to do so only with the incorporation of new child development research and an expansion of the content areas now covered in most early childhood curricula. Kathy Charner, NAEYC's current editor-in-chief for Books and Related Resources, embraced the idea of updating the book with enthusiasm and offered the full support I had come to expect and value from NAEYC. That support has included several others of NAEYC's talented editorial and production staffs: Derry Koralek, chief publishing officer; Mary Jaffe, managing editor; Holly Bohart, senior editor; Liz Wegner, associate editor; Ryan Smith, editorial assistant, and Eddie Malstrom and Malini Dominey, Creative Services staff.

A major reason for the simultaneous hurdles and satisfactions in writing both editions of this book was learning about each content area in greater depth, particularly the knowledge and skills that preschoolers acquire primarily through child- or adult-guided learning experience. As I explain in the preface, a primary source of information was a group of consultant researchers, curriculum specialists, teacher educators, and practitioners with expertise in one or more areas. In the first edition, these individuals responded to an informal written survey. In both editions, they also talked me through the issues in their domain and early childhood as a whole, and some reviewed manuscript drafts. Although I thank each of them here according to their main area of expertise, many offered ideas across developmental domains. Their excitement about the project helped sustain my own commitment to completing the comprehensive task I set for myself.

The following individuals played a significant role in one or both editions of the book. For help in framing the issues and synthesizing the general principles, my sincerest appreciation goes to Sue Bredekamp and Larry Schweinhart. In the area of language and literacy, I extend thanks to Linda Bevilacqua, Cathy Calamari, Jim Christie, Andee DeBruin-Parecki, Mary Hohmann, Leslie Morrow, Susan Neuman, Tomoko Wakabayashi, and Linda Ranweiler. Those who provided input on mathematics and science included Herb Ginsburg, Beth Casey, Rosalind Charlesworth, Doug Clements, Juanita Copley, Sue Gainsley, Charles Hohmann, Stuart Murphy, and Polly Neill. The consultants on approaches to learning, social and emotional learning, and social studies were Maury Elias, Betsy Evans, Alice Galper, Debbie Handler, Lilian Katz, Shannon Lockhart, Sherri Oden, Bob Pianta, Emily Vance, and Julie Wigton. Expertise in physical development and health came from Frances Cleland, Rhonda Clements, Joy Kiger, Rae Pica, Steve Sanders, Karen Sawyers, Sharon Schneider, and Phyllis Weikart. The creative arts chapter benefitted from the insights of Ursula Ansbach-Stallsmith, Chris Boisvert, Margaret Johnson, Beth Marshall, Kay Rush, and Eli Trimis. Their knowledge of theory and research, and the examples they provided from their own experience as practitioners, made everyone in this group a valued contributor. I thank them for their interest in the project and their insights into how intentional teachers can best help young children learn.

Finally, I thank the many teachers and young children with whom I have shared a love of learning in my nearly 50 years as a developmental psychologist and educator. My admiration for their dedication, enthusiasm, and delight in discovery was the inspiration for this book. Writing *The Intentional Teacher* has been a journey to learn more about how the human mind understands and appreciates our wonderful and complex world. I hope this second edition inspires a new generation of educators to carry on the essential and valuable work of teaching our children.

Contents

Why a Revised Edition of *The Intentional Teacher?*

When then-publications director Carol Copple encouraged me to write a book for NAEYC, I took that opportunity to explore the difficult but timely issue of how to purposefully and effectively teach content to young children, particularly preschoolers, since that was the age range of the most focused debate in the early childhood field and the main area of my own work. The result was the first edition of *The Intentional Teacher: Choosing the Best Strategies for Young Children's Learning.*

Since its initial publication in 2007, tens of thousands of educators have used the book to learn more about how young children develop and the best ways to support learning in the early years. Thus, when NAEYC and I explored the possibility of my writing another book, it seemed to be the perfect opportunity to publish a revised edition that would build on the shift in thinking that the first edition of *The Intentional Teacher* contributed to. Kathy Charner, NAEYC's new editor-in-chief of Books and Related Resources, was enthusiastic about the idea, and she and her staff seconded my proposals for updating and expanding the range of topics originally covered.

In the years following the publication of the first edition, the intentional teaching of content to young children has gained greater acceptance in the early childhood field. Yet questions remain about how to do so meaningfully and appropriately. The number of learning domains considered suitable for preschoolers has expanded. Whereas science previously was often grouped with mathematics, it has now come into its own as a subject of fascination for young children. Educators used to think that social studies was too abstract for preschoolers. Now they regard early childhood settings as small democracies in which young children experience diversity and learn about decision making—the underpinnings of social studies learning later in school. Early learning standards reflect these evolving ideas about the subject matter suitable in preschool. Likewise, this revised edition of *The Intentional Teacher* now includes a chapter on science (separate from mathematics) and one on social studies (separate from social skills and understandings).

In other domains, new research confirms what early educators have insisted all along. School readiness is not limited to preacademic subjects (such as literacy and mathematics) but is also highly dependent upon young children's social and emotional development. Consequently, in addition to the prevailing emphasis on academics, there has been a renewed interest in the creative arts. The arts engage children of all backgrounds—dual language learners, as well as those of different developmental and ability levels—in expressing themselves and communicating with others. Approaches to learning—*how* children learn—are also now considered an important area of the curriculum because these approaches affect the acquisition of knowledge and skills in all areas. This revised edition, therefore, includes a chapter on approaches to learning and expands the creative arts chapter to cover not only visual arts but also music, movement, and dramatic (or pretend) play.

Finally, developmental psychologists and early childhood educators simply know more now about how young children learn than when the first edition of *The Intentional Teacher* was published. Advances in our knowledge about early brain development, executive function, and emotional self-regulation, for example, provide insights into how we can effectively scaffold early learning by supporting children at their current level and gently extending their exploration and understanding. This new edition of *The Intentional Teacher* thus presents current research on all areas of child development and effective teaching practices that promote early learning.

The Origins of Intentional Teaching

Questions about the best ways to teach young children are hardly new. The subject waxes and wanes in public interest, but since 2001—and the passage of the federal No Child Left Behind Act (US Department of Education 2002)—it has received renewed attention in the popular press as well as in the professional literature. The controversy pits extreme interpretations of child-initiated learning (passive teacher) against adult-directed instruction (scripted lessons). Given the intensity of people's beliefs, with young children often caught in the middle, finding a balanced position is in everyone's best interests. Such a balance is also supported by research, as the Committee on Early Childhood Pedagogy concluded in its report *Eager to Learn*:

> Children need opportunities to initiate activities and follow their interests, but teachers are not passive during these [child]-initiated and directed activities. Similarly, children should be actively engaged and responsive during teacher-initiated and -directed activities. Good teachers help support the child's learning in both types of activities. (National Research Council 2000a, 8–9)

In the intermediate stance I advocate in both editions of *The Intentional Teacher*, both young children and adults have active roles in the learning process.

In addition to raising questions about *how* to teach young children, educators are also, as noted previously, continually rethinking *what* skills and content to teach them. Most are now convinced that certain learning domains not historically prominent in early childhood education, notably literacy and mathematics, are essential parts of the preschool curriculum. But they remain committed to also meeting young children's needs for meaningful social, physical, and artistic experiences. Above all, teachers want to interact with children in ways that respect the children's different personalities, varying levels of development, diverse cultural and linguistic backgrounds, and individual modes of inquiry and learning.

This book, then, is written for teacher educators and reflective practitioners—at all levels, from novice to veteran—who, in grappling with the issue of how and what to teach young children, seek a balance between extremes.

Drawing on the latest theory and research, *The Intentional Teacher* sets forth the rationale for a blended approach that combines what I call *child-guided learning* and *adult-guided learning* experiences. I use the term *child-guided learning* to refer to experience that proceeds primarily along the lines of children's interests and actions, although teachers often provide the materials and other support. The term *adult-guided learning* I use to refer to experience that proceeds primarily along the lines of the teacher's goals, although that experience may also be shaped by children's active engagement. For example, children develop ideas about sinking and floating or what they can do with clay through direct exploration and investigation (child guided), but to learn the names of letters requires that adults provide this information (adult guided). Regardless of whether children are engaged in child-guided or adult-guided experiences, however, teachers always play a vital educational role by creating supportive environments and scaffolding learning.

Further, a central premise of the book is that, from what we currently know about how young children learn, within each content area certain objectives or skills seem to be best acquired in the course of child-guided experience, whereas other objectives and skills seem to require adult-guided experience. But these two learning contexts are not mutually exclusive.

This Book's Objectives

My first objective in writing this edition of *The Intentional Teacher* is to take a reasoned and reasonable look at the instructional divide in early childhood education and attempt to find common ground. It's likely that not everyone will be satisfied with where I come out. But for those focused on when and how various approaches and strategies are most effective, the material I present here should help us move forward in this endeavor. This book is, therefore, intended to *encourage reflection about our principles and our practices.*

The second, related objective is to *broaden our thinking about appropriate early curriculum content and related teaching strategies.* The focus on early literacy, mathematics, and science is beneficial and essential, but we must still keep social-emotional, physical, and creative development in the curriculum, too. Children need to acquire important information and skills in *all* these content areas, with teaching strategies pegged to how they can best understand and apply what they learn. *How* young children learn (approaches to learning) is as important as *what* they learn. And in our diverse society, young children need to develop the flexibility to work with people from all backgrounds. Understanding and getting along with others comes not from abstract social studies lectures but from firsthand experiences with sharing activities and ideas in a warm, accepting classroom community.

Recent and past NAEYC publications, including the classic *Reaching Potentials: Appropriate Curriculum and Assessment for Young Children* (Bredekamp & Rosegrant 1992), emphasize that child-initiated learning never meant that teachers wouldn't teach:

> Good early childhood programs are, of necessity, highly organized and structured environments that teachers have carefully prepared and in which teachers are in control. The difference is that children are also actively involved and assume some responsibility for their own learning. (5)

While rejecting narrow drill-and-practice methods of teaching, NAEYC's curriculum position with regard to developmentally appropriate practices and accreditation standards stresses the importance of setting learning goals and providing experiences based not only on children's interests but also on other knowledge and skills teachers know that children need to develop. To enable children to achieve the desired outcomes, teachers must always keep these outcomes in mind and plan on that basis. Developmentally appropriate practice, as articulated by NAEYC, values the importance of play but also recognizes that teachers need to plan specific experiences for children so they can become literate by grade 3. Play and other contexts in which children explore and construct ideas are vital to their development and learning, but teachers must know how to enhance the quality of these child-guided experiences. Equally important, teachers must know what other experiences and instruction children require in order to learn to read and write and to acquire knowledge and skills in other learning domains.

My third and primary objective for *The Intentional Teacher* is to *provide specific ideas and strategies* for interacting with children in key subject areas. I attempt to address the question of what content learning is likely to occur from children's own activities and what content usually requires explicit adult instruction. As emphasized previously, these are not mutually exclusive. For example, children's solitary and peer play present many opportunities for teachers to promote learning, and teachers can plan explicit instructional activities based on the interests they observe in children's spontaneous play. Nevertheless, an awareness of what content young children are more likely to acquire through one mode or the other can give adults a leg up as they strive to be planful, thoughtful, and intentional in their teaching.

Basis for the Book

In the first edition of *The Intentional Teacher*, three sources of information provided the basis for the ideas regarding how and what children learn and how adults support that learning. First and foremost, I undertook an extensive review of the literature in the key subject domains covered in the earlier publication. The sources I consulted covered child development theory, the most current research of that time, and recommended preschool practices.

A second valuable resource was input from some 40 informants. These project consultants included researchers, curriculum specialists, teacher educators, and practitioners with expertise in one or more content areas. (Their names are listed in the Acknowledgments.) In an informal written survey, conversations, or both with these individuals, I asked them to identify which content children seemed most likely to acquire in a child-guided learning context and which in an adult-guided context. I also solicited concrete examples from the respondents' own research, training, and teaching experiences. At least two informants in each domain then reviewed the chapter drafts.

In undertaking the survey, I frankly anticipated some resistance to my request to classify the content areas of each domain into those primarily acquired in child-guided experience and those largely acquired in adult-guided experience. Yet all the consultants thought the question was legitimate and were intrigued by the challenge it posed. Also surprising was the amount of consensus in their responses. Despite occasional differences in degree, I was never faced with the dilemma of resolving diametrically opposed answers. So, while the material derived from the surveys requires further systematic research, input from these consultants nevertheless provided face validity for the book's basic premises.

The third source of information was the many decades of my own professional experience in curriculum development, staff training, and educational research. Trained as a developmental psychologist, I have never claimed to be an expert in every content area covered in this book. However, in addition to input from the literature and helpful colleagues, through my association with HighScope Educational Research Foundation I have access to a library of observational data, anecdotal notes, audiovisual records, and commentary from diverse research, training, and program sites around the country and abroad. These resources provided a rich archive from which to draw real-life examples.

This revised edition of *The Intentional Teacher* was informed by additional sources. I myself have written a book on social and emotional learning (Epstein 2009a) and developed a preschool mathematics curriculum (Epstein 2009b). In addition, I worked with a team of early childhood specialists to revamp an infant and toddler curriculum (Post, Hohmann, & Epstein 2011) and a preschool curriculum (Epstein & Hohmann 2012) based on the latest research in every domain covered in both editions of this book. In the intervening years, more states have incorporated early learning standards into educational policies, reflecting the collective wisdom of the field across a broad range of subject matter. Professional organizations in diverse content areas have begun to issue early learning standards. Finally, the Common Core State Standards (2012) for kindergarten in literacy and mathematics have also influenced thinking (if not always appropriately) on how preschool programs can prepare children to enter school ready to engage with these subjects.

Given these multiple data sources, I trust the information presented here is an accurate reflection of current thinking and agreement in the field—at least until the field discovers that our current thinking about a particular content area needs to be revised. Perhaps then a new generation of early childhood educators can write a third (or subsequent) edition of *The Intentional Teacher.*

Scope and Organization

As noted previously, this revised edition of *The Intentional Teacher* covers all domains of learning. Each area addressed in the first edition has been updated, and other domains have been added or expanded. Some topics partially addressed in one area now receive complete treatment in their own area. Notably, science, previously addressed under mathematics, is now a separate chapter. Likewise, social skills and understanding is now expanded and divided into three distinct chapters: approaches to learning, social and emotional learning, and social studies. The chapter on visual arts has been expanded to address creative arts in general. Some material from the chapter on physical movement has been moved to the creative arts chapter, while the retitled chapter on physical development and health recognizes the growing national concern with proper diet and appropriate exercise during the early years.

The Intentional Teacher: Choosing the Best Strategies for Young Children's Learning has two main parts. The first chapters lay out the meaning of intentional teaching. Chapter 1 introduces the concept of intentional teaching and explains the rationale for promoting children's learning of knowledge and skills through a blend of both child-guided and adult-guided experiences. These terms and others used throughout the book are defined and discussed, in particular *intentionality, teaching,* and *content.* Chapter 2 briefly reviews the best practices that underlie all developmentally based programs as teachers engage children with content across diverse areas of early learning. Although several references have been updated, the basic principles and practices discussed in this part of the book hold true to those presented in the first edition.

Next, curriculum chapters address the intentional teaching of content. They constitute the bulk of the book, exploring young children's learning and the intentional teacher's role in that learning in eight domains: Chapter 3, Approaches to Learning; Chapter 4,

Social and Emotional Learning; Chapter 5, Physical Development and Health; Chapter 6, Language and Literacy; Chapter 7, Mathematics; Chapter 8, Science; Chapter 9, Social Studies; and Chapter 10, Creative Arts. Each chapter begins with an overview of the area and then identifies the knowledge and skills children seem to acquire primarily through child-guided versus adult-guided learning experience.

Many practical teaching strategies are presented and illustrated with anecdotal examples. The teaching strategies I offer in these chapters certainly do not constitute a complete list. Based on your own personal observations and teaching experiences, you are encouraged to add your own strategies and to learn more about those recommended by other researchers and expert practitioners. Because this book intends to explore new ground, each chapter ends with a set of questions titled For Further Consideration. It is hoped that these questions will spur ongoing debate and inspire readers to continually examine their ideas and practices.

The book closes with Chapter 11, Reflections on Intentional Teaching. First, I offer general guiding principles of intentional teaching to help practitioners apply these ideas across all learning domains and situations. Finally, by sharing a series of thoughts and beliefs that crystallized in my own mind while writing both editions of this book, I invite you to consider the value of intentional teaching in imparting knowledge and skills to young children.

I hope *The Intentional Teacher* opens minds, inspires further research, and spurs the sharing of ideas. If you develop a renewed appreciation for content and think about how you can intentionally engage young children with the world of knowledge and skills in each domain, then I will have accomplished my objectives in writing this book. If you become a lifelong learner, continually seeking to discover what more the field has unearthed about the fascinating world of early childhood, then I will have achieved my goal in compiling this revised edition.

Chapter 1

Introducing Intentional Teaching

During choice time, Brandon, age 5, stands at the sink, soaking a sponge in water and squeezing it out. His teacher, Sam, kneels beside Brandon and imitates his actions.

"It's really heavy!" says Brandon after resoaking his sponge.

"I wonder what makes it so heavy," muses Sam.

"I think it's the water," answers Brandon.

"How can you tell?" asks Sam.

Brandon thinks for a moment, then squeezes out his sponge. "Hey! It's lighter now!" he says. "The water! The water makes it heavy!" Brandon fills and squeezes out his sponge again, as if to make sure. "Now you make yours lighter," he tells Sam.

"How?"

"Squeeze out the water."

Sam does so and hands the sponge to Brandon, who weighs one sponge in each hand. "There you go," he says to Sam. "Now your sponge is light like mine."

Sam then turns to Joon, age 4, and holds out two sponges. When Joon takes one of them, Sam pours water on to soak it. He puts the lighter, drier sponge in Joon's other hand and gestures to show that the wet sponge is heavier. Joon has watched his friend Brandon, so now he squeezes the wet sponge and weighs both sponges in his hands to feel the difference, smiling with his newfound understanding.

This book is about how an *intentional teacher*, like the one in this opening vignette and those that follow, acts with knowledge and purpose to ensure that young children acquire the knowledge and skills (content) they need to succeed in school and in life. **Intentional teaching** does not happen by chance. It is planful, thoughtful, and purposeful. Intentional teachers use their knowledge, judgment, and expertise to organize learning experiences for children; when an unplanned situation arises (as it always does), they can recognize a teaching opportunity and take advantage of it, too.

Intentional teaching means teachers act with specific outcomes or goals in mind for all domains of children's development and learning. "Academic" domains (literacy, mathematics, science, and social studies) as well as what have traditionally been considered early learning domains (social and emotional, cognitive, physical, and creative development) all consist of important knowledge and skills that young children want and need to master. Intentional teachers, therefore, integrate and promote meaningful learning in *all* domains. On the next page are additional examples of intentional teaching.

Katie, almost 5 years old, draws a picture of a garden with many different plants and asks her teacher, Sara, to write down the story that she will tell her about it. Katie hands Sara a small index card and a pencil and dictates, "This is a picture about my mommy's garden." Sara writes down exactly what Katie says.

"Now," says Katie, "I'm going to tell you the names of all the flowers and vegetables in my picture."

Sara points to the index card and asks Katie, "Do you think they will all fit?"

"Yes," says Katie, who begins to enumerate them as her teacher carefully writes down each one. As she nears the bottom of the card, Sara again asks Katie if she thinks all the names will fit. Katie reconsiders. "I think I need more room." She takes the card and turns it over.

"Should I continue writing on the back?" asks Sara.

"But then my mommy won't see it," worries Katie.

"Mmm, I wonder what else you could do so your mommy can see your whole story."

Katie thinks again, then gets another index card and tapes it to the bottom of the first one. "Will that be enough?" asks Sara. "There are still lots of plants left to name in your picture."

Katie tapes one more card on the bottom, and sets two more on the table "just in case." Katie continues to name the flowers and vegetables, and Sara writes down each one.

At small group time, the children in a 4s classroom make patterns with squares of colored construction paper. Hakim makes a complex pattern of red-blue-yellow-yellow, red-blue-yellow-yellow, red-blue-yellow-yellow. "Make one like mine," he tells his teacher, Maria. All the children stop to watch. Maria copies Hakim's pattern but on the third repeat she deliberately sets out pieces of red, blue, yellow, and then blue paper and waits for the children to notice. When no one comments, Maria says, "This doesn't look right. Can you help me?" The children offer different solutions until Hakim replaces the last blue square with a yellow one. "That's right!" the children chorus. "Now you make one for me to copy," Hakim says.

Intentional teaching requires wide-ranging knowledge about how children typically develop and learn. Teachers must have a repertoire of instructional strategies and know when to use a given strategy to accommodate the different ways that children learn and the specific content they are learning. At some times or for some content, children seem to learn best from *child-guided experience*—that is, they acquire knowledge and skills mainly through their own exploration and experience, including through interactions with peers. At other times and for other content, children learn best from *adult-guided experience*—that is, in planned situations in which their teachers introduce information, model skills, and the like. (See the box on p. 3.)

The division between child-guided learning and adult-guided learning is not a rigid one. Rarely does learning come about entirely through a child's efforts or only from adult instruction. Further, in any given subject, how a child learns will vary over time. For example, young children begin to build their speaking and listening skills through spontaneous and natural conversations (child-guided experience). However, they also learn syntax and vocabulary from the adults around them, and teachers often make a point of introducing new words and more complex sentence structures (adult-guided experience). Children also differ individually in how they like to learn. Some do a lot of

Child-Guided Experience + Adult-Guided Experience = Optimal Learning

An effective early childhood program combines both child-guided and adult-guided educational experiences. These terms do not refer to extremes—that is, child-guided experiences are not highly child controlled, nor are adult-guided experiences highly adult controlled. Rather, adults play intentional roles in child-guided experiences, and children have significant, active roles in adult-guided experiences. Each type of experience takes advantage of planned as well as spontaneous, unexpected learning opportunities.

	A child-guided experience . . .	
is **not** entirely child controlled (with the teacher passive)	proceeds primarily along the lines of children's interests and actions, with strategic teacher support	is **not** entirely adult controlled (with the children passive)
Example: Two children want to divide a bowl of beads equally between themselves.		
Child controlled: The teacher does not get involved, even when the children become frustrated and begin to get angry at each other over who has more.	**Child guided:** The children first try to make two equal piles by eyeballing them, but they are not satisfied. The teacher suggests they count their beads. They do so, and then move beads between their piles, count again, and make adjustments until the piles are equal.	**Adult controlled:** The teacher counts the beads and divides by two, telling the children how many beads each should take.
	An adult-guided experience . . .	
is **not** entirely child controlled (with the teacher passive)	proceeds primarily along the lines of the teacher's goals, but is also shaped by the children's active engagement	is **not** entirely adult controlled (with the children passive)
Example: The teacher wants the children to learn about shadows and their properties.		
Child controlled: The teacher allows the children to deflect the focus from shadows to a discussion of what toys they like to play with in the sandbox.	**Adult guided:** The teacher plans the lesson and leads a small group in exploring shadows with flashlights and a sheet. The teacher encourages and uses the children's input—for example, when they want to make animal shadows.	**Adult controlled:** The teacher controls all aspects of the lesson and delivers it to the whole group.

exploring and thinking through problems on their own, while others very readily ask adults for information or help. But every child learns in both ways.

Similarly, the division of content into the knowledge and skills that seem to be best acquired primarily through child-guided experience versus those acquired primarily through adult-guided experience is not an exact process. For example, most children acquire basic language abilities largely through child-guided learning experiences (albeit with linguistic input from the adults around them); they are born with the capacity to hear and reproduce the sounds of speech and are inherently motivated, as social beings, to communicate with others. By contrast, identifying the letters of the alphabet is something that children cannot do intuitively; as arbitrary creations of a culture, letter forms and their names clearly are learned through adult-guided experiences. In other content areas, however, the division is not so clear. Yet even in cases where assignment to "primarily child guided" or "primarily adult guided" is more difficult, knowledgeable educators can make a determination that most will agree on. I found this consensus in consulting with my expert informants for this book.

Although these divisions are imprecise, they are still useful when teachers are considering when and how to support children's own discovery and construction of knowledge, and when and how to convey content in teacher-guided activities and instruction. That consideration is a major focus of this book. *The Intentional Teacher* explores which type of learning experience is likely to be most effective for which content areas and what teachers can do to optimize learning in that mode. It also emphasizes that regardless of whether children engage in child- or adult-guided experience, teachers always play a vital educational role by creating supportive environments and using instructional strategies to help advance children's thinking to the next level.

In other words, both child-guided and adult-guided experiences have a place in the early childhood setting. It is not the case that one is good and the other bad, or that one is developmentally appropriate and the other not. Intentional teachers understand this and are prepared to make use of either or both in combination, choosing what works best for any given subject, situation, or child.

Intentional Teaching Terms

At the top of the class's daily message board, the preschool teachers write this sentence: "Who is here today?" Underneath it, they draw a column of stick figures, and next to each figure they write the name of a child or adult in the class. Each day the teachers indicate who is absent that day by making an erasable **X** in front of that name. Each day they also draw stick figure(s) and write the name(s) of any guest(s) who will be visiting the classroom. If the guest is free to play with the children, they draw a toy, such as a ball or block, in the stick figure's hand. If the guest is there only to observe, they draw a clipboard in the hand.

Each morning the class begins by talking about who is present and who is absent. Then, together with their teachers, the children count the number of stick figures with no mark (those in school) and those with a mark (those not in school). They also discuss any guest who is coming and whether that person will be a "player" or a "watcher." Sometimes the teachers ask the children to predict whether an absent child will be back the next day. For example, after informing the class that Tommy had left yesterday for a three-day vacation, a teacher asks, "Do you think he will be here tomorrow?"

Dual Language Learners

The term *dual language learners* refers to children who have a language at home that is other than English.

Later in the year, as the children's literacy skills begin to emerge, the teachers replace the stick figures with the children's names. Some children write their initial letters or their full names themselves. Children who are present make a mark (such as a dot, check, or plus sign) next to their names. Together with their teachers, they count how many names have a mark and how many are unmarked to determine how many are in school and how many are absent. One day, when Jose's mother will be coming to show the class how to make tamales, he tells a teacher, "Escriba a 'mi madre.'" "You want me to write that your mother is coming," she says, and draws a stick figure of a woman with a spoon in her hand. Jose nods. "Mi madre!" he repeats, and smiles.

These teachers are acting with intention throughout this daily activity. They take advantage of both child-guided and adult-guided experiences. The children are naturally curious about the members of their classroom community, and using a daily message board helps to solidify their social awareness. The children know everyone's name and notice when a peer is missing. The children come to this awareness on their own—that is, through child-guided experience. For adult-guided experience, the teachers use the children's knowledge and interest to introduce literacy ideas and processes—writing each person's name on the message board, encouraging those who are able to write themselves, and helping children who are dual language learners make connections between their home language and English.

They also embed mathematical concepts and processes into the activity. The children use classification (present versus absent; players versus watchers), counting (one-to-one correspondence of names and stick figures; tallying those with and without marks), and relational time concepts (yesterday, today, tomorrow). Children are asked to predict, a process used in science; later they will discover whether or not their prediction is confirmed.

Throughout the activity, adults and children engage in conversation, which enhances language development. Using adult-guided strategies, the teachers intentionally introduce new vocabulary words, such as *present* and *absent*. And the natural flow of talk, in which adults capitalize on the child-guided desire to communicate, boosts fluency.

Earlier in this chapter I introduced the concept of the intentional teacher and the organizing idea of child- versus adult-guided experience using three terms that reappear throughout the book: *intentional, teaching,* and *content*. Because they play such a key role in understanding the chapters that follow, let me clarify now how I define them and how they fit together.

The Meaning of *Intentional*

To be **intentional** is to act purposefully, with a goal in mind and a plan for accomplishing it. Intentional acts originate from careful thought and are accompanied by consideration of their potential effects. Thus, an intentional teacher aims at clearly defined learning objectives for children, employs instructional strategies likely to help children achieve the objectives, and continually assesses progress and adjusts the strategies based on that assessment. The teacher who can explain *why* she is doing what she is doing is acting intentionally—whether she is using a strategy tentatively for the first time or automatically from long practice, and whether it is used as part of a deliberate plan or spontaneously in a teachable moment.

Effective teachers are intentional with respect to many facets of the learning environment, beginning with the emotional climate they create. They deliberately select inviting equipment and materials that reflect children's individual interests, skills, needs, cultures, and home languages, and they put these in places where children will notice and want to use them. In planning the program day or week, intentional teachers choose which specific learning activities, contexts, and settings to use and when. And they choose when to address specific content areas, how much time to spend on them, and how to integrate them. All these teacher decisions and behaviors set the tone and substance of what happens in the classroom.

Intentionality refers especially to how teachers interact with children. Pianta defines *intentionality* as "directed, designed interactions between children and teachers in which teachers purposefully challenge, scaffold, and extend children's skills" (2003, 5). Berliner (1987, 1992) emphasizes that effective teaching requires intentionality in interactions with children, with an understanding of the expected outcomes of instruction. He summarizes research on the relationship between classroom environment and learning outcomes in a list of elements characteristic of good intentional teaching:

- **High expectations**—When teachers *expect* children to learn, they do.
- **Planning and management**—While guiding the class toward defined and sequenced learning objectives, teachers remain open to children's related interests.
- **Learning-oriented classroom**—Children, as well as teachers, value the classroom as a place to learn.
- **Engaging activities**—Teachers connect activities to children's experiences and developmental levels.
- **Thoughtful questioning**—Teachers pose questions to get insight into children's thought processes and stimulate children's thinking.
- **Feedback**—Effective evaluative feedback focuses on children's learning rather than merely offering praise or disapproval.

The Meaning of *Teaching*

Teaching is the knowledge, beliefs, attitudes, and especially the behaviors and skills teachers employ in their work with learners. An effective teacher is competent in three areas:

- **Curriculum**—the knowledge and skills teachers are expected to teach and children are expected to learn, and the plans for experiences through which learning will take place. Effective teachers know the subject matter covered in their program's curriculum and how children typically develop with regard to each domain addressed. Efforts to specify what preschool children need to know and be able to do have been made by states in their early learning standards and by specialized professional organizations such as the International Reading Association (IRA; 2005; IRA & NAEYC 1998), National Association for Sport and Physical Education (NASPE; 2009a), Head Start (US Department of Health and Human Services 2013), World-Class Instructional Design and Assessment (WIDA; 2014), and the National Council of Teachers of Mathematics (NCTM; 2000; NAEYC & NCTM 2010). Standards for kindergarten, including the Common Core State Standards (now adopted by the majority of states) and the Next Generation Science Standards, may also affect future standards developed or revised for prekindergarten programs (National Governors Association Center for Best Practices & Council of Chief State School Officers 2010; Next Generation Science Standards 2013).

- **Pedagogy**—the ways teachers promote children's development and learning. Effective teachers ensure that children experience a learning environment that promotes their development in all areas of the curriculum. To begin, teachers establish a nurturing environment in which children are healthy and safe and feel secure. Beyond this basic responsibility, teachers respect differences in children's preferences, cultures, home languages, and so on; are inclusive with respect to special needs; partner with families; and use instructional approaches and strategies effectively to support children's learning and thinking. The essential elements of pedagogy are highlighted in the standards for teaching and for teachers in *NAEYC Early Childhood Program Standards and Accreditation Criteria: The Mark of Quality in Early Childhood Education* (NAEYC 2007) and in the *Basics of Developmentally Appropriate Practice* books for teachers of children ages 3 to 6 and teachers of kindergartners (Copple & Bredekamp 2006; Phillips & Scrinzi 2013, respectively). A quarter of a century of research, summarized in the panel report *Eager to Learn: Educating Our Preschoolers* (National Research Council 2000a), establishes that how adults interact with children is a significant determinant of developmental outcomes for children. More than any other variable, instructional interactions define a program's quality and its impact on children's intellectual and social development (Dombro, Jablon, & Stetson 2011; Pianta 2003).

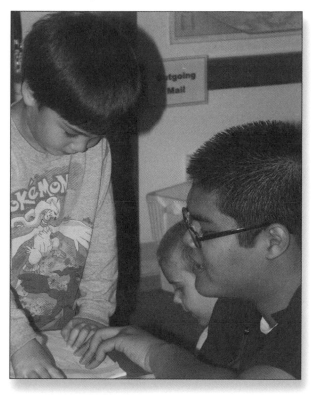

- **Assessment**—the ongoing process of determining how children are progressing toward expected outcomes of learning and development, using multiple sources of information. Assessment can take many forms, from observational measures and portfolios of children's work to standardized tests and instruments. Effective teachers know how to collect, administer, interpret, and apply the results of assessment as they plan learning experiences for individual children and the class as a whole, and to monitor individual and group progress. Teachers share assessment results with parents to ensure home and school work together to support children's early development. (Assessment also is increasingly used for program and teacher accountability.) Some assessments are dictated by administrators or policy makers, and then the information is collected by teachers or outside specialists; other assessments are developed by individual teachers to fit their classroom needs. Guidelines for the appropriate assessment of early learning are defined in a joint position statement of NAEYC and National Association of Early Childhood Specialists in State Departments of Education (NAEYC & NAECS/SDE 2003) and in the assessment of child progress standard of *NAEYC Early Childhood Program Standards and Accreditation Criteria* (2007).

The Meaning of *Content*

Content is the substance or subject matter that teachers teach and is, therefore, the object of children's learning. For the purposes of this book, *content* refers more specifically to the knowledge (certain vocabulary and concepts) and skills in an area of learning:

- **Vocabulary**—the language used in a content area. For example, vocabulary in the area of language and literacy includes the names of the letters in the alphabet as well as words such as *alphabet, book, author,* and *rhyme.* Social and emotional development vocabulary includes words for feelings *(angry, happy)* and the language used to invite someone to play or to ask someone to stop throwing blocks. Visual arts vocabulary includes descriptors for color, shape, and texture, as well as names of artists, genres, and techniques.

- **Concepts**—the important ideas or principles within a content area, its "big ideas." For example, basic language and literacy concepts include that a relationship exists between spoken and written language, that in English books are read from front to back, and that in English print on a page is read from top to bottom and left to right. In social and emotional development, basic conflict resolution concepts include that it is better to solve problems by talking than hitting and that solutions should be fair to everyone. Visual arts concepts include ideas such as realism versus abstraction, and how cultural beliefs and values are represented through art.

- **Skills**—the specific abilities needed within a domain of learning and development. In language and literacy, reading skills include recognizing the component sounds in words and the letters of the alphabet from their written shapes. In the area of social and emotional development, conflict resolution skills include expressing feelings, listening to others, and negotiating a compromise. Examples of visual arts skills are manipulating a paintbrush to make art, and observing and comparing the work of two artists.

Content and Dual Language Learners

Make content easier and more meaningful for dual language learners by using their home languages where possible and by using nonverbal cues, gestures, and visuals to help them understand what you are saying in English.

Of course, there are knowledge (vocabulary and concepts) and skills that cut across one or more content areas, and early childhood education strives to maximize such broad and general learning. Because this book is organized by content area, however, the challenge for the intentional teacher is to identify the "what" and "how to teach it" in each content domain. But, while this book looks at content in area-specific ways, in the classroom the cumulative result of a comprehensive and integrated education should be developing children's total vocabulary, enhancing their overall conceptual understanding of the world, and expanding their full repertoire of skills.

The field of early childhood education has been sometimes accused of being anti-content. If the accusation has some truth to it, it's partly because of carryover from a time when much of the emphasis in early education was on sharing, cooperating, and playing nicely to help children as they transitioned from the home to a group setting. It's also partly developmental appropriateness misinterpreted, typified by well-meaning teachers who feel they cannot display the alphabet because it pressures young children to memorize letters.

If early childhood education has been criticized for neglecting content, primary-grade education has been accused of going the opposite way and ignoring children's social and emotional development (and, in response to current academic pressures, of reducing support in other domains such as physical development and the arts). This tension prompted NAEYC and the NAECS/SDE to develop a joint position statement on curriculum for young children through age 8 (NAEYC & NAECS-SDE 1991, 2003). The 1991 statement aimed to address two basic problems of the time: "the 'early childhood error' (inadequate attention to the content of the curriculum) and the 'elementary error' (overattention to curriculum objectives, with less attention to the individual child)" (Bredekamp & Rosegrant 1992, 3).

A curriculum that meets the needs of young children is comprehensive (NAEYC & NAECS/SDE 2003):

> [It] encompasses critical areas of development including children's physical well-being and motor development; social and emotional development; approaches to learning; language development; and cognition and general knowledge; and subject matter areas such as science, mathematics, language, literacy, social studies, and the arts (more fully and explicitly for older children). (2)

Each of these content areas has its own vocabulary, concepts, and skills for children to master. Because young children typically are encountering these content areas for the first time, they need their teachers to "set the foundation for later understanding and success" (NAEYC 2001, 19).

❁   ❁   ❁

"If all children are to succeed, teachers need to create an effective balance between learning that's child initiated and learning that is guided by adults" (Hyson 2000, 60). This book advocates a balanced approach, acknowledging that children learn through both child-guided and adult-guided experiences and that teachers are most effective when they are able to choose among and apply any of a range of teaching approaches without going to the extreme of either type of experience. As shown in the box on page 3, that approach is neither laissez-faire, in which all learning is left to the child, nor entirely top-down, in which the child is seen as an empty vessel into which the teacher pours knowledge. Interactions between teacher and children are neither overly teacher directed and didactic nor overly child centered and left to chance. Instead, intentional teaching means systematically introducing content, in all domains, using developmentally based methods and respecting children's modes of learning.

Naturally, there will be individual differences in how children learn most effectively. What some children discover on their own or through interactions with peers, other children will encounter only through direct adult intervention. Therefore, the suggestions offered in this book cannot substitute for teachers' observing and knowing the experiences and learning styles of the individual children in their programs.

At present, the early childhood field lacks a label for such a balance between child-centered and adult-directed approaches. *Eclectic* seems too random. *Combination* and *middle-of-the-road* are vague. In this book, I have suggested a term that is not original to me but one that is useful in this context, I believe. I suggest *intentional teaching*—because it indicates that teachers play a thoughtful role during both child- and adult-guided learning. Whatever label we use, it is important that the words convey our commitment to child development principles as well as to educational content.

Defining and following such a balanced approach may help us to get past polarizing debates and arrive at more effective practice. Further, this approach will inspire us to continually update our knowledge and reflect on our practices—that is, to be intentional teachers whose methods ensure successful outcomes for young children.

For Further Consideration

1. What terms other than *intentional teaching* might describe the kind of thoughtful, multifaceted instruction advocated in this book?

2. In what contexts does *child-guided* experience seem to predominate? In what contexts does *adult-guided* experience seem to predominate? In what situations do adults themselves learn primarily through their own efforts, and in what situations is their learning primarily guided by others? How can understanding adult modes of learning inform how we intentionally teach children?

3. How can the early childhood field reverse a common perception that it is anti-content?

4. How can the early childhood field demonstrate to the public that content for young children should cover all areas of learning, not just literacy, mathematics, science, and social studies?

5. How can intentional teaching help to support *all* young learners, including children who are dual language learners and those with special needs?

6. What strategies, in addition to writing books such as this, can the early childhood field employ to encourage the adoption of intentional teaching?

7. What can you as a beginning or experienced teacher do to guarantee that intentionality has a place in your daily interactions with children?

Chapter 2

Best Practices for Intentional Teaching

"The children are really enjoying running in the sunshine at outside time now that we're over the rainy winter," says Simon to his preschool coteacher. "I wonder if there's a way to also make them aware of light and shadow as the days get brighter and the trees leaf out." The next day, as the children chase one another around a wide oak tree, Simon comments that sometimes he sees their shadows and other times he doesn't. "Why do you suppose that is?" he asks.

"You have to move," suggests Vinod. "It won't make a shadow if you stand still."

"Uh, uh," says Natalie, standing in place. "I'm not moving and I see my shadow."

"I know," says Mikhail, "You have to stand away from the tree."

Simon moves away from the tree and stands facing into the sunlight. The children comment that he doesn't have a shadow, but Sunil, who is facing Simon (with the sun behind him), says excitedly, "Look! I have a shadow."

Some children stand alongside Simon, others alongside Sunil. They observe which group does or does not have shadows but can't explain why. Then Simon squints and points up at the sky. "Maybe the sun has something to do with it," he muses.

Natalie says excitedly, "When you see the sun, you don't see your shadow."

Mikhail hides behind the tree. "I can't see the sun or my shadow," he observes.

The children try standing in different positions relative to the sun, each time noting whether or not they make a shadow (except Vinod, who continues to experiment with moving and keeping still). Over the next several days, the children notice whether the tree trunk and its branches make shadows and how the shadows change as more leaves grow out. The following week, on a cloudy day, they comment that there are no shadows at all! Their growing interest in light and shadow also leads Simon and his coteacher to plan a small group activity using flashlights and a hanging sheet.

Simon is being an intentional teacher. He thinks about a content area (the natural world—an aspect of science) and how he can build on the children's spontaneous delight in being outdoors on a sunny day to also focus their attention on light and shadow in the environment. He makes casual observations, in the context of their play, to draw the children's attention to the topic. He asks them to explain why shadows do and do not appear, and lets the children evaluate—and sometimes contradict—one another's ideas. When the children are still puzzled, he doesn't give them an answer but gently guides them to consider another line of reasoning (the position of the sun) as they continue to make sense of what they observe. Simon takes advantage of the many opportunities the outdoor learning environment provides for learning about light and shadow (trees, the sun, clouds, and movement). He also plans a small group experience so the children can explore other materials (flashlights and sheets) as he builds on their curiosity about a scientific phenomenon.

Simon's teaching exemplifies early childhood education **best practices.** That is, he has a goal in mind for the children's learning, he identifies interesting and open-ended materials (outdoors and in the classroom) that support learning, he encourages children to explore the materials and concepts at their own developmental level, he interacts with them to support and extend their discoveries, he encourages children to interact with and learn from one another, and he provides opportunities for them to generalize their ideas across different situations and with varied materials. These practices are based in child development theory, educational research, and the reflections of generations of teachers. We use them because we know they work. We value them because they reflect common ideals and beliefs about human development. And we advocate their use in every classroom, regardless of the curriculum.

With the increased focus on early childhood programs in recent years has come increased professional and public concern about teacher quality. Some policy makers have called for "teacher-proof" methods of instruction, and some curriculum developers have responded with packaged or scripted lessons that can be implemented with little training and almost robotic consistency. Understandably, many educators resist the idea that good teaching can be so mechanical or superficial: "Teachers must have a deep understanding of how children learn, as well as what is important for children to learn" (Espinosa 1992, 163).

Ready-to-use resources should not be dismissed out of hand, however, if the curriculum is designed with an understanding of how young children learn and it provides opportunities for both child and teacher input. Such materials can offer a welcome and useful starting point for the novice teacher or even for an experienced teacher approaching an unfamiliar subject area. But they do not relieve teachers of the need to be intentional. Teachers must still decide how to apply the curriculum to individual and groups of children. And with time and experience, most teachers will be able to bring more of their own creativity to teaching.

An Overview of Best Practice

Best practice requires us to think about what we are doing in the classroom and how it will foster children's development and produce real and lasting learning—the definition of intentional teaching. Much has been said about what constitutes best practice in early childhood education, the principles underlying it, and how to measure the implementation of it (particularly Copple & Bredekamp 2009; Hyson 2003; NAEYC 2007). These discussions constitute too much material to be covered thoroughly here. What this chapter does provide, however, is an overview of how intentional teachers use these best practices in the classroom.

Intentional teachers apply best practice principles in six key areas of responsibility. One of them, planning *curriculum* (the content of learning), is dealt with extensively in Chapters 3–10. Three others—structuring the physical learning *environment, scheduling* the program day, and *interacting* with children—concern how teachers implement the curriculum in the classroom. These are each reviewed in the sections that follow, comprehensively but through the focused lens of intentional teaching.

The remaining two areas—building relationships with *families* and *assessing* children's development—are also reviewed in this chapter but are covered even more nar-

How the Learning Environment Affects the Complexity of Children's Play

When teachers set up their classrooms, they commonly worry about matters of health and safety. Less obvious, but no less true, is that creating a safe and secure learning environment can also affect how children play in the setting. Children's feelings of security and confidence in a space affect the complexity and length of their play, as noted by Tegano and colleagues (1996):

> When children are in a large space, they feel small in comparison to their surroundings, and time seems to pass more slowly for them. When children are in a playhouse, in a play yard tent, or under a table, they feel large in comparison to their surroundings, and attention seems to be sustained. . . . Perception of the size of the space in which children play affects the quality of the play and thus the potential for learning. Altering space to make children feel large in relation to their environment may enable children to enter complex play more quickly and to continue complex play for longer periods of time. (136, 138)

rowly with regard to their intentional aspects. The section on families discusses communicating with children's families about the program's balance between adult-guided and child-guided experiences, as well as encouraging families to also be intentional in providing their children with both kinds of experience outside the classroom. With respect to assessment, the focus in this chapter is on using results to intentionally plan for children's learning and to identify areas for professional development. (For further guidance on families and assessment, as well as the other topics addressed in this chapter and the book, see the Resources list.)

Structuring the Physical Learning Environment

The first thing an intentional teacher does, even before the children arrive, is set up the classroom. Creating this setting should be undertaken with careful consideration of children's development, curriculum goals, teaching strategies, and characteristics of the families and community—the families' cultures and languages; whether the community is urban, suburban, or rural; and so on. The setting must promote not only children's learning but also their pleasure in learning and the motivation to pursue it. Because the classroom is a teacher's main work space, it should be welcoming and inspiring to the teacher, too.

Provide a safe and healthy indoor and outdoor environment

To be licensed by a county, state, or other authorized body, a program must comply with applicable standards for sanitation, ventilation, lighting, and temperature control. This is a primary responsibility of the teacher as well as the program (NAEYC 2001, 2007). In particular, children's safety depends on teachers being able to see and hear what is happening from anywhere in the room.

The classroom and outdoor play area should have adequate space to move freely and incorporate elements of universal design. Programs commonly consider the children's need for space and mobility, but teachers also must have space to move with children, join their play, and take advantage of learning opportunities as they arise.

Organize the space in interest areas or centers

Distinctive areas encourage different types of activity and expand the range of content children are enticed to pursue. They also promote thoughtful decision making, as children survey the room and choose where, with what, and with whom they want to engage. Taken together, a program's indoor and outdoor areas should address all aspects of children's development and allow groups of various sizes to play in each area. It should accommodate activities of different noise and physical energy levels, including offering places where children can find quiet and solitude during the day. Relative position should also be considered—for example, locate the art area near a sink and separate the quiet and noisy areas.

Typical indoor areas might include the following:

- Books and other materials for early reading and writing, in English and children's home languages
- Blocks and related building materials
- Dramatic play (house, dress-up)
- Visual art
- Music and movement
- Mathematics
- Science
- Sand and water; puzzles, games, and toys
- Computers (although these may be in the writing area)

Outdoor spaces might include these:

- Exercise equipment (climbers, slides, tricycles)
- Open areas for moving in various ways
- Areas for gardening, investigating wildlife (plant and animal), exploring art in nature, and engaging in sand and water play

Supply plentiful and diverse equipment and materials

Indoors and outdoors, intentional teachers provide sturdy, open-ended materials that children can use in many ways and that reflect the diversity of their homes and communities. While most materials should be present each day to encourage in-depth exploration, some may be rotated periodically to expand children's experiences and respond to new skills and interests. Reintroducing familiar materials can also inspire new uses. Items should have different textures, smells, sounds, and tastes. Materials that can be handled ("manipulatives," such as blocks, beads, shells, puzzles, and playdough) allow children to explore with all their senses, transform (change), and combine (put together and take apart). Label and store equipment and materials so they are visible and easily accessible to children. It encourages children's initiative and independence when they can find, use, and return supplies on their own.

Often it is better to have fewer different types of items but more of the same or similar things. Young children are eager to get started on an activity, and waiting for a turn is difficult for them, even for preschoolers who are beginning to share or understand that they will eventually get a turn. Boredom, loss of interest, and frustration from waiting can make for unhappy and unproductive play, whereas being able to put one's ideas into immediate action capitalizes on a child's excitement and sense of initiative. Children who are all working with the same or comparable materials (such as varied types of blocks—wooden, cardboard, rubber, foam, and so on) are also more likely to compare and share observations about their experiences. The exchange promotes social interaction and provides insights, as children note what their peers do, see, and say. In addition, having duplicates of dress-up clothes and props promotes higher-level play and communication, as there are multiple roles available for children to assume—two firefighters or two chefs, for example.

Reflecting Diversity in Classroom Materials

Reflecting cultural diversity in the classroom involves more than simply displaying unusual objects that set one group apart from another or celebrating a variety of holidays. Diversity applies to who and what we are every day. Here are some ideas for materials that will acknowledge and respect the cultural diversity of the children and families in your program. For all areas, labels and other written materials should appear in English and children's home languages.

Art area—Crayons in different skin tone colors; materials that showcase and encourage children to make the arts and crafts found in their culture and community (for example, ceramic bowls and statues, clay to make pottery, woven wall hangings and placemats, yarn and frame looms)

Block/construction area—Animal figures representing both typical and unusual pets (such as dogs, cats, snakes, pigs); toy vehicles representing different types of jobs (such as construction equipment, farm tractors, taxicabs); diverse building materials used locally (such as wood, bricks, ceramic tiles, boards made of recycled plastic)

Book area—Books in English and children's home languages; books depicting a variety of family constellations, races and ethnicities, cultures, and ages (including the elderly); books showing both men and women engaged in a variety of activities at home, work, and leisure; books depicting children and adults with various disabilities

Dramatic play area—Boy and girl dolls representing several ethnic groups; kitchen utensils and food packages like those found in children's homes; dress-up clothing with items from different cultures and occupations; child-size disability aids (for example, walkers, crutches, eyeglasses with lenses removed)

Music area—Recordings with songs reflective of children's cultures; musical instruments used in different cultures

Science area—Real examples and/or photos of plant and animal wildlife native to the area; tools and other items related to local weather patterns (such as for snow removal, sun protection, rainy season, hurricane preparedness)

Display work created by and of interest to children

Seeing concrete reminders of their own work prompts children to recall and reflect on what they and their peers have done. It can also lead them to expand on their ideas and pursue an interest or a project on subsequent days. Walls, shelves, and pedestals are all places to display examples of children's artwork and emergent writing, products of their science experiments and discoveries such as models or simple charts, photographs of children working together and of their play constructions, rules they create for a game they invent, family photographs, mementos of field trips, turn-taking lists for distributing snacks or choosing a song, and so on. The displays should be changed periodically, so "children's recent work predominates" (NAEYC 2007, Criterion 3.A.06). Displays that have been up too long cease to attract attention.

Displays should focus on the activities, products, and interests of the children, not the adults, which means information for parents and teachers should be posted somewhere other than the classroom, if possible, or in a small area of the room. But displays of children's work are an excellent way to document and share with parents, administrators, visitors, and others what children are learning.

Scheduling the Program Day

The intentional teacher's goal here is to offer children a rich and varied mix of learning opportunities within a supportive framework of routine.

Establish a consistent yet flexible daily routine

Routine provides young children with emotional stability and security. They know what will happen, when it will happen, and what is expected of them. Routines such as their teachers' morning greetings can help soothe any anxiety young children might feel in separating from their parents: "[It] may seem like an obvious ritual, but being fully greet-

ed in a conscious, sincere way sets a positive tone for a child's day" (Evans 2005, 50–51). A warm greeting from a teacher and time for children to say goodbye to their families for the day is also reassuring for family members as they entrust the care of their child to someone outside their home. For dual language learners and their families, hearing a greeting in their home language adds to the sense that the program is a place where they can feel safe and respected.

The number and nature of the day's components should be carefully chosen, in the same way that areas and materials should strike a balance between too much and too little. Dividing the day into a few meaningful blocks of time avoids transitions that are too frequent, which can be disruptive for young children. The sequence and length of activities also provide children with important experiences in temporal relationships and help to develop early mathematics concepts. A reasonable amount of flexibility is also needed to allow teachers to capitalize on spontaneous teaching opportunities and extend children's interests.

Further, recurring routines let children revisit materials and repeat activities. In our eagerness to broaden their experiences, we sometimes forget that children need to deepen their understanding of familiar materials and subjects, too.

A consistent routine also gives teachers a framework for planning, as they think about how to integrate content into each component of the day. For example, children can explore the use of numbers through one-to-one matching at greeting time (counting the number of children present), choice time (tallying how many children are playing in each area), and small group time (charting how many children use each paint color). The daily structure also prompts teachers to think about content broadly so they can include the full range of cognitive domains (introducing different subjects across activities) and social components (altering group size and composition; creating communities of children with shared interests and experiences) over the course of a day.

Every day, some parts of the schedule should offer children options, allowing them to share control with teachers. Even during adult-led activities, they should be able to count on having choices—for example, in how to use the materials or with whom to partner.

Allow for a variety of types of activities

Effective teachers schedule each program day to offer opportunities for the following:

- Choice and self-directed play (including time for children to make plans and antcipate what they will do)
- Cleaning up and taking care of individual needs (including use of self-help skills)
- Group activities in which teachers introduce key concepts and skills or read aloud
- Indoor and outdoor play, including movement activities
- Socializing with adults and peers
- Problem solving with materials and people
- Sharing snacks or meals

- Rest time (depending on children's ages and the length of the program day)
- Transitions
- Consolidating and reflecting on learning

A range of learning activities such as these allows children to learn content using all their senses, abilities, and interests, and to make meaningful connections.

A consistent schedule means the sequence of components is predictable, but what happens within any one component varies from day to day, depending on the children's interests and teachers' objectives. For example, small group time occurs at a fixed time of day, but the particular activity is different from one day to the next. This variety is important to accommodate children's range of interests and ways of learning, so that all children can find many engaging things to do throughout the day. Also, variety, like consistency, allows children to share control with adults.

At the same time, effective teachers know that too much variety can overwhelm young children. A varied routine does not mean trying to cram every possible experience into each day. Rather, the daily schedule, executed repeatedly over weeks and months, creates the structure within which content can be varied, sequenced, repeated, supported, and extended.

Use a variety of groupings

Children need opportunities to work alone, alongside each other, in pairs, and also in small and large groups. Some groupings happen spontaneously. Teachers create others, particularly small and large groups, to encourage different learning opportunities. Most obviously, groups present situations in which social learning occurs as children watch, listen, play, solve problems, and share their observations and ideas with peers. Group times also provide many rich opportunities for language development. Children hear new words introduced by teachers or used by peers, and refine their own ways of speaking to more effectively communicate their needs and intentions to others. These types of social interactions are particularly valuable for dual language learners, whose eagerness to be part of the group is an important motivator for learning the language of their peers. Groupings of various sizes are also another way that young children become aware of quantity—one of me, two of us, a few children in a small group, lots of children in a large group.

Effective teachers attend to individual and group dynamics. From observing children's comfort levels and preferences with various groupings, they can plan strategies to ensure that each child feels secure and supported in trying out new or uncomfortable situations. For example, a teacher might put quiet children in the same small group, where they might be more likely to speak up knowing they won't be talked over by louder, more verbal children. Or a dual language learner whose English-speaking skills are comparatively well developed can help another child whose English is not yet as advanced. The same might apply to grouping children who share a home culture, where those who have been in the school community longer can help newcomers feel comfortable as they adjust to new surroundings and a new culture. Such strategies give each child the opportunity for a rewarding and positive experience during each segment of the day.

Allow just enough time for each type of activity

The time allotted for each activity should not be so short that children are frustrated in achieving their objectives (whether exploring or creating), nor so long that they become impatient or bored. Children's individual preferences and developmental levels will naturally vary. For example, preschoolers are able to sustain choice time for a longer period than they could when they were toddlers. Another way to accommodate variations is by overlapping time frames. For example, one child might need a few extra minutes to finish an art activity during choice time while the other children wash up for snack time. Quick eaters could clean up and go outside with one teacher while slower eaters linger and chat with a second teacher.

This flexibility can make transitions smoother and avoid the abruptness and loss of control that can upset young children. When a classroom is beset with problem behaviors, often it is the schedule that needs managing, not the children. At other times, the content, not the length of the activity, needs to be adjusted. Perhaps children are being asked to accomplish too much, or the task hasn't captured their interest.

Interacting With Children

Children's interactions with teachers and peers, more than any other program feature, can determine what children learn and how they feel about learning (Dombro, Jablon, & Stetson 2011; Driscoll et al. 2011; National Research Council 2000a). In the early years, learning is largely a social process. Connecting with young children means recognizing that relationships are the basis of instruction and learning (NAEYC 2001, 35). Even children's encounters with materials are often mediated by others. It is, therefore, critical that teachers understand how children develop and offer them the kinds of support and encouragement that promote growth and progress.

The following sections outline the core strategies by which intentional teachers establish and maintain an interactive environment that supports children's learning and development. (See also the box on p. 19.)

Meet children's basic physical needs

All children have basic physical needs regarding food and nutrition, toileting, physical and psychological comfort, and safety and health. Having one's essential needs met, beginning in infancy, forms the basis for the fundamental trust all humans need to grow and develop. Attending to children's needs for physical care also helps meet their psychological need to feel safe and secure.

Children's needs change through their early years, but adults maintain an important role in helping to meet those needs. Infants need feeding, changing, cuddling, and playing; toddlers venture out to explore on their own but check back frequently to verify that their trusted caregiver is still there and available. At 3 and 4 years old, children can function independently or with peers for longer periods of time if they have established this basic trust early on. The security of knowing that caring adults will meet their basic needs prepares young children to venture beyond the familiar, setting the stage for all future educational experiences.

Create a warm and caring atmosphere

Children feel secure and successful when teachers interact positively with them, both verbally (listening, conversing with interest and respect, using a calm voice to problem solve) and nonverbally (smiling, hugging, nodding, making eye contact, getting down to children's eye level).

Warm, sensitive, and nurturing interactions are more beneficial for children's development than harsh, critical, or detached adult behavior (e.g., Kontos et al. 1994; Whitebook, Howes, & Phillips 1989). Effective teachers "create a climate of mutual respect for children by being interested in their ideas, experiences, and products" (NAEYC 2007, Criterion 3.B.03) and "develop individual relationships with children by providing care that is responsive, attentive, consistent, comforting, supportive, and culturally sensitive" (NAEYC 2007, Criterion 3.B.03). Such behaviors promote "positive development and learning for all children" (NAEYC 2001, 35).

Encourage and support language and communication

Teachers can support children's language development with many different strategies, including taking conversational turns with them, observing and listening while children take time to formulate and express their thoughts, and asking questions (even open-ended ones) sparingly so children can initiate as well as respond in conversation. For dual language learners, teachers can speak in the children's home languages (as much as teachers are familiar with) and English, beginning with common everyday words that will help children express their needs and intentions. Exposing young children to a rich, varied vocabulary and the rules of discourse helps them develop the language facility that underlies the later acquisition of literacy, interpersonal problem-solving skills, and other cognitive and social abilities.

Children talk when they have something to say. Providing children with interesting materials and experiences they want to talk about, therefore, is a good way to promote language. A positive classroom climate provides opportunities and encouragement so children feel free to talk. Intentional teachers invite children to talk with one another (see the Support Peer Interactions section on p. 22 in this chapter), and they themselves converse with all the children, including those who are quiet or whose behavior or demeanor make them more challenging to talk with. These strategies will increase the amount and complexity of children's language and create a classroom in which lively conversations accompany busy hands and minds. (For other suggestions on encouraging language and communication in children who are dual language learners, see the Dual Language Learning section on p. 106 in Chap. 6.)

Encourage initiative

"Initiative [means] children are eager to learn. They exhibit curiosity, independence, and self-direction as they learn about relationships, materials, action, and ideas. They take reasonable risks as they investigate the environment" (Epstein 2012a, 20). From an early age, children signal and act on their intentions. An infant reaches for a bright toy; a toddler holds out a cup and asks, "More juice?" Preschoolers develop and articulate more elaborate intentions, such as their plans to play in the block area and build a house. With freedom to express choices and engage in successful undertakings, children gain the confidence to continue learning under their own power and initiative.

Teachers create the kinds of learning opportunities that encourage initiative by respecting children's interests and choices. They should be enthusiastic about what children are doing, follow their lead, and participate as partners in their play. Teachers should welcome children's ideas during group activities as well as individual choice times. They should give children opportunities to make plans and reflect on what they

Children with special needs can benefit from most or all program activities when adaptations are made to ensure their participation. The following are some suggestions for accommodating children with different types of needs.

Learning differences and disabilities—Provide extra help by organizing information and assisting with tasks:

- Eliminate or reduce background noise and clutter as much as possible.
- Post picture and word sequences of schedules and routines in prominent places.
- Make suggestions that give children clues or choices for the next step in an activity.
- Have quiet places in the room.
- Show children how to use the tools and materials in the classroom.
- Keep transitions to a minimum.

Cognitive impairments and developmental delays—Accommodate a slower pace of learning. Concrete modeling and demonstration are key strategies:

- Allow lots of time for children to respond with actions or speech.
- Use lots of repetition and demonstration throughout the day.
- Give frequent feedback.
- Combine visual and verbal directions; increasingly use verbal cues alone as children become better able to interpret them.
- Sing directions for a task.

Speech and language impairments—Communication in any form is an important goal. Plan experiences that will motivate children to give and receive messages:

- Verbalize what children are telling you with their actions.
- Give only one verbal direction at a time.
- Reduce background noise as much as possible; avoid background music.

- Provide language experiences with repetitive sounds, phrases, and sentences, such as simple poetry, repetitive stories, and action stories and songs.
- Show pictures of what children have just been doing to encourage them to talk about it.

Hearing impairments—Use visual attention-getters to help orient children to what is happening:

- Avoid background noise.
- Face children whenever possible; speak using a clear voice and facial expressions.
- Use manual gestures or motions when talking, singing, or telling stories.
- Show objects to demonstrate what you are talking about.
- Sing along with song tapes to encourage children to lip-read.
- Learn basic signs (for yes, thank you, please, stop, and so on) to communicate with children and model appropriate social behavior.

Visual impairments—Encourage the children's use of hearing and touch to explore the environment:

- Keep pathways in the room wide, consistently located, and free of obstructions.
- Describe what you are doing as you do it; include actions as well as things.
- Use large, clear, tactile labels (including braille) to identify areas, tools, and materials.
- Use playdough and other modeling, molding, and sensory materials.
- Provide many put-together/take-apart toys and building sets throughout the room.

- Provide many tactile-auditory experiences, and use language in conjunction with them.

- Encourage children to explore all parts of an object; discuss part-whole relationships.

- Help children feel motions; for example, put your hands on a child's shoulders while he or she is swaying to music.

- Demonstrate activities that involve spatial concepts, such as on/off, up/down, and in/out.

- Encourage sighted children to be observers for visually impaired children by explaining what they are doing and how. (This is mutually beneficial.)

- Encourage other children to identify themselves and their actions as they approach their classmate.

- Record each child's voice and have children guess who it is. This helps visually impaired children match names with voices and is fun for the other children, too.

Orthopedic impairments—Match strategies to the children's range of physical disabilities:

- Make pathways wide enough to accommodate wheelchairs, body boards, and other devices.

- Keep the classroom uncluttered, with easy-to-reach shelves, cubbies, sink, and so on.

- Use lots of nonlocomotor movement activities (anchored movement such as moving the arms with feet in place).

- Provide ample space at group time for children to maneuver.

- Modify classroom tools by adding handles or grips that are easier to grasp (for example, add triangular grips to brushes and felt pens, rubber bicycle handles over doorknobs).

- Encourage other children to provide physical assistance when asked (such as picking up a crayon, closing a child's fingers around a handle).

- Plan floor activities for all the children.

- Use adapted battery or electric toys (such as remote-controlled cars) that allow children to control the toy's movement.

Emotional disturbances—Children who have frequent behavioral difficulties, mood swings, and problems forming relationships need predictable routines and extra interpersonal support:

- Shadow children inconspicuously and offer encouraging smiles and phrases.

- Develop mutually understood signals to indicate when the child should stop a behavior or needs help.

- Provide for calming activities such as sensory materials, water play, and soothing music.

- Allow a withdrawn child to watch from a "safe" distance.

- Prevent aggressive children from hurting others; this benefits everyone.

- Provide soft lighting and cozy spaces.

- Label the feelings behind the child's actions; help children to label feelings themselves.

- Read books about strong feelings, such as anger, and discuss them individually and with the group.

- Model coping strategies for when a child feels overwhelmed.

- Be sure to give the withdrawn child as much attention as the aggressive child.

Adapted, by permission, from K. Gerecke and P. Weatherby, "HighScope Strategies for Specific Disabilities," in *Supporting Young Learners 3: Ideas for Child Care Providers and Teachers*, ed. N.A. Brickman (Ypsilanti, MI: HighScope Press, 2001), 255–266.

have learned. "When children plan, carry out, and review their own learning activities, their behavior is more purposeful and they perform better on language and other intellectual measures" (Epstein 2003, 30).

Introduce information and model skills

It would certainly be inaccurate to say that content (that is, substantive learning in different subject areas) was absent from the early childhood curriculum before now. However, the recent trend has been to both expand the content and more clearly articulate goals or educational outcomes for all domains of early learning. Some ambivalence about content remains, however; early childhood teachers are not always sure how to provide information and model skills in a developmentally appropriate way.

Yet providing content by explicitly introducing information or modeling specific skills is not only appropriate but essential. Young children construct knowledge by combining their own experiences with the instruction and examples offered by more competent peers and adults. This book seeks to help teachers recognize that even content that can only be taught by telling and showing things to children (direct instruction) can be included in the early childhood curriculum by using teacher-guided strategies appropriate to young children's developmental levels and learning styles. Rather than quash children's initiative and spirit of inquiry, teaching with intention gives them the tools to spark further discovery and mastery.

Acknowledge children's activities and accomplishments

It is preferable for teachers to show that they value children's work through interest and encouragement rather than praise, which can have negative effects. Praise invites comparison and competition, raises anxiety about taking risks, and limits children's ability to evaluate their own work. By contrast, encouragement promotes initiative and self-confidence and develops children's ability to look at their own work objectively rather than just doing something to please adults.

Effective teachers use many ways to recognize and encourage children's intentions and accomplishments, including the following:

- Commenting specifically on what the child has done
- Asking questions to learn more about the child's plans and thoughts (not stock questions to which the adult knows the answer but authentic queries to elicit information)
- Repeating the child's ideas and imitating his actions
- Writing down or recording the child's ideas; photographing the child's creations
- Drawing connections between the child's current words and actions and events or information that came up at other times or places
- Referring one child to another for information or assistance
- Displaying the child's work or photographs of it
- Sharing the child's ideas, contributions, and creations with peers, other staff members, and family members

Support peer interactions

Preschoolers typically are highly motivated to establish and maintain relationships with their peers as well as adults. These relationships offer multiple benefits. Peers can become partners and collaborators in play, allow children to try out the roles of leader and follower, serve as sources of information and entertainment, help children establish a sense of identity through a growing awareness of similarities and differences, learn about a new language or an unfamiliar culture, and provide emotional support, especially when adults are not available.

The primary way teachers facilitate peer relationships is by themselves building authentic, supportive, and reciprocal relationships with children. By treating children with kindness and respect and engaging in conversations with them, teachers set the tone for how children interact with one another. Teachers can be important role models for communicating respectfully with children who come from different cultures or who speak different languages. By using some words in each child's home language, by treating all of the children's home languages and cultures as equally important, and by demonstrating patience and respect while trying to have conversations, teachers can help children learn important skills that will help them get along with each other.

The physical setting the teacher creates can also contribute to positive peer relationships. Materials should invite collaborative play (for example, rocking boats, large wagons, long jump ropes, equipment that takes two or more children to carry or operate, board games, dramatic play props). There should also be enough space in each interest area for a number of children to play together.

Another strategy teachers can use to support peer relationships is maintaining stable groupings— that is, the same children meeting as a group over an extended period of time, at least several months. Children who are in sustained experiences with the same group of peers develop greater social competence than those in shifting configurations (Corsaro & Molinari 2005; Howes 1988). Teachers should also watch for peer relationships that develop at other scheduled times (choice time, outside time), and offer children who have gravitated toward each other opportunities to interact throughout the daily routine.

Finally, teachers can refer children who have questions or need help solving problems to their classmates for assistance. For example, a child having difficulty with a certain piece of equipment (for example, the pump on a jar of paint, a new computer program or app) can be referred to a classmate who has mastered it, or two children can collaborate to figure it out. Teachers help children appreciate the contributions of their peers, for example, by giving them the task of generating a group story, rhyme, or chant. All these strategies encourage children to listen to and build on each other's ideas.

Encourage independent problem solving

Encouraging children to identify problems and try out solutions on their own helps them develop a range of cognitive, social, emotional, and physical skills. A teacher who doesn't let children struggle at all or who intervenes too quickly robs them of the chance to see themselves as competent and independent people. On the other hand, if a teacher waits too long or never offers help, children can become anxious or discouraged.

Effective teachers use several techniques to find the right balance. First, they encourage the child to acknowledge and describe the challenge he has encountered, whether with materials, peers, routines, or expectations. By waiting for the child to articulate the problem, teachers foster both cognitive and language development.

Second, effective teachers are patient, letting the child generate and try out solutions. Children get more satisfaction and learn more by figuring things out on their own. Then, as long as a child's solution satisfies him without causing problems for others, it should be accepted.

Finally, effective teachers are sensitive to instances where the child has tried but is unsuccessful after several attempts. A well-timed suggestion can help ("Have you looked for another truck in the block area?"). But sometimes teachers' direct assistance is needed to prevent frustration or harm (such as undoing a difficult knot or holding a toy two children are fighting over while they work out a solution). Even when the teachers intervene, though, they offer the child choices or let her follow through on her own in order to support her self-image as an independent problem solver.

Building Relationships With Families

Some dimensions of best practice when building and sustaining reciprocal relationships with families are the responsibility of the program rather than the teacher (for example, including parents on advisory boards, linking families with community services, helping families transition to other educational settings, publishing or posting program informa-

---

Trusting Children to Solve Problems on Their Own

Often when a problem arises among children an adult's first reaction is to solve it for them. It's more effective to resist this approach because children learn more when we help them define the problem, brainstorm solutions, and agree on a solution. In this example, the children come up with an original idea on their own.

Teacher: (Kneeling between two boys with an arm around each) You look angry, Lyle, and Hank, you seem really upset. (The boys nod in agreement.) What's the problem?

Lyle: I want to be the dad. I said so first.

Hank: You're always the dad. I want to be big.

Lyle: I'm the biggest, so huh! You can't be the dad. You're too little.

Teacher: So the problem is, Lyle, you want to be the dad, and Hank, you want to be the dad too. (Both boys nod their heads.) What can we do to solve this problem?

Lyle: I could be the dad today, and then you can be the dad the next day.

Hank: Well, I could be the dad today.

Teacher: It sounds like you both want to be the dad today.

Lyle: We don't need two dads. Hank, you could be the ladder guy *and* wear the tool belt!

Hank: And the gloves?

Lyle: Okay, the gloves. (Both boys smile.)

Teacher: So, Lyle, you're going to be the dad, and Hank, you're going to be the ladder guy who wears the tool belt and the gloves.

The boys nod and go off to play. When the teacher checks in on them later, the dad and the ladder guy have built a "swamp boat" and are giving rides to the other children.

tion in the families' home languages), although teachers can also be involved in these areas. Teachers can also do many things to build reciprocal relationships with parents and encourage them to participate actively in their children's learning. These include interacting with families in both informal and formal ways (chatting at pickup and drop-off times, sharing information at parent–teacher conferences, sending emails or tweets); providing different kinds of opportunities for parents to become involved in the program; and encouraging parents to participate in program activities with their children, such as by volunteering for fix-up-the-playground Saturday. The Resources list contains helpful ideas for working with families in all these ways.

This section focuses on two additional teacher strategies for involving families that relate most directly to intentionality. One is helping parents understand how a classroom curriculum that balances child-guided and teacher-guided experience promotes early development that is both broad and deep. The other is encouraging parents to themselves be intentional in the range of learning opportunities they provide for their children at home.

Exchange information about the curriculum and how it promotes children's development

Effective teachers share curriculum information with families in various ways, including through meetings, newsletters, mail and email, blogs, lending libraries with books, articles, and video recordings. They explain the curriculum and what children learn—for example, by posting signs in each area that list the kinds of learning taking place there. Teachers might also solicit parents' ideas and goals for their children's learning and answer parents' concerns, including their anxieties about their child's school readiness. After setting goals together with families, teachers can document and review with parents how children are progressing toward those goals.

Depending on their own school experiences, families may look for teachers to use highly directive teaching strategies as evidence that their child is being taught the information and skills needed in kindergarten. When families look for obvious signs of such instruction (such as worksheets) and don't find them, it is even more important for teachers to explain how they use a balance of child- and adult-guided experience to help children learn. Parental concerns should not be dismissed, nor should parents be seen as the enemy of appropriate practice. Even when families come from different cultural backgrounds and follow different childrearing practices at home (for example, with regard to eating or sleeping patterns), all families share with teachers a desire for their children to succeed in school and in life. Teachers and families can use this common ground to communicate with, support, and respect one another. Displaying and explaining children's work (such as writing samples, charts, experiments, constructions) will further help families recognize evidence that the learning they care about is occurring.

Share suggestions about how to extend learning at home

Many families provide a rich home environment that supports children's learning in different ways. Many also wonder what more they could do. Offering concrete and feasible suggestions about behaviors and activities parents can use with their children at home can help them consolidate and extend the learning taking place in the classroom. Effective teachers offer parents simple strategies they can use during everyday interactions with their children, as it is easier for most parents to follow through on ideas that fit into their families' daily home routines (such as during shopping, mealtimes, bedtime). If teachers find that families aren't using suggested ideas, they need to "evaluate and modify these approaches rather than assuming that families 'are just not interested'" (NAEYC 2001, 32).

For example, language is the underpinning of literacy. Teachers can offer parents many suggestions for carrying on conversations with their children as they drive them to school or wheel them down the supermarket aisles. If parents of dual language learners are concerned about their own lack of English, help them to see that developing their child's language skills in general will help them progress in learning English. Help families see the value of all the rich, wonderful vocabulary they have to offer their children in their home language through stories, songs, and conversations. Remind them that any new idea or concept a child learns in the home language actually builds the child's ability to learn English later on, but focusing too much on English at home does not seem to have any learning advantage for young children (Espinosa 2013).

Similarly, daily reading is essential. If reading at bedtime is not feasible (for example, if the parent works an evening shift), teachers and parents can discuss the situation and identify other times of the day when the parent or another family member can read to their children (again, in the home language as well as English). Opportunities for early mathematics experiences also abound in the home—setting the table (one-to-one correspondence), sorting laundry (classification and seriation), and taking a walk (looking for numerals on street signs and buildings). Children can learn numeral or shape names in more than one language, and basic math concepts (such as the rules for measuring, how to create patterns) are universal and independent of the particular language spoken.

Helping parents identify these naturally occurring learning situations will signal that teachers view parents as an active, intentional part of their children's learning and will help parents view themselves this way as well. If parents think of themselves as frontline teachers, they are more likely to continue in this role when their children enter elementary school.

In addition to offering suggestions to parents, teachers can offer opportunities for families to exchange ideas and network with one another. Different family backgrounds and experiences provide a wealth of knowledge that can be shared, while discovering similarities can be encouraging to those from different cultures. This approach acknowledges parental expertise and can greatly expand the range of strategies and resources families can draw upon. Everyone is enriched in the process.

Assessing Children's Development

Assessment, appropriately implemented and interpreted, provides valuable information about children's development to teachers, policy makers, researchers, and families. "Ongoing . . . assessments enable [teachers] to appreciate children's unique qualities, to develop appropriate goals, and to plan, implement, and evaluate effective curriculum" (NAEYC 2001, 33). Best practice requires teachers to demonstrate a range of competencies with respect to assessment. Among them are objectively documenting children's progress on a regular and consistent basis, maintaining children's portfolios, measuring progress using only developmentally appropriate and validated assessment tools, and sharing assessment results with families. Since dual language learners know and can do some things in English and some in their home language, truly accurate assessment for them must include observations and measures in both of their languages. Guidelines and strategies for carrying out assessment activities can be found in the sources outlined in the Resources list.

This section focuses on two other aspects of assessment. One is how teachers can intentionally apply what they learn from it to improve their understanding of children's development and plan appropriate ways to further individual and group learning. The other is how, with the intention of helping children grow, teachers can use assessment results to enhance their own skills through professional development.

Use assessment results to plan for individual children and the group as a whole

In addition to collecting objective assessment data (that is, based on reliable and verifiable observed behavior, not subjective impressions), teachers should be able to interpret and apply the data objectively.

> The excellent teacher uses her observations and other information gathered to inform her planning and teaching, giving careful consideration to the learning experiences needed by the group as a whole and by each individual child. By observing what children explore, what draws their interest, and what they say and do, the teacher determines how to adapt the environment, materials, or daily routines. The teacher can make an activity simpler or more complex according to what individual children are ready for. (Copple & Bredekamp 2009, 44)

Putting these pieces of knowledge together, an intentional teacher can choose the best combination of child-guided and adult-guided instructional strategies to scaffold further learning.

Use assessment results to identify areas for professional development

Teachers and their supervisors can also use the results of children's assessments to identify areas where professional development might help them better meet children's educational needs. That is, by enhancing their own expertise—in specific content areas, in the use of instructional strategies, or both—teachers will be able to more effectively plan and carry out activities that enhance children's knowledge and understanding. For example, if a valid assessment of literacy skills shows several children making progress in identifying letter names and sounds but not in comprehension, perhaps mentoring or attending a workshop on encouraging recall and prediction during book reading can help teachers develop these skills in children. Similarly, if objective observations indicate that the children regularly lose interest at circle time, staff members can brainstorm and consult resources on designing and implementing large group times to improve this type of learning experience for children.

Using Best Practices to Support Intentional Teaching

Best practices and intentional teaching work in synergy. The mission of the intentional teacher is to ensure that young children acquire the knowledge and skills they need to succeed in school and in life. To fulfill this mission, intentional teachers conscientiously address every area of early learning—intellectual, social and emotional, physical, and creative—with sufficient range and depth. They apply the best practices summarized in this chapter in a balanced offering of child-guided and adult-guided experiences. Moreover, intentional teachers attend to their own professional development. They regard themselves as lifelong learners—studying the children in their care, updating their knowledge of the latest child development theory and research, and examining the implications for practice. They are also collaborators, teaming with coworkers and families to apply their expertise and resources toward children's optimal development.

Along with a spirit of inquiry and dedication to children's well-being, intentional teachers engage in reflection and self-evaluation. They ask themselves what kind of teachers they want to be. And to answer that question, they consider what kind of adults they want today's children to become. Only by having this vision of our society's future, populated by the children of today, can we as early childhood advocates fully address the role that teachers can and should play in shaping young minds, hearts, and bodies.

It is my hope that some of the answers to these questions are contained in this book. What and how teachers teach as they interact with young children will help determine the intellectual, social, emotional, physical, and creative development of next year's students and the next generation's adults. A thoughtful, well-grounded approach to resolving these questions can lead to a thoughtful, well-rounded population of tomorrow's citizens.

The general principles and strategies of intentional teaching discussed in this chapter can and should be applied across all the content domains of early learning. You can refer to these overall strategies as you read the next chapters, which offer specific ideas for promoting early education in approaches to learning, social and emotional learning, physical development and health, language and literacy, mathematics, science, social studies, and the creative arts. Considering and using these best practices will help administrators and teachers create early childhood programs in which adults and children are partners in the learning process.

For Further Consideration

1. How can packaged curriculum materials help teachers provide essential content yet enable them to remain intentional in their teaching? What risks and short-comings come with packaged curricula, and what can teachers and programs do to address these?

2. How can early childhood practitioners overcome any anxiety they might have about teaching certain content areas, such as mathematics and science, or art appreciation (as a cognitive discipline)?

3. With so many content areas to cover, how can teachers possibly include everything in the daily schedule? Must programs be full day to provide a comprehensive early education?

4. What preservice and inservice professional development opportunities are needed to train and support intentional teachers in implementing best practices?

5. What beliefs and/or practices might experienced teachers need to unlearn to be more intentional in their teaching? What attitudes and/or assumptions might novice teachers need to change to be more intentional in their teaching?

Chapter 3

Approaches to Learning

Dwight, a young 3-year-old, stands at the easel, painting the same corner over and over until he wears a hole in the paper. He pokes his finger in the hole, dips his brush in the cup, and continues to paint over the same spot. He smiles with satisfaction.

❋ ❋ ❋

When Lourdes, age 4, is reluctant to touch the "icky" finger paint, her teacher offers her disposable gloves. After a few minutes, Lourdes removes one glove and dips her forefinger in the paint. She rubs her fingers together and then wipes them with a towel. She continues dipping and wiping.

❋ ❋ ❋

At outside time, Marica, 4, watches an ant carry a bread crumb twice its size across a patch of dirt. "He's awful little," she comments. "I wonder how he moves something bigger than him." She crouches and studies the ant for the next 10 minutes.

❋ ❋ ❋

The teacher waits patiently as 3-year-old Kalil puts on his jacket. It takes three tries to get his left arm in the sleeve. Then the zipper slips out of its notch several times. Thinking he might be frustrated, the teacher asks if Kalil wants help. He keeps working until, on the sixth try, he closes it. "I did it!" he says. "You worked hard to zip it yourself," says the teacher, acknowledging his effort.

The way preschoolers approach learning affects their educational experiences in every content area during early childhood and beyond. Researcher Ross Thompson (2002) says that when young children are curious, interested, and confident about discovering the answers to their questions, they are best able to benefit from learning opportunities. Studies show that ratings of children's **approaches to learning** at school entry predict their reading and math achievement throughout the primary grades (Li-Grining et al. 2010).

Defining approaches to learning is not easy. According to the National Education Goals Panel (NEGP; Kagan, Moore, & Bredekamp 1995), it includes the following components: curiosity, creativity, confidence, independence, initiative, and persistence. Psychologists also refer to the related term *styles of learning* or *dispositions*, which are "enduring habits of mind and characteristic ways of responding to experiences" (Katz & McClellan 1997, 6).

Approaches to learning also involve breaking down a task into its components, organizing a plan of work, and reflecting on the success of one's endeavors. Here again, a child's approach to learning affects her performance in other content areas. For example, it can determine whether the child asks a teacher for help with writing a letter of the alphabet or finds a sample of one to copy (language and literacy).

Styles of Learning

Psychologists and educators use the term *styles of learning* to describe how people acquire knowledge and skills, solve problems, and generally deal with information and experiences. Individual differences in styles of learning appear early in childhood and persist into adulthood. These differences vary along several dimensions.

Sensory mode. Research on brain development (Medina 2008) and the impact of technology on young children (Guernsey 2012) shows that visual stimulation—especially motion—tends to trump other types of input. Nevertheless, some children are still more visually oriented than others when it comes to choosing experiences or processing information. These children learn best by observing objects, people, and images (words and pictures). Other children process information auditorily and respond well to verbal descriptions and directions. Still others need to handle and manipulate objects to grasp how things work and understand concepts. While using the latter tactile mode is characteristic of young children in general, a preference for learning through touching and doing can last a lifetime.

Pacing or timing. Some children do well in a fast-paced learning environment and can shift rapidly from one activity to another. As adults, they may move from task to task more readily or willingly, or be more open (flexible) to change. Other children are slower and more deliberate in the way they process information. They focus on one thing at a time and transition gradually between activities or ideas.

Social context. People differ in whether they learn best by working on their own or interacting with others. Some children thrive on independent pursuits, quietly and methodically investigating things or practicing skills. Others learn well in a group context. The social give-and-take helps them consider new ideas and master new skills. Most of us can function in both types of situations, depending on the content of the activity (for example, writing is most often done independently, while inventing the rules for a game profits from group input) and the people we are working with (for example, the degree of trust present, the division of roles, the presence and style of a group leader).

Everyone uses virtually every style of learning at some point. However, a preference for certain modes predominates in their approaches to learning. And while some of these differences are due to innate temperamental differences—the dispositions or tendencies we are born with—the learning environment also plays a major role in shaping the ways we can and do learn.

Young Children's Development in Approaches to Learning

Infants are born with innate temperamental differences that persist into adulthood (Chess & Thomas 1996). Factors such as a child's level of inhibition and emotional reactiveness (the child's sensitivity to emotional triggers, or the strength with which the child exhibits feelings) can strongly affect his approach to learning. Because early experiences often occur in group settings, children's social dispositions (their openness to being engaged with the group) can also affect their exposure and willingness to acquire new information. However, the Collaborative for Academic, Social, and Emotional Learning (CASEL; Elias et al. 1997) emphasizes that the environment also plays a major role in determining how these biological traits are expressed. For example, an innate trait of persistence enables a child to solve problems, but consistently thwarting a child's desires can bend this trait toward stubbornness, interfering with the child's ability to face challenges and form satisfying relationships.

A healthy approach to learning is an important component of school readiness and is enhanced when young children are encouraged to explore the environment and materials, ask questions, and use their imaginations (Kagan et al. 1995). Encouraging young children to make choices builds their sense of initiative and self-confidence. Appropriate early experiences predispose children to take reasonable risks because they focus on the enjoyment of learning rather than on the fear of failure. (For dual language learners, this includes offering support and learning opportunities in their home language.) They perceive learning as a positive challenge, not as an insurmountable barrier or a threat. They engage in learning with the expectation of success, which enables them to benefit from their educational experiences.

Teaching and Learning Using Approaches to Learning

Adults can help children develop a positive approach to learning by respecting their individuality and creating an environment that acknowledges their emerging sense of themselves as doers and thinkers. A program setting that provides choices and supports initiative allows all children, using the traits they were born with, to act satisfyingly and successfully with different materials, people, activities, and events. Each child, and the class as a whole, can thrive in this environment and anticipate that learning will be interesting and rewarding. Language and culture can be important components of any child's learning style. As you prepare the environment to encourage each child to learn in his own way, be sure that there are materials, activities, and language models that reflect the languages and cultures of all the children.

To create a setting that supports a child's positive predisposition to learn and recognizes each child's preferred learning style(s), consider the following dimensions (see also the box on p. 30).

- **Sensory mode.** Provide an environment that is rich in materials and appeals to all the senses. The greater the variety of materials, the more likely that one or more will interest each child. A classroom that is carefully arranged and equipped with diverse materials (see Chap. 2) allows children to explore many options using their preferred modality and to safely try other choices.

- **Pacing.** Young children need time to try new things, solve problems, practice skills, or think about what they are learning. It is, therefore, important for adults to be patient. When adults step in too quickly, they deprive children of a chance to discover things for themselves. Children may lose interest, become anxious, or even resent the interference. They also learn to rely on adults instead of first seeking resources independently and using their own skills. On the other hand, some children prefer to do things quickly and move on to the next activity. Forcing them to slow down—and repeat or do something "more carefully"—may inhibit their energy and excitement for learning.

- **Social context.** Children should always have the option to play alone or with oth-

What the Research Says About Approaches to Learning

Research on approaches to learning (e.g., Fantuzzo, Perry, & McDermott 2004; Rothbart & Bates 2006) is clear on at least five points:

1. Children begin to develop these characteristics and behaviors at an early age.
2. Even in the early years, children differ in their approaches to learning.
3. These differences influence children's school readiness and school success.
4. Children's experiences at home and in early childhood programs can strengthen or undermine their positive approaches to learning.
5. Early childhood programs can implement specific strategies that will promote positive approaches to learning in areas such as strengthening relationships with children, working together with families, designing supportive classroom environments, and selecting effective curriculum and teaching methods.

Reprinted, by permission, from M. Hyson, *Enthusiastic and Engaged Learners: Approaches to Learning in the Early Childhood Classroom* (New York: Teachers College Press 2008), 3.

ers. However, it is also important to schedule group times during the program day when preschoolers can safely try working alongside or with their peers. This allows young children, especially those still building their interpersonal skills, to experience social contexts they might not choose on their own.

Fitting the Learning Experience to the Learning Objective

While there are many dimensions to approaches to learning, they can be divided into two general categories. One, which I refer to as *openness to experiences,* describes a child's initial willingness to explore materials, ideas, people, and events. Some children readily enter into an experience, others approach slowly on their own, and still others need coaxing from a peer or an adult. Most preschool children eagerly engage with materials, but it takes prompting for them to consider ideas. Further, many young children are impulsive, while others take action one step at a time, testing the waters along the way. Individual temperament aside, however, preschoolers eventually develop the ability to form mental representations. That is, they can picture something they have not yet seen or done. This emerging capacity allows them to be more planful about their actions.

The second overarching category in approaches to learning is what I call *processing experiences.* This dimension addresses how children deal with the physical and interpersonal environment both during and after the experience. For example, some children eagerly solve problems on their own, using whatever resources are available. They may make repeated attempts until they are successful (success being defined according to their own goals, not the adult's), or they may give up after one or two tries. Other children may turn to someone else for assistance as soon as they encounter a problem. Following an experience, children also differ in whether they move on to something else or take time to process what they have learned. A child may follow up on a discovery (for example, by repeating it to see if it happens again or by varying an action to see if it changes the outcomes), or she may simply accept the experience without much reflection. Again, however, regardless of individual dispositions, cognitive and language development allow young children to think back in more detail about what they have learned and to consider how they can expand on an experience that was interesting and challenged them at just the right level.

Openness to Experiences

The desire to explore, discover, and learn is inherent in human nature. Children are likely to take the initiative to explore on their own, especially when approaching interesting materials in the environment. These encounters tend to be spontaneous, as children are drawn to the sights, sounds, and other sensations that attract their attention. However, for them to approach learning with more forethought, or planning, depends on adult prompting. Likewise, children's engagement with the world of ideas is likely to require more active intervention, using words and nonverbal communication, from adults than their engagement with actions and materials.

Child-guided experience is especially important for learnings such as:

Taking the initiative

Children are "eager to learn" (National Research Council 2000a). In her book on approaches to learning, Marilou Hyson (2008) says that young learners are inherently enthusiastic about and engaged with the world. They don't need external rewards to entice them to explore new materials, exercise mastery and control over their actions, interact with others, and discover the effects of their actions on the environment (Stipek 2002). Preschoolers show initiative when they choose to participate in a variety of activities that, over time, engage all their senses. They are increasingly comfortable with trying new things, taking risks, and generating their own ideas.

Teaching strategies. In a supportive environment, children freely approach tasks because they are confident that their initiatives will be met with enthusiasm and support from adults. This allows them to display growing levels of originality, flexibility, and imagination. To help young children express and expand their inherent sense of initiative, try the following teaching strategies:

- Focus on children's efforts, not the outcomes of their actions. Emphasize the satisfaction of the learning itself. Expect children to succeed, and remember that success or failure is defined according to the goal the child has in mind, not what an adult thinks the child should do. Rather than give children praise, which implies judgment, encourage them by getting down on their physical level, imitating their actions, and commenting on what they are doing. Ask open-ended questions so children know you are interested in their thinking, not looking for a correct answer.

- Encourage—but never force—children to explore new materials (such as scissors or the computer), try out their knowledge and skills (by sorting beads or riding a trike), or share an idea or opinion (about why ice melts or the feelings expressed in a painting). Taking the initiative requires confidence and trust. Let children know that you see and value their courage as well as their curiosity.

- Balance freedom and structure in the environment. An overly structured classroom can inhibit children who are afraid of messing up the order imposed by adults. On the other hand, a disorganized or chaotic setting with too many materials can overwhelm some children. Balancing these extremes lets children exercise their curiosity without feeling anxious. Children's initiative is also supported by having independent access to materials so they can act with autonomy while pursuing self-directed goals. A highly structured classroom may deprive them of these choices. (See pp. 20–21 in Chap. 2 for suggestions on making materials accessible to children with special needs.)

○ During teacher-planned times of the day, give children choices about how to use the materials or carry out their ideas. For example, when working with children in a small group, introduce the materials with a brief story or demonstration, but then let children explore them according to their own interests and curiosity ("Here are the pebbles, leaves, and twigs we collected yesterday. I wonder what you can make with them"). At circle time, start with a movement or song for the children to join in, but then encourage them to contribute their own ideas for others to imitate or add to.

Engaging with materials

Engagement is the "action-oriented dimension of approaches to learning" (Hyson 2008, 17). The older children get and the more experience they have with demonstrating initiative, the longer they are able to maintain their engagement with materials and the more successful they are at completing a task. They work and play with more attention and persistence and are less susceptible to distractions. Engagement is an important component of school readiness (Fantuzzo, Perry, & McDermott 2004). It requires self-regulation, which researchers Elena Bodrova and Deborah Leong (2007) describe as children's "ability to act in a deliberate planned manner in governing much of their own behavior" (127). When some educators refer to "paying attention," they mean watching or listening to someone else. However, engagement is best described as children pursuing their own goals and using the materials and other resources at hand to achieve it.

Teaching strategies. For many children, engagement can be self-reinforcing. The more they get involved with materials, the more ideas spring to mind, and the more successful they are in pursuing those ideas. Nevertheless, adults can encourage and extend children's engagement with strategies such as these:

○ Provide a variety of materials and activities so each child can find something to engage her interest every day. New or reintroduced materials can also attract and sustain children's attention. Find the right balance between familiarity and novelty. Too much of the same thing can result in boredom, while too much newness induces overload. Observe children to find what works for each individual and for the group as a whole. For example, younger children might intently explore one color of paint—experimenting with the concept of redness, for example—at small group time. Older children may be ready to compare or blend two or more colors, or explore the effects of different painting tools.

○ Give children ample time to carry out their intentions. Even if children do not initially stay with one activity, scheduling a long playtime lets them know that they have the time if they need it. Be flexible about when individual children move to the next activity, and allow them to transition gradually (for example, perhaps they can finish a painting before cleaning up and joining the group for circle time). By the same token, be sensitive to when children lose interest in an activity. Either modify the activity (for example, introduce backup materials or have restless children move around instead of sing) or bring the activity to an end. If children feel forced to continue, that activity may take on unpleasant associations, and they may resist becoming engaged in it thereafter.

○ Minimize interruptions and transitions. Adults may inadvertently hamper children's concentration by assuming that young children have short attention spans and therefore need a constant change of pace or stimulation. Let children stay with their chosen activity as long as possible and decide when they are ready to move on to something else. Avoid setting up special projects during choice time that pull individual children away from their ongoing activity. Scheduling as few transitions as possible between parts of the day gives each component its due and allows children to settle in and pursue their intentions.

Adult-guided experience is especially important for learnings such as:

Planning

Supported by research, educators increasingly recognize the importance of children's **planning** to their early development. For example, Epstein (1993) found that "opportunities to plan, carry out, and review activities of their own choosing were positively associated with almost all aspects of children's social, cognitive, and motor development" (152). The Head Start Performance Standards (Administration for Children and Families 2002), as well as many state standards (Gronlund 2006), include planning as a measure of program quality and child learning. Planning is also an important component of executive functioning—the command-and-control ability that allows one to manage and execute tasks (Zelazo & Mueller 2002).

Planning becomes more complex and detailed as children are increasingly able to hold a mental image of objects and actions. A young preschooler's plan is simple ("I want to play with the trucks"). An older preschooler can specify a broader range of materials, actions, or people, and describe the sequence necessary to carry out the plan ("Yolanda and I are going to make tacos with playdough and paper. First we'll roll out the dough, then we'll tear the paper for lettuce"). The child might even anticipate problems and possible solutions.

Teaching strategies. Too often, teachers confuse planning with making choices. For example, they might ask whether a child plans to go to the house area or the art area during choice time but not allow the child to voice an independent idea of what she envisions doing there. Epstein (2003) emphasizes the distinction: "Planning is *choice with intention*. That is, the chooser begins with a specific goal or purpose in mind that results in the choice" (29). To offer young children true opportunities to make plans, try the following ideas:

- Provide opportunities for children to make intentional choices throughout the day. For example, as children hang up their coats, ask them to think about which book they want to look at during arrival time or who they want to sit with at breakfast. At the beginning of choice time, ask children what materials they plan to use, what they might do with them, and who (if anyone) they will play with. When children run into a problem, talk with them about what materials and/or actions they could use to solve it and how they might avoid a similar problem in the future. At group times, encourage children to describe ahead of time how they might use the materials or to plan how they might move depending on the type of music that is played. As the children get ready to go outdoors, ask them what they plan to do ("Where will you play? Do you think you'll move fast or slow? Will you be quiet or noisy?").

- Treat children's plans with respect. Show interest in their choices and decisions. Repeat and extend their ideas, imitate their actions, accept their suggestions, and let them be the leaders. Explain to parents the cognitive and social benefits of allowing their children to make plans at home. Most of the time, adults make plans for children (for example, the day's schedule). It is, therefore, important for children to set their own agenda when possible.

○ When there are children who are new to English in the group, learn to ask a general question in the children's home languages, such as "Where will you play?" or "What will you play with there?" or "What will happen next?" This will acquaint them with important things to think about, even if you don't fully understand their answers. Teachers and children can practice together so everyone becomes used to showing as well as telling their answers to questions about planning, reviewing, and solving problems and questions that express curiosity.

Engaging with ideas

Preschoolers may not consider how or why something happened unless prompted to do so by adults. Many times they simply accept discoveries or observations without seeking an explanation. Adults can encourage them to pay attention to the reason(s) behind what they observe through **scaffolding**, a term introduced by psychologist Jerome Bruner (1986) and based on the work of Lev Vygotsky (1978). Scaffolding has two parts. The first is to support children at their current level of understanding; the second is to gently extend their learning. Finding the right balance requires sensitivity to each child's approach to learning and developmental level. Supporting a child without extending learning can mean the child stays at a safe (successful) level without taking on a new challenge and progressing. On the other hand, too much pressure to advance may confuse or frustrate the child or turn him off completely by creating a failure situation.

Teaching strategies. Scaffolding children to engage with ideas means involving them in authentic, give-and-take conversation. Adults and children should be equal partners in the conversation, with both voicing their own sense of wonder about what is happening and why. To encourage children to take on the world of ideas, try the following strategies:

○ Describe, and encourage children to describe, what they are doing. Comment on the materials they use, their actions, and the effects of their actions. Adult commentary serves two purposes. First, it shows that the adult is aware of and interested in what the child is doing, which sends the message that the child's learning is important. Second, it invites the child to converse with the adult. In the process of describing their own activities, children are more likely to consider their choices and observe the outcomes of their actions. In other words, they begin to think as well as do.

- Use questions sparingly. Questioning young children is tricky. It can dampen a conversation if the inquiry is about facts that are obvious ("What color is that?") or unrelated to the situation at hand (such as asking a child who is painting if it's her turn to pass out cups for snack time that day). On the other hand, questions can stimulate thoughtful conversation if they are used sparingly, convey genuine interest in what the child is doing, and leave it open to the child whether and how to respond. Best of all is to let the child ask the adult questions rather than the other way around!

- Invite children to explain their thinking. Conversations that inspire children to engage with ideas focus on thought processes rather than facts. Only the child has the answer to a question about what he thinks, so the dialogue is in the child's control, not the teacher's. Further, in the process of making a comment or answering the question, the child can consolidate what he knows and recognize how he knows it. Statements that engage children with ideas include these:

  > "I wonder why . . . ."
  >
  > "How can you tell?"
  >
  > "How do you know that?"
  >
  > "Tell me how you got [the object] to . . . ."
  >
  > "What do you think made that happen?"
  >
  > "Suppose you tried it another way . . . ."
  >
  > "What do you think would happen if . . . ?"

- Take advantage of opportunities to explain your own thinking and reasoning (for example, "If I want these two pieces to stick together, I'll think I'll need something stronger than tape. I wonder what else I could use"). Exclaim over your own discoveries ("The chirping got louder when I got close to the nest!") and encourage children to help you explain why something happened ("Why do you suppose the mama bird sounds so upset?").

Processing Experiences

When children have a goal in mind, particularly one they have set for themselves, they can be quite persistent in achieving it. If they encounter a problem, they are motivated to solve it without external prompting. As preschoolers' cognitive processing skills develop, they are increasingly able to analyze the problem and draw on various materials or assistance to take care of it. In fact, they readily make use of whatever resources are available to carry out their play ideas. When it comes to reflecting, however, children benefit from adult scaffolding to help them think about what they have learned from their experiences. They also depend on adult encouragement and suggestions to consider how they can extend or follow up on an idea, an action, or a discovery.

Child-guided experience is especially important for learnings such as:

Solving problems

Children often encounter problems as they carry out their play ideas. [*Note:* This section refers to problems children have with materials. For problems that arise between children, see the Engaging in Conflict Resolution section on p. 60 in Chap. 4.] Differences in how children approach problem solving emerge early (Dweck 2002). Those who are anxious about getting things right tend to avoid situations that may result in failure and are concerned with how others, including adults, regard them. By contrast, children with an orientation toward learning or mastery focus on increasing their knowledge or abilities and are willing to take on new challenges, regardless of feedback or past failure. Children in the latter group tend to do better when they enter school (Schunk & Pajares 2005).

In addition to individual differences, there are also developmental changes in the way children approach problems (Flavell, Miller, & Miller 2001). Younger preschoolers do so with more enthusiasm and self-confidence but less persistence. They rely on trial and error. Older preschoolers are more persistent and flexible, as well as somewhat more systematic in their attempts to solve a problem. Self-regulation (another factor in executive function) also plays a role. Older children are better able to manage frustration, focus their attention, and apply a range of cognitive skills to solving problems (Zelazo & Mueller 2002). Ages 3 to 5 are key to the development of these executive functions because of concurrent changes in the brain's frontal cortex, which is responsible for regulating and expressing emotion (Shore 2003).

Teaching strategies. The approach young children take to solving problems will not only affect their willingness to take on new challenges in the school years but also will likely determine their behavior in the face of risk-taking opportunities and setbacks throughout their lives. To prepare preschoolers to deal with problem-solving situations, use these strategies:

○ Encourage children to describe problems that arise during play. They may not see a problem the same way as an adult, but by using their own words, preschoolers learn to trust their skills as observers and analyzers. They are also more likely to propose and try solutions. For children who are not (yet) verbal, simply state the problem for them ("It looks like the button isn't working"). This helps the child recognize what is wrong and encourages her to try to fix the problem on her own.

○ Give children time to come up with solutions. While the adult's solution may be more efficient or effective, simply telling the child what he should do would deprive him of an opportunity to learn and develop confidence in his independent problem-solving abilities.

○ Call children's attention to what is and is not working. Talking about what did or did not solve the problem helps children establish a cause-and-effect connection, which they can apply to similar problems in the future. It helps them become more systematic in their problem-solving attempts.

- Assist children who are frustrated. Sometimes children do need adult help, especially when their inability to solve a problem keeps them from moving forward with their plans. Provide just enough assistance for children to continue solving problems on their own, as shown here:

Cole, age 4, tells his teacher, "The computer's not working." She asks him how it isn't working and he says, "It keeps going back to where I started." When she asks Cole what he wants the computer to do, he answers, "Go to the next part of the game." She points to the arrow icons on the screen and says, "I wonder what these do." Cole clicks on them, and when he presses the forward arrow (–>) icon, the game advances. He says, "Now I got it working!"

Using resources

Children become increasingly adept at identifying and using resources, including manipulating objects, watching and imitating others, and specifying what kind of help they need. As Lilian Katz (1993) points out, the dispositions, or "habits of mind," they bring to these endeavors are the desire to find things out, make sense of experience, strive for accuracy, and be empirical (prove something works). Although temperamental differences affect children's willingness to try new resources, there is a developmental trend toward greater experimentation and curiosity (Kagan 2005). A toddler asks reflexively, "*What* is that?" while a preschooler wonders, "*Why* is that?" The importance of providing age-appropriate and hands-on resources to young children cannot be overstated. For example, an international study of programs in 10 diverse countries found that the availability of open-ended materials in the preprimary years was a significant predictor of children's cognitive and language performance at age 7 (Montie, Xiang, & Schweinhart 2006).

Teaching strategies. While we want preschoolers to begin grappling with ideas, it is important to provide the raw materials, or resources, on which their ideas are built. Young children are concrete in their thinking. Experiences with a wide range of resources form the foundation for the conceptual understandings they are gradually developing. To help them with this process, try the following strategies:

- Provide open-ended materials that appeal to all the senses. Children learn meaningful lessons when they can experience materials in many ways (see, hear, smell, touch, and taste them). Diverse materials also cater to children's individual sensory modes or preferred styles of learning. Closed-ended materials, with one correct way of being used, restrict the possibilities for discovery, and children quickly lose interest in them. By contrast, open-ended materials, which can be put to multiple uses, lead to sustained engagement and spur a child's imagination.

- Some children, particularly dual language learners in a wait, watch, and listen phase, may need to see that it is okay to explore materials in different ways. Demonstrate this by simply sitting next to the children and playing or exploring alongside them. When they see the teacher using a soda straw to poke holes in clay or using the wheels of a toy truck to paint interesting patterns, they will gain the reassurance they need to proceed on their own.

○ Talk with children about how they use resources—for example, the objects and people they work with, how they use materials to solve problems, what they observe (using all their senses), and the conclusions they draw. Verbalizing their actions and observations helps children make lasting neural connections in their brains (Shore 2003). That is, attaching words (language) to the images helps the brain encode and remember them.

○ Encourage children to use resources to answer their own questions. For example, if a child asks you how to do something, say, "I wonder what you could use to find out" or "How do you think it might work?" to encourage her to experiment with materials and observe the results. Supporting children in finding the answers to their own questions often leads to meaningful and lasting insights.

Adult-guided experience is especially important for learnings such as:

Reflecting

Reflection involves more than "memory or a rote recitation of completed activities. Reflection is *remembering with analysis*" (Epstein 2003, 29). Unlike rote memorization, reflection helps children discover and apply underlying concepts. For example, grasping the alphabetic principle that every letter has a unique appearance and sound allows a child to apply this idea to each new letter. Generalizing information like this is an efficient way to learn. During the preschool years, cognitive and language developments make children increasingly able to reflect on their experiences and apply what they learn in related contexts. As they

construct mental images (representations) of objects, events, and interactions, children become less tied to the here and now. They can review the past and anticipate the future. Words help them encode experiences in their memory, so they can entertain "what if" thoughts about things that have not yet happened.

Teaching strategies. To engage children in meaningful reflection, adults should be careful not to quiz them on their activities. Rather, talking with children both during and after they are involved in pursuits that interest them will encourage children to become more thoughtful on their own. Here are some ideas to help children reflect on what they learn from their experiences:

○ Make comments and ask open-ended questions that encourage reflection and help children connect current and previous experience. As you play alongside them, use questions and statements such as the following: "What does this remind you of?" "How else could the story end?" "What if . . . ?" "How else could you have . . . ?" and "I wonder where else you could use this."

○ Create opportunities for children to describe their actions to peers. For example, refer them to one another for help ("Jonetta got her tissue paper to stick. Maybe she can tell you how she did it"). This encourages children to think about what they did in order to communicate it to someone else. When children act as leaders at circle time, encourage them to tell as well as demonstrate their ideas. Again, this will help them think about (analyze) and describe a movement in a way that others can understand and imitate.

o Use photographs and other mementos to help children remember and reflect on experiences. "A picture is worth a thousand words" means one image can evoke the entire story behind it. Images are particularly useful for dual language learners, who can begin to attach simple labels (names of objects or actions) to their experiences. A sequence of photographs helps children recall the order of events of a situation and also highlights if-then connections. For example, viewing pictures of children building a bridge across a stream helps them recall the series of steps that led to the final structure. They may have discovered that they needed an extra support in the middle of the stream to hold up the bridge (*if* they didn't shore up the middle, *then* the bridge collapsed). Likewise, an object representing an event, such as something brought back from a field trip, can elicit reflections about the objects and incidents most memorable to each child, such as in the following example:

The day after the kindergarten class goes on a field trip to the art museum, the children look at the reproduction postcards they bought in the gift shop. One child studies a painting in somber tones and says, "It's gray because he was sad when he made it." Another child examines a metal sculpture of a large figure and comments, "It's so tall, you can't see its eyes. It's scary, like a monster." A third child, rather than reflecting on the art or the time in the museum, remembers the trip to the museum cafeteria. "Tommy spilled his juice on my shoe," the child recalls.

Following up

As preschoolers pursue an interest or a discovery, most do not spontaneously choose to continue doing so in greater depth. Once finished with an activity, they tend to lose interest, look to see what others are doing, or simply move on to something else. When a child remains absorbed by a set of materials or an activity for a prolonged period of time, however, it indicates the child is ready to go deeper—to follow up this interest. This capacity tends to increase with age.

Follow-up, however, should not be confused with the unvarying and repetitive play teachers may complain about ("All they want to do is play superheroes!"). In these cases, the adult's creativity and ingenuity can help a child expand, rather than constrict, learning in an area of interest.

Teaching strategies. Adults can encourage children to follow up their interests and discoveries by structuring the program day to enable children to do this, providing ready access to both the same and different materials each day, and showing genuine interest in and curiosity about each child's pursuits. Try the following strategies:

o Provide time and materials for children to continue pursuing their interests. Ask if they would like to use a set of materials, practice a skill, or expand on a pretend play scenario later that day (for example, carrying appropriate materials outside) and/or the following day. Remind them that the materials and opportunities to use them are available *if* they choose. Provide work-in-progress signs for children who want to store an ongoing project in a safe place to finish at another time.

○ Provide opportunities for children to elaborate on the play themes that interest them. Rather than discourage repetitive play, think of creative ways to build on it. For example, if the same group of children plays superheroes every day, offer a variety of materials they can use to make props. Pose questions such as, "Suppose he lost his power to become invisible; how else could he sneak inside?" Encourage them to move like superheroes at circle time or invent a song a superhero might sing about his special powers. Ask them questions about what superheroes eat for snacks or what they do when they are not fighting the bad guys.

○ Share in children's interests and curiosity. Your genuine involvement in what they are doing communicates to them that their activities and what they learn from them are worth following up. Using the strategies described previously, demonstrate your interest by engaging in authentic conversations, asking questions sparingly, playing with children as partners, sharing their activities with families, and suggesting ways parents can extend a child's interest at home.

For Further Consideration

1. How can teachers recognize and respect their own approaches to learning while allowing children to approach learning in ways that are consistent with their own personalities and developmental levels?

2. How can adults play as enthusiastic partners with children while respecting their initiative and not taking over the children's play themes?

3. Think of one learning center in the classroom (such as the house area, art area, or music and movement area). What types of materials should teachers provide to accommodate differences in preschoolers' preferred sensory modes (learning styles), paces of learning, desire to play alone or with others, special needs, and developmental or ability levels? How can teachers provide the necessary variety for the group as a whole without overwhelming individual children?

4. Consider the differentiations emphasized in this chapter between planning and making choices (*planning is choice with intention*) and between reflection and memory (*reflection is remembering with analysis*). What strategies can adults use so that children's opportunities to make plans and recall their experiences are not rote but instead result in genuine and meaningful learning?

5. In scaffolding children's learning, how can teachers find the right balance between supporting children at their current level of understanding and providing gentle extensions that encourage children to use additional resources, engage with ideas as well as materials, try alternative ways to solve problems, and follow up on their experiences and discoveries?

Chapter 4

Social and Emotional Learning

Manuel, age 4, watches his mother leave after she drops him off and says to his teacher, "Estoy triste." She replies, "Estás triste. You are sad because your mother left." Manuel nods and says, "Sí" The teacher asks, "Would you like a hug, un abrazo?" She opens her arms and he cuddles inside them. "A hug," the teacher repeats. "Hug," says Manuel, trying out the word, and he smiles.

❀ ❀ ❀

At snack time, 5-year-old Maria says, "I'm happy because my babcia [Polish for grandmother] is making pierogies tonight, but Lucas [her brother] is mad!" When the teacher asks why her brother is mad, Maria answers, "She stuffs them with potatoes, but Lucas only likes the kind with meat."

❀ ❀ ❀

At the beginning of small group time, Travon, a younger 4-year-old, observes his teacher wrapping a wide rubber grip around a red pencil before placing the pencil on the tray of Keira's wheelchair. Later, when Keira says she wants to use a blue pencil, Travon says, "I'll get you one!" He fetches a blue pencil from the pile on the table, wraps it with a rubber grip, and puts it in the middle of Keira's tray.

❀ ❀ ❀

When Annette, a teacher, observes Malia (age 4) and Rhyann (age 5) playing together in the block area every day for a week, she begins to ask for their help on tasks that require two people. For example, she asks them to carry some big boards outside when the class decides to make a balance beam. When they set the board down on the grass, Rhyann tells Annette, "That's teamwork!"

Social and emotional learning has always been an essential—even the primary—domain of early childhood education. Today more than ever, teachers need to help children develop skills that will enable them to face a world filled with challenging situations and extreme pressures. In addition to acquiring social norms from home and school, young children are increasingly exposed to influences from the media and technology, where they face evolving and often contradictory expectations for personal and interpersonal behavior (Levin 2013).

Thus, the importance of paying attention to children's social-emotional development receives attention in the professional literature. Its significance in education policy is highlighted in major reports such as *From Neurons to Neighborhoods: The Science of Early Childhood Development* from the National Research Council (2000b) and "Emotions Matter: Making the Case for the Role of Young Children's Emotional Development for Early School Readiness" from the Society for Research in Child Development (Raver, Izard, & Kopp 2002). Organizations such as Fight Crime: Invest in Kids (2013), as well as individuals like James Heckman,

Nobel laureate in economics (Heckman & Masterov 2007), are also playing a role in raising public awareness that appropriate early intervention can help set children who are at risk on a path toward better social adjustment throughout their school years and into adulthood (e.g., Reynolds et al. 2001; Schweinhart et al. 2005; Yoshikawa 1995). Ongoing projects apply the lessons from research to Head Start, child care programs, and other early childhood settings. One example is the Center on the Social and Emotional Foundations for Early Learning (CSEFEL) in its series of What Works briefs (2003); another is the Collaborative for Academic, Social, and Emotional Learning (CASEL), which publishes a guide to effective social and emotional learning programs (2013).

Young Children's Development in Social and Emotional Learning

Social-emotional competence has been defined as

> [T]he ability to understand, manage, and express the social and emotional aspects of one's life in ways that enable the successful management of life's tasks such as learning, forming relationships, solving everyday problems, and adapting to the complex demands of growth and development. (Elias et al. 1997, 2)

Put another way, "socially competent young children are those who engage in satisfying interactions and activities with adults and peers and through such interactions further improve their own competence" (Katz & McClellan 1997, 1). Both of these definitions emphasize that social development underlies and affects all other areas of learning and development, and so it is an important part of the early childhood curriculum (Hyson 2004). With minor variations, child development researchers and practitioners (in publications as well as personal feedback provided for this book) agree that social-emotional competence is made up of the following four components, which clearly are closely related:

- **Emotional self-regulation**—responding to experiences with an appropriate range of immediate or delayed emotions. In preschool, this component is characterized by children's growing ability to focus and organize their actions, exhibit greater forethought and less impulsivity, and show enhanced awareness of and ability to follow rules, routines, and common procedures. Young children's language development and ability to hold mental images (representations) enable them to label their emotions, defer gratification, anticipate the eventual satisfaction of their needs, and be more flexible in creating alternative goals and solutions to problems (Denham 2006). A related aspect that is developing over the preschool years is self-awareness, the understanding that one exists as an individual, separate from other people, with private thoughts and feelings. Seeing oneself as independent and self-motivated is essential to understanding the ability to control one's own behavior.

- **Social knowledge and understanding**—knowledge of social norms and customs. Acquiring this knowledge in the early years is called *socialization*, or becoming a member of the "community." The classroom as a community, and the teacher's role in establishing a supportive group environment, is central in early childhood practice (as is establishing ties with families and the community beyond the school). To become a participating member of the group, children must be able to give up some individuality for the greater good, transitioning from the "me" of toddlerhood to the "us" of preschool. This shift is also the underpinning of civic competence, a key aspect of social studies (Jantz & Seefeldt 1999).

- **Social skills**—the range of appropriate strategies for interacting with others. Cognitive development, especially becoming able to take another's perspective and to empathize, facilitates the development of social skills. Preschoolers' emerging classification skills—understanding similarities and differences and concepts such as some/all—mean they become aware of how they are both like and not like others. Teachers can play a crucial role in helping young children respect differences they observe in gender, ethnicity, language, ability, ideas, and so on (Derman-Sparks & Edwards 2010).

- **Social dispositions**—enduring character traits. These include socially valued ones, such as curiosity, humor, and generosity, as well as less appreciated ones, such as closed-mindedness, argumentativeness, and selfishness. Babies are born with innate temperamental differences that manifest themselves immediately and endure into adulthood. However, environment also plays a significant role in shaping whether a difference is expressed constructively or not (for example, as persistence or as obstinacy).

Teaching and Learning in Social and Emotional Development

Educators often seem conflicted about the relative importance of child- versus adult-guided experience in contributing to early social and emotional development. On the one hand, many educators would agree with Katz and McClellan's (1997) observation:

> [I]n the preschool and early school years, children probably do not learn social competence through direct instruction—lessons, lectures, magic [discussion] circles, workbook exercises, or suggestive and sometimes exhortatory approaches . . . [especially] attempted with the class as a whole. (20)

Instead, children learn through the guidance they get from their interactions and behaviors, it is argued, because such guidance is individualized. It maximizes the child's participation in constructing new knowledge and allows teachers to be warm and supportive during the interaction (Gartrell 2012).

On the other hand, researchers and early childhood practitioners recognize the value of explicit adult intervention in such areas as conflict resolution and violence prevention (Levin 2003). Furthermore, young children can learn how to solve problems collaboratively and contribute to classroom policies through group strategies such as class meetings (Vance 2014).

Drawing on work that integrates the best of both approaches, I offer some general strategies for teachers as they work with the class as a whole, as well as with small groups and individual children, to encourage social and emotional development:

- **Modeling.** Modeling can be done at the group as well as the individual level. "Teaching by example, or modeling, is the most powerful technique that educators employ, intentionally or otherwise" (Elias et al. 1997, 56). So, for example, children learn positive behaviors when they see teachers being empathetic, solving problems, taking risks, admitting mistakes, and so on. And, while children can pick up knowledge and skills on their own from observing positive behaviors, their learning is enhanced if teachers occasionally make explicit what they themselves are doing—for example, pointing out that they are listening to each child.

- **Coaching.** Like modeling, coaching can be done with either individual children or groups. Coaching entails teachers dividing a positive behavior into its component parts, providing children with explicit instruction on how to perform and sequence the parts, creating opportunities for them to practice the behavior, and offering feedback on their efforts. Coaching social skills is thus comparable to providing instruction in domains such as literacy or physical movement.

Coaching may be especially helpful with children who don't seem to be accepted by their peers and whose reaction to this only increases peers' rejection of them. For example, a teacher might coach a child who is having trouble entering an ongoing play group. She might help the child to first observe from the sidelines, and then use strategies such as offering help with some task that will further the group's play (for example, fetching a blanket to wrap up a baby) or accepting a role assigned by the leader. Children can also learn to notice cues (such as moving over to make room) that indicate the group is open to the child's entering.

- **Providing opportunities for practice.** As in any domain of learning, repetition and practice are vital to mastering appropriate social behavior. However, more so than in some disciplines, social-emotional learning not only "entails the learning of many new skills, it may also require the unlearning of habitual patterns of thought and behavior" (Elias et al. 1997, 55). Unlearning may be easier at the preschool age than in later years, when habits are more ingrained. Nonetheless, norms in preschool and other settings can be incongruent and, thus, confusing for children; for example, listening to others may be more valued, or at least more practiced, in the classroom than at home for some children. Teachers need to give young children repeated opportunities to integrate social skills into their everyday behavior until the skills become natural and routine. Once social skills become automatic, they are more likely to generalize from the early childhood setting to kindergarten and beyond.

Above all, to help preschoolers become socially and emotionally competent, we must remember that a lack of such skills does not mean children's attitudes or behaviors are bad or naughty, any more than a toddler is being ignorant or willful by not reading or doing arithmetic! Young children simply do not know any better—yet. But through child-guided and adult-guided experiences, preschoolers can acquire the social and emotional knowledge and skills that promote individual and collective well-being. As their mastery of social skills and knowledge increases, young children's positive interactions, as well as social dispositions such as curiosity, become an effective mechanism for learning in all other domains.

Fitting the Learning Experience to the Learning Objective

The remainder of this chapter identifies the emotional learning and social learning that children typically develop around preschool age. By emotional learning, I mean the knowledge and skills related to children's recognition and self-regulation of their feelings. Social learning means the principles and strategies young children need for interacting successfully with others.

Both of these areas are further divided in this chapter into skills and knowledge that seem most likely to be learned, or best learned, through child-guided experience (including through peer interactions) versus those that seem to depend more on adult-guided instruction. As with every other curriculum area covered in this book, there is not a hard line between the two modes. Both child-guided and adult-guided experiences require adult support, and both occur in an atmosphere the teacher has created. The knowledge and skills discussed in the adult-guided experience section are those that seem to require more explicit teacher intervention.

As a general rule, dealing successfully with one's emotional state is a prerequisite to socializing effectively with others. Admittedly, these dimensions often overlap. Conflict resolution, for example, involves both emotional self-regulation and social problem-solving skills. Yet the division between emotional and social in this chapter can help early childhood teachers think about which instructional components to emphasize in promoting learning in each area.

For both emotional and social learning, a central role of teachers in child-guided experience is to create a warm and caring program environment, as discussed in Chapter 2 (see p. 18). Preschoolers' primary emotional attachments are to their parents or other important caregivers. With the help of family members, teachers play a crucial role in making a child's transition to the school setting successful. Adults need to understand the challenges young children face when they find themselves among strangers, in an unfamiliar place full of unfamiliar social and behavioral expectations. Even if the personal and social norms of a child's home and school are congruent, there is still an adjustment to the group nature of the classroom. Teachers who establish a supportive climate help young children to discover themselves and begin to form positive relationships with others. To the extent that children can navigate this territory on their own—with adults providing support only as needed—their social and emotional confidence will be enhanced.

In addition to creating a supportive environment, the role of teachers in adult-guided experience is to explicitly guide young children in acquiring various social-emotional skills and knowledge. They can take concrete and conscious steps to promote children's positive attitudes about themselves and their abilities in a way that allows children to develop the self-control and motivation to solve problems with others and to become respectful, contributing members of the community. While these goals may sound lofty when applied to preschoolers, the early years lay the groundwork for these children's later beliefs and behaviors as friends, family members, coworkers, and citizens.

Emotional Learning

Of the key knowledge and skills in the area of emotional learning, a positive self-identity and the ability to empathize with the feelings of others seem especially dependent on interpersonal interactions and other child-guided experience. In comparison, young children seem less likely to develop emotional competence or to learn to recognize and label emotions without adult teaching and other intervention.

Child-guided experience is especially important for learnings such as:

Developing a positive self-identity

Self-identity is how one defines and feels about oneself as a person. A sense of self begins to emerge in infancy; its healthy development depends on the child establishing trusting and secure relationships with the important caregivers in her life, including her parent(s), grandparent(s), teacher(s), and others. Identity formation continues during the toddler and preschool years. When it forms positively, it means the child recognizes and respects his own name, gender, role in the family, physical appearance, abilities and limitations, ethnicity, and language or languages. It may include other elements such as religious group, neighborhood, and family structure (for example, two-household family, single-parent home, foster home, grandparents or other relatives as head of household, parents of the same sex, blended family).

Teaching strategies. Teachers help children develop a sense of who they are by supporting their transition from home to the early childhood setting, providing labels for the many facets of their identity, and establishing a classroom atmosphere in which every child feels valued. Children's positive self-images are fostered when teachers use strategies such as these:

- Support children through their separations from family members as they gradually gain confidence that they can handle them on their own. Acknowledge and accept their feelings (e.g., anxiety, sadness). Those feelings predictably surface at drop-off time, but they also can arise at unexpected times during the day. Work with family members to help in the transition process—for example, to make it clear to children when they will be back. Allow children to enter classroom activities at their own pace or to reenter them later if they get upset and withdraw.

- Let children know they are valued by giving them your positive, respectful attention. Focus primarily on the children throughout the day; that is, spend most of your time attending to them and what they are doing rather than arranging materials, cleaning up, or interacting with other adults. Interact with children in calm and respectful tones; avoid shouting, shaming, or using harsh words and actions. Rather than talk about children in front of them as though they weren't there, address comments directly to them.

- Address diversity and differences positively. Children are curious about differences, so don't shy away from naming and discussing them. Supply identity labels and use them in respectful ways (for example, "Tomoko has trouble walking so she uses a wheelchair," or "Hassan is Muslim, Angel is Catholic, and Marva is Jewish" or "Chloe lives with her mommy and daddy, and Milo lives with his two daddies"). Talking with children about differences in gender, skin color, religious observances, family composition, and so on can be affirming and instructive as long as the teacher's tone is accepting and factual, not judgmental. (See also the Valuing Diversity section on p. 182 in Chap. 9.)

- Provide children with nonstereotyped materials, activities, and role models. For example, read picture books that include women in nontraditional professions and men doing housework and nurturing children. Provide clothes and props for children of both sexes to role-play different occupations. Encourage children of both sexes to work with all types of equipment (for example carpentry tools, cooking utensils).

○ Include materials and experiences that reflect different cultures. For example, stock the house area with food containers and utensils from a variety of cuisines; include items the children are familiar with (such as a saucepan or griddle) as well as those that may be new to them (such as a rice steamer or clay pot). Read books with stories and pictures depicting a variety of countries, including those that families of children in your program come from.

○ Encourage family members to become involved in the program. Be sure to include parents, grandparents, and other regular caregivers. Provide many options for involvement so family members can choose what suits them. Examples include volunteering in the classroom (interacting with children, not just performing custodial chores), contributing materials, attending parent meetings and workshops, writing for a program newsletter, serving on advisory councils, meeting with teachers formally and informally to discuss the program and children's progress, sharing a family's valued custom with the group, and providing resources that can extend children's classroom learning into the home. Where feasible, provide transportation and child care as needed for families to participate in program activities. (See also the Building Relationships With Families section on p. 24 in Chap. 2.)

○ Establish ties with the community. Community members may be willing and able to contribute time and support by serving as mentors and role models to children, hosting visits to their workplaces, helping translate written communications into other languages for families, serving as interpreters or advisors on culture, or interacting with children in the classroom. Community members might include artists, tradespeople, business owners, community service workers, medical and other professionals, senior citizens, and others involved in the community. The more diverse these community connections, the better we communicate to children that people of all backgrounds are valued and welcomed in the program.

Feeling empathy

Empathy is comprehending another person's feelings, being able to put yourself in that person's shoes. Being empathetic includes traits such as caring, compassion, and altruism. Empathy has both a cognitive and an affective dimension. To be fully capable of experiencing and demonstrating empathy, the child must be developmentally capable of seeing a situation from someone else's perspective, which Piaget ([1932] 1965) called decentering. This is an ability that is just emerging in the preschool years. Yet there is evidence that even infants and toddlers have some ability to pick up on another's emotions (Hoffman 2000; McMullen et al. 2009; Quann & Wien 2014; Spinrad & Stifter 2006).

Teaching strategies. The main strategies intentional teachers use to support children's discovery of empathy are modeling, acknowledgment, and encouragement. Here are some examples:

- Show (model) concern for children who are upset or angry. Use verbalizations, facial expressions, and body language to show you are aware of the way others feel. Describe your reactions and actions; for example, you might say "I'm giving Taryn the fuzzy monkey to cuddle. She's sad because her grandma is leaving today." For dual language learners, label emotions in both a child's home language and English. Use what you know about the children to comfort them in ways that suit their individual temperaments and preferences and so are likely to be effective. Children will follow your example, as this preschooler did:

> Alexandra sees her teacher move over to make room when Leo joins the circle of people sitting on the rug. After a few minutes, when Inez comes over, Alexandra slides to her right and says, "Now there's room for you, too."

- Allow and encourage children to express their feelings. Make them aware that others in similar situations share such emotions; for example, you could say, "Claudia is mad because her dog chewed a hole in her new shoe. Tommy also felt angry the time his brother's puppy tore up his baseball hat."

- Introduce perspective-taking activities and questions about subjects other than feelings. For example, ask children to give directions for their classmates to follow or wonder aloud about how something would look to a person sitting on the other side of the table. Practicing the cognitive and perceptual skills required by perspective taking can help children generalize those skills to social-emotional situations.

- Pair children of different ability levels or ages to help them see that older or more skilled people can help others, while younger or less skilled people can learn from others. If children find themselves in either position at one time or another, they can better adopt different perspectives as the occasion warrants. Because young children are more often on the receiving end of help, it is especially empowering for them to be able to give it. They come to see the recipient of their assistance as an individual and feel good about their ability to bring about change. For example, a supervisor in an inclusive preschool recorded this anecdote:

> The children were very impatient with Michael, a child who was often confused and took longer to accomplish things. So each day over a two-week period, the teacher asked a different child to help Michael with a task (such as cleaning up, pouring juice, putting on his coat). By the end of this period, most children showed less impatience or anger with Michael. A few asked the teacher if they could continue to help; some asked Michael directly if he wanted help. The child helpers began to take pleasure in Michael's incremental but meaningful accomplishments, such as the first time he poured his own juice while a helper held the cup. They encouraged him to try more things on his own, which he did. In fact, Michael was more willing to try things with encouragement from his peers than he was with similar support from adults.

Adult-guided experience is especially important for learnings such as:

Developing feelings of competence

Competence is being able to do something well. Feeling competent means having the self-confidence to undertake tasks with the expectation of success. For young children, it is important to judge success not according to adult standards but by what the child sets out to accomplish. Helping young children develop feelings of competence is important to their current and future learning. How children feel about themselves and their abilities when they enter school has a great influence on their motivation and willingness to undertake challenging learning tasks.

Teaching strategies. Helping young children develop a positive and realistic sense of confidence in their abilities is arguably the single most important task of early childhood teachers. Many of the following strategies were introduced in Chapter 2 as best practices for early childhood teachers generally; they are especially pertinent in this discussion of self-confidence:

○ Create a classroom space and schedule that promote children's sense of efficacy and control. Establish and follow a consistent daily routine so children feel they know about and have some control over what happens in their environment. To enable children to find, use, and return materials independently, label the materials in English and in children's home languages, and add picture cues.

○ Encourage self-help skills in ways that are consistent with children's abilities and developmental levels. Give them time to do things on their own (such as putting on their outdoor clothing or cleaning up spills). Resist the temptation to complete these tasks yourself because doing so would be easier, faster, or better; don't worry if tasks are not done perfectly because improvement will come with practice and maturation. Similarly, let children practice a task as often as they want to achieve mastery. Don't rush them or insist they do something else instead. The goal is for children to believe in their ability to take care of their own needs.

○ Introduce the next level of challenge once children have mastered the current one and are ready to move on. For example, at cleanup time, a younger child may be able to return blocks to the correct storage area but not yet be able to sort them on the shelf by size. For an older child, a teacher might ask, "Can you put this block with the others just like it?" Coach or model ways children can make everyday tasks easier or more efficient—for example, bundling paper scraps together and wrapping them in a paper towel to throw away all at once instead of bringing them to the trash can one at a time.

○ Support children's ideas and initiatives. Welcome their contributions during discussions and activities, and encourage them to share ideas with peers.

During choice time and other individual activities, encourage them to make plans and choices (for example, deciding in what area or areas they will play, what materials they will use and how, whether to play on their own or with others and with whom, or how long they will engage in each activity). Equally important, during group activities, even during teacher-led group times, encourage children to make choices and use materials in their own way. For example, provide just a general context (such as a finger play) but let children determine exactly how the activity will unfold.

O Acknowledge and encourage children's efforts and accomplishments. While praise ("What a nice picture you've painted") can make them depend on the judgment of others to feel good about themselves, encouragement helps them evaluate their own competencies positively ("You really put a lot of detail into your painting"). To encourage young children, watch and listen, imitate their actions and repeat their words, comment on what they are doing, and, with their permission, display their work to peers and parents. Involve families further by sending work home, sharing it at parent conferences and during informal contacts such as pickup time, and explaining what it shows about their children's learning.

O Provide opportunities for children to be leaders; for example, ask them to suggest movements during large group time or ways they might transition from one activity to another. Invite a dual language learner to teach the group the word in his home language for a toy or activity that is popular with the children. Ask children from different cultures if there is a simple song they sing with their families that they would like to lead the class in singing (learn it first yourself so you can help teach it, asking families for help if necessary). Do not force or require children to lead, but give everyone the opportunity to do so. If you sense children are not listening to or do not fully understand what the leader is saying or doing, repeat children's ideas (making sure you have correctly understood them yourself) so their classmates can listen and try to carry out the ideas.

O Tune in to the involvement level of the children during large group activities. Be open to making group time longer or shorter, depending on how children respond. To allow extra time for children who are very involved, schedule something afterward that doesn't require participation by the entire group at the outset (such as outside time) so that children can join when they are ready (Perrett 1996). By doing so, you communicate that persistence at tasks is a worthwhile trait and instill a sense of confidence that they can carry out their intentions to completion.

Recognizing and labeling emotions

Emotional awareness involves understanding that one has feelings as distinct from thoughts, being able to identify and name those feelings, and recognizing that others have feelings that may be the same or different from one's own. [*Note:* These abilities are components of emotional intelligence, but emotional intelligence is a broader concept that also encompasses identifying and addressing the emotions of oneself, other individuals, and groups (Goleman 1995).]

Teaching strategies. One's emotions arise naturally, but knowing what they are, what they mean, and how they are labeled by one's culture are things we must learn from others. Intentional teachers are ready to take advantage of events as they arise to introduce children to specific knowledge and skills in this area. Because preschoolers are capable of forming mental representations, teachers also can refer to hypothetical, past, and future situations in helping children master emotional experiences and vocabulary. Here are some strategies:

- Attend to children's emotional states. When children express emotions in words or actions, convey with your words, facial expressions, and gestures that you are paying attention. Make eye contact, get down on the children's level, and focus on them.

- Accept children's full range of emotions as normal. Do not judge emotions as good or bad. However, do stop cruel or unsafe behavior that may result from emotions such as hurt, anger, fear, and frustration.

- Label children's emotions and your own with simple words, such as angry, happy, or sad. (For dual language learners, pair the word in their home languages with the word in English, and use a picture if possible.) Encourage children to name their own emotions; repeat the words they choose to use (for example, "You said you feel all squiggly inside?"). Wait to introduce children to new labels for emotions until the heat of the moment has passed. During times of upset, children are usually too distracted by or invested in their feelings to absorb words that are new to them. For example, at group time, use puppets or persona dolls to act out strong feelings or conflict situations that you have noticed occurring among the children, and invite children to discuss how the puppets or dolls could address these issues. Or introduce new words for feelings before conflicts arise—for example, while reading and discussing a book in which emotions are part of the story.

- Point out to children that others also have feelings (but first make sure you correctly understand what each child is feeling). For example, say, "Jimmy said it made him angry when you grabbed the watering can from him." Point out to children their peers' body language, facial expressions, and verbalizations ("Carla banged her fist on the table. People sometimes do that when they are angry"). This is particularly effective during social problem-solving situations. Adult interpretation works well for children who are not yet adept at picking up these cues themselves or who are too overwhelmed and self-focused at a particular moment to notice others' feelings.

- Comment conversationally on the emotions you observe children expressing throughout the day. Be sure to notice and remark on all types of feelings. For example, "You look like you might feel sad this morning," "What a big smile (sonrisa)! I think you're very happy (feliz)," "You sound excited about playing at Nicola's house after school today," and "You sure looked surprised when the guinea pig popped out at the other end of the tunnel!"

- Plan small group activities that focus on feelings. Preschoolers do not often talk about emotions in the abstract, but they can do so readily by reading books, acting out situations with puppets or persona dolls, or creating and discussing artwork about people and events that evoke emotions (for example, a visit from a grandparent, a car trip for a child used to taking public transportation, the arrival of a sibling, the loss of a pet).

Validating and Putting Words to Children's Feelings

Some children talk readily about their feelings. Some do not, perhaps because they are not encouraged to vocalize feelings at home, this behavior is not valued by their culture, or for a variety of other reasons. Here, a teacher helps a preschool class, and one child in particular, deal with the sadness of a friend's moving away.

Jack's family was moving to a distant city, and he would be leaving the preschool at the end of the week. Before Jack left, the teachers talked about his upcoming departure at greeting circle and asked the children how they felt about it. They used words like *sad* and *unhappy* and said they would miss him. After Jack was gone, they kept his name on the board for a couple of weeks (with an arrow pointing to a house to indicate he was living someplace else), talked about the fact that he had moved away, and shared things they remembered about him.

The week after Jack left, a teacher noticed that Sean, who generally collaborated well with other children, was kicking over their blocks, grabbing toys away from them, and engaging in other similar acts. After solving a few immediate crises, she remembered that Sean had often played with Jack and wondered if he was having some unexpressed feelings about his friend's leaving. During a calm moment, she sat on the couch with Sean:

Teacher: I'm still sad that Jack moved away.

Sean: It's not fair.

Teacher: You think it isn't fair that he moved away.

Sean: Yes. Now I have no one to build big towers with.

Teacher: That's no fun.

Sean: I'm mad at Jack.

Teacher: You're mad because Jack moved away and now you can't play with him.

Sean: Yeah. He shouldn't have done that!

Teacher: Jack had to go because his mommy got a job in a different city. But it makes us sad and mad that he had to move away.

Sean: Yeah, really, really mad.

Teacher: It's okay to feel that way.

Just expressing his anger helped Sean to be less angry, but it didn't fully solve his problem. A few days later, the teacher had another one-on-one talk with him about what would make him feel better. Sean thought of two other children who liked to play with the blocks and used his existing social skills to enter their play.

Later, when Jack's mother sent a photo of him and his family, the teachers and children commented on how *happy* he looked in front of his new home. Sean told his teacher, "I still miss Jack, but I'm happy too because now I have two new friends."

○ Discuss with families children's need to express and label their feelings appropriately. In workshops and informal exchanges, explain to families that labeling and showing a range of emotions in acceptable ways are an important part of early learning. Doing so will help their children adjust to the wide range of people and experiences they will encounter in school and beyond. It can also help them deal better with situations at home, such as conflicts with siblings, limit setting by parents, or disappointments when hopes and plans do not work out. Parents should also be encouraged to nurture their children's expression of positive emotions—joy, happiness, love—in such situations as a parent returning from deployment or a grandparent visiting from the family's home country. While different cultures have different norms about the acceptability of emotional expression, families and teachers agree that they want their children to succeed. Explaining to parents why emotional competence is a component of school readiness opens the door to exploring a range of comfortable avenues for encouraging appropriate emotional expression at home.

Social Learning

Of the key knowledge and skills in the area of social learning, developing a sense of community, building relationships, and engaging in cooperative play all seem to typically develop in the course of child-guided interactions. But young children seem to need adult-guided experience to learn to use problem-solving strategies when they have social conflicts and to develop a framework for moral behavior.

Child-guided experience is especially important for learnings such as:

Developing a sense of community

A community is a social group with common interests. Community members receive and give one another support for individual and group undertakings. Having a sense of community means seeing oneself as belonging to the group and sharing all or a significant number of its characteristics, beliefs, and practices. Through their interactions with peers in the classroom community, young children also deepen their understanding of social norms and conventions.

Teaching strategies. Intentional teachers create a sense of community in the classroom and help young children feel they belong to that community by employing strategies such as these:

- Create an atmosphere in which children and adults are expected to be kind to and supportive of one another. Refer to the children and adults in the classroom with phrases such as "our class," "all of us," "our group," and "all together." Express your own pleasure at being part of the classroom.

- Arrange the room to include both open areas where large groups can assemble and enclosed areas with comfortable furniture conducive to more personal interactions.

- Establish a consistent daily routine. When everyone is engaged in the same type of activity at the same time each day, it creates a sense of community. However, participating in the same type of activity does not mean everyone necessarily is doing the same thing. For example, all children can be engaged but involved with different activities during choice time; at small group, they may use the same materials but in different ways. During each activity, set an unhurried pace that lets children enjoy one another's company instead of feeling pressured to finish a task.

- Call attention to occasions when children are working or sharing an experience together as a group. The occasions can be routine ("We got everything put away at cleanup so we can find them tomorrow at choice time") or special ("Look at all the shells we gathered at the beach. I wonder what we could do with them?"). Take photos of the group activities and put them in a class album, labeled with simple captions.

- Organize activities that foster children's participation with others. Even those who tend toward solitary play can feel safe in groups that are noncompetitive and don't call attention to the individual. During brief whole group activities (such as greeting time or class meeting), encourage children to share problems and solutions, invite them to share something they are looking forward to, or plan a special event together and write down the children's ideas. Here are some additional thoughts on opportunities for children to engage with one another:

> [Adult-initiated] group times offer special social opportunities. During the child-initiated parts of the routine, children can choose how solitary or social they want to be—working by themselves, with a friend or adult, or with a group. Since some children will choose not to play with others during these times, the group times offer additional opportunities for them to participate in a social experience. At small group time, for example, where everyone is working with the same materials, children often share and discuss what they are doing, learn from one another, and help one another. At large group time, where everyone is engaged in a common action game or song (all of which are safe, low-risk social experiences), children have opportunities to contribute and demonstrate their ideas to the group as well as imitate and learn from their peers. (Epstein & Hohmann 2012, 326–27)

○ Involve children in the larger community. For example, children might do projects around the building, such as recycling classroom materials or picking up playground trash (with adults closely monitoring to avoid broken glass, contamination, or other dangers). Use stories, poems, songs, and chants ("narratives") to illustrate classroom and community activities. For example, sing "This is the way we put away the blocks" at cleanup time, and invite the children to make up their own verses as they share cleanup tasks. Welcome community guests to the classroom; make them feel comfortable by, for example, having children give them a tour of the learning centers. Walk around the neighborhood and draw children's attention to how residents decorate their windows and yards and to what businesspeople put in storefront displays. Visit local places (such as the public library or farmers' market) and take part in community activities (such as street fairs). Clip newspaper photos of familiar people, places, and events; write simple captions; and post them near the door so children and families can see and discuss them at drop-off and pickup times. Include clippings from foreign-language newsletters and magazines commonly found in the community (many weekly or monthly publications are available for free in local stores) and translate the captions—or key words—into English.

Building relationships

Human relationships are rewarding in their own right and facilitate every other type of learning. *Relationships with peers* are evident by age 2 and become more reciprocal during preschool (Ladd, Herald, & Andrews 2006). Preschoolers can describe why they like their friends (for example, shared interests and desirable traits, such as being funny or kind). The increased contact between children, however, often means there are more opportunities for conflict. *Relationships with adults*—critical in the infant and toddler years—continue to be important during preschool, although their nature changes. Preschoolers become more selective in the kinds of interactions they want with adults, whether it is seeking comfort, getting help, sharing a discovery, or simply enjoying a conversation. In *One Child, Two Languages,* Patton Tabors (2008) shares some conversation skills that young children can be taught so they can communicate more effectively with children who speak different languages. For example, teach children to initiate conversations with other children even if they seem shy or resistant at first. Show them how to speak slowly and clearly (but naturally rather than in an exaggerated manner). Demonstrate how to restate a question or statement with slightly different wording to help the other child understand.

Teaching strategies. Adults play a vital role in encouraging and supporting young children as they navigate the complex terrain of human relationships. Accepting overtures from others, and reaching out to them, can be risky for preschoolers. They need to know they are socially and emotionally safe, and that their autonomy will be respected as they interact with others. To help children establish relationships with others, try these ideas:

- Be genuine and authentic in your interactions with children. Talk with them to learn what and how they think, not to manage their behavior. Place yourself at their level rather than stand over and talk down to them. Children sense when adults are disinterested, impatient, or mechanical during conversations. Rather than dominate the interaction or ask a lot of questions, listen to what they are saying. Give children plenty of time to think through their ideas. Pose a real question now and then (that is, one that you don't know the answer to) and respond honestly to children's questions. If you talk to children with warmth and respect, they will learn to converse in kind with others. Children from different language backgrounds or cultures may have different ways of showing emotions or responding to adult questions. Getting to know children may mean simply spending time with them and showing interest in what they are doing without putting pressure on them to respond.

- Maintain a stable group of children and adults so relationships can build over time. Create clusters in which one adult and a small group of children (no more than 10) stay together for several weeks or months to share meals or snacks and small group activities. Stable groups allow children to get to know the personalities and interests of their peers and the adult. They also help preschoolers feel safe and secure, which further encourages them to reach out to others.

- Support children's friendships. Be aware of when preschoolers are forming relationships with one another. For example, you might observe children sharing materials, engaging in pretend play, talking, or showing concern for one another. To encourage and support these budding relationships, begin by simply acknowledging them ("Delia, I saw you and Sammy playing store in the house area"). Provide an ample supply of the materials they like to incorporate in their pretend play. Put the children together when it is time to (re) form small groups. Mention the friendship to the children's families so they can try to arrange playdates outside of school.

- Provide opportunities for children to interact with less familiar people. Although preschoolers often develop clear peer preferences, they can benefit from interacting with others they don't typically choose to play with on their own (for example, those with different interests; a native English speaker for children who typically gravitate toward others in the classroom who also speak their home language). Adults can create situations in which this might occur, such as by asking two children to help with a task ("Daniel and Abby, can you help me carry the scarves outside?"). However, avoid asking children who are bilingual to serve as interpreters for children who are not as fluent in English—this sets a new purpose for their relationship and is often not developmentally appropriate for young children's level of language development. Also, never require children to be friends. This denies their right to make choices. However, providing opportunities to interact allows them to discover new people with whom they might then choose to form relationships.

Engaging in cooperative play

Cooperation is acting together toward a common goal. Cooperative play and collaboration in the early childhood classroom means playing and working with others. It includes sharing toys, space, friends, conversations, resources, skills, and ideas.

Teaching strategies. Young children learn to play with others by watching and imitating, and by trial and error. Because humans are social beings, we are intrinsically motivated to master techniques for human interchange. Nevertheless, it would be a mistake to assume children, therefore, engage in role-playing and collaborative behavior without any adult intervention. In fact, teachers perform a vital function in helping children elaborate their roles in interactive play. Here are some strategies:

- Promote interaction through your use of space and materials in the classroom. Examples include providing dress-up clothes that inspire group role-play and playground equipment that requires two or more children to operate. Avoid arbitrarily limiting the number of children who can play at one time in a given area because it models exclusionary behavior. Whenever possible, provide enough of the same type of materials so children are not preoccupied with having access to them and can freely interact with the materials and each other. If space or supplies are limited (for example, the classroom has only one couch or only two computers), problem solve with the children on how to accommodate everyone who wants to use them. (See the Engaging in Conflict Resolution section on p. 60 in this chapter for individual and group problem-solving ideas.)

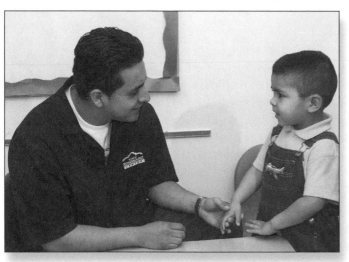

- Create opportunities for collaborative interaction. Allow sufficient time for children to elaborate on their play ideas and incorporate peers into their role-playing. Encourage collaboration by pairs in some activities by suggesting children work with a partner if they choose. Plan small and large group activities that naturally involve working in dyads or triads. These can include movement and music activities where children move or dance as partners, construction activities where two children hold something steady while a third builds on it, conversations where children alternate asking and answering questions, and data-gathering activities where one child collects information and the other records it. Refer children to peers when they need assistance.

- Help children who tend to be aggressive or withdrawn to join their peers. For example, coach children who enter a group too forcefully by suggesting noninvasive strategies; you might say something like, "Maybe if you help carry

Referring Children to Each Other for Assistance

Child-guided learning does not happen only when children play on their own; it often occurs when they interact with other children. One way teachers can facilitate this interaction is by referring a child to another child for assistance when a need arises. Not only does the recipient of the assistance benefit from the learning, but the provider also gets a sense of confidence from being able to help a peer, as shown in the following example.

At small group time, the children are exploring playdough. Their teacher notices that Kyle (4) is having trouble and refers him to Gabriella (also 4) for help:

Teacher: Kyle, you look frustrated. What do you want to do with your playdough?

Kyle: I'm trying to make it go down but it won't.

Teacher: You want your playdough to go down. You want to make it lie flat on the table?

Kyle: Yes, but it's not staying.

Teacher: Show me how you are using your hands to make it stay flat.

Kyle: (He shows how he presses down on the playdough.)

Teacher: Gabriella, I see your playdough is lying down flat. Can you show Kyle how you did it?

Gabriella: Look, Kyle, I used this roller to push it. I think there's another roller in the bucket. (She gets a roller and gives it to Kyle.)

Kyle: (Tries the roller but still does not get the effect he wants.)

Gabriella: You have to push down really, really hard. (She puts her hands over Kyle's and pushes down with him.)

Kyle: Hey, it's working. Let me try. (He does and the playdough stays flat.)

Gabriella: There. You got it to go way down. (She smiles.)

Kyle: I did it! I made it flat like a pizza. Here, Gabriella, I'll slice you a piece.

Encouraging children to help one another is also an effective strategy for helping dual language learners learn English. Pair a native speaker with a dual language learner, or if there are children with varying levels of English proficiency, pair one who is more advanced with one who is less advanced. This gives both children an opportunity to practice and hone their English language skills while building a sense of community (a shared language and perhaps also a shared culture) between them.

---

a chair, they'll let you sit on the bus with them." Reticent children may benefit from using a tool such as a talking stick during group time (only the person holding it may talk; everyone else must listen). Here's an example:

At greeting circle, the teacher invites children to tell the group about something they saw on their way to school. She gives the first child the talking stick, and each child passes it to the next one who wants to speak. Those who do not want to speak are not pressured to do so. However, the teacher notices that even children who are often shy or reserved feel empowered when they hold the talking stick and take a turn speaking before passing it to a peer. (Emily Vance, personal communication, 2004)

○ **Allow children to discover the consequences of their actions**—provided no one is being hurt or endangered. They will adjust their own behavior accordingly, especially if they are rejected by their peers. Here's an example recorded by a preschool teacher:

Jim brings his new fire truck to school and announces that no one is allowed to touch it. When he brings the truck over to where Zack and Maggie are playing with toy cars and ramps, they tell him he cannot join their game. This continues for two days. On the third day, Jim puts his truck on the ramp and says to Maggie, "You can push it if you want." She does and then gives it to Zack. Maggie asks Jim, "Do you want to play racing cars with us?" Jim says yes and joins their play, letting his friends take turns with his truck.

This teacher didn't jump in to give social directions, offer opinions or interpretations, or solve problems for the children. If the teacher had insisted Maggie and Zack let Jim play with them, Jim might not have figured out how to alter his behavior to achieve his social goal of inclusion. Teachers also can point out the beneficial consequences of cooperative behavior to encourage children to continue or increase it. However, the focus should be on how the behavior makes the child feel rather than on how it pleases the adult. For example, you could say, "You're having fun building that tower together," rather than "It makes me happy to see you sharing."

○ Model cooperative play by partnering with children. Get down on their level, imitate their use of materials, and follow their ideas and play leads. Act out the roles and attributes they assign ("You're the dog, and you chase me"). Offer suggestions and extensions for the play as appropriate, but be careful not to take over and direct the play.

○ When possible, share control in the classroom in other ways, too. For example, solicit ideas for a rotation system for children to pass out snacks, choose a song, or lead an action at large group. Ask children how they can make sure everyone who wants a turn using the new computer program gets a chance, and for how long. Give children conversational control by listening to and commenting on what they say, and by not overloading them with questions.

Adult-guided experience is especially important for learnings such as:

Engaging in conflict resolution

Conflict resolution—known by other names, such as problem solving and guidance—refers to using appropriate, nonaggressive strategies to discuss and develop solutions to interpersonal differences. Resolving conflicts when needs and emotions are running high is a challenge; sometimes even adults cannot or choose not to use their own skills at such times.

Teaching strategies. Because preschool-age children developmentally still are quite egocentric and thus focused on their own needs, they often get into conflicts with others. Typically they do not intend harm or mean to act selfishly; they are simply goal oriented ("I want that truck, so I'll grab it"). Intentional teachers, therefore, explicitly model, coach, and teach children the behaviors necessary to resolve conflicts. Understanding that children are not misbehaving but rather making mistakes as they learn how to behave appropriately, we avoid using value-laden or negative terms with them (such as "Stop being mean" or "When you act up like that, you can't sit with the other children") (Gartrell 2012).

As in many other areas, young children need *concrete* experience with conflicts to learn how to resolve them. Once conflicts arise, as they inevitably will, teachers can use the occasions to begin teaching children conflict-resolution skills and proactively help them learn how to avoid future conflicts. To become skilled at conflict resolution takes a great deal of repetition, but preschoolers can begin to implement problem-solving strategies on their own with sufficient modeling and support from their teachers. Consider the following strategies for helping children learn to successfully resolve their conflicts:

The Intentional Teacher

- Establish a safe classroom. Let children know they will not be physically or verbally hurt. Stop children's hurtful or dangerous behaviors immediately, including aggression and rejection. Set and discuss a few clear limits ("No hitting") and expectations ("Everyone gets a turn") with children, and post these where children can easily see them (add a picture or symbol as well to clarify the expectation). Be consistent in implementing rules and following through on expectations.
- Convey calmness through your voice, body language, and facial expressions during a conflict. Show concern but not alarm. Be aware of your own emotional

One Approach to Conflict Resolution

Recommended approaches to conflict resolution vary somewhat, but they all contain the same basic elements. Here is one six-step procedure. Applying steps one and two sets the tone for the rest of the process, as shown in the example that follows.

Mediating Conflict

1. Approach calmly, stopping any hurtful actions. Place yourself between the children, on their level. Use a calm voice and gentle touch. Remain neutral rather than take sides.
2. Acknowledge the children's feelings. If the conflict is over an object, let the children know you need to hold the object ("neutralize" it) until the conflict is resolved.

   Say something like "You look really upset."
3. Gather information from each child.

   "What's the problem?"
4. Restate the problem.

   "So the problem is..."
5. Ask for ideas for solutions, and choose one together that all can agree to try.

   "What can we do to solve this problem?"
6. Be prepared to give follow-up support. Stay near the children.

   "You solved the problem!"

An Example

Shari is feeding her doll a bottle. Daniella grabs it away and says, "I need that." When Shari takes it back, Daniella punches her in the arm and says, "I hate you, you stupid baby!" Their teacher comes over and kneels down between the two girls.

Teacher (to Daniella): You're angry because you want to feed the bottle to your doll. But you cannot punch Shari or call her stupid.

Teacher (to Shari): Let me hold the bottle while we talk about this. (He takes the bottle to neutralize it during their discussion.)

Shari: I had it first.

Teacher (to Shari): You're upset because you were using the bottle and Daniella grabbed it away from you.

Shari: (Nods)

Teacher (to Shari and Daniella): So you both want to feed this bottle to your dolls.

As the children calm down, the teacher takes them through the rest of the problem-solving steps. Each child says in her own words what happened, and then the teacher repeats and verifies their statements and asks them to suggest solutions. The girls decide to make another bottle. Shari holds a block while Daniella tapes on a red LEGO "nipple." Shari uses the original bottle while Daniella uses the one they made together, happy because "My bottle is bigger." When the teacher checks back later, the dolls are taking a nap in the carriage and Shari and Daniella are building a cradle out of blocks.

Adapted, by permission, from B. Evans, *You Can't Come to My Birthday Party! Conflict Resolution With Young Children* (Ypsilanti, MI: HighScope Press 2002), 117–18.

triggers beforehand to help prevent your overreacting during a conflict situation. When you are in control of yourself, you help children regain or maintain control of themselves and you communicate that having strong feelings need not be scary. Your remaining calm, rather than being upset with or critical of the children involved, also focuses attention on solving the problem.

o Soothe children who are upset; children's emotions can run high during a conflict. Rely on your previous observations of them to choose individual strategies you know will be effective. Acknowledge and respect children's feelings. Encourage children to name their own emotions, and then use the words they use. Help children to become aware of one another's feelings by calling attention to their body language, facial expressions, and statements. (See the Recognizing and Labeling Emotions section on p. 52 in this chapter.) Act and speak sincerely; for example, make eye contact with all the children involved, and reflect warmth and concern in your voice. In nonthreatening ways, touch or hold children to reassure them and help them regain self-control.

o Observe children's behavior while mediating the conflict, and collect information to arrive at an insightful interpretation. Remain neutral; don't assign blame or take sides. For example, take time to assess whether a child has knocked down another's tower of boxes because of a misguided attempt to enter the play, because the child is angry with the builder, or because the child simply wasn't watching what she was doing. Involve children in describing problems and proposing solutions. Listen actively. Repeat accurately what children say or paraphrase their words for clarity. Check with children to confirm the accuracy of what you are restating.

o Develop solutions together with children by soliciting their ideas and deciding which one(s) to try. If the children have difficulty coming up with problem-solving solutions on their own, coach them by offering one or two suggestions. Sometimes, if the children involved cannot generate ideas or agree on a solution, they may agree to ask one or two other children for help or even bring the problem before a class meeting. (See also the Creating and Following Rules section on p. 184 in Chap. 9.) Respect children's definition of "fairness." Their definition may differ from yours, but as long as all the parties involved agree on the solution, accept it and help them carry it out. Follow up to see whether the solution is working. If conflicts reemerge, repeat the problem-solving steps until all the children appear settled and reengaged in play.

o Help children reflect on the problem-solving strategies they are learning at times other than during actual conflicts. It may be easier for children to absorb information when they are not emotionally involved. For example, read books and sing and listen to songs about characters coping with anger and other conflict-producing feelings. Role-play conflict resolution scenarios with puppets, dolls, or other props. Pose simple, familiar "what if" situations for small group discussion. To elicit their ideas on how to solve problems, suggest situations you know the children will find unacceptable; for example, "What if I decided that only teachers could mix the paints?" Review with children successfully resolved episodes from their past; for example, do this at snack time or when reading a book that addresses a comparable situation.

The same general approach to conflict resolution can also be used when children exhibit problem behaviors, such as throwing toys when they are frustrated or refusing to follow routines. In such cases, the problem solving would be between the adult and the child. Begin by stopping any hurtful behavior (such as throwing) and validating the child's feelings (for example, "I know you want to keep playing with the blocks, but it's time to get ready to go outside now"). Give the child an opportunity to express her feelings or desires. Stay calm, even if the child becomes emotional ("I don't want to go outside!"). Recap the problem briefly ("You want to keep playing with the blocks, but I can't leave you alone in the room. We need both teachers outside with all the children"). Ask the child for solutions and (if necessary) suggest one or two yourself (for example, "You could put a work-in-progress sign on your tower so no one will touch it, and you can continue building it after lunch" or "Would you like to take some of the blocks outside to play with? I can help you put them in the wagon"). Stay with the child until she calms down, help the child carry out the chosen solution, and follow up to make sure the child is reengaged in play. Acknowledge that the child helped to solve the problem.

Developing a framework for moral behavior

Morality is a system for evaluating human conduct. Conscience is an internal sense of right and wrong that is not dependent on external censure or punishment. Moral development is a long process that extends well into adolescence and even early adulthood. Preschoolers, especially older ones, are beginning to wrestle with questions of moral behavior, particularly with regard to the treatment of others. They are interested in, and capable of, reflecting on their own and others' deeds and misdeeds, especially when encouraged to do so by adults.

Teaching strategies. Our moral sense develops to a great extent through our following (or sometimes explicitly rejecting) the examples set by significant others in our lives, particularly in our home setting. Nevertheless, teachers help lay the groundwork from which children build their own value systems by modeling appropriate behavior in the classroom and conveying moral principles. To support children as they begin to construct a moral framework, teachers can employ several strategies, including these:

- Be consistent and fair-minded. Provide clear expectations about behavior, but emphasize problem solving rather than blame or punishment.

- Verbalize in simple terms the reasons for your actions and decisions that involve moral matters, such as fairness. For example, "I'm making sure every child who wants a muffin has one before giving out seconds. It isn't fair if someone gets two before every child has had one."

- Work with children's families to achieve as much congruence between home and school values as possible. When you find that a child's home beliefs about right and wrong diverge from your classroom's moral principles, explain clearly and simply to children and families why this is so. Try not to put a negative value judgment on beliefs families may hold that conflict with yours; rather, problem solve the conflicts that may arise over how situations are handled in the two settings. (For more on problem solving, see the Resources at the end of the book.) For example, messiness is an area of potential difference. In some cultures, parents may see it as a sign of disrespect if a teacher covers a child's new outfit with a spattered smock, and they may become quite upset if some paint nevertheless gets on the child's clothes. In this case, while acknowledging the parent's discomfort, you should also do your best to explain how chil-

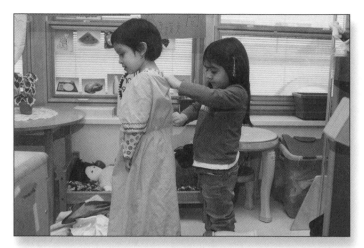

dren learn important concepts in math, science, and other areas by exploring messy materials. If the parent agrees, you might talk about having a spare set of the child's old clothes on hand or ask if the parent would prefer a different or more effective cover-up.

❊   ❊   ❊

Social and emotional learning is an essential developmental domain for young children. They need to understand, regulate, and express their feelings appropriately in order to feel good about themselves. To experience satisfying interpersonal relationships, they need to develop social competence. Such skills are also the mechanisms through which learning in other domains occurs, via observation and imitation, requests for assistance, direct interactions, collaborative exchanges, and the like.

We help young children construct and master emotional and social skills by bolstering their sense of competence and initiative and by creating a classroom environment in which their independent problem-solving abilities can thrive. Teachers also provide explicit guidance in the complex rules of social intercourse by helping children grasp and adhere to classroom and societal norms and offering suggestions when children's own resources prove insufficient to achieve their goals.

Between their intrinsic motivation to be social and our desire to socialize them, young children can and will develop the skills they need to be ready for interpersonal and civic relationships inside and outside of school.

For Further Consideration

1. How can early childhood educators promote emotionally positive self-images for all children in the face of conflicting messages children often encounter in the media?

2. How can we respect the right of children to choose their friends while encouraging them to be open to meeting and interacting with new people?

3. What strategies can teachers employ when children refuse to participate in conflict resolution, rule setting, or other social processes in the classroom?

4. If you are an experienced teacher, what are your emotional triggers in the classroom? If you are a novice teacher, what do you expect will be your emotional triggers in the classroom? How can you recognize them in order to remain calm and in control when helping children deal with their feelings and the situations that upset them?

5. Given that young children vary in emotional and social development, can we develop reliable indicators for teachers to use to screen children with potential problems in these areas? What are the trade-offs with the benefits of early detection and intervention versus the dangers of false and premature labeling?

Chapter 5

Physical Development and Health

On the preschool playground at outside time, Cody tells his teacher Rachel that he is a "crooked horse" and starts galloping in a zigzag pattern. "I see," says Rachel, "You galloped in a crooked path to the tree. I'm going to move like you did." Rachel imitates Cody's movements and says, "Sometimes I call this 'going zigzag.'" Several other children, drawn by the activity, begin to gallop in a zigzag path, too. After several minutes of doing this, Rachel says to them, "I wonder what other kinds of paths we could gallop in." One child suggests "circles," and the children gallop in a series of curves. Other ideas that the children try out include sideways, "baby" (small) gallops, and "monster" (big) gallops. When Malcolm joins the group in his wheelchair, he suggests "forward and back." Malcolm maneuvers his wheelchair back and forth as the other children gallop forward and backward beside him.

The idea that children need to be taught physical movement skills and concepts may seem odd. We assume children develop physically on their own, provided they receive adequate nutrition and have safe opportunities to move around in the environment. Certainly, there is a typical progression in what children are capable of in terms of their gross motor and fine motor development (see Copple & Bredekamp 2009, 116–17). However, it is a mistake to view the development of children's physical skills as being purely maturational in the early childhood years.

Research confirms that young children do not learn fundamental physical skills simply through play (Manross 2000). Left on their own to respond to music, for example, preschool children tend not to make use of all the movement possibilities. In this situation, a 3-year-old typically remains stationary; a 4- or 5-year-old tends to move around more (Stellaccio & McCarthy 1999). But whatever they do, young children tend to limit their movement to the repetition of a few patterns.

To ensure that children gain the basic physical skills they need, adults plan movement experiences and structure physical activities that introduce a range of movement options. They also provide children with time, space, and equipment to practice those skills. "Play provides children with the opportunity to practice movement skills in a variety of contexts. [However], some structuring of physical activity is necessary to help children maximize their movement experiences" (Sanders 2002, 31). Children may also be willing to take more risks with physical activity when they know an adult is nearby to assist if they run into trouble. Amid concerns that hovering adults, concerned about safety or lawsuits, are making play "too safe" (Brussoni et al. 2012), feeling secure in the presence of grown-ups who actually encourage reasonable risk taking may free children to test and extend their physical limits. Play areas for children should be "as safe as necessary," not "as safe as possible" (3134).

Movement education has received increasing national attention because of its potential health benefits. The United States has seen an unprecedented rise in childhood obesity, which is associated with an increased risk for diabetes, heart disease, high blood pressure, colon cancer, and other health problems in adulthood. According to the Centers for Disease Control and Prevention (CDC), the percentage of children identified as overweight more than doubled between 1976 and 2006 (CDC 2009), although obesity among preschoolers in families with low income declined slightly in 19 of 43 states and territories from 2008 to 2011 (CDC 2013). According to the White House Task Force on Childhood Obesity (2010), one in five children today is overweight or obese by age 6. The preschool years are crucial to preventing obesity because ages 3 to 7 are prime years for the development of fat tissue. For that reason, the National Association for Sport and Physical Education (NASPE; 2009a) recommends that preschoolers get *at least* one hour a day of vigorous physical activity (a combined total including the home and other settings).

Unfortunately, sedentary time spent watching and interacting with media often reduces the time children spend in physical activity—and physical inactivity, along with poor diet, has contributed to a large increase in the prevalence of childhood obesity in the United States. By contrast, children who develop basic motor skills (such as throwing, catching, skipping, galloping) and are physically active are more likely as adults to be healthy and participate in daily physical activity (National Center for Health Statistics 2004).

Developing and exercising basic physical abilities are also important in their own right. Gross and fine motor skills serve multiple functions. Physical coordination is essential to accomplishing many, if not most, everyday tasks. In addition, movement is, or should be, inherently pleasurable. There is joy in moving the body, whether one is feeling the freedom of using different muscles or expressing creativity through music and dance. For children with physical limitations, the satisfaction of using and testing the capacities of "workable" body parts may be particularly gratifying, and allow them to compensate for specific disabilities.

Physical development can also promote growth in other domains:

> Not only does movement stimulate learning physiologically, but it also helps young children to experience concepts so they can process them cognitively. Teachers must offer children opportunities to solve movement problems, invent their own solutions to challenges, and make abstract concepts (like high and low) concrete by physically experiencing them. (Pica 1997, 4)

For example, patterning, an underlying phenomenon in brain development, is echoed in the body's physical rhythms. Preschoolers often respond to music with physical movement or gestures, suggesting they may need to "replicate the musical stimuli to get at the substance" of music's underlying pattern (Scott-Kassner 1992, 636). Many areas of intellectual development are linked to physical abilities. When children act out stories, they enhance two essential components of early literacy development—comprehension and representation. As the opening vignette illustrates, movement activities also offer many possibilities for increasing vocabulary. Writing requires physical coordination and dexterity. Movement is also intrinsically tied to forming concepts about space, which is in turn the foundation for understanding geometry. Other mathematical concepts are reflected in movement vocabulary terms, such as *up* and *down*, *straight* and *curved*, or *flat* and *angled*. Bending, crawling, stretching and other flexible movements are vital in scientific investigations of the natural world and help children construct basic principles about physics.

Movement also offers many opportunities for developing and expressing creativity. Children move to music in dance-like ways, and experiment with direction and speed as they maneuver objects through space. Such freedom of expression can boost self-esteem and social confidence.

Conversely, being less physically adept is somewhat associated with mental health problems in children (Sanders 2002). The source of this relationship is unclear; more research needs to be done to determine whether the connection between low physical competence and mental health problems (where that relationship exists) reflects nature, nurture, or some combination of the two. Perhaps children who lack movement competence are ostracized by peers and lack the play opportunities in which young children develop many social skills. Maybe peer ridicule or rejection adversely affects their self-esteem, with troubling implications for their willingness to take on other interpersonal or cognitive challenges. As a result of this diminished self-confidence or lack of social acceptance, the overall school performance and social adjustment of children with un-developed physical skills can suffer.

Young Children's Development in Physical Movement and Health

Implementing appropriate teaching strategies for physical movement and health requires an understanding of how young children develop physically. Learning new movement skills is a process, and during this process children move through four "generic levels of skill proficiency" (Graham, Holt/Hale, & Parker 2004). Preschoolers are generally somewhere in the first two levels, depending on the skill and the child:

1. **Precontrol level** (beginner)—Children cannot consciously control or intentionally replicate a movement. At this stage, they need many opportunities to explore and discover movement.
2. **Control level** (advanced beginner)—Children's movements become less haphazard as their bodies begin to respond to their intentions. Exploration and practice are still central at this stage.
3. **Utilization level** (intermediate)—Children's movements are increasingly automatic. They can join one movement skill with another in a game-like situation.
4. **Proficiency level** (advanced)—Children's movements are mostly automatic and begin to seem effortless. They are now ready to participate in a formal game situation. (Sanders 2002, 48)

Children who do not get opportunities to learn and practice a particular physical skill may grow up unable to perform that skill. Perhaps they just never had an occasion to throw or dribble, for example. Or they may not have had sufficient time or motivation to practice. Research suggests that young children are not motivated to practice a new skill unless they experience success close to 80 percent of the time—that is, the task can't be too hard or too easy, because in either situation the child will lose interest (Sanders 2002, 45).

Several documents provide administrators and practitioners with summary statements about early physical development, as well as guidance on how to apply the information in program settings. The Council on Physical Education for Children (COPEC) published a position paper titled *Appropriate Practices in Movement Programs for Young Children Ages 3–5* (NASPE 2009b). NASPE issued its early childhood standards in a publication titled *Active Start: A Statement of Physical Activity Guidelines for Children Birth to Five Years* (2002, updated in 2009).

Both publications, as well as other contemporary writings in the field of movement education, emphasize the same appropriate child-centered practices that are a part of other developmental domains (for example, active learning, adults and children enjoying physical activities together). In addition, they all stress two points specific to early physical education. First is that the development of any motor skill is sequential. "No matter what the activity, one cannot take part successfully if the essential fundamental movement skills contained within that activity have not been mastered" (Gallahue 1995, 125). So, for example, a child who doesn't achieve basic competency in running, stopping, kicking, and dodging can never become competent at soccer and is unlikely to enjoy or participate in it as an older child or adult. Consequently, there has also been a shift away from discrete learning units focused on one instructional area at a time (for example, three weeks of throwing followed by three weeks of skipping) toward a variety of motor experiences throughout the year for practice and cumulative mastery. Like other content areas, then, the movement curriculum should be designed so that later learning builds on earlier experiences and skills.

A second principle is that movement programs and youth sports are different. Sports programs are appropriate only for older children who have matured to a proficiency level and have refined the basic physical skills necessary to compete. Most children do not attain this readiness until age 6 or 7, and for quite a few it is even later. By contrast, movement programs for young children are meant for everyone. They emphasize self-improvement, participation, and cooperation instead of competition. Following this principle would mean the early childhood physical education curriculum should shift toward a focus on building basic skills and away from games and sports—that is, activities should focus on large muscles instead of large group games.

> Inclusion of [adult-oriented activities such as sports] in early childhood or preschool movement programs has little support among educators because these activities are considered developmentally inappropriate. . . . Simply stated, group games and gymnastics, traditional dance, or fitness experiences have no place in preschool movement programs. (Sanders 2002, 40)

Even for seemingly safe practices, such as simple yoga poses, while the American Academy of Pediatrics and the American Academy of Orthopaedic Surgeons do not have an official position, parents and teachers are advised to check with a doctor with regard to children younger than age 6.

An effective physical education curriculum, one that follows the aforementioned principles, should provide appropriate opportunities for young children to develop in two separate but related gross motor areas: **movement skills** and **movement concepts.** Children learn about the concepts as they practice the skills, so teachers need to incorporate both in preschoolers' physical activities (Sanders 2006, 130).

Gross Motor Development

Movement skills

This first curriculum area refers to the actual physical/motor movement skills (also called *skill themes*) that young children need to develop and refine. There are three categories of movement skills (Gallahue 1995; Sanders 2002):

- **Locomotor**—The body is transported in a horizontal or vertical direction from one point in space to another. Children's locomotor skills, the first of the three types of movement to develop, are walking, running, hopping, skipping, galloping, sliding, leaping, climbing, crawling, chasing, and fleeing.

- **Stability**—The body remains in place but moves around its horizontal or vertical axis, or it balances against the force of gravity. These skills develop next; they include turning, twisting, bending, stopping, rolling, balancing, transferring weight, jumping/landing, stretching/extending, curling, swinging, swaying, and dodging.

- **Manipulative**—The body moves to apply force to or receive force from objects. These skills develop last and are throwing, catching/collecting, kicking, punting, dribbling, volleying, striking with a racket, and striking with a long-handled instrument. Manipulative skills are important in many games and sports, such as kickball and catch. The fine motor skills needed for tasks such as writing and drawing are also manipulative skills, although they are less vigorous than the gross motor ones (see the Fine Motor Development section that follows).

Movement concepts

The movement concepts are the knowledge component of the curriculum. If movement skills relate to *what* the body can do, movement concepts relate to *where, how, and in relationship to what* the body moves. Put another way: If movement skills are "body verbs," then movement concepts are "body adjectives and adverbs." Learning these movement concepts helps to modify or enrich the range of movement skills and the effectiveness of children's use of skills (Graham, Holt/Hale, & Parker 2004). There are three categories of movement concepts (Sanders 2002, 91):

- **Space (or spatial) awareness**—Where the body moves in space. Space awareness concepts are space, directions, levels, and pathways.

- **Effort awareness**—How the body moves in space. These are awareness of the components of time (speeds, rhythms), force (degree, creation, absorption), and flow/control (dimensions).

- **Body (or relational) awareness**—Relationships that the body creates. These are relationships with the self (body parts, body shapes, roles) and relationships with others and the environment (locations).

Fine Motor Development

Young children use various fine motor movements to manipulate materials and tools. Common preschool actions that require these types of movements include molding, squeezing, poking, smoothing, positioning, writing, stacking, pouring, and cutting. Between the ages of 3 and 5, children gain in strength, eye–hand coordination, and endurance. They grow more skilled at manipulating age-appropriate materials such as scissors, pencils, markers, crayons, blocks, puzzles, string, beads, pegs, hammers, screwdrivers, paintbrushes, clothes fasteners, eating utensils, snap-on and screw-on lids, switches, buttons, levers, and gears on toys and technology. The more proficient and confident preschoolers become in their fine motor skills, the more eager they are to try working with new tools and materials.

Despite these impressive advances, there are physical limits to preschoolers' fine motor abilities. For example, they cannot make fully circular wrist motions because the cartilage in their wrists does not harden into bone until about age 6 (Berk 2008). Therefore, writing, drawing, and cutting with precision are still difficult for them. Handedness is generally established by age 4, yet children still experiment with using the nondominant hand beyond this age. It is important for adults to keep these developmental limitations in mind to avoid holding unrealistic expectations for children. (For ideas on how fine motor exploration can help prepare children for writing, see Huffman & Fortenberry 2011.)

Developing Personal Care Routines and Healthy Behavior

Young children enjoy taking care of themselves and often practice self-help skills intently and repeatedly. They learn to serve food and eat on their own, get dressed, use the toilet, wash their hands, brush their teeth, use and dispose of tissues, and so on. Even children with physical or other limitations enjoy—and insist on—doing as much for themselves as possible. The development of fine motor skills enables children to assume more of these self-care responsibilities. As they learn to care for themselves, children may also show interest in taking care of others, including pets as well as people. They may not always perform these tasks to adult standards (such as missing a spot of paint on their hand), but their pride is evident and should be accepted (not corrected) and acknowledged by adults.

Performing daily self-care routines, along with learning about the natural world as part of science explorations (see Chap. 8), also makes children aware that they have to take of their bodies just as they take of toys and equipment. They hear and begin to understand that exercise is good for them. Preschoolers also start to grasp that some foods are more healthful than others. Physical activity and good nutrition are not only essential to healthy development, but they are also inextricably linked:

> Activity has a lot to do with appetite and nutritional status. Active children need more calories than inactive ones; this means that they have a better chance of getting all required nutrients. Adequate physical exercise year-round, preferably on a daily basis, is important to a child's nutrition (as well as development) because it stimulates a healthy appetite, uses calories, and maintains muscle tissue. (Aronson 2012, 79)

Teaching and Learning in Physical Development and Health

NASPE (2009a) offers the following specific recommendations for preschool physical activities.

1. Preschoolers should accumulate at least 60 minutes of structured physical activity each day.
2. Preschoolers should engage in at least 60 minutes—and up to several hours—of unstructured physical activity each day and should not be sedentary for more than 60 minutes at a time, except when sleeping.
3. Preschoolers should be encouraged to develop competence in fundamental motor skills that will serve as the building blocks for future motor skillfulness and physical activity.
4. Preschoolers should have access to indoor and outdoor areas that meet or exceed recommended safety standards for performing large muscle activities.

5. Caregivers and parents in charge of preschoolers' health and well-being are responsible for understanding the importance of physical activity and for promoting movement skills by providing opportunities for structured and unstructured physical activity. (24)

Developmental and educational wisdom supports the use of both child- and adult-guided experience in physical education.

> Teachers should employ both direct and indirect teaching methods. Direct methods provide instructional models for children to replicate. Indirect teaching methods encourage children to explore and discover a range of movement possibilities. Teachers provide opportunities for children to make choices within and between tasks, while actively exploring their environment. Teachers serve as facilitators, preparing a stimulating environment with challenging activities. (Sanders 2002, 13)

In other words, physical education, like any other content area, requires that adults take an active and deliberate instructional role.

Intentional teachers fulfill these recommendations by creating an appropriate learning environment and using effective interaction strategies with young children. Providing an appropriate learning environment is essential regardless of who guides the learning.

Needs such as time, space, and equipment for practice are universal for children's learning. Similarly, each interaction strategy can be used with both child-guided and adult-guided experiences, but their frequency and intensity should vary depending on the skill in question. For example, the strategies of modeling and using explicit cues may be useful to support child-guided experience, but they are more often necessary in adult-guided experiences. Likewise, challenges make learning fun in both instances, but they become more salient in adult-guided instruction to suggest movement possibilities and raise awareness of health issues that children are unlikely to think of on their own.

Physical Education Learning Environment

NASPE (2009a) defines the movement environment as comprising these components: scheduled activity, class size, equipment, play, facilities, allowance for repetition and success, participation for every child, and integration of movement into other subject areas. While several of these have already been touched on in this chapter, a few points are worth emphasizing and expanding here.

First, movement education should be a **scheduled activity,** like small group time, snack time, or any other part of the daily routine.

Second, regarding **class size,** "large classes are accidents waiting to happen" (Sanders 2002, 24). The number of children in large group physical activities should not exceed class size, which is another way of saying that two or more classes should not share a gym or playground at the same time. Best practice says maximum group size with two teachers for 3-year-olds is 18 children; for 4-year-olds, it is no more than

Basic Equipment and Materials for Early Childhood Movement Programs

Some of the following items are only available commercially but are worth the basic investment. Others can be made or collected at minimal cost, especially with contributions from children's families and local businesses. Materials should be varied and plentiful. It is not always necessary to have one of each item for every child.

Balancing equipment—beams 4 to 6 inches wide and no more than 30 inches off the ground; boards or platforms raised off the ground with a narrow base of support; railroad ties, bricks, blocks, or rocks arranged in various configurations

Balloons in different sizes and weights—sometimes recommended for indoor use only to avoid potential environmental hazards; children should be closely supervised to avoid choking hazards

Balls of many types—lightweight foam, rubber, and plastic balls; old tennis balls; yarn and cloth balls; smooth and textured balls; whiffle balls; beach, tennis, and soccer balls; balls in different diameters up to 10 inches

Baskets, bowls, and boxes—various heights and widths, to throw things into

Basketball hoop or other types of anchored net—child size

Bats—plastic and foam, rather than wood; 2 to 4 inches in diameter and 28 inches in length; foam bats have a larger head and make connecting with the ball easier

Beanbags—square and cubed; about five inches per side; filled with dried beans, rice, sand, birdseed, or plastic pellets

Boards—good for carrying (strength) and walking on (balance)

Bowling pins—foam; 3 to 4 inches in diameter

Carpet squares—good for practicing jumping; many carpet businesses will donate old samples

Climbing equipment—jungle gym, ladder, tree stumps, boulders, snow piles

Crawl-through shapes and tunnels—of heavy-duty foam, or cut your own out of cardboard in different geometrical shapes and colors; approximately 3 by 2 feet

Disks—Frisbees, paper plates, plastic paint can lids, clean pizza cardboard

Gardening tools—tools for digging, raking, and so on; these help to develop upper body strength

Hockey sticks—foam; 24-inch handles are good for young children

Hoops—plastic; in 24-, 30-, and 36-inch diameters; smaller diameters are better for young children

Jump ropes—7 feet long; preferably weighted along length with plastic beads

Launch boards—child steps on one end and beanbag at other end flies up for child to catch

Mats—don't teach rolling without them!

Recorded music and simple instruments—percussion, string, wind

20 children (NAEYC 2007, Table 2). It is even more important to have smaller groups when the children don't all speak the same language. In this situation, a greater portion of teaching strategies will involve individual feedback, such as touching the children, guiding their movements, and keeping them engaged. To do this effectively, it is better to divide the children into smaller groups rather than try to teach new skills and movements to the whole group. If larger groups must be used, assign buddies so a child who understands English can help guide and support a child who is not as fluent.

Third, **space to play and practice** is particularly important in the development of gross motor skills. Because the amount of space required is more than the dimensions of a typical classroom, physical education is often moved elsewhere, such as a gym, multipurpose room, large hallway, or outdoors. Wherever movement learning takes place, safety is a primary concern. Environments should be free of obstacles (tables, chairs, shelves, sand and water tables, easels, computers). Equipment specific to large motor activity (hoops, balls, mats) should be located around the perimeter or stored nearby with easy access. Having to haul gear long distances is a disincentive to its frequent and spontaneous use by both children and teachers.

Paddles—foam; with handles of different lengths

Parachute—6 to 12 feet in diameter

Pull and push toys—wagons, toy lawnmowers, shopping carts, doll strollers, vacuum cleaners, wheelbarrows

Rhythm sticks—wood or plastic; about 5/8 of an inch in diameter and 1 foot long

Ribbons, ribbon wands, ribbon sticks—to perform expressive rhythmic movements; sticks are 18 inches long and ribbons 6 to 12 feet long; use shorter ribbons with younger children

Rocking toys—wooden or plastic horse, boats

Scarves—for throwing, catching, and rhythm activities; lightweight scarves fall slowly, so they are ideal for catching; 11 to 16 inches square

Scoops—plastic; construct homemade ones from empty milk jugs; act as extensions of arm to assist in catching

Sleds—length should be shorter than the child

Sliding equipment—commercial slide, fireman's pole, waterslide

Stilts—foam; 8 inches off the floor

Swings—commercial swings, tire swing, rope swing

Target board—can be constructed of plywood or other sturdy material, with targets painted on them; to practice overhand and underhand throwing

Tires—for obstacle courses, locomotor challenges, and so on (see the box on p. 82 in this chapter)

Traffic cones—good to mark boundaries or serve as base to practice knocking something off

Wedges—foam

Wheeled vehicles—tricycles, toy cars and buses, scooters; always wear helmets

Compiled from the following:

R. Clements & S. Schneider, personal communication, 2004.

A.S. Epstein, *The HighScope Preschool Curriculum: Physical Development and Health* (Ypsilanti, MI: HighScope Press, 2012c), 46–47.

V. Harris, "The Playground: An Outdoor Setting for Learning" in *Supporting Young Learners: Ideas for Preschool and Day Care Providers*, eds. N.A. Brickman & L.S. Taylor, 167–173 (Ypsilanti, MI: HighScope Press, 1991), 172.

P. Neill "Open-Ended Materials Belong Outside Too," in *HighScope Extensions*, 2013, 27 (2), 1–8.

S.W. Sanders, *Designing Preschool Movement Programs* (Champaign, IL: Human Kinetics, 1992), 116–118.

P.S. Weikart, *Round the Circle: Key Experiences in Movement for Young Children*, 2nd ed. (Ypsilanti, MI: HighScope Press, 2000), 94–107.

Equipment is another key component. "Learning to move is like learning to read, write, or understand principles of math and science in that each requires a manipulative of some type to best develop skills and knowledge in a content area" (Sanders 2002, 25). In acquiring movement resources, consider scale, accessibility, and quantity. Equipment should be child size and appropriate for children with special needs. Have a sufficient amount of equipment so that every child can participate without waiting. That means if the activity is throwing and there are 12 children in the class, have 12 items to throw (balls, beanbags). Every child does not need to have the same item, as long as there is something appropriate for each child. Another option is to create multiple activity stations for children to visit so that fewer items of each kind are needed. Remember too that outdoor equipment does not need to be limited to permanent structures. Loose parts— "materials with no specific set of directions [that] can be used alone or with other materials" (Neill 2013, 1)—can also be used to promote vigorous physical activity and gross motor development. Loose parts include natural materials (such as stones, tree stumps, logs, leaves, water, dirt) and manufactured materials (such as milk crates, gutters, rope, traffic cones, hoops).

Finally, the principle of **active involvement** is crucial, and it is a distinguishing difference between a movement program and sports. Rather than winning, a movement program's goals are to have children "experience the joy and satisfaction inherent in movement . . . [as well as to] foster a positive attitude toward physical activity, self and body images, and physical skill competency" (Sanders 2006, 127). So elimination games such as Duck, Duck, Goose; Musical Chairs; and Simon Says are poor choices, as players spend most of their time sitting or standing, and they exclude some children altogether. These games can be adapted, however, so there are no winners and losers (for example, after each round, all the children continue to play). Likewise, races can promote feelings of inadequacy and discouragement for all except the winner and are, therefore, not appropriate for young children. Instead, teachers should select activities and attend to issues of scheduling, space, and equipment to ensure every child is an active participant and experiences that 80 percent level of success.

Physical Education Interaction Strategies

"Providing appropriate adult encouragement and support not only enables young children to learn about movement but also ensures the success of their many movement ideas and experiences" (Weikart 2000, 28). The following interaction strategies promote movement learning of all types in young children:

Facilitate access and exploration by providing materials, space, and time for young children to explore movement. Feedback from the sensations of moving will help them discover and adjust what their bodies can do.

Teachers can **model a skill** to demonstrate for children how to use their bodies or equipment to accomplish a physical objective. This demonstration technique is especially useful for children who do not easily process verbal instruction, who have limited vocabulary, or who are dual language learners. The goal is not for children to copy exactly what the teacher or a more skilled peer is doing but rather to help them get the idea and then practice it on their own. Teachers should also use modeling to prevent or correct children's errors, describing and modeling the correct way to hop, skip, and so on.

> [K]now what common errors to watch for, even with simple skills like walking (pronated feet that roll in with [the outermost] toes lifting off the floor) and jumping (landing with knees straight and on balls of feet only). Motor skill errors and delays do not go away on their own. (Rae Pica, 2004, personal communication)

Teachers or other professionals (such as physical education specialists, occupational therapists) and parents, therefore, should be ready to intervene.

Add descriptive language. Describing movement serves a dual purpose. It makes children more aware of what they are doing, so they pay attention to their bodies and the feedback they receive from their nerves and muscles. It also increases their vocabulary. Once they hear movement words from teachers, children can begin to use labels such as *over* and *under, fast* and *slow, straight* and *bent*—not just in physical education but also to convey concepts in literacy, mathematics, and other content areas. Movement awareness and verbal skills serve children later, too, as they combine skills to master new challenges. For example, when the teachers says (pausing between directions), "Put your foot *in front of* you and lean your body *forward* with your arms out to the *side*. . ." a child who has learned these physical skills and verbal labels can accomplish a throwing or balancing act.

While children are practicing and refining a new skill, teachers can **provide small bits of key information (*cues*)** about that skill to help them learn it more quickly and correctly. A well-timed cue can also prevent the formation of bad habits (a point that movement educators say should be applied to other curriculum areas as well). Cues can take three forms (Weikart 2000): verbal, visual (demonstration), and hands-on guidance. A *verbal cue* might be, for example, telling a child, "Hold your hands in front of your body to catch the ball." *Visual cues* can replace or supplement verbal cues; for example, pointing to your eyes as a reminder to the child to look at the target when throwing a beanbag. For *hands-on cues,* the teacher, with the child's permission, gently moves the child's body into a more efficient position; for example, centering the child's body over a balance beam. Good teachers are sensitive to which type works best for each child, skill, and situation and then individualize the cues they provide.

Create skill challenges. Challenges are "tasks or activities made measurable (or more fun) by the teacher. In making a task measurable, the teacher motivates a child to try it in a different way" (Sanders 2002, 55). For example, the teacher might say, "I wonder how many different ways you can bounce the ball?" or "Can you hop from here to the wall and back?" Challenges can increase children's interest and enjoyment and encourage them to stay with a task longer. Challenges also can extend their physical learning and help children apply a skill to other situations.

Invite children to lead the movement activity. As leader, the child might make verbal suggestions or demonstrate an action to be copied by the class. Being leaders develops children's confidence and independence, and also makes them more aware of verbal labels and motions because they have to communicate them to others. Most children will want to be leaders, but never require them to be; let them volunteer. You may find that children who typically don't speak up in a group will feel comfortable leading. Even children who are pre- or nonverbal or who are dual language learners can lead physical activities.

Promoting Personal Care Routines and Healthy Behavior

Eating and physical activity patterns are established at a very young age. For that reason, early childhood programs play a vital role in helping children establish healthy habits. Because their stomachs are small, young children do best with several smaller meals and snacks spread throughout the day. Water intake is also important. Variety is another aspect of healthy nutrition, and allows children to experience different tastes, textures, and smells. Likewise, good exercise habits are built on children enjoying a variety of large motor activities as a normal part of the daily routine. When teachers are active alongside them—not watching from the sidelines—children get the message that an active lifestyle is vital for adults too. Finally, eating and exercise have important social dimensions. Eating in a pleasant and relaxed setting develops positive attitudes about food. These attitudes are fostered when meals and snacks in the classroom are conducted family style, with adults and children passing around the food, serving themselves, and conversing while they eat. Sharing physical activities that are not competitive is also fun for both grown-ups and children and builds a sense of community in the classroom.

Fitting the Learning Experience to the Learning Objective

The rest of this chapter examines *movement skills* (gross motor and fine motor), *movement concepts*, and the developmental of *personal care routines and healthy behavior*. Each section is in turn divided into those skills or concepts acquired primarily through child-guided or adult-guided experience. Keep in mind that, as with all areas of development, this division is not rigid.

Movement Skills

Movement learning (both gross and fine motor), more than the other content areas in this book, can be difficult to attribute to either child- or adult-guided experience. Because many movement skills appear spontaneously, at least in rudimentary form, the assumption (as noted at the beginning of the chapter) is that adult intervention is unnecessary. Yet movements that are more difficult or complex and involve greater eye–hand

coordination or coordination of muscles and senses require a certain amount of direction and refinement. As well, children are more likely to learn the correct version (a version that is performed safely, without stressing the body and with maximum efficiency/accuracy) of any movement skill through direct adult intervention. Yet they are also more prone to mistakes (and therefore more likely to need or benefit from adult assistance) in the more complex adult-guided skills listed in this chapter. It is the relative importance of independent versus assisted learning that underlies the assignment of movement skills to either the child-guided and adult-guided category.

Locomotor skills, for example, often mature on their own, and children spontaneously practice and improve them as long as teachers give them opportunities to explore and discover. Similarly, children are likely to learn many stability skills independently. However, there are some locomotor and stability skills that require adult intervention before children can come to a more mature form and eventually combine and apply them in games and sports. On the other hand, only a couple of manipulative skills seem to be acquired primarily through child-guided experience, and they are acquired only if the appropriate equipment and support are available to the child. Otherwise, manipulative skills depend more on adult-guided experience than do skills in the other two movement areas.

Whether a skill fits in one category or the other is currently an empirical issue; that is, it is based on the observations and systematic research of those who work in the field of movement education. As the concept of the intentional teacher takes hold with respect to physical development and more work is done to generate theories and research, a higher-order explanation for what constitutes each type of skill should emerge.

Child-guided experience is especially important for learnings such as:

Locomotor skills: Crawling, walking, running, climbing

These four locomotor skills seem to be primarily learned by children through exploration and discovery. Although adults typically take walking for granted, it actually requires considerable balance and strength (Weikart 2000). Running, because it is faster and contact with the ground is not continuous, requires even more strength and balance than walking. Children typically begin walking at about age 1, but running doesn't begin until around age 2. Climbing, which combines crawling and walking skills, involves both arm and leg strength—and often strength of mind, as the parent or teacher of a determined toddler can attest! Preschoolers become increasingly coordinated in their running, and they are also able to maintain better balance while climbing.

Teaching strategies. Young children bring a high level of motivation to mastering basic locomotor skills. Quite simply, they enjoy moving. Nevertheless, teachers play a critical role in creating a physical environment that supports movement exploration. Their attitudes are also important in helping children overcome their fears and in sharing their joy of discovery, including acknowledging the adaptations that children with special physical needs make to carry out their movement intentions. To provide this wide-ranging support, teachers can implement a variety of strategies, including these:

- Provide ample space and time. Buy or construct appropriate equipment, including ramps, bridges, and playground climbers, as well as large blocks you and the children can use to build your own structures.

- Promote children's free exploration and practice of locomotor skills. Accept and respect children's originality and creativity. To encourage children to move in new ways, make interesting or novel suggestions; for example, say, "Imagine you are a squirrel scampering along the ground" or "Pretend to be . . ." Or select a favorite action storybook (or make up an action story) at group time and suggest children mimic the actions of the characters while you read or tell the story. Pause to allow time for the children's movements, and then summarize the events before proceeding with the narrative.

- Model locomotor movements and encourage children to imitate them (but don't insist on exact duplication). For example, demonstrate a crawling movement using your knees and forearms (instead of hands) and say, "Let's all crawl around the table."

- Provide specific cues as needed to help children improve the quality of their movements. For example, walking cues could include "keep your head up," "look where you want to go," and "swing your arms."

- Challenge children to practice and extend a movement, such as "How can you walk to the sink faster?" or "How else can you . . . ?" or "Who has a different way to . . . ?"

- Use these basic locomotor skills to enhance other areas of learning. For example, if children are exploring short and long strings during small group time, encourage them to take short and long steps at outside time. Stopping and starting, which are time concepts, can also be combined with movement activities; for example, have children stop and start moving when a piece of music starts and stops.

Stability skills: turning, twisting, bending, straightening, curling, stretching/extending, swinging, swaying, pushing, pulling, rising, falling, dodging, stopping

These stability skills seem to be primarily acquired through exploration and discovery. Children typically use these skills while standing in place. For example, turning rotates the body in a 360-degree movement; a twist is a partial rotation before returning to the starting point and rotating in the other direction. Bending is a movement around a fulcrum such as the wrist, knee, elbow, or waist (because it can stress the spine, bending at the neck is discouraged). Swinging means moving a suspended body part (such as a leg or an arm) back and forth. Swaying means a smooth shifting of one's weight from side to side or forward and back (also called *rocking,* especially if done repetitively and rigidly). Dodging and stopping are two stability movements that can involve the child traveling (for example, dodging behind a tree or stopping in mid-run) but not necessarily (for example, ducking one's head or stopping in mid-twist). While any of these stability skills can be practiced by children individually, they are often done in groups, such as swaying together to music.

Teaching strategies. Teachers can build on young children's spontaneous movements to suggest many games and challenges that will further develop their basic stability skills. Many of these activities can be done during large group time, with each child on a carpet square or small mat or on a soft surface outdoors. Pretend play also offers opportunities for children to act out the stability movements natural to animals or illustrative of characters in stories. Try strategies such as these:

- Buy or construct equipment to facilitate practicing stability skills—for example, ramps, beams, low risers, pull and push toys, rocking toys, swings, and wheeled vehicles. Search for online catalogs that provide equipment explicitly designed for children with a wide range of special needs to practice or adapt carrying out these motor skills.

- Provide cues for performing specific stability skills. Cues for bending include "spread your legs," "hold out your arms," and "bend in stages for balance." Cues for stopping include "allow enough time," "try to slow down gradually," and "lean back slightly."

- Demonstrate and practice stability skills with children. For example, bend and straighten different parts of your body, describing the movements as you do. Ask the children to do this with you. Have them suggest body parts to bend and straighten. Together practice curling and stretching/extending fingers and toes. Explore the words *curl* and *stretch* with familiar situations. For example, ask children to pretend to be sleeping kittens that wake up. Or have them pretend to sleep in a curled-up position, and then wake them with an alarm clock sound; they can take turns making the wake-up noise.

- Challenge children to practice and extend a movement, such as "Who can stretch only one side of your body?" or "Show me how you can lie on the floor and stretch your legs."

- Have a child lead the group in an activity exploring a stability skill such as swinging, letting him choose which body part to swing and how. Encourage the leader to describe the movement before performing it. Supply the words for body parts and motions.

Manipulative skills: throwing, kicking

These are the manipulative skills children typically discover on their own. Throwing is the easier skill, and children may naturally use an underhand, overhand, or sidearm motion. Kicking develops later because children's lower-body control typically lags behind upper-body control. Initially they kick using a lateral pushing motion along the ground, often from a stationary position. Later, children approach their target with one or more steps and swing their foot upward, which gives momentum and height to the kick.

Teaching strategies. Children naturally throw and kick things, curious about the effects of such motions. They may also imitate the actions of older siblings or sports figures. Although their abilities are rudimentary at first, children enjoy seeing their accuracy improve with practice. Teachers can encourage this practice with strategies such as these:

○ Provide appropriate equipment and materials for children to throw and kick during choice time, group time, and outdoor time. Equipment should be child size and accommodate children's wide range of abilities and interests (such as softballs, beanbags, balloons, Frisbees). Children may also kick objects they find lying on the ground, such as sticks and pebbles.

○ Provide cues for performing specific manipulative skills. Cues for throwing include "look at the target," "hold your arm far back," and "step forward with the foot opposite your throwing arm." Cues for kicking include "swing your foot back," "make contact with the top of your foot," and "stop your body after you kick."

○ Encourage children to practice and explore manipulative skills. For example, they can toss a beanbag overhand and underhand, or kick a ball with their toe (in a sturdy shoe) or the side of their foot. Encourage them to use their non-dominant as well as dominant leg or arm. After children master basic motions, provide targets for them to throw or kick objects at (such as hoops, baskets, bowls, boxes, or target boards). Begin with large/close/low targets, moving to smaller/farther/higher targets; also progress from stationary to moving actions.

○ Challenge children to extend and vary their skills; for example, say, "Try to throw the ball farther" or "I wonder how you could kick it a different way."

○ Use children's interest in throwing and kicking to explore movement concepts. For example, challenge them to throw a beanbag up or down, stand near or far away from the target, or throw with a straight or curved arm. Invite them to suggest other variations. Encourage their use of position and distance words.

Fine motor skills and eye–hand coordination: grasping, pinching, tearing

Fine motor skills require eye–hand coordination. Typical skills that preschoolers develop on their own include grasping, pinching, and tearing. They practice these motions with diverse materials such as small objects (animal and people figures, food), clay and playdough, collage materials, and different types of paper. At first, young children enjoy mastering fine motor skills for their own sake. Later they apply them to fulfill their intentions as they build structures, create art, engage in pretend play, and carry out self-help tasks.

Teaching strategies. Space, time, and materials are as important to the development of fine motor skills as they are to the growth of gross motor skills. The following strategies will support young children as they practice, master, and apply a variety of fine motor abilities:

○ Provide quiet and protected spaces for children to practice fine motor skills. To focus on tasks requiring eye–hand coordination, young children benefit from spaces without competing visual or auditory distractions. Uncluttered tables at the children's height provide flat surfaces for working with small toys, writing tools, art materials, and so on. Preschoolers can also work comfortably on the floor, at easels, on paper tacked to the wall, on outdoor pavement, at sand and water tables, in flower and vegetable gardens and digging areas, and many other such spaces where they can use their small muscles and hone their eye–hand coordination with a variety of interesting materials and tools.

○ Provide a variety of fine motor materials, tools, and equipment, such as art materials, writing tools, dress-up clothes, household utensils, blocks and other construction toys and tools, puzzles, stacking and nesting toys, beads, and items that can be taken apart and put back together. While some items are best purchased commercially (for example, it is worth investing in a good set of wooden unit blocks), others can be made or collected at minimal cost. Families and local businesses are often willing to contribute items.

○ Give children time to exercise their small muscles throughout the day. For example, when children arrive, they can turn the pages of a book while reading with an adult. At choice time, children may draw, do a puzzle, or put on safety goggles to hammer nails or golf tees into wood, cardboard boxes, or playdough. At snack time, they can use serving and eating utensils. Outside, they can pour and fill in the sandbox or sort collections of small objects such as fallen leaves or pebbles. Virtually any time of the day can be a chance for children to develop fine motor skills.

Adult-guided experience is especially important for learnings such as:

Locomotor skills: hopping, galloping, sliding, slithering, marching, plodding, leaping, chasing, fleeing, skipping

Plodding is a heavy walk where the feet drag. Hopping usually is done one-footed (two-footed it's also called jumping). Galloping is an uneven transfer of weight while traveling; the same front foot leads and takes the weight as the rear foot comes up to meet it. Sliding is like walking but without lifting the feet. Slithering is crawling with the entire body pressed to the ground. Chasing and fleeing are purposeful running, using cognitive as well as movement strategies to anticipate or avoid the other person. Skipping is the most difficult locomotor skill because both legs must perform equally well and in alternation.

Teaching strategies. Once children have mastered basic locomotor skills through child-guided experience, there is an almost endless range of variations to explore. However, children may not create or chance upon more complex movements on their own. Adult interventions such as the following can help open up the world of movement:

○ Provide cues for performing specific locomotor skills. Cues for skipping include "lift the knees" and "step, hop, and land on one foot and then the other." Cues for galloping include "put the same foot forward every time" and "begin with a big step forward." You can also emphasize the beat of locomotor activities, such as chanting, "DA-da, DA-da, DA-da" during galloping.

○ Issue movement challenges and encourage children to make up their own. Provide targets or goals to locomote to; for example, say, "Let's gallop to the fence" or "Hop to the coat rack to get ready for outside time." Ask children to suggest targets. Provide time and number challenges for locomotor movements or ask the children to issue the challenges; for example, "How many times can you skip to the bookshelf and back before the music stops?" or "Let's see how fast you can skip around the circle." For activities that favor one side, such as hopping or galloping, encourage children to practice on one foot and then the other.

Create opportunities to navigate difficult spaces. For example,

> In the activity "A Walk Through the Woods" (Sanders 2002, 22), children take a pretend trip through the woods, walking around foam pins, cones, and two-liter soda bottles representing trees. Children first "plant" trees, by placing the objects themselves (you may need to move some "trees" farther apart). Then they practice different locomotor skills such as walking, skipping, and hopping through the "woods."

For children with mobility or vision difficulties, problem solve with them alternative ways they can meet movement challenges, such as how many times they can roll a wheelchair back and forth between two points before the music stops, or how they can use tactile feedback to navigate moving through a narrow space.

○ Provide space, time, and equipment for children to practice these locomotor skills. In addition to purchasing standard playground equipment (slides, swings, climbers), use furniture or recycled items (such as empty cartons or old tires) to enhance movement opportunities.

Stability skills: transferring weight, balancing, jumping/ landing, rolling

Adult-guided stability skills extend those learned primarily through child-guided experience and may build on the young child's growing muscle control and coordination. Transferring weight involves shifting one's center of gravity; it is a controlled movement that is essential in many movement activities. Balancing means evenly distributing the body's weight on each side of a vertical axis. "For young children, being in balance simply means not falling over. This is critical in developing physical skills" (Sanders 2002, 40). Rolling is traveling by transferring weight to adjacent body parts around a central axis; children can roll like a log, rock on their backs, and roll headfirst.

Teaching strategies. Stability—bodily control—underpins many movement tasks. For that reason, the teacher's role in helping children master these foundational skills is particularly important for lifelong physical activity. For example, try the following strategies:

○ Buy or construct equipment to practice stability skills, such as an inclined mat for rolling, a wide beam or strip of tape on the floor for balancing, or a string for jumping over. For example, stretch two pieces of tape or string along the floor that start close together and get farther apart. Have children jump over them, beginning at the narrow end and progressing as far as they can toward the wide end. Children can suggest other ways to cross over, such as leaping or jumping sideways.

○ Offer stability challenges and encourage children to invent their own. For example, say, "Roll like your legs were glued together" (demonstrate if neces-

Practicing Skills With Old Tires

Recycled items provide many creative opportunities for young children to march, hop, skip, and leap. (Make sure all materials are clean and safe before using them with the children.)

Garages often give away old tires. Try to get one tire for each child or two children, but certainly enough tires to make a straight and staggered line. (If tires aren't available, all the locomotor skills can be practiced using Hula-Hoops instead.)

Give one tire to each child or pair of children and pose the following locomotor and stability challenges:

"Hop [or march, skip, gallop, or slide] around the tire." *(locomotor skill)*

"In pairs, chase each other around the tire." *(locomotor; give starting/stopping signals)*

"Jump into the middle of the tire. Now jump back outside of it." *(locomotor)*

"Stand on the edge of the tire." *(stability)*

"Crouch inside the tire like a frog and jump out." *(locomotor, stability)*

"Crouch like a duck and waddle around the tire." *(locomotor)*

Arrange the tires in a straight line and/or zigzag path and pose the following locomotor challenges:

"Walk [or march or hop] from the middle of one tire to another."

"Walk [or march, hop, run, or gallop] up one side of the row and back down the other."

"Walk [or march, hop, run, or gallop] around the edges of the tires in a weaving [zigzag] pattern."

"Slide [slither] over the first tire and into the next tire in the row. Go to the end this way, and come back."

---

sary) or "Who can roll in one direction? in the other direction? in a circle?" Suggest balancing challenges for the floor or a low beam, such as varying the position of a raised leg. Ask children to suggest other positions. Again, explore alternative stability challenges for children who need mobility assistance and encourage them to come up with their own ideas (for example, crossing a wide, low plank with their walker, shifting their weight while leaning on a cane). Challenge children without physical limitations to try these variations as well.

o Build on children's interests and imaginations to develop stability skills. Design a balance trail with an interesting arrangement of items that children can stand or walk on. As they become more competent, gradually add more difficult items. For example, begin with wide planks on the floor and taped pathways; later add twisted ropes and low elevated beams. Or make up and act out group stories. For example, say, "We're searching for buried treasure. Everyone get on the boat. Uh-oh. I can feel big waves rocking the boat." Pause while children are "rocked" back and forth by the waves. Encourage children to imagine scenarios that challenge their stability, such as maintaining balance on the rolling seas, jumping onto land or back in the boat, or rolling away from "sharks" in the water.

o Provide cues for performing specific stability skills. Cues for rolling like a log include "keep your legs together" and "keep your arms at your sides or over your head." Cues for transferring weight include "keep your movements smooth" and "don't lean too far in one direction." Cues for balancing include "keep your head and body still" and "extend your arms." Cues for jumping/landing include "crouch before jumping" and "land on both feet at the same time with your legs apart." Practice at jumping/landing should start in safe places such as low steps, curbs, or boxes; if children wish, hold their hands and jump/land with them.

Manipulative skills: catching/collecting, dribbling, volleying, punting, striking with a racket, striking with a long-handled instrument

Catching/collecting (sometimes called fielding) is difficult because it involves visual tracking plus motor coordination. Children may be startled by the approaching object and close their eyes or freeze. Dribbling involves moving an object forward by striking it repeatedly using hands or feet while following along behind. Children can dribble, if primitively, with their feet (such as by kicking a pebble along the path) before they have the control to dribble a ball with their hands. Volleying involves passing an object back and forth using the hands or feet.

Teaching strategies. The development of these fundamental manipulative skills is critical for children's later participation in sports or games. Because some involve interacting with others (throwing, catching, volleying), their mastery also opens a world of social relationships. Try these strategies to support children's manipulative skills:

○ Provide equipment and materials for practicing manipulative skills with the hands and feet. For example, children can use a launch board to practice catching; they place a beanbag on the low end of the board and then stand at the high end and stomp on the board, making the beanbag fly into the air. They can also play this game in pairs. Items to catch, volley, and strike should be soft and slow moving at first, such as scarves, beanbags, and oversized balls. Children who have difficulty standing can practice these skills from a sitting position. Pair children with and without disabilities to work together.

○ Provide cues for performing specific manipulative skills. Cues for catching a rolled or thrown ball, for example, include "watch the ball," "move to where it is," and "bring the ball toward your body and hug it to you." Cues for hitting with a racket include "turn the flat side of the paddle toward the object," "keep your wrist stiff," and "follow through on the swing."

○ Incorporate manipulative skills into different parts of the daily routine. For example, incorporate catching into transitions by saying, "I'm going to throw the beanbag to a girl in a red shirt and after she catches it, she can go the small group table." During large group time, have children choose partners to practice catching, volleying, or hitting something back and forth with a paddle or racket. Encourage their suggestions; for example, they might catch down low and up high, or stand face to face or side to side.

○ Build children's skills in sequence. For example, at first children should use their hands to strike stationary objects (such as a balloon placed on a table or batting tee), and then they can progress to striking objects suspended from a string or rope. Next would come dropping the object in front of the child and finally throwing a moving object to the child. When introducing an implement to strike an object, first use one that is large and flat (such as a paddle or racket). Using long-handled instruments (such as a child-size bat or golf club made from materials safe for young children, such as plastic rather than wood) comes last, since it involves estimating distances as well as physical movements.

Fine motor skills and eye–hand coordination: cutting, folding, writing

Some fine motor movements, such as cutting, folding, and writing, require both greater eye–hand coordination and the precise use of small muscles. While children are highly motivated to master these abilities on their own, they may need guidance and encouragement from adults, particularly if they are perplexed or frustrated in their independent efforts. Children can also benefit from being shown these skills by peers who have already mastered them (see the box on p. 59 in Chap. 4, Referring Children to Each Other for Assistance). When adults refer children to each other for assistance, the helper is more reflective about the steps involved, while the one being helped learns a skill that he in turn can pass along to others. Finally, provide assistive devices (such as magnifying lenses or large or easy-grip writing tools) for children with special needs. Younger preschool children may also find such aids useful as they develop these skills.

Teaching strategies. Mastering complex fine motor skills depends on children having access to a variety of interesting and gently challenging materials and experiences. Consider the following ideas as you supply the classroom and create opportunities for children to use their small muscles:

- Provide similar objects in a range of graduated sizes and shapes so children can feel a sense of accomplishment as their fine motor skills develop. Examples include Duplo and LEGO blocks, knob puzzles with one to three pieces, jigsaw puzzles with pieces that vary in number and size, Peg-Boards with large and small holes (and corresponding pegs), large and small stringing beads, people and animal figures in different sizes, paintbrushes with thick and thin handles, fat and skinny crayons and markers, and doll clothes with different types of fasteners. Encourage children to begin with the easiest materials and then gradually attempt to work with more challenging ones. (Materials in larger sizes, brighter colors, with rubber grips, and so on are also useful for children with motor or sensory problems.)

- Appeal to children's diverse interests when supplying materials that promote fine motor skills. Provide a variety of materials in each area that entail the use of small muscles, such as scissors (art area), thin rods (block area), magazines (book area), small figures (toy area), eggbeaters (house area), measuring spoons (sand and water table), and chalk (outdoor playground).

- Appeal to children's diverse interests when planning small and large group times that exercise their small muscles. Vary both the materials and the content of these activities so children can use their hands and eyes to make and build, transform, investigate cause and effect, and represent things (write, draw, sculpt). Incorporate materials and activities that promote fine motor skills at other times of the day, too, such as hooks for children to hang their coats on at arrival time, sign-in charts to write their names, markers to slide or dials to turn to signal a transition, filling and emptying toys to use outside, and small food items to serve and eat at mealtimes.

Movement Concepts

From infancy on, children begin to differentiate the space they occupy from that filled by others. As motor skills develop, they form an initial awareness of how and at what rate (speed) their body moves. Young children also develop many aspects of body awareness, such as body parts and body shapes, through their own exploration and feedback, especially when adults supply appropriate labels (see the Orienting Self and Objects in Space section on p. 143 in Chap. 7). Because they are interested in their own bodies, preschoolers are generally motivated to learn body vocabulary. This applies equally to dual language learners and native English speakers. (Ask parents for the appropriate words in their home language, because digital translators often provide words that are inaccurate for program use.) As with any vocabulary set, learning the names for body parts, shapes children can create with their bodies, and other concepts requires direct instruction or conversation. (For more on vocabulary learning, see the Vocabulary section on p. 110 in Chap. 6.)

Most movement concepts seem to be learned through adult intervention, although children's initial experiments and observations form the foundation for understanding them. For example, beating on a drum with a stick explores hard and soft (levels of effort); climbing steps is an experience with low and high (space awareness); and observing a bird flying overhead but a fish swimming in a pond below creates an awareness of location (body awareness or relations). Even for such basic concepts, adult guidance is essential to help children become aware of, label, and apply what they learn.

Child-guided experience is especially important for learnings such as:

Space awareness: self space, shared space

Children learn primarily through self-discovery about the space they themselves occupy versus the space they share with other people and objects. In infancy, children perceive themselves and their caregiver as one entity, but one of the earliest spatial understandings that develops is the capacity to distinguish the space they alone occupy from that shared by others. Preschoolers have long since mastered this basic concept, but they continue to explore the boundaries between themselves and others, especially when trying out movements they do not yet fully control.

Teaching strategies. Viewing the world from their own (egocentric) perspective, young children naturally test the boundaries of their bodies. Teachers can facilitate this exploration by providing both limited and wide-open spaces for them to navigate. For large group activities, large, open spaces, where children are less likely to bump into one another or objects as they experiment with movement, are needed. Some activities are best accomplished outdoors; others will work well in uncluttered indoor spaces. For example, the area used for circle or music time might be suitable. Minimize sharp edges and provide soft surfaces (such as carpeting) so that bumps, when they do happen, do not result in injuries.

To develop an awareness of personal space necessarily means paying attention to the space filled by others. Hence, this area of physical development has both individual and social aspects. Here are some strategies:

○ Introduce self- and shared-space activities gradually. Begin with large group activities where children stay in their own space and perform movements such as swaying or bending. You may need to provide visual markers, such as carpet squares or tape on the floor, to help some children stay in their own area.

○ Have children move through space. Line up half the group on each side of the room and say, "Now see if you can move to the other side without touching anyone or anything else." Begin with a simple locomotor movement the children have mastered (such as crawling or walking) and progress to more advanced movements (such as plodding or skipping). Encourage children with mobility challenges to invent other ways to navigate across the space and ask their peers to offer (and themselves try) other suggestions.

○ Provide children with opportunities to discover their personal body boundaries; for example, have them move through narrow and wide spaces, or low and high ones. Use existing spaces and create others with furniture, cartons, sheet-draped tables and chairs, beanbag chairs, Hula-Hoops, and the like. For example, challenge children to perform increasingly difficult motor movements while inside a hoop. Begin with movements that require little balance (such as raising the arms) and progress to ones that require more control and stability (such as lifting one leg). Ask the children to suggest movements.

○ Ask each child to choose a partner and perform the motions while inside the same hoop together. This activity also presents a good opportunity for children to engage in social problem solving, such as agreeing on rules about how to avoid actions that might hurt the other person.

Effort awareness: time (speeds)

The aspect of effort awareness primarily learned in exploration and discovery is the time concept of speeds. (The other time concept is rhythms, discussed on p. 89 in this chapter under adult-guided learning.) For preschoolers, speed concepts include slow, moderate or medium, and fast, as well as accelerating and decelerating (going faster and slower).

Teaching strategies. Children love to play with speed—the more extreme, the better. They challenge themselves and one another to go faster or be the fastest. However, children also enjoy experimenting with slow movements, especially if they are exaggerated (for example, "verrrry sloooow!"). Teachers have many options for supporting this natural fascination with rates of movement, including these:

○ Call children's attention to moving things and comment on their rate of speed. Ask them to imitate the fast and slow movements they observe. Describe the speed of various activities; for example, say, "Those are slow-cooking cookies. I'm getting hungry" or "The water from Jamie's faucet is coming out faster than the water from Nicola's. Jamie's bucket will fill up sooner." Comment on the speed of creatures and events in nature, such as the rate at which animals travel, clouds move, seeds germinate, and leaves fall. Point out the speed of objects in the environment, such as a fast-moving jet or a slow-moving freight train.

- Ask children to name things that move at a slow, fast, or medium speed and demonstrate the corresponding movement. Then copy the children's movements and ask, "Am I moving too fast or too slow?" Follow their suggestions for making a movement faster or slower.

- Invent games or transitions that feature moving at different speeds. For example, suggest to a child, "Can you move to the snack table as slow as a turtle?" Or say to the group, "Let's see how fast we can clean up and get ready to go outside." Scarves are wonderful for observing and experimenting with slow movement, as in the following example:

> Several children become very interested in dropping scarves from the climber and are quite amazed at how *slowly* they drift to the ground. "It takes a long time for them to go down," one child notes. This observation leads the children to try out being "slow scarves" during large group, in which they exhibit an understanding and tolerance for moving slowly, a capacity they had not shown before.

Body awareness: with self (body parts, body shapes)

At its most basic, body awareness is the relationship we each have with our own body. Children come to understand that their body comprises various parts, meaning that they understand that the thing attached to their shoulder is their arm, at the end of that is their hand, and at the end of that are their fingers.

Those individual parts take various shapes, as does their whole body in relation to the world around them (including relational movement concepts, such as whether they move on top of or underneath something). The shapes (or characteristics) that preschool children can create with their bodies and comprehend with minimal adult intervention include round, straight, tall, long, short, small, and big. With a bit more guidance, they can grasp such concepts as narrow, wide, stretched, twisted, square, rectangular, triangular, diamond, thin, thick, pointed, oval, flat, angular, curved, curled, crooked, sharp, smooth, tiny, gigantic, and skinny. They can also experiment with and experience the concept of like and unlike (see also Chap. 8 and 9).

Teaching strategies. Young children's fascination with their own bodies offers many natural openings for teachers to support their learning of relational movement concepts, including the following strategies:

- Refer to children's body parts by name in natural conversation. For example, "Tristan, I see you're wearing a new red hat on your head" or "Lyla, can you show Ian how you kicked the ball by turning your foot to the side?" Comment when a change in position creates a change in body shape; for example, "When I sit down on this chair, I'll make a flat lap for you to cuddle in while we read."

- Use the arts to enhance children's awareness. Read books and tell stories that feature body parts. Sing songs and chants that use body parts, such as "I Got a Wiggle." Encourage children to name a body part to put in and take out when you sing "The Hokey Pokey." Use various noisemakers, and ask children to represent the sounds with their bodies. For example, they might show a jingly sound by wiggling, a gong sound by standing up straight, and a ticking sound with head bobbing. Describe the sounds, acknowledge children's labels, and provide additional vocabulary words.

○ Pose movement challenges and problems to enhance body awareness. This problem-solving approach is more effective than showing or telling. For example,

> When you present children with a challenge, such as "Show me how crooked you can be," chances are that no two responses will be alike. Divergent thinking, one of the cognitive skills required for creativity, is enhanced through problem-solving challenges that allow for various responses. In addition, when you validate the different responses received, children realize that it's okay to find their own individual solutions and to not to have to compete with one another. Their confidence grows, and they continue to take greater creative risks. (Pica 2009, 60–61)

Adult-guided experience is especially important for learnings such as:

Space awareness: levels, directions, pathways

Levels refers to the position of the body or a body part in space—that is, high, middle or medium, and low. Directions concepts include up/down, forward/backward, beside, and sideways. (They also include right/left and clockwise/counterclockwise, but most preschoolers are not yet ready to learn these concepts.) Pathways are straight, curved or circular, and zigzag movements.

Teaching strategies. These areas of spatial awareness have important implications not only for physical education but also for other domains. As teachers help young children move in different ways through space, they are also creating the foundation for many areas of mathematics (geometry), science (physics), and social studies (geography). Teachers can use the following strategies to help develop these areas of spatial awareness:

○ Suggest ways children might use or place their body parts at different levels. For example, suggest to children, "Walk around the playground with your nose as high in the air as you can" or "Think of a way to move with your elbows down low." Invent activities in which children move their bodies or manipulate objects in different directions or along different pathways. For example, suggest they crawl across the room forward and backward. Ask them to suggest ways to move forward and backward, up and down, sideways, and in straight or zigzag patterns. Encourage children to invent their own activities and follow their suggestions.

○ Play musical instruments of varying pitch and ask children to position their bodies according to the sound. For example, they might stand on tiptoe for a high pitch or crouch for a low one. Describe the sounds and label children's actions.

○ Create pathways that are circular, straight, or zigzag using chalk, tape, traffic cones, large blocks, and other materials. Suggest ways to move in, out of, and around these paths. Follow children's ideas. Encourage children to observe and comment on the differences in paths and movements, and extend their language. For example, if a child says, "One road is straight, and the other is funny," say, "Yes, this one is a straight line, and that one is a zigzag." Encourage children to walk or move in other ways along the paths.

○ Set up obstacle courses involving changes of direction, different levels, and various types of pathways. Use things such as blocks, carpet squares, shelves, ramps, chairs, tables, and tape marks on the floor to create the course. Outdoors, also incorporate natural materials. Encourage children to create their own obstacle courses.

○ Incorporate into the daily routine pathways and ways of moving along them, such as during transitions (going from the table to wash up) and cleanup (moving between areas to put away toys). Suggest movement ideas and ask children to contribute their own. For example,

> Children in HighScope preschools make plans to indicate what they will do at work (choice) time. Part of planning is deciding what area of the room to work in. One teacher suggested this idea: "The teacher lays a 'planning path' (made from long sheets of fabric) on the floor and asks children to choose a way to move their bodies along the path (e.g., crawl, hop, go backwards, jump, walk like a crab) to an area where they plan to work." (Strubank 1991, 106)

○ Use naturally occurring situations to supply vocabulary words that describe level and direction as children move about the room and play outdoors. Encourage them to use these vocabulary words as they describe their own actions. For dual language learners, supply these words in both their home language and in English.

Effort awareness: time (rhythms), force, control/flow

The component of time in which adult intervention plays a salient role is rhythms—that is, beat, cadence, and pattern. Beat is the "consistent, repetitive pulse that lies within every rhyme, song, or musical selection" (Weikart 2000, 122). Cadence is the musical measure of movement, while pattern is its systematic or regular repetition. The force component of effort awareness has three aspects: degree (strong, medium, light); creation, when the body is the source of a force (starting, sustained, explosive, gradual); and absorption, when the body reacts to a force (stopping, receiving, stabilizing). The control component (sometimes called flow) refers to the complexity of movement—that is, single movements, combinations of movements, and transitions between movements.

Teaching strategies. Just as space awareness concepts apply to other domains of learning, effort awareness concepts do as well. They contribute to children's musical development, mathematics (patterning) understanding, and the ability to carry out increasingly complex directions (Geist & Geist 2008). Try strategies such as these to support children's learning in effort awareness:

○ Incorporate different strategies to increase children's familiarity with rhythms. Use poems, chants, and songs with steady beats. Instrumental music is best because children are not distracted by the lyrics. Emphasize beats with your gestures and words, such as by clapping your hands, tapping your foot, nodding, and accenting syllables. Call children's attention to actions that involve steady beat, as in the following example:

One spring day during outside time, Jessie, an adult, was pushing 4-year-old Timmy on the swing. She noticed that his legs were beginning to perform the bending and straightening motion used in pumping. She began to reinforce Timmy's natural movement with language, saying "BACK" as his legs went back and "OUT" as his legs went out. As Timmy felt the timing of the words, his movements became larger and more pronounced, and he moved to the steady beat. From that day on, Timmy was able to pump himself on the swing. (Weikart 2000, 138)

○ Provide children with different experiences that involve weight and force. As they work with objects of different weights, comment on their level of effort: "Lucy carried that heavy box all the way across the room!" Ask children to pretend to carry things of different weights: "Let's imagine we're lifting a hammer over our heads. Now pretend it's a feather from a tiny bird."

○ Offer children hard and soft materials to transform, and comment on how much effort it takes. For example, they might compare hammering nails into wood with pounding golf tees into pumpkins or gourds (use safety goggles and take other appropriate precautions). Use clay or dough that varies in plasticity, and encourage children to comment on how easy or hard the materials are to shape.

○ Gradually increase children's ability to follow and sequence movement directions. Children often follow and respond to movement directions better if adults separate the verbal and visual components (Weikart 2000). Therefore, demonstrate the movement without talking *or* describe it in words without moving, and then ask children to try it. Children may differ in which type of cue is most effective for them, so alternate visual and verbal cues. After children master a movement, you can combine the two components when you give the direction.

○ Build a movement sequence by always beginning with one motion at a time and encouraging children to practice it for a while. Add a second motion only after the children appear comfortable and confident with the first one. When sequencing, keep each movement simple and familiar (for example, patting the knee and touching the shoulder). Encourage children to suggest pairs of movements.

Body awareness: with self (roles), with other movers and objects

The concept relating to the self that requires adult intervention is roles. Roles that children create with their bodies include copying; leading/following; meeting/parting; passing; mirroring; and acting in unison, alternately, solo, with partner, or as a group. Children also use their bodies to create relationships with other people and objects; this concept is called locations. Locations includes above/below, near to/far from, over/under, in front of/behind, on/off, together/apart, facing/side by side, around/through, between, and into.

Teaching strategies. Like advanced manipulative skills such as volleying, awareness of body relationships also has social and cognitive implications for young children's development. Thoughtful teachers can use the following strategies to support the learning of these movement concepts with those impacts in mind:

- Give children opportunities to manipulate equipment (such as Hula-Hoops, pool noodles, scarves, cartons) to help them discover relationships between themselves and objects. For example, here are some suggestions to use with hoops:
  - "Walk (or march, hop, gallop, or jump) around the outside of the hoop."
  - "Lift the hoop up around the outside of your body. Now lower the hoop down around the outside of your body."
  - "Walk away from the hoop. Walk toward the hoop."
- Create imaginative ways for children to use their bodies, and ask them to suggest other ideas. Invent games in which they change the location of their bodies relative to others and to objects (for example, jumping in and out of a large circle, facing toward and away from a partner, or stepping in front of and behind a chair).
- Encourage children to use their bodies to express emotions such as friendly, sad, mad, frightened, brave, shy, silly, and adventurous. Say, "How do you move your body when you are happy?" or "Let's move to the snack table as though we're tired and sleepy." Ask them to suggest feelings to represent with their bodies.
- Provide vocabulary words to describe the body's position relative to people and objects. Give children simple definitions. Insert location words into conversations; for example, "Tawana is moving her finger along the shelf to find a book that begins with the letter *T*" or "Let's stand farther apart while we do 'Hokey Pokey' so everyone has room to *shake it all about!*" For dual language learners, provide these words in their home languages and English. Encourage them to use these words (in either language) themselves.
- Give children opportunities to lead and follow during movement activities. For example, ask them to suggest ideas for "Everybody Touch Your Head" or other familiar songs. Dual language learners can give directions in their home languages as a way of teaching these words to their peers. Repeat or clarify their ideas to make it easier for other children to listen and copy. Have children observe others and perform the same movements (they need not duplicate them exactly). For example,

> In [the game] *Mirrors*, children pair off and stand facing each other. While standing in place, partners trade off performing and imitating a series of simple movements. Variations include having one child stand in back of the performer and another in front or having one child lead a group. (Sanders 2002, 35)

Personal Care and Healthy Behavior

In their eagerness to be like adults and become more independent, young children devote a great deal of energy and attention to mastering self-help skills. As their physical awareness grows, they also pay more attention to how their behavior affects what their bodies can do. Children practice many personal care routines, such as eating and dressing themselves, and engage in some healthy behaviors, such as moving energetically, with little prompting or help. Other behaviors, such as following good hygiene and safety practices, or learning what is (and is not) healthy, require more explicit adult guidance.

Child-guided experience is especially important for learnings such as:

Feeding and dressing oneself (using serving and eating utensils; putting on and taking off outerwear, shoes, dress-up clothes)

Children have many opportunities at home and in school to practice self-help skills related to feeding and dressing themselves. For example, they use serving and eating utensils (and sometimes their hands) to dish out solids, pour liquids, and convey food from plate or bowl to mouth. They put on and take off outerwear when they arrive at or leave school or go outside, and they add and remove dress-up clothing during pretend play. They also practice using various fasteners when they create or put clothes on dolls and stuffed animals. Although children sometimes turn to adults for help with these skills, they are likely to learn them on their own and/or by watching how others carry them out.

Teaching strategies. Given children's high level of internal motivation to master basic personal care behaviors, the role of adults is primarily to provide time and appropriate materials. Here are some strategies that teachers can use to accomplish this:

- Let children do things for themselves. Adults often dress or serve food to children because it is faster or neater or a behavior that is valued in their culture. However, young children need multiple opportunities and ample time to learn to perform these actions on their own. Daily schedules—the time allotted to get ready to go outside, for example—should accommodate this need. Moreover, preschoolers should not be expected to carry out these tasks according to adult standards. Acknowledge when children meet the goals they have set for themselves, such as buttoning a sweater, even if some buttons are misaligned. Correcting or improving on what children do may discourage them from further attempts. Provide many opportunities for children to practice and refine these skills.

- Provide activities and equipment for children to practice self-feeding and dressing skills. Preschoolers practice many self-help skills during pretend play. For example, they prepare food and wash dishes while playing house, put clothes on dolls, or dress up as firefighters and chefs. In addition to encouraging this direct practice of skills, adults can provide other tools and activities that help children develop the manual dexterity to zip a jacket or hold a pitcher steady. Examples include beads and string, pegs and Peg-Boards, scissors, staplers, hole punches, screwdrivers, hammers, sponges, tape, wooden spoons, brooms, and shovels. Likewise, art and building activities allow children to exercise the fine motor abilities needed to care for themselves. For example, they handle a toothbrush to apply paint to paper or tie tape around a stack of blocks. Even turning the pages of a book is practice for separating the top paper towel from the stack.

Exercising

Without the distractions of technology, children readily engage in vigorous physical play. They run and jump, roll and hop, and twirl and slide. Even children with physical disabilities work hard at moving those parts of their bodies that function partially or fully. While these actions have the advantage of strengthening their

muscles, to the children the satisfaction of moving is benefit enough. The movement is itself a pleasurable sensation, and it creates other sensations—a vision of spinning trees, the wind against one's face. In the process of exercising, young children also learn about their bodies and the many ways it can move. They gain mastery over their muscles, learning to control and coordinate the direction, speed, and precision of their movements.

Teaching strategies. As mentioned previously in this chapter, there is increasing concern today about the lack of physical exercise in the daily experiences of young children. Adults can help to correct this imbalance by providing time and interesting materials that take advantage of children's instinctive desire to play. They can also set an example by exercising themselves. Here are some helpful strategies:

- Provide time and materials for young children to engage in vigorous activity. Opportunities for exercise abound throughout the program day, particularly during large group time and outside time. Preschoolers can also move in safe ways during choice time and transitions. While running through the room may pose safety hazards, children can glide, twirl, and explore ways of moving in place or from place to place. Interesting materials to support large motor play (see the box on pp. 72–73 in this chapter) inspire children to explore different types of exercise. They can jump in and out of tires, run to make scarves stream behind them, or march to the steady beat of lively instrumental music. Children who do not walk may be able to roll, crawl, pull themselves along by their arms, and/or travel from place to place using assistive mobility devices.

- Join in active exercise yourself. Don't just watch the children move—get going alongside them. Children pick up healthy behavior by imitating adults. When they see you exercising regularly, preschoolers are apt to adopt these behaviors too. In addition to modeling the actual movements, convey a positive attitude. If you express displeasure, as though exercising were a distasteful task forced upon you, children will internalize the same negative sentiments. However, if you express pleasure in actively using your body, children will trust the joy they experience in exercise too.

Adult-guided experience is especially important for learnings such as:

Washing hands and brushing teeth

While dirt is visible, most germs are invisible and therefore may seem abstract to young children. The need to wash our hands to free them of disease-causing bacteria or to prevent decay by brushing our teeth is not obvious to preschoolers. On the other hand, most do have firsthand experience with getting sick and can comprehend that concrete behaviors might lessen the need for a trip to the doctor's office. The specific techniques needed to clean one's hands and teeth are not intuitive, however, so this is an area where explicit adult guidance and modeling can help children learn healthy practices.

Teaching strategies. Children are less likely to resist cleaning their hands and brushing their teeth if they perceive performing these acts as them taking on adult responsibilities, rather than as tasks imposed upon them by adults. The following strategies can help preschoolers develop positive attitudes toward these self-care behaviors.

- Model and guide emerging physical skills in bodily self-care. Although preschoolers' physical abilities have come a long way since toddlerhood, they are still learning about their changing bodies and how to take care of them. They will watch your hand washing and toothbrushing with interest and attempt to copy you. Describe your actions in simple terms and demonstrate them as often as needed ("I'm spreading the soap all the way to my wrists"). Don't expect young children to be as thorough in these rituals as you, but do encourage and appreciate their attempts.

- Provide daily opportunities for children to practice hand washing and toothbrushing. These activities can be fun, since they are types of water play. Understand, however, that if something more interesting beckons, children's efforts at cleaning themselves may be cursory. Therefore, don't pull them away from other activities for these routines. Keep the routines low-key and schedule them after one activity has wound down and before another begins. Preschoolers can also develop the skills needed for cleaning their hands and teeth by practicing related skills. For example, they can wash dishes during pretend play or develop an understanding of the up-and-down motions of a toothbrush by moving their bodies up and down to music at large group time.

Practicing interpersonal hygiene

If self-hygiene skills do not come naturally to young children, the kinds of hygienic practices necessary to protect the health of others is even less obvious to them. Behaviors such as using and discarding tissues, or covering one's mouth when coughing (or coughing into one's elbow) appear arbitrary to them. In essence, they are trusting the adult's word that such practices help to guarantee the health of others. As preschoolers develop empathy (see the Feeling Empathy section on p. 49 in Chap. 4), however, they are concerned with doing what is right and helpful for those they care about. Therefore, they will become more motivated to follow such practices, provided adults demonstrate and explain how to do so.

Teaching strategies. Adults encourage young children to follow hygienic practices when they routinely use such behaviors themselves. Acknowledging children's efforts, even when less than perfect, also encourages the use of healthy interpersonal hygiene. Try these ideas:

- Call attention to the hygienic practices you follow yourself. Briefly describe how and why you blow your nose into a tissue and throw it away, or cover your mouth with your hand or elbow when you cough. For example, you might say, "The tissue catches my germs so no one else gets them" or "I'm making sure no one gets sick by covering my cough." At first, children might copy the behavior without understanding why it is important, but gradually, as they begin to comprehend cause-and-effect relationships, they will accept that certain behaviors lead to better health. They will also take pride in performing actions that are good for the community.

- Acknowledge when children use hygienic practices. Make simple statements describing and accepting when children use tissues appropriately or cover their cough. Don't praise them, since the purpose of engaging in such practices is *not* to be rewarded by an adult. Instead, show you are aware that they are behaving in a helpful manner. Calling attention to a child's hygienic actions also makes other children aware of the behavior and more likely to carry it out themselves. If children forget to use a tissue or cover a cough, don't criticize them but offer a gentle reminder. It is easy for preschoolers to forget such niceties when there are many other concrete distractions!

Differentiating between healthy and unhealthy foods

To young children, food is simply food. Their preferences are based on taste and texture, not health. In this regard, they are similar to adults. The prevalence of food advertisements and ready access to unhealthy food (one of the earliest literacy accomplishments in children is recognizing the logo of a fast-food chain) further subverts the widely growing push to improve the diet of young children. Children therefore depend on adults, who must often first educate themselves, to help them distinguish between foods that are and are not good for them to eat. Fortunately, preschoolers' interest in classification (see p. 163 in Chap. 8) makes them as curious about sorting food into "healthy" and "not healthy" groups as they are about sorting beads by color or classmates by gender. The US Department of Agriculture (USDA) Center for Nutrition Policy and Promotion (2011) publishes materials (such as the illustrated MyPlate) that can help teachers introduce simple concepts about good nutrition to preschoolers.

Teaching strategies. As adults who have attempted to change their own eating habits know, it takes time and vigilance to make healthy eating a routine part of the day. The following ideas will help both teachers and children approach food as a health-promoting option that can be shared and enjoyed in a relaxed social atmosphere:

○ Integrate healthy food into the daily routine. Work with the individuals who are responsible for planning and purchasing food for your setting to select a variety of healthy options, emphasizing vegetables, fruits, whole grains, and low-fat dairy and protein, that meet USDA guidelines for young children. Plan small group times in which children can describe and discuss the properties of healthy foods, including their appearance, sound, smell, feel, and taste. Provide foods that children are familiar with in their cultures as well as some new ones to try. Also, don't be afraid to cook with children. Colker (2005) offers these simple tips to protect children's health and safety: Use sharp knives (dull knives are actually more dangerous), thick potholders, and warm (no more than 120 degrees Fahrenheit) rather than hot water; wash ingredients thoroughly and keep foods at the recommended temperature to prevent bacterial growth; and discourage nibbling during cooking activities. If you keep the activity short and provide a concrete measure (such as a timer) of when it will be done, preschoolers can delay gratification.

○ Label foods as more or less healthy. Providing labels serves a dual purpose. It makes children more aware of what they are eating and its effect on their bodies ("Candy and oranges are both sweet, but oranges are healthier for our bodies"). The verbal labels also increase vocabulary and classification skills (words such as *vitamins* and categories such "good for you" and "not good for you"). Preschoolers will begin to apply the words they hear to identify and sort foods on their own. Left to themselves, they may not always choose the healthier option (cookies may win over carrots), but they will begin to reflect on the implications of their choices.

Following safety procedures

Most health and safety rules are imposed by licensing agencies or by adults following guidelines or applying common sense. Often it is the adults themselves who are responsible for establishing and implementing these policies. However, there are some practices that children can appreciate as directly applying to them because they have witnessed, or even experienced, the consequences of not following them. These include such procedures as wearing a bike helmet, not walking in front of a moving swing, or walking around a spill until it is cleaned up. The more preschoolers develop a sense of cause and effect, they more they can see the need for certain rules. Also, as they form mental images of the past and future, children can better understand the reasons behind these procedures. They may even offer their own ideas about how to improve or enforce them!

Teaching strategies. Because the logic behind many safety policies is not self-evident, young children must depend on adults to explain, demonstrate, and gently enforce them. Often a simple explanation or calm reminder is enough to encourage compliance. The following strategies will help teachers create a safe classroom while not overly restricting children's explorations:

○ Model safety procedures yourself. As with the health and hygiene practices discussed in the previous sections of this chapter, children are eager to emulate adult behavior. Periodically, however, ask yourself whether a safety rule is really necessary or whether it exists to reassure or simplify things for adults. Unnecessary policies might unduly restrict children's explorations.

For example, rather than having a safety rule forbidding the use of water in the house area, problem solve with the children ways to minimize or wipe up spills. Children are more likely to follow rules when they discuss and participate in setting guidelines.

○ Acknowledge when children follow safe practices. As with interpersonal hygiene, encourage rather than praise (or criticize) their efforts. Children will become more reflective about their behavior when you describe it and casually mention its benefits ("Carl, you walked around the edge of the playground instead of in front of the swing so that you wouldn't be hit by it").

○ Provide picture cues—preferably using photos of the children in your program—as reminders of safety rules and procedures for children who may not understand spoken reminders. Add phonetically spelled phrases in the children's home languages so that teachers, substitute teachers, or visitors can verbalize the safety cue in the appropriate language.

○ Encourage children to remind one another about safety procedures. Once children have learned to follow safety policies themselves, they are often eager to remind their peers to obey them, too. Don't be overly concerned about children being tattletales. In most instances, being reminded by a peer is more effective than being reminded by an adult. If children are too critical with one another, problem–solve ways they can deliver the message without being hurtful (see p. 61 in Chap. 4).

Facilitating children's development of physical skills and healthy behaviors during the preschool years is "fundamental and crucial to the goal of helping all children become physically active and healthy for life" (Sanders 2002, 58). Movement experiences and health awareness can also enhance learning in other domains, such as mathematics and peer interactions. But mastering motor skills, developing healthy habits, and applying these skills and habits to cognitive and social content will not happen through maturation alone. Teachers play a vital role by arranging and equipping the learning environment, scheduling physical education activities in addition to free play, issuing physical challenges, offering concrete cues to help children develop physical knowledge and skills, modeling and remarking on healthy behaviors, and offering daily opportunities to exercise and eat healthy foods.

For Further Consideration

1. What arguments can early childhood advocates use to preserve physical education in the face of budget allocations favoring academic disciplines at the expense of other content areas?

2. What role can and should early childhood education play in preventing obesity, inactivity, and other physical conditions that predispose children to later health and related problems?

3. Think about the kinds of physical activity you enjoyed as a child. How can you, as a new or experienced teacher, plan ways to include these types of activities in your program on a daily basis? What kinds of physical exercise do the children in your program or programs you have observed seem to enjoy? How can you, as a teacher, create opportunities for them to build on their interest and pleasure in such movements?

4. If developmental theory and research show it is inappropriate for preschoolers to participate in sports, how can the early childhood field address the current trend toward involving children in organized athletics at increasingly younger ages?

5. What advocacy and practical roles can early childhood professionals play to promote large motor activity in neighborhoods where children do not have access to safe outdoor play areas? Can and should early childhood agencies serve as community organizers, advocates, mediators, and builders?

6. What role can or should the early childhood community play in bringing fresh, healthy foods to areas where there is a lack, and in encouraging healthier eating options?

Chapter 6

Language and Literacy

The preschoolers are going for a walk around the block. As they get ready to leave, their teacher, Linda, leads them in a rhyming game about what they might see, using the children's first names.

"Walker, walker, what will you see?

Maybe a house. Maybe a tree.

I'm a walker; my name is [child's first name, such as Benny],

I think that I will see a [insert rhyming word, such as penny]."

Gus says he will see "a bus," Tracy thinks she will see "something lacy," and Pete comes up with "street." After each child responds, the teacher makes a comment such as "Yes, *bus* rhymes with *Gus*" or "*Tracy* and *lacy* end with the same sound. They rhyme." Linda offers "Binda" and everyone laughs, acknowledging that the made-up word does rhyme with her name. When Jake says he will see a "dog," the teacher does not correct him but instead says, "I wonder if you'll see something else that rhymes with Jake." When he replies uncertainly, "Cat?" she asks the other children for ideas. They suggest "rake" and "cake." Elena, whose English language skills are developed enough to understand the opening rhyme (*see* and *tree*) and the basic idea of the chant, nevertheless has trouble thinking of an English word that rhymes with her name. Her teacher says, "En español" to encourage her. Elena's face brightens and she says, "Reina!" The teacher tells the class, "*Reina* is the Spanish word for *queen*. *Elena* and *reina* rhyme."

The landmark report *Preventing Reading Difficulties in Young Children* (Snow, Burns, & Griffin 1998) observes that "preschool teachers represent an important, and largely underutilized, resource in promoting literacy by supporting rich language and emergent literacy skills" (6). Since then, numerous articles, books, and reports have emphasized how critical the early years are in laying the groundwork for later literacy learning (e.g., National Governors Association 2013; Schickedanz & Collins 2013; Strickland & Shanahan 2004). However, the best way to help children learn these skills during the early years is the subject of lively and sometimes touchy debate. The reading wars that often divide primary-grade educators are now being fought on the preschool playground, and the debate is reignited with every report on the state of children's literacy in this country (Strauss 2013). However, there is a degree of common ground in the midst of this debate, and teachers should be encouraged to start young children on the path toward literacy.

The basis of this common ground is the "consensus in the research community that reading is a *constructive* and *interactive* process aimed at meaning-making and involving the reader, the text, and the contextual setting in which the reading takes place" (Gambrell & Mazzoni 1999, 80; see also Schickedanz & Collins 2013). In other words, learning to read is like mastering any other skill. Young children are motivated to do it because they want to make sense of their world, and they learn best by using real materials in real situations. Children acquire much of this learning through teacher-provided information, but children also develop knowledge and skills on their own during play as well as through their interactions with peers.

Because we now understand that younger children are interested in reading, there has been a major shift in what we call **reading readiness.** Previously, children did not receive reading instruction until first grade. But in the past three decades, early education has taken up the idea of **emergent literacy.** In this view, literacy is not an all-or-nothing type of skill acquisition (that is, it does not begin only with the introduction of the alphabet), but rather it is a gradual progression that begins in infancy with learning language and looking at books. The preschool years can build on early experiences, or fill in gaps when necessary, to prepare young children for the next steps. Literacy learning continues through the formal reading and writing instruction of elementary school. Though Snow, Burns, & Griffin (1998) caution against replicating in preschool the formal instruction of later grades, they do note that while providing "optimal support for cognitive, language, and social development . . . ample attention should be paid to skills that are known to predict future reading achievement, especially those for which a causal role has been demonstrated" (5).

Young Children's Development in Language and Literacy

Reading research has yielded much useful information about how language and literacy develop, from which the following are summarized (Ranweiler 2004):

- Language and literacy are connected from infancy onward. Speaking, listening, reading, and writing develop concurrently rather than sequentially.

- Children differ in their learning. Some pick up literacy skills easily and quickly; others need more explicit help and time.

- Some language and literacy learning is incidental. It arises naturally during play and other everyday experiences. Other learning depends on the explicit instruction that occurs during formal teaching. Thus, children actively construct their own knowledge, but they also need support from adults to further their development.

- Children acquire language and literacy as they interact with others. Young children learn to talk, read, and write because they are social beings. They want to communicate with adults and peers at home, school, and other familiar places.

- Children learn best when instruction is relevant and meaningful to them. When children can apply language and literacy to their everyday interests and activities, that learning will be genuine, deep, and lasting.

- Language and literacy learning happens through activities children might initiate, such as role playing, exploring print materials, and doing inventive writing. It also happens through instruction such as book reading, letter identification practice, and performing or composing songs and poems using alliteration and rhyming.

- Differences between children's home language and culture and those of the program can affect their language and literacy development. Any good program of support and instruction must take these differences into account.

In 1997, in response to a Congressional directive, a National Reading Panel (NRP) was convened by the National Institute of Child Health and Human Development and the US Department of Education. Its report, built on the work of Snow and her colleagues (1998) as well as on other research, was issued in 2000. Its recommendations were incorporated into the federal No Child Left Behind Act and Reading First and Early Reading First grant guidelines.

Particularly noteworthy for early childhood practitioners are the four abilities that the report (NRP 2000) says preschoolers must develop to become speakers, readers, and writers:

- **Phonological awareness**—the general ability to attend to the sounds of language as distinct from its meaning. Initial awareness of speech sounds and rhythms, rhyme awareness, recognition of sound similarities, and phonemic awareness are all elements of this ability.

- **Comprehension**—understanding the meaning of spoken and written language. Comprehension is "intentional thinking during which meaning is constructed" (14).

- **Print awareness**—understanding how print is organized and used in reading and writing. Children learn that speech and written language carry messages and that words convey ideas.

- **Alphabet knowledge** (or the "alphabetic principle")—understanding that there is a systematic relationship between letters and sounds. Whole words have a structure made up of individual sounds and of sound patterns or groupings.

It is also the case that to become literate, young children must see reading and writing as not only useful but also pleasurable. Adults play a key role in promoting this positive attitude (Neuman, Copple, & Bredekamp 2000).

Teaching and Learning in Language and Literacy

As with all curriculum areas, a balance of child-guided and adult-guided experiences is essential in early language and literacy development, and the division between the two is not cut-and-dried.

> Literacy, whether oral or written language, is a social and cultural phenomenon. By definition, then, the most productive child-initiated activities will still be those that involve [the child in] some kind of interaction with an adult or other children at some point during the activity. (Linda Bevilacqua 2004, personal communication)

In other words, even though children have language and literacy experiences and acquire many literacy skills on their own, the presence and support of thoughtful adults is critical to sustain their motivation and supply essential information.

Just as child-guided learning cannot happen as effectively without adult support, it is also the case that "even knowledge and skills acquired through intentional and explicit adult-guided instruction require child-guided exploration and practice to gain depth and extension" (Lesley Mandel Morrow 2004, personal communication). So while teachers take the lead when adult-guided activities are called for, they should also encourage child choice and discovery in those areas.

The NRP (2000) says that both incidental and explicit reading instruction are necessary and can be effective. It cautions, however, that "educators must keep the *end* in mind" (10) and provide "methods [that are] appropriate to the age and ability of the reader" (14). So, for example, systematic phonics instruction cannot stop with decoding exercises (dissecting the sounds and parts of words); ultimately it must allow children to derive meaning and achieve fluency in their everyday reading and writing activities.

Similarly, the main purpose of vocabulary instruction is not to build random word knowledge but to produce gains in children's comprehension of spoken and written language. For young children, "a primary motivation for acquiring vocabulary and developing rules of syntax [is] a desire to communicate with others"; further, research consistently shows that children who make the most progress in literacy "had teachers who stressed vocabulary learning *in context,* that is, in all content areas" (Genishi & Fassler 1999, 62).

NAEYC's professional standards for initial licensure (NAEYC 2001) apply research findings to create a list of expectations for teachers. These standards say that to help young children become readers and writers, practitioners need to plan experiences that help children develop the ability to converse, use, and understand a wide vocabulary; enjoy reading and writing and see their usefulness; understand stories and texts; and develop basic print concepts and understanding of sounds, letters, and letter-sound relationships.

The joint position statement of the International Reading Association and NAEYC (1998) also provides context and practical examples for helping children develop specific knowledge and skills in these four areas, stating, "The ability to read and write does not develop naturally, without careful planning and instruction" (3). Fortunately, the literature is rich with practical suggestions on how to accomplish these ends, including guidance for those working with children whose first language is not English and those from other cultures (Genishi & Dyson 2009; Nemeth 2012).

Fitting the Learning Experience to the Learning Objective

The following discussion—grouped according to skills in *language* (listening and speaking), *reading,* and *writing*—should help practitioners sort out the "what" and "how to" in early literacy instruction and learning. Within each of the three areas, the sample teaching strategies are grouped according to knowledge and skills gained primarily through child-guided or adult-guided learning, but this is not a rigid division. Careful attention to children's emerging abilities will help teachers decide which approach works best for each child at any given time.

Language

Of the key knowledge and skills in the area of language, child-guided experience seems particularly important in children's acquisition of sound awareness and production as well as conversational skills. Dual language learning is also included in the child-guided category because dual language learners gain a great deal from their English-speaking peers. However, adults are also vitally important, for example, in helping dual language learners develop English vocabulary and in facilitating communication between monolingual children and dual language learners when gestures and context do not suffice. Furthermore, adults as well as children are critical in encouraging dual language learners to maintain their home language at the same time they are acquiring proficiency in English (Nemeth 2012). Adult-guided experience seems especially significant for gaining phonological awareness, vocabulary, and knowledge of narrative/comprehension.

Child-guided experience is especially important for learnings such as:

Sound awareness and production

This skill area refers broadly to awareness of sounds (including nonwords) and is the simplest level of phonological awareness (more on that on p. 108 in this chapter). It also includes being able to produce various sounds with the vocal cords. Development of sound awareness begins in infancy with recognizing the sounds made by people and things. This includes learning to distinguish the noises made by significant individuals (such as the voice qualities of different caregivers, determining mood by tone of voice), animals (sounds of family pets, zoo animals), everyday activities (cooking and cleaning noises, stroller wheels on pavement), vehicles (starting the car, a garbage truck backing up, brakes on a bus), and other noisemaking items (household appliances, machines, musical instruments). Early and frequent exposure to sounds, especially the sounds of language, is crucial for a young child's development of language and literacy skills.

Young children also naturally make their own sounds. Infants babble and play with their voices. Toddlers and preschoolers enjoy experimenting to hear the variety and range of sounds their vocal cords can create. This playfulness also appears later when young children begin to produce recognizable language. For example, preschoolers enjoy making up nonsense words or combining words with sounds that vary in loudness or pitch. By interacting with children as they create and play with these sounds, adults further support and extend early language and literacy learning.

Teaching strategies. To ensure that young children are exposed early and often to a variety of sounds, consider and elaborate on the following ideas:

- Provide many noisemaking items inside the classroom, including musical instruments; timers that tick and ring; noisemaking toys; CDs and CD players or MP3 players; interactive media with appropriate noisemaking software or apps; tools and workbench; and things that make noise during filling and emptying, such as pea gravel, stones, beads, buttons, dice, shells, bottle caps, running water, and beanbags or bags filled with other types of materials. Ask children to vary the sounds they make with instruments, other materials, or their voices. For example, ask them to make sounds that are loud and soft, fast and slow, high and low, long and short, or continuous and interrupted.

- Expose children to a wide variety of sounds outside the classroom, including those in nature (wind, birds, waves, running streams), throughout the building (bells, buzzers, telephones, footsteps in the hall), and in the neighborhood (cars, construction vehicles, sirens, barking dogs).

- Call children's attention to sounds throughout the day (such as a sneeze, doors opening and closing, footsteps, balls bouncing, water running). Comment on what you hear and encourage children to be alert to different sounds.

- Ask children to identify the sounds they hear. At group time, have them close their eyes as you or a child make different sounds with tools and materials, and ask the children to guess the source of the sound. This game promotes language development and sets the stage for recognizing differences between the sounds of the letters of the alphabet. Record sounds to use in this game, such as whistles, clapping, stomping of heavy boots, a baby's crying, crackers (or other crunchy food) being eaten, hammering or sawing, a cat's meowing, the blast of a car horn, a door slamming, and a truck rumbling down the street. As you take a walk outdoors together, listen for different sounds and record them. Invite families to record sounds they hear indoors and out, and then play them back for all the children to guess what made each sound.

○ Use nursery rhymes, finger plays, and songs that play with sounds.

○ Provide puppets and other props that encourage children to explore sounds in dramatic play.

○ Read books and tell stories that include sounds (*grrr, whoosh, waa, mmm*). Add your own sound effects. Encourage children to imitate and make up sounds that go with the story.

Conversational skills

Conversation is the verbal exchange of information, observations, thoughts, and feelings. Having a conversation means using the give-and-take of language for social intercourse. Conversational skills comprise listening (especially active, engaged listening), initiating talking with adults and peers, and responding appropriately to the talk of others.

Teaching strategies. The most important thing to remember about conversation is that it requires at least two participants. Beware of the adult tendency to dominate when talking to young children. Patience and silence are virtues when we want to encourage preschoolers to express themselves. Here are some strategies:

○ Model active listening as well as talking with children. Remind yourself not to take over in conversations. Preschoolers are not always fluent in their speech. Wait patiently while they frame and express their thoughts. Get down on their level, make eye contact, pause to listen, repeat or clarify what they say, summarize their thoughts, and accept and expand on their ideas.

○ Play games that use verbal directions, such as Simon Says, to encourage children's listening. The gestures that accompany the verbal directions are especially helpful for dual language learners to understand body and action vocabulary words.

○ Speak clearly and intelligibly. Model standard language (vocabulary and pronunciation, grammar and syntax). Use more complex sentences as children's verbal skills increase.

○ Expand children's verbalizations. For example, if a preschooler says, "More juice," you might say, "You'd like me to put more juice in the pitcher." Expanding a one- or two-word statement into a short sentence is especially valuable for dual language learners as it builds on their language in context and is, thus, easier to understand.

○ Create natural opportunities for conversations throughout the day, such as during meals and snacks as well as greetings and departures. Use these times to talk with children about their interests.

- Encourage children to talk to one another. Plan group activities that promote collaboration rather than solitary activity. Support peer conversations by redirecting children's attention to one another, restating the topic of the conversation, and suggesting they share ideas. Support sociodramatic play among children by providing props for role playing and pretending. The desire to join in such play is a strong motivator for dual language learners to communicate in a way that their peers can understand. Often they will observe and listen intently, and then try out their emerging English-speaking skills so they can participate in the play.

- Use **information** talk to describe what children are doing when playing, and invite their comments. For example, say, "Kanye, you used lots of blue in your painting. I wonder how you made these swirly marks at the top." For dual language learners, make simple informational statements in both their home language and English.

- Engage children in **decontextualized** talk. Converse about objects, people, and events that, while familiar to children, are *not* immediately present or occurring. Talking about things that children cannot simply show you or point to encourages them to use more language. (Think of information talk as "here and now," and decontextualized talk as "there and then.")

- When children who can or should talk rely too much on gestures, gently encourage them to speak. Do not immediately comply with nonverbal requests if you think a child can use words. Although it is fine for children to communicate without words now and then (just as adults do), the more they talk, the better their language skills will become. Humor is a good way to get them to talk without forcing them to do so. Consider this example:

> [Child hands adult a shoe.] **Adult:** "Oh, your shoe. What do you need?"
> [Child gives no response.] **Adult** [with actions]: "Hmm, I could put it on my head . . . or on my foot." [Child giggles.] **Adult:** "Well, what should I do with this shoe?" **Child:** "My foot." **Adult:** "Oh, on your foot? Okay, I'll help you put the shoe on your foot." (Ranweiler 2004, 28)

In this exchange, only after speaking does the child bring about the desired result (help with the shoe). Also, the teacher uses this as an opportunity to expand the child's two words ("My foot") into two sentences that are easily understood by the child.

- Use questions appropriately and not to excess. Bombarding children with questions tends to end dialogue, whereas making comments invites further talk. When you do use questions, make them open-ended questions to invite thoughtful and expanded answers (for example, ask "How will you make your soup?"). Avoid questions that have a single or brief correct answer (for example, do not ask "Will you put beans in your soup?").

- Talk to parents and coworkers in the presence of children. Hearing adult conversations helps children expand their own vocabularies and syntax.

Questions and Comments That Open—or Close Down—Thought

Convergent or closed-ended questions, to which the adult already knows the answers, tend to discourage children from expanding on their answers. Divergent or open-ended questions and comments, used when adults want to learn what children think, are more likely to open up conversations. The following are examples of questions and comments that encourage children to think and also permit adults to introduce new vocabulary words.

When dual language learners answer your open-ended questions with sentences you don't understand, enjoy the fact that they are practicing their oral language even if you don't know whether what they are saying is correct. By keeping a recording device handy, you can capture these episodes of expanded language and find a parent or colleague to translate them for the child's portfolio.

Questions that encourage children to think and reason, and use expanded language:

"How can you tell?"

"How do you know that?"

"What do you think made that happen?"

"Can you tell me how you made that?"

"I wonder would happen if . . . . ?"

"How can you get it to stick [or roll or stand up]?"

Examples of questions that allow adults to introduce vocabulary words and concepts:

"How can we move the truck [or ball or sand] *without* using our hands?" [If children respond only with motions, label the body parts and movements children suggest.]

"Kenisha says we can put the bowl [or wet painting or seed cup] on top of the shelf or inside her cubby. Where else do you think we can store it so people don't bump into it?"

"Antoine says he sees a lot of monkeys in this picture. I count five of them. [Point to and count each one.] What else do you see a lot of?"

"What kinds of fruits do people in your family like to eat?"

"What things in the science area [or house area or block area] are *heavy*? Which do you think is the *heaviest*? How could we find out?"

Dual language learning

In 2005, nearly 25 percent of children in Head Start or Early Head Start programs came from families where only one or neither parent spoke English (Iruka & Carver 2006). Five years later, Head Start reported that 30 percent of its enrollees were dual language learners and in some states, half or more of the families of young children identified a language other than English as their primary language (Espinosa 2013).

Children's earliest experiences with a second language profoundly affect later literacy learning. Research shows it is important for early childhood settings to build on children's home languages. The more sophisticated a child's skills are in vocabulary, phonological awareness, alphabet knowledge, concepts about print, and writing skills in the child's first language, the more these skills transfer to English (Bialystok 2001). Learning English is facilitated when children can both retain communication skills in their home language and receive support in the acquisition of their second language (Cheatham & Ro 2010).

Dual language learners typically progress through several stages (Tabors 2008):

   ○ **Stage one**—Children attempt to use their home language but gradually realize they are not being understood and must adapt their communication strategies.

   ○ **Stage two**—Children actively listen, observe, and process the features of the new language. This is often done silently. Meanwhile, they try to communicate nonverbally using gestures, facial expressions, and nonlanguage vocalizations such as shouts, cries, or laughter.

o **Stage three**—Children have mastered the rhythm and intonation of English, plus key phrases. They use telegraphic speech ("Up!" to mean "Look up at the bird!") and formulaic speech (such as "I want ___" and filling in the blank). These strategies are often still accompanied by gestures.

o **Stage four**—Children express themselves in their own words using English rules but may still make errors (in vocabulary, pronunciation, or grammar) typical of young native speakers.

> When children are learning two languages, they develop *interlanguage*—a "transitory grammar" based on the rules they have observed in their home language and those they observe in their new language. Remarkably, even with limited English proficiency, these children find ways to communicate. (Cheatham & Ro 2010, 19)

A child's progression through these stages may take anywhere from six months to two years, depending on differences in the home and school cultures (Rogoff 2003) and languages (Cheatham & Ro 2010). For example, transferring to English from Spanish is easier than it is from Chinese because the letter sounds and grammatical constructions in English and Spanish are more similar. Adults should therefore hold reasonable expectations for children and remember that even native speakers take between 4 and 10 years to become fluent (Bialystok 2001).

Teaching strategies. To support young children as they maintain knowledge of their first language while they acquire proficiency in a second language, try the following:

o Encourage children to communicate regardless of the language(s) they use. Acknowledge and support all verbal interactions, including those with other bilingual children in their shared home language, as well as with native speakers of English. When possible, pair children who do not speak English with dual language learners who do speak at least some English to help them make the bridge between languages. Don't be concerned when children "code switch" (mix the two languages) because it is evidence they are learning to adapt to different listeners and situations.

o Sing songs, read books, and tell stories in children's home languages as well as English. Invite families to share the songs and stories they enjoy and to teach them to the class. Encourage children to make up their own stories. These need not be formal narratives. For example, invite the child to tell you a story about what he did during choice time.

o Encourage pretend play to expand English vocabulary. Because dramatic play uses actions and props, dual language learners can supplement their home language with gestures and materials, reducing their frustration in trying to communicate. Children who are native English speakers will often spontaneously fill in the words, providing a natural learning opportunity. Pretend play also allows dual language learners to pick up the rhythms and intonations of English dialogue. They can stand on the sidelines, listening and watching, until they are ready to join in and try out their new language.

○ Use both English and a child's home language when possible, but be selective about when you do this (Nemeth 2012). For example, decide which language to emphasize at different times of the daily routine (perhaps the home language during meals but English during small group). Using both languages all the time can not only be overwhelming for dual language learners but can also make other children impatient. If you do not speak a child's home language, use visuals, facial expressions, and gestures to "bring your words to life" (Nemeth 2012, 53). Focus on vocabulary rather than grammar or sentence structure. Nouns, verbs, and adjectives and adverbs (descriptive words) allow the dual language learner to begin communicating with others. The success of being understood will encourage the child to continue learning and talking in English.

Adult-guided experience is especially important for learnings such as:

Phonological awareness

Phonological awareness, as described previously in this chapter, is the ability to attend to the sounds of language as distinct from its meaning. At its simplest level, it includes the awareness of speech sounds and rhythms. It also extends to rhyme awareness (word endings, also known as *rimes*) and sound similarities (such as the initial sounds of words, also known as *onsets*, emphasized in alliteration).

Recall also that **phonemic awareness** is one type (or subset) of phonological awareness, an important skill for preschoolers to develop. A phoneme is the simplest unit of sound, such as the /b/ sound in *bat.* Phonemic skills involve blending—that is, combining individual sounds to make a word, such as putting together the sounds /b/ and /a/ and /t/ to make *bat.* Phonemic skills also involve a "reverse" process called segmentation—separating the sounds within a word, such as breaking *bat* into /b/, /a/, and /t/.

Teaching strategies. Phonological awareness is crucial to the development of literacy. When teachers introduce children to multiple experiences with oral language and systematically engage them in activities such as alliteration and rhyming, they help children develop the skills to become readers and writers. Consider the following strategies:

○ Point out language sounds that are meaningful to children. For example, say, "I'm throwing the ball to Brian. *Ball* and *Brian* start with the same /b/ sound."

○ Share songs, poems, stories, nursery rhymes, and chants that feature rhyming, such as *The Cat in the Hat,* by Dr. Seuss. As you go, ask children to supply the rhyming words, especially once they are familiar with the verse or text. Substitute a different word at the end of a familiar rhyme and ask children to come up with a next line. For example, you might set an example by saying, "Hickory, dickory, door. The mouse ran up the floor." When children grasp the idea, invite them to make their own substitutions ("Hickory, dickory, pear. The mouse ran up the _____.") Accept children's rhymes, even when they contain nonsense words. Encourage dual language learners to think of a rhyming word in their home language if they cannot think of one in English (as in the opening vignette for this chapter).

○ Share songs, poems, stories, nursery rhymes, and chants that feature alliteration, such as "Baa, baa, black sheep" or "Fee, fie, fo, fum." Substitute a different sound at the beginning of the words in a familiar song, poem, or chant— for example, "Wee, wie, woe, wum"—and ask children to do the same. When children grasp the idea, invite them to make up their own alliterative changes and songs. (See the box that follows.)

○ Use rhymes and alliterations throughout the day. Many books, CDs, and web resources contain ideas; feel free to make up your own. For example,

> It's snack time, it's snack time,
> Everyone gets a treat.
> It's snack time, it's snack time,
> I wonder what we've got to eat!

Playing Alliteration Games

Alliteration is the repetition of the initial or beginning sound of words. Because alliteration highlights phonemes that start a word, it helps young children develop phonemic awareness. Here are some alliteration games you can use in the classroom to have fun and promote learning at the same time.

Who Is It?—Ask children to guess who in the group has a name beginning with a certain phoneme. You can also play this game with the names of characters in a book familiar to the children.

"There are two people in this circle whose names begin with the /b/ sound. Who are they?"

"I'm thinking of a person in this room whose name starts with /sh/. Guess who."

"I remember someone in [book title] whose name begins with an /r/ sound. Who do you think it is?"

Doing the Names—Combine the initial sound of children's names with the initial sound of actions for them to perform.

"If your name begins with a /t/ sound, touch the floor. Yes, Tyler and Taylor are tapping the floor."

"Anyone whose name starts with the sound /w/, let's see you wave. Wen and Waseem are waving. Everybody wave with Wen and Waseem. Now let's see everyone wiggle."

Word Starters—Ask children to think of words that begin with the same sound.

"Let's think of words that start like *car*, *cat*, and *call*."

"What words begin with /d/ like *daddy*?"

"How many words can you think of that start with a /p/ sound?"

Letter Substitution—Pick a sound and substitute it at the beginning of words during an activity, such as snack time or a transition. This game is especially good to make cleanup time silly and fun. When children get the idea, let them pick the sound.

"It's gircle time. Everyone go to the gug. Let's all gap our gands!"

"Let's begin flean up time by putting away the flocks. Now we can do the faints and frushes. Who wants to stack the fuzzles?"

"Miguel, it's your turn to pick a sound to help us get ready for outside time. [Miguel replies he wants /m/ like in his name.] Okay, let's put on our moats and wait by the moor until everyone is ready to go moutside." [Act out or point to some of the objects and wait to see whether children can fill in the words on their own. For example, pretend to put on a coat. Look at or gesture toward the door.]

Keep in mind that although this is an enjoyable and useful activity for children who are native English speakers, it is likely to confuse dual language learners. A child who is confident in her understanding of a language will recognize that when the teacher says, "gircle time," it is funny because *gircle* is not a real word. If, however, a child is new to the language, he will struggle to learn *gircle* as a new word and question his prior belief that the word is pronounced "circle."

○ Use letter sounds during transitions. For example, say, "Everyone whose name starts with the same sound as *book* and *box,* go to the circle."

○ Play games that encourage children to segment the sounds in words. For example, "I'm going to say some words, and I want you to say back just the first little part. Can you say the beginning of *shoe* [*shower, ship,* etc.]?" Do the same thing for the endings of words. For example, "Tell me what's left if I take off the first part of *shop* [*shine, shoulder,* etc.]." Play these games with common non-English words, especially words dual language learners use with one another or have taught to their English-speaking peers (such as the beginning or end of *casa*, which is Spanish for *house*).

○ Lead guessing games that encourage blending sounds in words. For example, "I'm thinking of someone whose name begins with the /k/ sound and ends with an /arl/ sound. Who do you think it is?"

○ Respond to children's requests for help with spelling a word by saying the sound of each letter aloud as you write it.

Vocabulary

Vocabulary is the sum of words understood or used by a person. Receptive, or listening, vocabulary is the number of words a child understands. It is generally greater than productive, or speaking, vocabulary, which refers to the number of words a child can say and use correctly. The size of a child's speaking vocabulary at school entry is highly predictive of success in reading.

Preschoolers' vocabulary depends on the language they have heard growing up. By age 3, this can vary widely—especially by social class. Children from families with low income tend to hear far fewer words, and fewer complex words, than those from more affluent families. Hart and Risley (1995) discovered that this difference can range from ten to thirty thousand cumulative words by the time young children enter school. More recent research suggests that this income-based language gap may appear as early as 18 months of age (Fernald, Marchman, & Weisleder 2012). Children grow their vocabularies when adults comment on what children say and do, answer their questions, and read with them. When they talk to people who have larger vocabularies, children learn more words. For dual language learners, this vocabulary growth can happen simultaneously in English and their home language, and they become increasingly adept at knowing which language to use when (for example, at home or school, with other dual language learners or monolingual peers; Tabors 2008). Dual language learners may not know as many words in English as their monolingual peers, but their combined vocabulary—the number of words they know in either or both of their languages—is generally comparable (De Houwer, Bornstein, & Putnick 2013).

Teaching strategies. Children's vocabularies do not get larger by adding isolated or stand-alone words. The best way to grow vocabulary is to build on what children are talking about by adding synonyms and other words related to the topic of conversation, including during reading (Christ & Wang 2012; Collins 2012). For children to learn new words, including their meaning and how to use them, they need repeated exposure and practice (once is not enough!) in one or more "communities of speakers." The preschool classroom is one such community. Here are some strategies you can use to accomplish this:

- Talk with children—a lot! Talk to them during routines and during play. Make sure the conversation is reciprocal; listen as well as talk. Be patient while children find the words to express their thoughts. Show that you value what they have to say.

- Use words that build on children's interests. Children like to talk about what they are doing. For example, many children are interested in pets. When one child asked, "Why is Sniffy [a guinea pig] eating the tube?" the teacher replied, "He gnaws on cardboard and wood fibers to wear down his teeth. Otherwise they would grow too big for his mouth." After another child commented, "We got a new puppy last night," the teacher introduced new words by sharing this: "When my dog was a puppy, she curled up beside me on the couch while I read the newspaper. She would push her nose into the pages and wrinkle them."

- Read children books that are rich in vocabulary words and interesting ideas that will spark their questions and engage them in conversation.

- Provide familiar synonyms and definitions when you use words that are new to children. This strategy is especially helpful for dual language learners as they build their repertoire of English words while continuing to master new vocabulary in their home language. Combining the familiar with the novel helps children grasp the meaning of the new word in context, so they can understand and use it themselves:

  > "We had a *debate* about where to display our rocks. When people have a debate, they talk about all the reasons they want to do something or not do something. We could also say we *discussed* our ideas about where to put our rocks so everyone can see them, or we *exchanged* ideas about good places to store our rocks." (Hohmann 2005, 250)

- Vary experiences to introduce new and unusual words. Field trips are good sources, and dramatic play also helps to illustrate a variety of words. Humor is another way to encourage exploring and having fun with language. Young children like jokes and silly names and rhymes.

- Create learning experiences in which children organize and relate concepts by using vocabulary words in classification (sorting and matching), seriation (ordering objects and making patterns), and spatial and temporal (space and time) phenomena. Doing these activities in small groups not only helps children use their own vocabulary but also allows them to hear and learn the words used by their peers. For example, give children items to sort and ask them to describe the items to one another using the traits by which they did the sorting (see the Geometry and Spatial Sense section in Chap. 7 for more examples).

- Show children how to use words to give one another directions during group projects or games. For example, when playing Simon Says (without winners or losers), give the direction, "Simon says to wriggle on the wood chips." This introduces interesting words (*wriggle*, *wood chips*) in a playful way. Even children who are not familiar with those terms (including dual language learners) will see and imitate those who do (or watch the teacher demonstrate), which facilitates the acquisition of the new words.

○ Announce your motivations and intentions: "I'm going to the house area to see what Bessie and Vinod are cooking. It smells like they're making something spicy for lunch."

Knowledge of narrative/comprehension

Comprehension (as in reading comprehension) involves understanding ideas and their connections in a spoken or written narrative. Children comprehend things by linking what they are learning to what they already know. Comprehension in preschool has four parts. *Understanding* is a child's ability to demonstrate through a variety of means what she knows; for example, to talk about what she sees (illustrations) and hears (oral narrative or written text read aloud). *Connection* is the ability to relate elements of the story to the child's own life, link new words and phrases to concepts and experiences the child knows, and discover new relationships, ideas, and knowledge. *Prediction* is the capacity to imagine what will happen next. *Retelling* is recounting the story in sequence and with an increasing level of detail.

Teaching strategies. Think of comprehension as the steps between what goes in and what comes out when children encounter a story. As young children develop, their brains are increasingly able to build the mental structures necessary to process this material, but they need explicit guidance from adults to establish connections and make sense of the narratives they hear and read. Reading comprehension improves when oral language in general is better developed. That is why it is so important to talk to children from the moment of birth. The more they hear, they more they learn. Try strategies such as the following:

○ Read children's favorite stories again and again. Repetition enhances children's awareness of character and narrative sequence.

○ Examine and discuss the pictures in books. Encourage children to tell or "read" the story in familiar books by looking at the pictures. Ask them to describe what they see. Converse about how the characters and situations depicted relate to objects, people, events, and ideas in children's own lives, both at home and in the classroom. For example, you might look together at the picture on the cover of a book like this:

Sit with a child or a small group of children in a comfortable spot where everyone can see the book being read. Say something like "Today we're going to read the book [read the title aloud]. Let's look at the cover. I wonder what the book is about." Show them the cover. Listen to and comment on their ideas. For example, say, "Jei sees a cow, so he thinks the book is about a farm" or "Shannon sees some corn, so maybe the story is about what a family eats for dinner." After talking about the children's ideas, say, "Let's open the book and find out."

○ Discuss the text in books. Talk about what happens. Make connections between a story's characters and situations to children's own lives.

○ Engage children in reviewing and predicting as you read. Stop occasionally to encourage children to recall what has happened so far. Rather than asking close-ended questions (such as "What did the duck say?"), invite comments by saying, "Let's see what we can remember so far" or "Can you help me remember what happened at the very beginning?" Ask children what they think the picture or words on the next page will be, or how they think a character will solve a problem. Encourage them to look and listen for clues that suggest what might happen next. Relate the picture and text at the end of the book to the title and first page. Recall what happened at the beginning, middle, and end of the story.

○ Encourage children to represent stories in various ways during art, dramatic play, movement, and other activities. Provide materials such art supplies, props, and music to facilitate their representation. Suggest ideas such as moving to the next activity like a character in a book or drawing a series of pictures to show the sequence of events in a story. Nonverbal representation is especially encouraging for dual language learners, who can participate fully; their engagement also provides teachers with insight into how much of a story they are able to understand.

○ Recall and talk about stories at times other than when the stories are being read or told—for example, during snacks or related field trips. Listen for children's comments that can lead naturally into discussions of familiar and favorite narratives.

○ Use ideas from favorite and familiar books to plan group times and transitions. For example, plan field trips to the settings depicted in books (such as a farm, supermarket, pet store, museum). If characters move a certain way (for example, snakes slither along the ground), ask the children to imitate that movement while going from reading to the next activity.

○ Provide opportunities for children to talk among themselves and look at books together. As one child shares ideas, the other can contribute additional story elements, and both children can expand their understanding of the narrative. Pair dual language learners with children fluent in English for this activity.

Reading

Of the key knowledge and skills in the area of reading, child-guided experience seems particularly important in acquiring visual discrimination skills, environmental print knowledge, print awareness, and motivation to interact with printed materials. Adult-guided experience seems especially significant in understanding the relationship between spoken and written language, as well as gaining alphabet knowledge.

Child-guided experience is especially important for learnings such as:

Visual discrimination skills

Reading depends on the ability to visually distinguish the structural features of letters and punctuation, and how they form words, sentences, and paragraphs. Children must recognize the types of marks that make up print, such as lines, dots, and closed shapes. They have to further distinguish between types of lines—straight and curved, vertical and horizontal. Finally, children have to perceive how printed marks are arranged on a page and in relation to one another.

Teaching strategies. Children's visual discrimination comes with physical maturation, but there are specific teaching strategies that can help young children acquire the particular visual skills needed for reading. Some of these ideas will seem obvious; others may inspire your creativity. Here are some recommended strategies:

- Provide a visually rich environment that includes not only many examples of print but also nonprint materials with diverse features. Most teachers know that having lots of printed materials in the classroom is important for early reading. (See the section on Print Awareness on p. 116 in this chapter for more information on this topic.) However, there are many things without letters that can also help young children become aware of the lines, marks, and contrasts they will find in print. Examples include artwork and reproductions of artwork (two- and three-dimensional; in different media; representative of many cultures, especially distinctive visual patterns and motifs), maps and diagrams, plants with flowers and variegated leaves, shells and stones, patterned fabrics, wood with distinctive grains, magnifying lenses, and different types of lighting (natural and artificial) positioned to create light and shadow.

- Use vocabulary words related to print's visual features, such as *straight, curved, circle, long, tall, short, blank, empty space,* and *line*. Call attention to visual features of objects indoors and outdoors, such as size, shape, form, color, foreground, and background.

- Encourage children to describe the visual attributes of materials, tools, artwork, and so on in their environment. Talk about the features that make things look the same or different.

- Play games and plan art activities that focus on visual characteristics. For example, partially hide objects and encourage children to find them; then ask them what features helped them find the object. Make imprints and rubbings (such as with sneaker soles, tree bark, keys, hands, and feet); then ask children to match these to the actual objects, discussing how they did so.

Environmental print knowledge

Children and adults encounter environmental print in the context of everyday life. Examples include company names, logos, and advertising copy in stores and on television, web pages, and vehicles; apps; product labels; menus; street names and traffic signs; storefronts; billboards; text and captions in magazines, newspapers, and catalogs; junk mail; invitations; and letterhead.

Teaching strategies. Because environmental print is everywhere, children already encounter it all the time on their own. However, teachers play a significant role in calling it to children's attention. They can draw an explicit connection between logos or other symbols and printed words, and between the shared properties of environmental print and books. Try strategies such as these:

- Create a print-rich classroom environment that includes environmental print materials: photo albums, magazines (for children and adults), catalogs, newspapers, brochures, flyers, telephone books, junk mail, instruction manuals, address books (especially with the letters of the alphabet written in large type), calendars, greeting cards, ticket stubs, business cards, and empty seed packets.

- Set up learning centers that incorporate reading and writing materials. For example, the house area can include empty food boxes and cans with labels (cleaned and with any sharp edges smoothed), store coupons, play money, cookbooks, a telephone directory, message pads, and pencils. A restaurant center could be equipped with menus, wall signs, and notepads for taking food orders.

- Ask families to contribute materials.

- Affix labels and captions on interest centers and materials throughout the classroom. Post signs and lists, such as weekly snack menus, the daily routine, or the names of children in each small group.

- Put printed materials at children's eye level and make them accessible.

- Include printed materials that reflect children's home languages and cultures.

- Introduce letters and words in ways that are personally meaningful to children. For example, letter links (DeBruin-Parecki & Hohmann 2003) pair a child's printed nametag with a letter-linked picture of an object that starts with the same letter and sound. A letter link for Annie might be *ant* and one for Pedro could be *paintbrush*. Letter links—which children help choose for themselves—can appear on children's cubbies, the bottom of their pictures, chore charts, and other places throughout the room.

- Visit places in the community that feature print (library, sign shop, bookstore, supermarket). Look for large print at the children's eye level. For example, product signs on shelves are easier for children to see than aisle signs hanging near the ceiling.

- Support dual language learners by translating between non-English and English words and phrases commonly found in your community (for example, on storefronts and product packages). Take walks around the neighborhood and encourage families to bring in empty containers of products representing their language and/or culture. Using masking tape and markers, add the correspond-

Children Creating Environmental Print During Play

Children use and make their own printed materials in the course of play, the same way they use and create other types of props. In the following example, a group of preschoolers makes tickets and signs for a pretend train trip.

Several 4-year-olds agree to take a make-believe train trip to France. They use an elevated loft as their train and move chairs up the stairs for passenger seats. Two of them go to an adjacent center and make tickets for the journey, using scribbles to represent writing. Once the tickets are ready, they are distributed to every child and collected by the engineer as passengers enter the train. While the children wait for their teacher to pack his bag and join them, they lean over the loft railing and read signs he helped them make earlier, including "Train," "No Smoking," and "No Ghosts." They have difficulty reading a sign with an arrow that says, "This way to the train" and ask, "What does that say?" The teacher reads it out loud and then climbs on board.

Jim Christie, 2004, personal communication. Used with permission.

ing English word(s) to home language labels and vice versa (for example, *cracker* and *galetta*). Invite parents to help with this labeling activity. Choose one color for each language and use the same color for that language throughout the room. When possible, add phonetic spellings so adults can say the words to the children in their home languages.

Print awareness

Print awareness, or concepts of print, includes general knowledge about the conventions of print and how books work. For example, preschool children learn that books have distinctive parts (cover and pages, beginning and end), an author or illustrator or both, and a written message separate from (though related to) the pictures. Through repeated experiences, they master directionality—that is, knowing books are held right-side up (orientation) and read front to back (turning pages in order), and each text page is scanned from top to bottom and left to right. Be mindful of children whose family reads to them in a language that uses print from right to left.

Teaching strategies. The logical structure of books is so well known to adults that we take it for granted. We sometimes forget that young children are not born knowing how books work. Repeated exposure to print helps bring about such awareness on its

own. Still, adults can play an intentional role in pointing out the main features of books with strategies such as these:

○ Provide a variety of books for children to hold, carry, look at, listen to, and talk about to aid in their understanding and application of the general rules of print. Provide many different types, such as illustrated storybooks, controlled vocabulary books (with word sets such as *cat, mat,* and *bat* that encourage sight reading), picture dictionaries, and informational (nonfiction) books on topics of interest to the children. Make the books easily accessible to children. Change the selection periodically to maintain their interest.

○ Provide lots of other printed products children can interact with, such as the environmental print materials discussed in the previous section of this chapter, dictated stories, and stories children have written (and illustrated) themselves.

○ Ask children to hand you a book "so I can read it." Accept or reorient the book as needed. Occasionally pick up or hold a book the wrong way and see how children react. Make a visual and vocal point of turning the book right-side up.

○ Point out book and print features while looking at books with children. For example, say, "This is the front cover and this [turning it over] is the back cover. This is called the 'title page' because it has the name, or title, of the book." Encourage children to talk about what they see on the front and back covers. Explain the concepts of author and illustrator. Before reading, say, "I'm going to read the book [read the title aloud]. It was written by [author's name], and [illustrator's name] drew the pictures." Encourage children to turn the pages as you read. When you're done, you might say, "That's the end of the story." Look for books that say "The End" on the last page. After finishing the book, go back and point out page numbers in sequence. (Once you begin reading, don't interrupt the story to point out book features. It can destroy the pleasure of reading. Also, children need narrative continuity to build comprehension skills. You can mention print attributes occasionally, but for the most part, point these out before and after reading the book.)

○ Make books with children that include all the parts (front and back covers, title page with their names as authors and illustrators, drawings with words). Leave commercially produced books on the table so that they can refer to them while they make their own books. Display the children's finished books; put them in the reading area so they can look at their own and their classmates' books. Invite them to read their books aloud at small group and to talk about how they made each part.

○ Favor print books, which children can manipulate, over ebooks, and encourage families to do the same at home. However, as ebooks (and other forms of print on electronic devices) become increasingly common, demonstrate basic practices to the children, such as how to scroll down or "turn" the page. Children with practice using eReaders at home will often provide instruction to children who are less familiar with these devices. Encourage children to use the devices together.

Motivation to interact with printed materials

This area refers to children's interest in—or disposition toward—engaging with printed materials and the things that are represented in print, such as stories and information. For example, it includes being positively disposed toward looking at books as well as listening to recorded books.

Teaching strategies. Interest in reading cannot be forced on children. Fortunately, if they have positive reading experiences with adults, children will naturally be motivated to want to read themselves. To foster positive attitudes toward reading, try such strategies as these:

○ Read to children frequently, both individually and in small groups.

○ Create cozy and comfortable places where you can read with children and they can look at books by themselves. Provide stuffed animals and dolls for children to read to.

○ Display books on open shelves, with attractive and colorful covers facing outward.

○ Encourage children to select which book(s) to read.

○ Choose books that interest children. Remember that they are curious, so virtually any subject, well presented for their age, can intrigue them. This includes nonfiction as well as storybooks.

○ Provide books that children will have success "reading" themselves, such as wordless books, easy-to-read books (with predictable word sets), and books in the children's home languages with color-coded stickers to help them identify the language they need.

○ Let children see you reading for enjoyment and information.

○ Let children know you expect them to succeed at reading.

○ Encourage parents to read to children at home. Start a lending library in the classroom. Make book backpacks for each child so they can choose books to take home and return.

○ If your program uses ebooks, choose appropriate titles and read them with children the same way you would a print book (that is, using the interactive procedures described in the previous section of this chapter). Provide this same guidance to families, emphasizing the importance of parents reading ebooks *with* their children.

Adult-guided experience is especially important for learnings such as:

The relationship between spoken and written language

This domain involves connecting what people say with the same words when written. It requires children to understand the one-to-one correspondence between the two modes of expression.

Teaching strategies. The relationship between spoken and written words may seem self-evident to adults. But grasping this abstract connection is a notable achievement for young children, whose concrete minds are just beginning to form mental representations. By demonstrating visual, auditory, and tactile connections, teachers can help young children relate oral and written modes. Here are some strategies:

○ Take children's dictation and read it back to them verbatim. (When you take dictation on paper, ask children where on the page to begin writing, to reinforce that print concept.) Or type it into the computer and print it out. The power and pleasure of seeing their words in print—provided it's voluntary and not coerced—encourages children to invent additional occasions for dictation. Opportunities for taking individual dictation include labels; captions on artwork; role-playing props (such as menus, traffic signs, party invitations); books the child creates; messages (cards, notes from the child); and original songs, rhymes, and chants. Opportunities for group dictation include original stories, songs, rhymes, and chants; rules for a game children have invented; lists and graphs (such as favorite foods, toys, and colors or places to go on a field trip); shared experiences ("Our trip to the pet shop"), with comments from each child; plans for a group experience ("What I want to do at the park"); and small group problem-solving discussions ("How can we stop fighting over the red wagon?"). Encourage dual language learners to dictate stories and captions in their home language and/or a combination of their home language and English.

- When you read to children, run a finger along the lines of print, point out and enunciate individual words, and model intonation. Do the same whether you are reading a print book or an ebook. Ebooks with narration in different languages can help both teacher and child learn to pronounce the words in each other's language.

- Engage children in speaking and acting out written stories from books of their own creation as well as commercial books.

- Make picture cards and write appropriate words (nouns, verbs, short sentences) underneath. These can be about individual items and actions or use related word sets (such as buildings, planting a garden). Point to the pictures and words as you read the text aloud. Encourage children to look at the cards on their own, as well as with partners, and to say the written words aloud. Again, encourage dual language learners to use whatever language, or combination of languages, they are comfortable with. Write and read the words in both languages (English and their home language).

Alphabet knowledge: Letter identification and letter-sound knowledge

Alphabet knowledge means knowing the names of letters and letter-sound matches (alphabetic principle). Although knowing letter names (visual discrimination) and sounds (auditory discrimination) are distinct abilities, they usually develop in tandem because children are given both pieces of information together, as in, "That's the letter *m,* and it makes the /m/ sound."

With informed guesses, as well as continued explicit instruction, children come to understand that other words they are interested in saying and writing begin with the same letter—for example, that *mom, me, mud,* and *motor* all begin with the /m/ sound. Children find it easier to identify letters at the beginning of words, especially if the letters are capitalized. For example, the initial *B* in the name Barbara is easier to find (and hear) than the embedded *b* in the middle of the name.

Teaching strategies. Like phonological awareness, alphabet knowledge is critical in early literacy. The alphabet is an arbitrary code of letters and sounds unique to one or more related languages. Children must learn the rules and conventions of their language(s); they cannot make them up. Adults, therefore, play an explicit role transmitting this body of information. At the same time, children need ample opportunity to experiment and practice the alphabet on their own. Try the following strategies:

- Display alphabet letters where children can see them, not posted far above their heads. Provide alphabet letters and blocks children can hold, copy, trace, and rearrange, such as cutout letters and letter stencils made of wood, plastic, and heavy cardboard; magnetic letters; letter-shaped cookie cutters that children can press into sand and playdough; and alphabet puzzles.

- Say the names of letters and sound them out in words children read, write, and dictate. For example, say, "That's a *b,* and it sounds like /b/." Sound out letters, letter strings, and letter combinations in the words children dictate. For example, if they dictate a party menu, write and enunciate, "/p/ /i/ /z/ /z/ /a/. That makes the word *pizza.* I like pepperoni on my pizza!" Include the letter strings and combinations at the beginning, end, and (later) the middle of words. For example, when Simone said to her teacher, "Write the word *daddy* for me," her teacher wrote the letters and said, "It starts with the sound /d/ and I write it D-A. And it ends with the sound /d/, D-D-Y. D-A-D-D-Y. That makes the word *Daddy.*"

○ Connect sounds to the letters children write to stand for whole words. For example, if a child writes *HB* and reads, "Happy Birthday," say, "You wrote 'happy birthday.' I see the *H* for the /h/ sound in *happy* and a *B* for the /b/ sound at the beginning of *birthday.*" Sound out the (invented) "words" children spell. If they ask, "What word is this?" or "What does this spell?" pronounce the word as it is written or arranged. For example, if a child arranges the letters KRGMS, say "This word sounds like /k/ /r/ /g/ /m/ /s/. You wrote *krgms.*"

○ Involve children in searching for letters by their sounds, as in the following example,

---

On a class walk, the teacher says, "I'm looking for a letter that makes the sound /s/. Can you find one?" Children points to signs for "gas station" and "South Street Market" and the license plate RS 0371.

○ Provide alphabet knowledge in context. Call attention to letter names and sounds when it is relevant to children's playing, reading, and writing. This strategy is more effective than offering such information isolated from children's ongoing and meaningful activities.

○ Identify initial letter sounds in children's names and other familiar words. Often the first letter and sound that children learn is the one that begins their own name, or it's a word they use often and find important, such as *Mom,* their dog's name, or a favorite food. Pair a child's written name and the sounds made by its first letter; transitions are a good time for this:

Teacher (holding up Darren's nametag): Here's Darren's name. It starts with the sound /d/. I wonder what letter makes the /d/ sound at the beginning of your name, Darren?

Darren: *D* makes the /d/ sound for *Darren.*

Teacher: The *D* makes the /d/ sound at the beginning of *Darren.* You can get your coat, Darren.

Teacher (holding up Lydia's nametag): Lydia, your name starts with the /l/ sound. I wonder what letter makes the /l/ sound?

Lydia: *Lydia* makes the /l/ sound!

Teacher: Yes, *Lydia* starts with the /l/ sound. I'm wondering what letter makes the /l/ sound?

Max: I know. *L* makes the /l/ sound.

Teacher: The *L* at the beginning of *Lydia* makes the /l/ sound. Lydia, you can get your coat. (Holds up Max's nametag.) Now, Max,

---

what letter makes the /m/ sound at the beginning of *Max*? (adapted from HighScope Educational Research Foundation 2004, 25)

- Link the remaining sounds of a word to the first letters in children's names. For example, while writing and spelling *box,* you might say "It begins with *b* like the /b/ in *Brian*. It ends with *x* like the /x/ in *Xavier*. In the middle is an *o* just like the /o/ in *Olive*."

- Make sure any technology programs you use with children are interactive, not simply drill and practice. For example, look for game-like software and apps that allow children to choose the letters and manipulate (move) them around the screen. Make sure the auditory component (pronunciation of the letter sounds) is clear and that the letters are large and distinct so they can be easily read.

Writing

Of the key knowledge and skills in the area of writing, child-guided experience seems particularly important in acquiring fine motor skills, as well as awareness of the purposes and functions of written words. Adult-guided experience seems especially significant in building letter- and word-writing skills, as well as awareness of the conventions of spelling, grammar, syntax, and punctuation.

Child-guided experience is especially important for learnings such as:

Fine motor skills

Writing, like reading, is dependent on children having certain perceptual motor skills. Prerequisite fine motor skills for writing include being able to grasp writing materials and the eye–hand coordination to make certain types of marks in specific locations on the writing surface. (See p. 69 in Chap. 5 for a discussion of fine motor skills in general, and Copple & Bredekamp 2009, pp. 116–17, for a developmental progression of fine motor skills for ages 3 to 5.)

Teaching strategies. The development of the fine motor skills needed for writing is, to a great degree, maturational. However, as with the visual acuity skills necessary for prereading, children depend on adults to provide materials and opportunities to practice their developing fine motor skills. Here are some examples:

- Provide manipulative materials in all areas of the classroom to develop children's manual dexterity and eye–hand coordination. Examples include items to assemble and take apart (nuts and bolts, shoes and laces); things to copy and trace; beads and string; jigsaw puzzles; small blocks and sets of small toys; dress-up and doll clothes with various types of fasteners; moldable art materials, such as clay and dough; drawing and painting tools (crayons, brushes, and pencils of graduated thickness); paper for children to manipulate and transform; scissors; hole punches; staplers; tape of various kinds; cooking utensils; safety knives for cutting snacks; carpentry tools and materials such as nails and wood (use appropriate safety precautions including safety goggles); and interactive technology with touchscreens and buttons/switches that are easy for preschoolers to see and manipulate.

- Provide writing materials of all kinds throughout the room (see suggestions in the next section of this chapter, including those for children with visual or special needs).

- Encourage children to play simple games of eye–hand coordination, such as aiming at a target with a beanbag or ball. (Remember that preschoolers need a large target and short throwing distance.)

- Model how to hold writing tools, scissors, and so on, especially for children who are having difficulty mastering these techniques on their own. Be sensitive to children's frustration levels. If you wait too long to intervene, children may simply become averse to writing.

- Refer children to one another for help. Children often learn dexterity and coordination skills better by watching and imitating peers than from direct instruction by adults.

Awareness of the purposes and functions of written words

This area refers to knowing all the ways and reasons people write. Like reading, writing is done for functional reasons (such as to communicate an idea, remember to do something, give directions) and for pleasure (such as to extend an invitation, express appreciation, tell a story, preserve a memory).

Teaching strategies. Young children want to do things for themselves and share their ideas and accomplishments with others. Writing helps them achieve these personal objectives. Strategies such as these build on children's inherent motivation to write:

- Provide a wide variety of writing tools and materials throughout the classroom. Include not only materials for making written marks (such as pens and pencils, paper) but also those that record ideas (writing software) and transmit them to others (email services, envelopes and stamps). Include regular and colored pencils; pens; and markers; crayons; chalk (white or colored) and chalkboards; unlined paper, color construction paper, and stationery; ruled notebooks; notepads; sticky notes and labels; used gift wrap; wallpaper samples; grocery bags; checkbook registers; inkpads and stamps; order forms; stickers; age-appropriate drawing software; and tape, staplers, yarn, and hole punches (so children can make their own books).

- For children with limited visual acuity or motor control, provide appropriate assistive technology, such as magnifiers, wide crayons and markers, rubber writing grips, adjustable writing platforms (for example, those that can be affixed to wheelchair trays and raised or lowered), large-type keyboards, and voice-recognition software.

- Provide contextualized examples of print that serves a here-and-now purpose. Examples include labeled centers and materials, rules created by children, a daily schedule, cookbooks in the house area, instructions for equipment in the woodworking or science area, lists of children's names, and lists of book titles checked out of the lending library.

- Model the use of written language for different purposes and call it to children's attention. Point it out to them when you write things—for example, a to-do list, parent newsletter, or a story dictated by the children. Similarly, make children aware when you use existing writing (for example, to follow directions or look up information in a book or on the computer).

- Encourage journal writing. Have children make their own journals with decorated front and back covers and blank pages in between. Make a class journal that individual children can add entries to. With children's permission, read entries from their previous day's entries at morning greeting.

- Display children's writing where children and families can see it.

Adult-guided experience is especially important for learnings such as:

Letter and word writing

Literacy includes the ability to write letters and combine strings of letters into words. Children make letter-like forms before they write conventional letters. Letter writing usually begins with writing one's own name, starting with writing the initial letter. Children are highly motivated to master this feat because of the personal value they attach to their name.

Between the ages of 3 and 6, name writing progresses from continuous horizontal scribbles to separate and recognizable letters arranged in the correct order (Hildreth 1936). While children are highly motivated to develop this ability, they do so only when parents and teachers continually make an explicit connection between the sounds in their names and writing the associated letters. Adults need to call attention to environmental print that uses the initial letter in a child's name, or they can write the letter: "That's a *P*, just like in your name, Paco."

Teaching strategies. Like alphabet knowledge, letter and word writing are highly dependent on explicit instruction, but to be effective, letter and word writing instruction must be provided in relevant and developmentally appropriate ways. Try the following strategies:

- Call attention to how letters are formed, particularly the lines and shapes that compose them.

- Engage children in writing and reading their writing. Write down children's dictation; then read the words back yourself, and ask children to read back the words you have written for them. Have them write for a purpose (for example, to write messages to one another, family members, and teachers).

- Engage them in name writing each day—for example, writing their name on a sign-in chart, task list, bookmark, or art project. Comment positively no matter how children go about writing their names, whether it's with up-and-down strokes, continuous linear scribbles, discrete letter-like units, partial and inverted letters, or conventional letters. For example,

   "Zarius, you wrote your name using dots and lines."

   "Anna, there's your name with two As and two ns—Anna."

   "Lee, I see you've written the L at the beginning of your name and two up-and-down lines with lots of lines crossing them, Es, afterward. That's your name, Lee."

"Myles, I see you've written your name, M-y-l-e-s." (HighScope Educational Research Foundation 2004, 23)

○ Draw attention to similarities between written examples of children's names (for example, on nametags and class lists) and their own signatures. Point out similarities between the letters in children's names and other names and words that use some of the same letters. For dual language learners, be sure to include words in their home language as well as in English.

○ Act as a writer as well as a teacher. When children see adults write, they want to write too. Label what you are doing as "writing" and explain to children both its purpose and what actual letters, words, and sentences you are writing.

Awareness of the conventions of spelling, grammar, syntax, and punctuation

The conventions of print include a culture's correct or accepted rules of written expression. As children become literate, they often construct unconventional rules first and then gradually move toward conventional ones. For example, they may invent spellings with the most salient sounds in words, such as *DG* for *dog*. Or they might understand the ideas of "past tense" and adding *-ed* but misapply those ideas to an irregular verb (as in "I goed to the store"). (Dual language learners will do the same with the conventions of their home language.) Young children cannot be expected to follow all the conventions initially; as we raise their awareness, they will begin to use the rules as they are ready. (Dual language learners might apply the conventions of their home language to English, such as the way plurals are formed, before they master the conventions of English). Our task is to build on what children know; that is, young children's understanding is more important than whether *goed* is correct or adding *s* rather than *en* at the end of a noun makes it plural.

Teaching strategies. Children's spontaneous and joyful writing should not be stifled by teachers repeatedly correcting them or insisting that rules must be followed. Strategies such as these help make children aware of the conventions and their application without discouraging their impulse to write:

○ Spell words aloud as you write them (whether in English or the child's home language) when you take dictation from children. Emphasize middle letters and especially vowels. Children tend to get initial letters and consonants first, so linger on other letter types to fill in the "blanks" in their spelling.

○ Respond to children's requests for help to spell words correctly. Once they realize that letters represent sounds, help them write the sounds they hear in words. As they get better at sounding out words, help them make the transition to conventional spellings. Here's an example:

> **Child:** "Did I spell *today* right?"
>
> **Teacher:** "T-O-D-A, you have all the sounds. Just add a *y* at the end and you'll have it. *Day, say, hay,* all those words have the *ay*." (Neuman, Copple, & Bredekamp 2000, 91)

○ With older preschoolers, provide word banks, word walls, and books with words that share spelling features. Post lists of "hard-to-spell words." Ask children to suggest words for the lists, and encourage them to add words throughout the year.

○ Make comments to highlight writing conventions as you read or write with children, such as "This is a new sentence, so it begins with a capital letter."

○ Use punctuation while writing with children. As they observe what you write, explain the marks and their significance. For example, "We're making a list of questions to ask the tour guide at the museum tomorrow, so I'm writing a question mark at the end of each one."

○ When children make spoken errors in grammar and syntax, repeat back their ideas using conventional language rather than correcting them. For example, if a child says, "I goed to the barbershop yesterday. He cutted my hair," you might say, "Oh, you went to the barbershop yesterday and the barber cut your hair." Do the same when children apply the rules of their home language to English. For example, say, "You want me to read both books" if a child whose first language is German asks you to read two *buchen* or if a child puts the adjective after the noun instead of before it (for example, if the child says "doll big," refer to the "big doll").

"Learning is enhanced when the classroom environment reflects a community of literacy learners" (Gambrell & Mazzoni 1999, 87). Teachers play a critical role in es-

---

Introducing the Idea of Punctuation in Context

The idea of punctuation is too abstract for young children to learn and apply its rules. However, they are often interested in punctuation marks and how they are used when the topic comes up in meaningful contexts. In the following anecdote, some children are impressed when their teacher uses an exclamation point to convey her feelings; later, she overhears the children imitating and discussing this punctuation mark in their own play.

A teacher is sitting in the writing center with a small group of children. She writes a get well card to a sick colleague:

"Dear Carol, We hope you get well SOON!!!" She describes and explains to the children as she writes ". . . exclamation mark, exclamation mark, exclamation mark. Because I want her to get well *soon*."

Moments later, Kira and Hana talk about exclamation marks.

Kira: And this is (pause) extamotion [sic] mark.

Hana: Three cause it's big letters.

Later still, Hana and another child, Christina, include exclamation marks in their own writing. Christina writes the letters *COI* over and over inside one band of a rainbow and exclamation marks inside another band. Hana writes her name and fills the bottom of the page with upside-down exclamation marks.

Adapted, by permission, from D. Rowe, *Preschoolers as Authors: Literacy Learning in the Social World* (Cresskill, NJ: Hampton Press, 1994), 168–69.

---

tablishing this community through their interactions with individual students and the collaborations they foster among peers. Intentional teachers use their knowledge of child development and literacy learning to supply materials, provide well-timed information, guide discussions, make thoughtful comments, ask meaningful questions, and pose calibrated challenges that advance children's learning.

Young children's motivation to learn to read and write comes from an intrinsic desire to communicate. But they need adult guidance and support to begin the journey toward full literacy with competence and enthusiasm.

For Further Consideration

1. What bsic language and literacy skills should early childhood educators teach young children, especially those whose backgrounds place them at risk for reading difficulties? Who determines basic requirements, and how should they be assessed?

2. In your program, how do you balance time for literacy learning with other content areas in a comprehensive curriculum? How do you integrate literacy learning with early learning in other domains? If you are not yet teaching, how do you expect that you will do these things?

3. What can teachers do to help children build varied vocabulary?

4. How might systematic reading instruction take away from—or add to—the joy of reading?

5. How can we use children's knowledge of their home language to help them learn English? How can we involve and support parents who are not native English speakers?

6. How can you help dual language learners develop and maintain proficiency in their home language at the same time they are learning English?

Chapter 7

Mathematics

Gretchen, nearly 5, says, "I need a big circle for the bottom of my snow lady." She finds a large wooden circle in the block area and brings it to the art area, where she traces it onto a piece of construction paper, cuts out the circle-shaped sheet, and tapes it on the lower edge of her paper. She asks her teacher for help finding a "medium circle for the middle." The teacher suggests that she look in the house area. Gretchen goes there and chooses two lids, one from a coffee canister and one from a yogurt container. "I found a medium and a small circle!" she tells her teacher.

❀　　❀　　❀

Luis's teacher Leon holds a piece of twine while Luis (4½) measures it with a ruler. Luis puts the end of the ruler near (but not quite at) one end of the twine, runs his finger along the ruler, and announces, "Cuatro! La cadena tiene cuatro centimetros de largo." Leon records this activity with a digital camera so that later he can ask a colleague to translate Luis's words.

❀　　❀　　❀

Fatima, a younger 4, glues alternating red and yellow construction paper squares around the border of the card she made for her grandmother. "I made a pattern," she tells her teacher. "See, it goes red and yellow and red and yellow around and around."

❀　　❀　　❀

Sheldon (4) sits at the computer, where he uses the mouse to trace triangles over a picture of pizza slices. He draws a circle around two of the nearby plates. "Look," he tells his friend Atef. "I made two circles, one for me and one for you. Pizza time!" Atef (nearly 4) uses the mouse to drag one triangle slice onto each plate, and the friends pretend to chomp the pizza.

Young children develop ideas about mathematics in the course of their day-to-day lives quite naturally and without recognizing them as such. The remarks of the children in this chapter's opening vignettes, for example, reflect an interest in mathematical subjects that matter to them—including size (height, width), number and order, design (pattern), shape (geometry), speed and age (measuring and comparing), and making sense of simple quantitative information (data analysis). Summarizing children's early mathematics knowledge base, Clements states, "Prekindergarten children have the interest and ability to engage in significant mathematical thinking and learning" (2004, 11). Copley notes that "young children continually construct mathematical ideas based on their experiences with the environment, their interactions with adults and other children, and their daily observations (2010, 5).

Thus, in the past 25 years, as "the intuitive, informal mathematical knowledge of young children often surprises early childhood teachers" (Copley 2010, 3), studies of the development of early mathematics have switched from looking at what preschool children *cannot* do to what they *can* do. "Indeed the research has so effectively introduced new insights into what children can do, that we can now chant a litany of competence, competence everywhere" (Ginsburg & Golbeck 2004, 191). Consequently, mathematics has risen to the top of the education agenda in the way that language and literacy did a decade earlier (National Research Council 2009), and evidence suggests that early mathematics may be an even better predictor of school achievement than early literacy (Stipek, Shoenfeld, & Gomby 2012). Observations of children during choice time, for example, often show them engaged in mathematical explorations and applications, and sometimes these are surprisingly advanced (Ginsburg et al. 2006). Moreover, because mathematical understanding is less dependent on language than literacy skills are, dual language learners can experience early success in this important area of learning (National Mathematics Advisory Panel 2008).

The typical early childhood curriculum, however, incorporates little in the way of thoughtful and sustained early mathematics experiences (Copley 2004). If mathematics is included, it tends to be limited to the topic of number, particularly counting. Yet young children also spontaneously explore topics such as patterns, shapes, and the transformations brought about by processes like adding and subtracting (Ginsburg et al. 2006; Tudge & Doucet 2004), and there are foundational mathematical understandings children need to develop in these areas.

Along with changing our ideas about *what* children can understand has come rethinking of *how* to foster early mathematical development.

> Because young children's experiences fundamentally shape their attitude toward mathematics, an engaging and encouraging climate for children's early encounters with mathematics is important. It is vital for young children to develop confidence in their ability to understand and use mathematics—in other words, to see mathematics as within their reach. (NAEYC & National Council of Teachers of Mathematics [NCTM] 2010, 4)

Researchers and practitioners have developed various systems for categorizing the mathematical areas in which young children demonstrate interest and ability (e.g., Campbell 1999; Greenes 1999). In 2000 NCTM published *Principles and Standards in School Mathematics,* which includes standards for prekindergarten through grade 2. And in 2002 NAEYC published a joint position paper with NCTM (updated in 2010) supporting those NCTM standards and offering recommendations for early mathematics education. The NCTM standards (2000), as well as the organization's follow-up publication, *Curriculum Focal Points for Prekindergarten Through Grade 8 Mathematics* (2006), are now widely cited in the field and used by many state departments of education and local school districts to develop comprehensive early mathematics curricula in preschool programs and the primary grades. They have also influenced the Common Core State Standards in mathematics for kindergarten through grade 8.

The NCTM standards (2000) define five content areas: number and operations, geometry, measurement, algebra, and data analysis and probability. The standards are described in this chapter, along with their application in the preschool years. NCTM also defines five process standards, consistent with the strategies suggested in this chapter: problem solving, reasoning and proof, connections, communication, and representation. Problem solving and reasoning, as the position statement phrases it, are the heart of mathematics:

While content represents the what of early childhood mathematics education, the processes . . . make it possible for children to acquire content knowledge. These processes develop over time and when supported by well-designed opportunities to learn. Children's development and use of these processes are among the most long-lasting and important achievements of mathematics education. Experiences and intuitive ideas become truly mathematical as the children reflect on them, represent them in various ways, and connect them to other ideas. (NAEYC & NCTM 2010, 6)

For further explanations of NCTM's process standards and examples, see the work of Clements (2004) and Copley (2004, 2010), as well as the NCTM website (www.nctm.org). For additional information on state early learning standards in mathematics, see Gronlund (2006) and the Common Core State Standards for kindergarten (National Governors Association Center for Best Practices & Council of Chief State School Officers 2010), for which state pre-K standards lay the groundwork.

Young Children's Development in Mathematics

Young children, like those quoted in the vignettes at the beginning of the chapter, start with only an intuitive or experiential understanding of mathematics. They don't yet have the concepts or vocabulary they need to be able to *use* what they intuitively know or to *connect* their knowledge to school mathematics. The preschool teacher's task, therefore, is

to find out what young children already understand and help them begin to understand these things mathematically. From ages 3 through 6, children need many experiences that call on them to relate their knowledge to the vocabulary and conceptual frameworks of mathematics—in other words, to "mathematize" what they intuitively grasp. (NAEYC & NCTM 2010, 4–5)

The goal of early mathematics education, then, is to build "mathematical power" in young children (Baroody 2000). This power has three components: a positive disposition to learning and using mathematics; understanding and appreciating the importance of mathematics; and engaging in the process of mathematical inquiry. Turning children's early and spontaneous mathematics play (child-guided experience) into an awareness of mathematical concepts and skills is at the heart of intentional teaching in this area.

In early mathematics, free exploration is important—but by itself it is not enough. There are concepts, principles, and vocabulary that children will not construct on their own. Even for those areas in which their investigations are key, children do not always construct mathematical meanings from them. Clements (2001) suggests teachers consider whether children's thinking is developing or stalled. "When it is developing, they can continue observing. When it is stalled, it is important to intervene" (Seo 2003, 31). In this way, adult-guided experience supplements child-guided exploration.

Teaching and Learning in Mathematics

Young children need many opportunities to represent, reinvent, quantify, generalize, and refine their experiential and intuitive understandings that might be called "premathematical," or emerging mathematics. Many of these processes (for example, representing and generalizing) can be done with objects or writing tools and do not require verbal labels, making them accessible to dual language learners. Further, counting can be done in the home languages of dual language learners, providing an opportunity for them to simultaneously learn English words for numerals.

To provide meaningful and effective mathematical experiences, intentional teachers design programs so that children encounter concepts in depth and in a logical sequence:

> Because curriculum depth and coherence are important, unplanned experiences with mathematics are clearly not enough. Effective programs also include intentionally organized learning experiences that build children's understanding over time. Thus, early childhood educators need to plan for children's in-depth involvement with mathematical ideas. . . . Depth is best achieved when the program focuses on a number of key content areas rather than trying to cover every topic or skill with equal weight. (NAEYC & NCTM 2010, 7)

This need to focus on a limited number of key concepts and skills is further highlighted in NCTM's amendment of its own standards, *Curriculum Focal Points* (2006). Intentional teachers use a variety of approaches and strategies to achieve this focused emphasis. They integrate mathematics into daily routines and across other domains in the curriculum, but they always do so in a coherent, planful manner. This means that the mathematics experiences they include "follow logical sequences, allow depth and focus, and help children move forward in knowledge and skills"; it does not mean "a grab bag of experiences that seem to relate to a theme or project" (NAEYC & NCTM 2010, 8).

In addition to integrating mathematics in children's play, classroom routines, and learning experiences in other parts of the curriculum that do not focus exclusively on mathematics, intentional teachers provide carefully planned experiences that focus children's attention on a particular mathematical idea:

> Helping children name such ideas as *horizontal* or *even and odd* as they find and create many examples of these categories provides children with a means to connect and refer to their just-emerging ideas. Such concepts can be introduced and explored in large and small group activities and learning centers. Small groups are particularly well suited to focusing children's attention on an idea. Morcover, in this setting the teacher is able to observe what each child does and does not understand and engage each child in the learning experience at his own level. (NAEYC & NCTM 2010, 9)

Research points us to the materials and activities that foster the development of mathematical concepts. Because young children are concrete, hands-on learners, they need to manipulate materials to construct ideas about the physical properties of objects and their transformation. Spontaneous investigations are most common with discrete play objects such as LEGOs, blocks, or puzzles and continuous (non-countable) materials such as sand, water, or clay (Ginsburg et al. 2006). Children tend to use mathematical inquiry most frequently during construction or pattern-making activities, types of play that are equally accessible to dual language learners and native English speakers. Interactive media can also play a role in early mathematics education as well as other content areas if the technology is used appropriately (Hyson 2003; NAEYC & Fred Rogers Center 2012; see the Learning About Tools and Technology section on p. 168 in Chap. 8.)

Perhaps less expected is the finding that mathematical thinking is fostered by social interaction. When children share hypotheses and interpretations, question one another, and are challenged to justify their conclusions, they are more likely to correct their own thinking (Campbell 1999). In fact, agreements and disagreements during peer-to-peer dialogue more often prompt reflection and reconsideration than adult-delivered instruction (Baroody 2004b), perhaps because many teachers are insufficiently knowledgeable about children's early grasp of mathematical principles (Kamii 2000).

For that reason, understanding how children learn in the areas of early mathematics is essential to meaningful teaching. Research points to the effectiveness of the following general support strategies:

- **Encourage exploration and manipulation**—Provide materials that have diverse sensory attributes and allow children to have a sufficient amount of time and space to discover their properties (see the box on p. 132 in this chapter). At the same time, "the ways children use objects are often very different from those that we intend or define" (Seo 2003, 30). Teachers might not see art materials or dramatic play props as math manipulatives, but children do (for instance, as they count the Velcro strips on a smock or the rooms in a dollhouse). Indeed, there is nothing they do not count!

- **Observe and listen**—Attend to the questions children ask. The problems they pose for themselves or to adults offer a window into their mathematical thinking.

- **Model, challenge, and coach**—Demonstrate hands-on activities that children can imitate and modify. Many such activities (for example, combining and dividing the items in a set and creating patterns) are not dependent on language and are, therefore, easily engaged in by dual language learners. Provide experiences that stretch children's thinking. Discuss what does (and does not) work (using facial expressions and gestures to indicate this to dual language learners—satisfied smiled, raised eyebrows, head scratching), pose questions, and suggest alternative approaches to finding a solution.

- **Encourage reflection and self-correction**—When children are stuck or arrive at an incorrect mathematical solution or explanation, do not jump in to solve the problem or correct their reasoning. Instead, provide hints to help children reconsider their answers and figure out solutions or alternative explanations on their own.

- **Provide the language for mathematical properties, processes, and relationships**— Introduce the language for children to label their observations, describe transformations, and share the reasoning behind their conclusions. Because the words will be provided in the context of hands-on, demonstrable concepts and problems, dual language learners will gradually pick them up along with native English speakers.

- **Play games with mathematical elements**—Games invented for or by children offer many opportunities to address such concepts as (non)equivalence, spatial and temporal relations, and measurement. Many such games (for example, throwing beanbags and measuring their distance from the base line) are not language dependent.

- **Introduce mathematical content**—Children enjoy good books about counting, especially when these invite participation. Storybooks and nonfiction texts are also a wonderful way to introduce real-life problems whose solutions depend on mathematical reasoning. This is also a good opportunity to support math learning in children's home languages to give them a good foundational understanding for grasping the English words used in other math activities. (For a list of suggested storybooks involving math concepts and ideas for using them with children, see Shillady 2012.)

Materials That Promote Mathematical Exploration

Children can use almost any object or type of material to manipulate, count, measure, and ask questions about. Yet there are some things teachers should make sure to have in their classrooms to promote exploration and thinking about the components of mathematics.

Number and Operations

Printed items containing numbers and mathematical symbols—signs, labels, brochures, advertisements with charts and graphs

Things with numbers on them—calculators, playing cards, thermometers, simple board games with dice or spinners

Numbers made of wood, plastic, or cardboard (make sure they are sturdy so children can hold, sort, copy, and trace them)

Discrete items children can easily count—beads, blocks, shells, poker chips, bottle caps

Paired items to create one-to-one correspondence—pegs and Peg-Boards, colored markers and tops, egg cartons and plastic eggs

Geometry and Spatial Sense

Materials and tools for filling and emptying—water, sand; scoops, shovels

Everyday things to fit together and take apart—LEGOs, Tinkertoys, puzzles, boxes and lids, clothing with different types of fasteners

Attribute blocks that vary in shape, size, color, thickness

Tangram pieces

Wooden and sturdy cardboard blocks in conventional and unconventional shapes

Containers and covers in different shapes and sizes

Materials to create two-dimensional shapes—string, pipe cleaners, yarn

Moldable materials to create three-dimensional shapes—clay, dough, sand, beeswax

Things with moving parts—kitchen utensils, musical instruments, cameras

Books that feature shapes and locations, with illustrations from different perspectives (for example, a farm field photographed from an aerial perspective, an apartment building observed from the sixth floor of a building across the street)

Photos of classroom materials and activities from different viewpoints

Materials that change with manipulation or time—clay, playdough, computer drawing programs, sand, water, plants, animals

Materials to explore spatial concepts (over/under, up/down) and to view things from different heights and position—climbing equipment, empty boxes (large cartons from appliances and furniture), boards

Maps and diagrams

- **Encourage peer interaction**—As noted in previous chapters, children can sometimes explain mathematical ideas to their peers more effectively than adults can. Sharing ideas, particularly conflicting ones, prompts children to articulate and, where necessary, modify their understanding.

In general, an investigative approach works better than a purely didactic one. Begin with a "worthwhile task, one that is interesting, often complex, and creates a real need to learn or practice. Experiencing mathematics in context is not only more interesting to children but more meaningful" (Baroody 2000, 64). It also makes learning in mathematics more likely and more lasting. As Ginsburg and his colleagues note,

> Rote instruction that does not emphasize understanding does little to inculcate the spirit of mathematics—learning to reason, detect patterns, make conjectures, and perceive the beauty in irregularities—and may instead result in teaching children to dislike mathematics at an earlier age than usual. Clearly the early childhood

Measurement

Ordered sets of materials in different sizes—nesting blocks, measuring spoons, pillows, paintbrushes, drums

Ordered labels so children can find materials and return them to their storage place—tracings of measuring spoons in four sizes on the Peg-Board in the house center

Storage containers in graduated sizes

Materials that signal stopping and starting—timers, musical instruments, musical recordings

Materials that can be set to move at different rates of speed—metronomes, wind-up toys

Things in nature that move or change at different rates—slow- and fast-germinating seeds, insects that creep and scurry

Unconventional measuring tools—yarn, ribbon, blocks, cubes, timers, shoes, ice cubes, containers of all shapes and sizes

Conventional measuring tools—tape measures, scales, clocks, grid paper, thermometers, measuring spoons, graduated cylinders

Patterns, Functions, and Algebra

Materials with visual patterns—toys in bright colors and black-and-white; dress-up clothes; curtains; upholstery

Materials to copy and create series and patterns—beads, sticks, small blocks, pegs and boards, writing and collage materials

Shells and other patterned items from nature

Original artwork and reproductions featuring patterns—weavings, baskets

Pattern blocks

Routines that follow patterns

Stories, poems, and chants with repeated words and rhythms

Songs with repetitions in melody, rhythm, and words

Computer programs that allow children to recognize and create series and patterns

Data Analysis

Tools for recording data—clipboards, paper, pencils, crayons, markers, chalk, computer or tablet

Materials for diagramming or graphing data—newsprint pads and easels, graph paper with large grids, poster board, interactive computer programs

Small objects to represent counted quantities—buttons, acorns, pebbles

Boxes and string for sorting and tying materials into groups

Sticky notes and masking tape for labeling

education community should not implement at the preschool and kindergarten levels the kinds of activities that the National Council of Teachers of Mathematics is trying to eliminate in elementary school! (Ginsburg, Inoue, & Seo 1999, 88)

Fitting the Learning Experience to the Learning Objective

The rest of this chapter describes what preschoolers learn as they begin to acquire mathematical literacy across NCTM's (2000) five content areas: number and operations, geometry, measurement, algebra, and data analysis and probability. Some of NCTM's standards, however, have labels that seem too sophisticated for what happens in preschool mathematics. That is, are young children really doing what older children and adults know as geometry, algebra, or probability? In writing its standards document, NCTM opted to use one label for each area across the entire age range, from prekindergarten to grade 12, for a purpose. It wanted to emphasize that for each content standard, children at *every* age are learning aspects of math that relate to that standard. However, in this chapter we have modified slightly the labels for three of the areas to be more descriptive of the specific learning occurring at the preschool level, so here they appear as geometry and spatial sense; patterns, functions, and algebra; and data analysis. Number and operations as well as measurement remain labeled the same. Of those five areas, number and operations, geometry and spatial sense, and measurement are areas particularly important for 3- to 6-year-olds because they help build young children's foundation for mathematics learning:

> For this reason, researchers recommend that algebraic thinking and data analysis/ probability receive somewhat less emphasis in the early years. The beginnings of ideas in these two areas, however, should be woven into the curriculum where they fit most naturally and seem most likely to promote understanding of the other topic areas. Within this second tier of content areas, patterning (a component of algebra) merits special mention because it is accessible and interesting to young children, grows to undergird all algebraic thinking, and supports the development of number, spatial sense, and other conceptual areas. (NAEYC & NCTM 2010, 7)

Each section of this chapter is divided into those concepts and skills that seem most likely to be learned, or best learned, through children's own explorations and discoveries (child-guided experience) and those concepts and skills in which adult-guided experience seems to be important in going beyond, as well as contributing to, what children learn through their independent efforts. As with every other domain described in this book, of course, this division is not rigid.

Number and Operations

This is the first of three areas that NCTM (2000, 2006) has identified as being particularly important for preschoolers. In the preschool years, number and operations focus on six elements or goals for early learning. (For further explanations and examples, see Clements 2004 and Copley 2004.) *Counting* involves learning the sequence of number words, identifying the quantity of items in a collection (knowing that the last counting word tells how many there are), and recognizing counting patterns (such as 21-22, 31-32, 41-42). *Comparing and ordering* is determining which of two groups has more or less of some attribute (comparing them according to which has the greater or lesser quantity, size, age, or sweetness, for example), and seriating or ordering objects according to some attribute (such as length, color intensity, loudness). *Composing and decomposing* are complementary: Composing is mentally or physically putting small groups of objects together (for example, two stones plus three stones makes five stones), while decomposing is breaking a group into two or more parts (for example, five spoons is two spoons plus two spoons plus one spoon).

Adding to and taking away is knowing that adding to a collection makes it larger and subtracting makes it smaller. When this understanding is combined with counting and (de)composing, children can solve simple problems with increasing efficiency. *Grouping and place value* are related: Creating sets of objects so that each has the same quantity creates groups, and grouping in sets of 10 is the basis for understanding place value later (that is, making groups of 10 and then counting the objects left over). *Equal partitioning* is dividing a collection into equal parts, a prerequisite to children's understanding of division and fractions.

To develop the mathematical understanding and skills encompassed in these six areas, preschoolers need an optimal blend of child-guided and adult-guided experiences.

Because early mathematical development depends so much on manipulating objects, it is important that young children have ample opportunities to work with materials that lend themselves to ordering, grouping and regrouping, and so on. Be sure to include materials representative of the children's cultures (for example, nesting dolls). Children intuit certain properties and processes from their spontaneous explorations, while adults provide conventional labels to describe the numerical properties and transformations they observe. Adults also challenge children to try additional transformations and reflect on the results. These experiences and the role of the intentional teacher within these experiences are described in the sections that follow.

Of the key knowledge and skills in the area of number and operations, intuiting number and its properties, as well as performing informal arithmetic, seem to develop best with child-guided experience. Adult-guided experience seems to prove helpful for counting and numeration, as well as for performing simple arithmetic.

Child-guided experience is especially important for learnings such as:

Intuiting number and its properties

Even before they learn how to count, young children come to an informal understanding of quantity and equivalence. For example, they can recognize small quantities (up to four or five) by eyeballing them. They can identify sets of one or two without counting; for higher quantities (three to five) they can pick out sets with the same number of items (Copley 2010). They do this using one-to-one correspondence to establish equivalence (for example, putting one acorn on each leaf to see that there are equal quantities). And they can make equal sets (i.e., make groups) by putting one in each pile, then another in each pile, and so on (for example, to distribute an equal number of crackers to each person at the table). Although lacking a formal knowledge of sets in a strict mathematical sense (defined as a collection of distinct elements, such as a set of squares versus a set of triangles), young children can create groups and recognize when items share all or some attributes with other items in a group.

Mathematicians, researchers, and practitioners agree that a central objective of early mathematics education is developing children's **number sense**—intuition about numbers and their magnitude, their relationship to real quantities, and the kinds of operations that can be performed on them. Early number sense includes this eyeballing ability, called *subitizing,* (recognizing quantities by sight alone, usually for quantities of four or fewer) and establishing one-to-one correspondence (linking a single number name with one, and *only one,* object). One-to-one correspondence is the foundation of counting.

An ability to identify **equivalence** is also fundamental to understanding number. Most 3-year-olds can recognize equivalence between collections of one to four objects (for example, two hearts and two squares) without actually enumerating items. They can also recognize equal collections in different arrangements as being the same (for example, three squares on the top and two on the bottom has the same number as one square on top and four on the bottom). Most 4-year-olds can make auditory-visual matches, such as equating the sound of three dings with the sight of three dots. These findings suggest that by age 3, children have already developed a nonverbal representation of number, although it's unclear what this mental representation is like or how accurate it is. Regardless, they can clearly represent and compare objects even before they can count them (Baroody 2004a; Copley 2010).

The *part-part-whole* concept is the understanding that a whole number (such as 7) can be represented as being made up of parts (such as 4 and 3, or 5 and 2, or 6 and 1). Part-part-whole representation is a precursor to number operations, helping children understand addition and subtraction. Most 3- and 4-year-olds can describe the parts of whole numbers up to 5, with an understanding of larger numbers developing around age 6 (Copley 2010, 59).

Teaching strategies. Intuition develops with experience. Teachers can help young children develop their number sense by surrounding them with a number-rich environment offering many opportunities to work with materials and processes that rely on numbers and their operations, as shown in the following examples (see the box on p. 132 in this chapter for further suggestions for materials):

- Display materials around the classroom printed with numerals and mathematical symbols. Make sure the numerals are large enough for children to see and are placed at their eye level. Include manipulatives in the shape of numerals made of wood or cardboard, as well as toys and other items with numerals on them. As noted previously in this chapter, these materials are not language dependent and, thus, are equally interesting and accessible to native English speakers and dual language learners.

- Offer materials and games that convey the concept of numbers, such as dominoes and dice. Encourage children to explore them and to find matches (for example, "Can you find another domino with the same number of dots?"). For dual language learners, demonstrate making a match (for example, point to the same number of dots on two dominoes) and encourage them to find or create their own matches.

- Label and describe number phenomena that occur naturally in the children's play (for example, "There are four wheels on Katie's truck and two more, or six, on Darnell's" and "You found the second mitten for your other hand"). Occasionally, recite numerals both in children's home languages and in English. Keep in mind that while reciting numbers helps children talk about math, learning how numbers work is much more important.

- Provide materials that allow children to explore one-to-one correspondence, such as nuts/bolts and seeds/holes in the dirt (large seeds work best). Children will also make one-to-one correspondences with any sets of materials they are playing with; for example, they might give each stuffed bear a plate or ball. Here again, the one-to-one concept can be explored independent of the child's proficiency in English. Children with special needs who have language delays can also engage with these materials to develop basic number sense.

- Include materials that can be broken down and divided into smaller parts, such as a lump of clay that can be divided into smaller balls or a piece of fruit that can be sliced or separated into sections. Unit blocks, LEGOs, and other toys with equal-size parts that children can build up and then break down into components also work well. (These materials and activities are also well suited to dual language learners and those with language delays.)

○ Offer materials that are the same in some ways but different in others, such as paintbrushes of the same thickness but whose bristles have different kinds of tips. When children use these materials, make observations that highlight their attributes, such as "All the paintbrushes are the same thickness, but some bristles have pointy tips and some have straight (flat) edges."

Performing informal arithmetic

Informal arithmetic is something similar to adding and subtracting nonquantitatively—that is, without using numbers or other written symbols. Even before receiving formal instruction, preschoolers often are able to solve simple nonverbal addition and subtraction problems (for example, two children are drawing at the table when a third child sits down, and then one child fetches "another" piece of paper for her). Children begin by acting out the problems with objects (such as by setting out two beads, and then "adding on" one more). Later they can substitute representations (such as tally marks on paper) for the physical objects and form mental representations (such as visualizing two beads, then adding one more). Teachers can be helpful in encouraging representation (NCTM 2000).

Children's formation of mental representations is significant: "They understand the most basic concept of addition—it is a transformation that makes a collection larger. Similarly, they understand the most basic concept of subtraction—it is a transformation that makes a collection smaller" (Baroody 2000, 63). Preschoolers can attain this basic understanding of operations on their own, especially when adults support its development. The understanding is fundamental to later success in school mathematics.

In kindergarten, children sometimes solve simple multiplication (grouping) and division (partitioning) problems by direct modeling with objects. With adult guidance, these informal strategies are replaced by formal number knowledge and counting strategies (Campbell 1999).

Teaching strategies. Because preschoolers tend to think concretely, handling objects and working with visual representations help them carry out and understand operations. The following are examples of strategies teachers can use to promote this learning:

○ Provide many small items that children can group and regroup, adding and subtracting units. Include toys, cooking and eating utensils, items of clothing, and other objects that children from different cultures or whose parents have different occupations might find at home (such as spools and thimbles, fasteners, flower and vegetable seeds). Ask parents to contribute such items to the classroom. When dual language learners work with familiar items they have seen at home, they can spend less time trying to figure out what the object is and more time focusing on learning the concept or skill. For all children, this use of real items to understand math ideas is a good way to help generalize school learning to home situations.

○ Pose simple addition and subtraction problems in the course of everyday experiences. For example, after a child sets the table, say, "Remember that

Micah is out sick today" or "Mrs. King is going to join us for snack" and see whether they subtract or add a place setting. Or as children are playing with blocks, say, "Jenessa wants to make her wall one row higher. How many more blocks will she need?"

○ Pose simple multiplication or division problems that children can solve using concrete objects. For example, give a child a collection of objects at small group and say, "Give the same number to everyone," or "There are five children and everyone wants two scarves to wave in the wind. How many scarves will we need to bring outside?"

Adult-guided experience is especially important for learnings such as:

Counting and numeration

For young children, counting and numeration (reading, writing, and naming numbers) involves understanding the following:

- Numbers, which is knowing the number names and the position of each one in the sequence, ordinal numbers (such as first, second, . . .), and cardinal numbers (such as one, two, . . .)

- Notation, which is reading and writing numerals and recognizing the simple mathematical symbols +, −, and =

- Counting, which is determining quantity and equivalence

- Sets, which involves creating and labeling collections and understanding *all* and *some*

As with learning letter names and shapes, children cannot acquire knowledge of number names and numerals unless adults give them this information. At times children will ask, "How do you write *three*?" or "What comes after ten?," but the intentional teacher also is proactive in introducing the vocabulary and symbols (notation) children need to understand and represent mathematical ideas (Campbell 1999). With adult guidance, children can then apply this knowledge to solve problems, including those of measurement and data analysis.

Early counting is finding out "how many," which is a powerful problem solver and essential to comparing quantities. Research (Gelman & Gallistel 1978) has identified five principles of counting: 1) stable order (two always follows one), 2) one-to-one correspondence (each object is assigned a unique counting name), 3) cardinality (the last counting name identifies how many), 4) order irrelevance (objects can be counted in any order without changing the quantity), and 5) abstraction (any set of objects can be counted). Adult-guided experience helps preschoolers develop these understandings.

Older preschoolers use counting to determine that two sets of objects are equivalent. Between the ages of 3 and 4, as they acquire verbal counting skills, children gain a tool more powerful than their earlier subitizing for representing and comparing numbers, including collections larger than four items. They recognize the "same number name" principle (two collections are equal if they share the same number name, despite any differences in physical appearance). Children generalize this principle to any size collection they can count. Similarly, by counting and comparing two unequal collections, preschoolers can discover the "larger number" principle (the later a number word appears in the sequence, the larger it is). By age 4, many preschool children can name and count numbers up to 10 and compare numbers up to 5. When they have ample opportunities to learn the counting sequence, children often learn to name and count to 20 by age 5 (Clements 2004). They are also fascinated by large numbers, such as 100 or a gazillion, even if they only know them as number names without a true sense of their value.

Equal partitioning builds on and is related to the concept of equivalence. Equal partitioning is the process of dividing something (for example, a plate of eight cookies) into equal-size parts (for example, to serve four children). Children as young as 4 or 5 begin to solve such problems concretely, using strategies such as dividing the objects into the requisite number of piles (four) and then counting how many are in each pile (Baroody 2004a).

Teaching strategies. Psychologist Howard Gardner says, "Preschoolers see the world as an arena for counting. Children want to count everything" (1991, 75). Being creative, teachers can invent or take advantage of many situations to count objects and events in children's daily lives. Here are some examples:

- Notice things that children typically compare (such as the number of steps from the climber to the sandbox, or their ages) and provide materials and experiences based on these observations. Think of fun and unusual things to count, such as the number of mosquito bites on someone's ankle or freckles on an arm.

- Make numerals prominent. Place numerals of different materials, sizes, and colors throughout the classroom. Provide cards with dots and numerals for children to explore, sort, and arrange in order. Use numerals on sign-up sheets so children can indicate not only the order in which they will take turns but also how many turns they want or for how long (such as two minutes, three flips of the sand timer). Children can indicate their preferences with numerals or other marks (such as stars, checks, hash marks).

- Use written numerals and encourage children to write them. For example, when they play store, encourage them to write size and price labels, orders, and the amount of the bill. Because dual language learners are often eager to enter into role-play scenarios, writing numerals gives them a language-free way to participate with their peers—as well as an opportunity for adults (and other children) to supply the English words for the numerals they write.

- Take advantage of everyday activities for number learning and practice. For example, as children gather or distribute countable materials, engage them in counting at cleanup (counting items as they're collected and put away), small group (handing out one glue bottle per child), and choice time (distributing playing cards). At snack or mealtimes, ask the table setter to count children to determine how many place settings are needed. Pose simple number problems such as "Our group has six, but Celia is sick today. How many napkins will we need?" or "How many cups of sand will it take to fill the hole?"

- Play games as a natural yet structured way to develop counting skills. Examples include board games with dice (moving a piece the corresponding number of places) or physical movement challenges (counting the number of times the tossed beanbag lands in the bucket).

- Respond to children's own questions as the springboard for teachable moments. For example, Baroody (2000) imagines an incident when a child named Diane says to her teacher.

"My birthday is next week, how old will I be? Will I be older than Gianna?" The teacher could simply answer, "You'll be 4, but Gianna is 5 so she's still older." Or, the teacher can respond by saying, "Class, Diane has some interesting questions with which she needs help. If she is 3 years old now, how can she figure out how old she'll be on her next birthday?" The teacher could follow up by posing a problem involving both *number-after* and *number-comparison* skills: "If Gianna is 5 years old and Diane is 4 years old, how could we figure out who is older?" (65)

○ Read and discuss children's literature. Not only are there many appealing counting books, but there are also storybooks in which mathematics is used to solve a problem. For example, read books where the story is about sharing a quantity of something fairly. Before the problem is solved in the book, ask children to suggest solutions by trying them out with materials or working through simple ideas in their heads. Children can work alone or in pairs. After reading the book, encourage them to comment on the solution(s) in the text. As a follow-up, they might role-play the same or similar situations using props that you supply or that they make themselves.

○ Encourage families to play counting games with their children, such as counting the number of passengers on the subway car, varieties of peanut butter on the supermarket shelf, or socks in the laundry basket. Not only will the children learn math concepts, but games will also infuse the everyday task with fun and make family outings and chores times for learning.

Performing simple arithmetic

Younger preschoolers perform simple arithmetic concretely—that is, by physically manipulating the objects they add to or subtract from a set. Older preschoolers, however, begin to add and subtract whole numbers quantitatively—that is, using numerals to abstractly represent numbers of objects rather than physically manipulating or visualizing the objects. They are able to do this because they can hold a representation of quantities in their minds. For example, they may say out loud, "Two and one more is three" or "If Logan isn't here today, I only need four trays." Although they can do this most readily with numerals up to 5, some preschoolers can handle numbers up to 10.

Research shows they may also be capable of adding and subtracting very simple fractions. For example, when researchers hid part of a circle behind a screen and then hid another fraction of the circle, children could visually identify what the total amount was. They understood, for example, that two halves made a whole, a half plus a quarter circle resulted in a three-quarters circle, and so on (Mix, Levine, & Huttenlocher 1999). Such research suggests that children can grasp the basic idea behind simple fractions if adults pose interesting challenges.

Teaching strategies. Arithmetic follows fixed rules or conventions. As with combining letters into words, performing operations on numbers depends on knowing these rules. With support from their teachers, preschoolers are capable of solving simple arithmetic problems that come up in play and exploration. They are also motivated to use arithmetic like grown-ups do. Teachers can therefore readily implement strategies such as the following to enhance young children's early understanding and use of arithmetic:

- Use real objects when helping children work through arithmetic problems. For example, if a child is lining up animal figures, ask how many how dogs there would be if he added two more to make the row longer. Wonder aloud how many dogs would be left if he made it three animals shorter. The child can add or subtract the actual animal figures and count the result to determine the answer.

- Pose challenges that build on children's interests. For example, if a child has drawn a picture of a flower, wonder aloud whether she can draw a flower "twice as big" or "half as big."

- Encourage children to use arithmetic to answer their own questions. For example, if a child says, "My daddy wants to know how many tortillas to bring for snack time tomorrow," you could reply, "Well, there are sixteen children and two teachers. Plus your daddy, and your brother will be here, too. How can we figure out how many tortillas you'll need to bring?"

- Engage children in reflecting on their arithmetic solutions rather than telling them if they're right or wrong. When children are stumped (though not yet frustrated) or arrive at erroneous answers, resist the temptation to give the answer or correct them. Instead, offer comments or pose questions that encourage them to rethink their solutions. Baroody (2000) gives this example:

Kamie concluded that 5 and two more must be 6. Instead of telling the girl she was wrong and that the correct sum was 7, her teacher asked, "How much do you think 5 and one more is?" After Kamie concluded it was 6, she set about recalculating 5 and two more. Apparently, she realized that both 5 and one more and 5 and two more could not have the same answer. The teacher's question prompted her to reconsider her first answer. (66)

- Start with one fraction at a time. For example, children are fascinated by the concept of one half. If they learn—really learn—through repeated experiences that half means two parts are the same and together they make up a whole, then they can generalize this concept later to thirds, quarters, and so on.

Geometry and Spatial Sense

This is the second of three areas that NCTM (2000, 2006) has identified as being particularly important for preschoolers. In the preschool years, learning about geometry and spatial sense focuses on four elements: *Shape* refers to the outline or contour (form) of objects and comprises identifying two- and three-dimensional shapes. *Locations, directions, and coordinates* refers to understanding the relationship of objects in the environment. *Transformation and symmetry* is the process of moving (sliding, rotating, flipping) shapes to determine whether or not they are the same. It also involves building larger shapes from smaller shapes, a common construction activity in preschool. *Visualization and spatial reasoning* is creating mental images of geometric objects, examining them, and transforming them. At first children's mental representations are static; that is, children cannot manipulate them. Later children can move and transform images mentally, such as deciding whether a chair will squeeze into a given space, how low to bend their bodies to slide under a shelf, or how to rotate a puzzle piece to interlock it with the one beside it.

Spatial concepts and language are closely related; words facilitate an understanding of such concepts as *on top of, next to, behind,* and *inside.* For example, where someone stands determines whether he is in *front of* or *behind* another object. "Communication centering on mathematical ideas stimulates children to extend their thinking and fosters development of a community of mathematical learners" (Greenes, Ginsburg, & Balfanz 2004, 161). Because society has specific conventions for labeling various shapes, transformations, and especially concepts of position, location, and so on, teachers especially need to enhance children's descriptive vocabulary in this domain. Because many spatial terms are new to all preschoolers, dual language learners can learn the words together with their English-speaking peers, assisted by visual cues and actions (with their bodies and materials). Be sure to provide dual language learners with spatial labels in their home language too so they can increase vocabulary and maintain fluency in both.

Of the key knowledge and skills in the area of geometry and spatial sense, child-guided experience seems most helpful for creating familiarity with two- and three-dimensional shapes and their attributes, as well as for orienting self and objects in space. To create, name, and transform shapes, on the other hand, as well as to articulate positions, location, directions, and distance, adult-guided experience seems necessary.

Child-guided experience is especially important for learnings such as:

Familiarity with two- and three-dimensional shapes and their attributes

For young children, shape knowledge is a combination of visual and tactile exploration, which begins in infancy. During the preprimary years, NCTM (2000) expects children to be able to recognize, name, build, draw, compare, and sort two- and three-dimensional shapes. Although most adults support children's recognition of two-dimensional shapes, they often overlook the need to give them experiences with three-dimensional shapes, which focus their attention on geometrical features. For example, exploring the rolling of cylinders and other shapes helps children to understand the properties of the circle versus the ellipse. These skills involve perceiving (differentiating) attributes such as lines and cubes; circles, cylinders, and globes; sides and edges; and corners, angles, and so on. Preschoolers are also engaged in investigating transformations with shapes (composing and decomposing), and they demonstrate an intuitive understanding of symmetry. [*Note*: Children need adult-guided experiences to learn to accurately label and describe transformations and symmetry.] It is important to give children multiple examples of these forms and attributes in different contexts and with different materials. For all children, but especially for dual language learners, many of these terms are completely new, and seeing only one example may limit their understanding of the term to that one example.

Teaching strategies. Communication skills are important in all areas of mathematics, but they are especially so in geometry. The following are some helpful strategies that teachers can use to help develop these communication skills in preschoolers:

- ○ Introduce both two- and three-dimensional shapes, giving children opportunities to explore them. Include both regular and irregular shapes. Engage children in drawing and tracing the shapes. Provide models (drawings, molds, scale models) and tools children can use to trace or copy them. Visual and physical shapes help young children grasp the essential attributes of each.

O Encourage children to sort shapes and provide reasons for their groupings. Invite them to describe why objects are *not* alike.

O Suggest to children that they combine (compose) and take apart (decompose) shapes to create new shapes, such as combining two triangles to make a square or rectangle (composing) and vice versa (decomposing). Engage them in discussions about these transformations.

O Provide materials that have symmetry that is vertical (meaning the left/right halves are identical) or horizontal (meaning the top/bottom halves are identical)—for example, doll clothes, a teeter-totter, a toy airplane, and a leaf with a center axis. For contrast, provide similar but asymmetric materials—for example, a glove, slide, toy crane, and an irregularly shaped leaf. Engage children in discussing how the two sides (or top and bottom) of objects are the same (symmetrical) or different (asymmetrical).

Orienting self and objects in space

Spatial relations—how objects are oriented in space and in relation to one another—are the foundation of geometry, which involves understanding and working with the relationships of points, lines, angles, surfaces, and solids. Compared with toddlers, preschoolers navigate their bodies and move objects with greater skill and confidence. Younger children still tend to see and describe space from their own perspective (egocentrism), but older preschoolers can begin to represent and describe things from another person's point of view (perspective taking).

Teaching strategies. Because mathematics is the search for relationships, early instruction should focus on physical experiences through which children construct understandings about space. Teachers do this primarily by providing materials and giving children ample time to explore them, as described in these strategies:

O Create different types of space in the classroom and outdoor area—small spaces for children to maneuver into and around; large open areas where children can move about freely; and spaces for children to crawl over and under, in and out, up and down, and around and through. Ask and talk with children about their relationships with objects and one another.

O Provide materials, time, and ample space for children to build with construction toys. Notice all the relative dimension and position concepts Trey and his friends used when they made a "bus" with large wooden blocks and invited their classmates and the teacher to get onboard:

> The group quickly decided the bus was too *small*, so they made it *bigger* by adding many more seats. The children worked hard *fitting* the big wooden blocks *end-to-end* to make the bus *longer*. They made a "driver's seat" *up front* and made a "steering wheel" to fit *on top* of the "dashboard." They also decided to build a "refrigerator" in the *back* of the pretend bus. Trey said it needed to be "on the back wall, but in the *middle* of the aisle." (Tompkins 1996b, 221)

- Offer other materials for children to move and rearrange (for example, dollhouse furniture or pedestals to display artwork). Provide materials children can use to organize and construct collages.
- Look for computer programs and apps that allow children to move and transform shapes. Manipulating shapes on a screen allows children to do what their hands may not yet have the dexterity to perform, and it is especially valuable for those with limited motor control or difficulties with eye–hand coordination.

Adult-guided experience is especially important for learnings such as:

Creating, naming, and transforming shapes

The ability to accurately name, describe, and compare shape, size (scale), and volume is important for children to acquire during the preschool years. With appropriate experiences and input, they can learn to transform shapes to achieve a desired result and describe the transformation (for example, "I'm making this bridge longer by adding more blocks at the end and holding it up in the middle"). They can also create and label symmetry in their two- and three-dimensional creations. Language is critical with all of these activities. Therefore, as vocabulary expands, so does geometric understanding.

Teaching strategies. Building on preschoolers' explorations of shapes, teachers should explicitly focus the children's attention on features and what the shapes will do (for example, "Which of these shapes can roll?") and provide words for these characteristics. Children should have opportunities to identify shapes in various transformations, including reflections and rotations and (de)compositions. For example, try these strategies:

- Comment and ask children about differences in the size and scale of things that interest them, such as their own bodies, food portions, or rocks. Encourage them to alter two- and three-dimensional materials and comment on the transformations, including whether their manipulations resulted in regular or irregular forms.

- Identify and label shapes and their characteristics throughout the children's environment (classroom, school, community). Go on a shape hunt in the classroom (for example, a "triangle search"). Use increasingly sophisticated vocabulary words; for example, say, "On our walk, let's look for all the square signs" or "You used cubes and rectangular blocks to build your dollhouse." Remember to supply names of three-dimensional as well as two-dimensional shapes. Identify shape names in children's home languages as well as English. (For example, use *triangle* and *triángulo*; *circle* and *círculo*; *cube* and *cubo* for Spanish speakers. Words that sound similar in two related languages are called cognates. Showing children the connections between these words has been shown to be an effective teaching strategy for dual language learners.)

- Encourage the exploration of shapes beyond conventional ones such as circles, squares, and triangles. Young children enjoy hearing and learning names such as *cylinder* and *trapezoid* (just as they love saying the names of big numbers). Even if they do not fully grasp the meaning and characteristics, they become attuned to the variety of spatial phenomena in the world. Also important is giving children diverse examples of triangles and other shapes, not just the equilateral triangle that is the only example offered in many classrooms.

- Use printed materials to focus on shape. Cut out photographs from magazines that feature shape pictures and encourage children to sort them. Look for shapes that may feature prominently in other cultures (for example, those used as design motifs in traditional costumes, banners, or symbols). Create a shape scrapbook for the book area. Encourage children to build structures like those in storybooks and information books. Refer to the books and talk with children about their choice of materials, how they match the attributes in the illustrations, and how the children are re-creating or modifying the structures or both.

- Challenge children to imagine what their structures would look like with one or more elements transformed (for example, in location or orientation). Encourage them to represent and verify their predictions. For example, in *Building Structures With Young Children*, Chalufour and Worth share this note from a preschool teacher:

I brought a whiteboard and markers over to the block area because Abigail was having a hard time imagining what her tower would look like if it were built with the blocks placed vertically instead of horizontally, as she had done. Not only did it help her to see a drawing of a tower built with verticals, but Adam came up to the drawing and pointed to one of the blocks near the top of the drawing, declaring that he didn't think it would balance on top of the one under it. So he and Abigail proceeded to use the drawing to build a tower and, lo and behold, Adam was right! Tomorrow I'm going to invite him to tell the group about the event. We can ask Adam how he knew that the vertical wouldn't balance. (2004, 45)

Articulating position, location, direction, and distance

With appropriate adult guidance, preschoolers can use position and direction words and follow orientation directions. They also are able to begin moving beyond their egocentric perceptions to predict another's perspective. For example, with experience they can describe how someone else would see something from their perspective, and they can give appropriate directions or instructions to another person.

Teaching strategies. Teachers need to supply vocabulary for position, location, direction, and distance concepts, of course. But preschoolers still master such ideas through a combination of concrete experience and mental imagery, so teachers need to provide many opportunities for them to represent these concepts in two- and three-dimensional ways. Consider the following suggestions:

- Make comments and ask questions that focus on location and direction, such as "You attached the sides by putting a long piece of string between the two shorter ones" or "Where will your road turn when it reaches the wall?" Comment on naturally occurring position situations, such as "Lazlo is climbing the steps to the slide, Cory's next, and last is Jessica."

- Use various types of visual representations to focus on these concepts. Engage children with making and interpreting maps—for finding a hidden object, for example. Children can draw diagrams of the classroom, their rooms at home, and other familiar places. Simple drawing programs on the computer can be used for this purpose, whether to supplement handmade maps or to replace them for children whose motor or coordination abilities are limited. Activities that focus on visual representation also allow children with limited verbal and/or English language skills to participate fully. Ask children about the placement of the objects. Comment on the location of things in their drawings using position words: "You have a big poster over your bed" or "What's poking out behind the curtain?"

○ Ask children to draw, paint, build, or use their bodies to represent favorite books featuring characters or objects in relation to one another. For example, ask them to draw the three bears from *Goldilocks and the Three Bears* sitting around the table or to lie down next to one another like the three bears in their beds. Because society has specific conventions for labeling various concepts of position, location, and so on, teachers are especially needed to enhance children's descriptive vocabulary in this domain.

○ Create occasions for children to give directions—for example, when helping one another or leading during large group. This requires them to use position and direction words, such as "Hold the top and push down hard into the dough" or "Stretch your arms over your head and then bend down to touch your toes." Encourage children to volunteer as the leader. Encourage dual language learners to give directions in their home language if they do not yet know the English words, and use translation and gestures to help them communicate directions to their peers.

○ Use movement to focus on spatial concepts. Provide objects that can be thrown safely, such as beanbags and foam balls, and interact with children about distance. Use simple movement directions for games and dances at large group time. Invent variations to games and dances by frequently modeling the addition of a new twist (for example, the "eensy, weensy, spider" might crawl "down" into a cave or wriggle "through" a tunnel instead of going "up" the water spout). Get the children engaged in making up variations of their own.

○ Talk about trips children take with their families or about walks and field trips with the class. For example, "Does your grandma live close to you or far away?" or "We took a long ride to the zoo on the bus, but after we parked, it was just a short walk to the monkey house."

Measurement

This is the third of three areas NCTM (2000, 2006) has identified as being particularly important for preschoolers. In the preschool years, learning about measurement focuses on two elements. *Attributes, units, and processes* refers to developing concepts about size and quantity, arranging objects to compare them, estimating differences (such as by eyeballing, lifting), and quantifying differences with nonstandard (such as footsteps) and standard (such as tape measure) tools. *Techniques and tools* comprises learning rules for measuring, such as starting at zero, aligning or equalizing beginning points, and not allowing gaps. It also includes becoming familiar with standard measuring tools such as rulers, scales, stopwatches, and thermometers. As with spatial concepts, measurement exploration benefits from the use of language, especially comparison words. Here too teachers should provide basic terms in English and children's home languages.

Of the key knowledge and skills in the area of measurement, comparing (seriating)—or estimating without counting or measuring—seems to develop best with child-guided experience. Adult-guided experiences seems integral for counting or measuring to quantify differences.

Child-guided experience is especially important for learnings such as:

Comparing (seriating), or estimating without counting or measuring

Young children are able to grasp the basic concept of one thing being bigger, longer, heavier, and the like, relative to another. Making comparisons is the beginning of measurement. According to NCTM's standards (2000), preschoolers should be engaged in comparing length, capacity, weight, area, volume, time, and temperature.

At first, children make *general* quantitative comparisons by matching or ordering things ("This pepper plant is the short one, and that pepper plant is the tall one" or "My cup holds more water than yours") rather than *specific* comparisons that use counting or measuring ("I have two more oranges than you"). To estimate, they use their various senses, such as eyeballing (visual), lifting (kinesthetic), or listening (auditory). They may compare length by aligning several twigs at the bottom and seeing how much they stick out at the top; listening to instruments to compare their loudness; or touching side-by-side patches of grass, one in the sun and one in the shade, to feel which is warmer.

Teaching strategies. Teachers can draw on children's interest in comparing to focus their attention on quantitative differences. (*Note*: Comparisons based on qualitative, or nonmeasurable, differences fall within classifying, a topic covered under science on p. 162 in Chap. 8.) Examples abound in mathematical applications, including the following:

- Make comments and ask questions using comparison words ("Which of these is longer?" or "Does everyone have the same number of apple slices now?"). Ask children whether they think something is wider (or softer, heavier, louder, or colder) than something else.

- Provide ordered sets of materials in different sizes (see the box on p. 132 in this chapter). Plant a garden with flowers and vegetables whose plants grow to different heights.

- Encourage children to move at different rates throughout the day and comment on relative speed. Make transitions fun by asking children to proceed to another area or activity "as slow as a snail" or "as fast as a rocket." Acknowledge their observations about speed and what affects it. A preschool teacher shared this anecdote:

  > At outside time, James was pushing two children around the playground on the toy taxi. When the adult asked if she could have a ride, he said "Sure." After going around two more times, James stopped the taxi and said, "Get off. You're too fat and I can't go fast." Acknowledging the validity (if not the kindness) of his observation, the teacher got off the taxi so he could move at a faster clip. (Graves 1996, 208)

- Call children's attention to graduated changes in nature. Comment on seasonal fluctuations in temperature (for example, "It feels colder now than it did when we went to the pumpkin patch. We're wearing heavier jackets"). Plant a garden and ask children how long they think it will take before the seeds germinate, the vegetables are ready to eat, and so on.

Adult-guided experience is especially important for learnings such as:

Counting or measuring to quantify differences

Many older preschoolers and kindergarten children are able to understand the idea of standard units, and with well-conceived learning experiences, they can begin to determine differences in quantity by systematic measurement. They use their knowledge of numbers to make comparisons. At first they use nonstandard units, such as how many steps it takes to cross the schoolyard in each direction or the number of song verses that are sung in the time that it takes to clean up different areas of the room. With teachers' assistance, they can acquire the understanding that it is useful to employ conventional units and measuring devices, such as inches on a ruler or minutes on a clock.

Teaching strategies. There are many opportunities throughout the day for children to engage in measurement, such as when they are building something or resolving a dispute. However, it usually does not occur to preschoolers to measure or quantify things to solve these problems. Adults can actively encourage children to use measurement in these situations with strategies such as the following:

○ Provide conventional and unconventional measuring devices and encourage children to use them to answer questions or solve problems. Conventional devices include rulers, tape measures, clocks, metronomes, kitchen timers, and spring and balance scales. Unconventional ones include string, plastic chains, or paper towel tubes for length; sand timers for duration; grocery bags for volume (for example, three bags of blocks were needed to make a tall tower, but only one bag to make a short one); and unmarked bags of clay or sand for weight. Children can also develop their own devices. When children ask measurement-related questions ("Which is heavier?") or have disputes ("I am too taller by a whole, big lot!"), ask them which of these tools might help them arrive at an answer or a solution.

○ Pose measurement challenges that children will be motivated to solve (for example, "I wonder how many cups of sand it will take to fill all twelve muffin tins?"). Ask "How many more . . . ?" questions, such as "How many more pieces of train track will you need to close the circle?" Here's an amusing challenge shared by a curriculum developer and writer who works with preschoolers:

> I was stretched out on the floor against a wall. I said, "I wonder how many me's long the wall is." The children thought this was very funny but they were intrigued to figure out the answer. Some estimated by simply "envisioning" the response. Others wanted to use the direct route, having me move and stretch out while they counted the number of repetitions. When I said I was too comfortable and didn't want to move, the children had to come up with another solution. They decided that two of them equaled one of me, so they stretched in a line along the wall and counted how many of them it took. With my help, they then divided the number of children in half. (Stuart Murphy, 2004, personal communication)

- When resolving social conflicts with children, ask how they could use measurement to guarantee a fair solution—for example, to make sure everyone gets to write on the computer for the same amount of time (see the box that follows).

- Use visual models to help children understand and quantify differences. For example, make a daily routine chart where the length of each part in inches is proportional to its duration in minutes. Such visual representations are especially helpful for dual language learners who are adjusting to the program's routine. Give time checks ("Five minutes 'til cleanup") with visual and auditory cues.

- Create opportunities for group construction projects, such as laying out a garden, making a bed for each doll within a defined space, or re-creating a supermarket after a class field trip. These often lead to situations where children have different opinions and need to measure to find out who is right or what solution will work. Sometimes you will need to suggest this method of resolving the difference of opinion.

- Include units of measurement when sharing information with children (for example, "I went grocery shopping for an hour last night" or "My puppy gained five pounds since the last time I took him to the vet" or "We need to space the seeds six inches apart so the beans have room to grow").

Measuring to Resolve a Social Conflict

Undertaking an investigation with adult help is one way to resolve disputes (for more on this, see p. 60 in Chap. 4). Some conflict situations lend themselves to collecting information that can be quantified and interpreted to reach a fair solution. In the following example, a group of older preschoolers resolve a dispute by measuring heights and are surprised by the result:

Julian, Liza, and Devon argue about the order of turn taking to drive the big truck around the playground. They decide that the biggest person should go first, then the next biggest, and then the smallest. They will make a list and check off each name as that person finishes a turn. Julian chalks *J, D, L* on the blacktop and moves to get on the truck. But the conflict is not yet over:

Devon: Hey! I'm bigger than you. I get to go first!

Julian: No, you're not. I'm the biggest one.

Liza: Let's measure and find out.

The children stand against the wall and ask their teacher to make a chalk mark where each of their heads touched. Then they get the tape measure and ask their teacher to write down how many inches tall each child is. She writes *41* next to the *J, 42* next to the *D,* and *44* next to the *L.*

Liza: It's me! I'm the biggest!

Devon: Yeah, and I'm next. Julian is last.

Julian: But I can stay on the longest because there's no one after me!

Patterns, Functions, and Algebra

In the preschool years, learning about patterns, functions, and algebra focuses on two elements. *Identifying patterns* involves recognizing and copying patterns and determining the core unit of a repeating pattern. It includes visual, auditory, and movement patterns. Deciphering patterns requires inductive reasoning, which is also a precursor to understanding probability. *Describing change* is using language to describe the state or status of something before and after a transformation, as in, "When I was a baby, I couldn't drink out of a cup" or "When we raised the ramp a little higher, my car went all the way to the bookshelf."

Of the key knowledge and skills in the area of patterns, functions, and algebra, child-guided experience seems to help children recognize, copy, and create simple patterns and also recognize naturally occurring change. To identify and extend complex patterns and to control change, on the other hand, children seem to benefit most from adult-guided experience.

Child-guided experience is especially important for learnings such as:

Recognizing, copying, and creating simple patterns

For young children, this area encompasses an awareness of patterns in the environment (visual, auditory, temporal, movement). Preschoolers can acquire the ability to copy or create simple patterns with two elements, such as *abab* or *aabb* (for example, alternating slices of apple-pear-apple-pear on a plate; a movement sequence that goes jump-jump-clap-clap-jump-jump-clap-clap). Even before they know the word *pattern*, children notice recurring designs or routines in their lives, whether it be on their clothing, the stripes on a kitten's back, or the order of each day's activities. Preschoolers generally need at least three repetitions of a pattern before they can recognize or repeat it (Clements & Sarama 2009).

Teaching strategies. Patterns and series of objects or events are plentiful in the world; simple observations and questions can lead children to notice and create regularity and repetition. Teachers can actively help children become aware of common patterns and series with the following strategies:

- Ask children to do or make things that involve series and patterns. For example, at small group time, give children drawing or sculpting materials and invite them to represent their families—from the smallest to the biggest members. Other materials that lend themselves to pattern making include string and beads in different colors and shapes (for example, to make a necklace), multicolored blocks in graduated sizes (for example, to make a train), and pegs and boards (for example, to make a design).

- Acknowledge the patterns children spontaneously create in art and construction projects. When they are busy building, acknowledge their work with a smile and a descriptive statement such as, "I see a pattern in your tower. First you used two rectangles, then you used a cylinder, and then you added two more rectangles and a cylinder" or "This reminds me of the Eiffel Tower. It's wide at the bottom and becomes narrow at the top" (Chalufour & Worth

2004, 38). Music provides many opportunities for calling attention to patterns: "You beat out two loud, one soft, two loud, and one soft beat with the rhythm sticks." So does movement; for example, comment on a series of two or three steps repeated in sequence (side, side, hop, side, side, hop). The verbal repetition, together with the visual representation, is especially useful for dual language learners exploring new vocabulary words.

○ Encourage children to move their bodies during large group time into graduated positions such as lying, sitting, and standing. Move through transitions at slow, medium, and fast paces.

○ Read and act out stories in which size, voice, or other graduated qualities play a role, such as in *Goldilocks and the Three Bears* or *The Three Billy Goats Gruff*. During small group time, ask children to make beds for the three bears with playdough. During large group time, have them choose which instrument the papa, mama, or baby bear would play, depending on variations in pitch or loudness.

Recognizing naturally occurring change

Noticing and describing changes includes identifying what natural variable or variables are causal. For example, children see changes in their own bodies (for example, getting taller) or the growth of a flower. Although they are often unable to identify the causal factor accurately, young children do make tentative guesses, both right and wrong, about the changes they see (for example, "I'm 5 today. That means I'm taller" or "The flower grew up because the wind blew on it from the bottom").

Teaching strategies. The most important strategy teachers can follow in this area is to notice and acknowledge children's awareness of changes in their environment and initiate situations in which change can be created, observed, and investigated. For example, discuss the growth of vegetables in the school garden or comment on children's experiments with color mixing at the easel. Repeating and extending children's comments about the changes they observe lets them know that you are listening to them. Calling their attention to change and showing that you are interested in their reactions and explanations is also a form of acknowledgment. Consider the following strategies:

○ Repeat children's comments to acknowledge their spontaneous seriation. For example, when LaToya said, "These giants are the most hungry because they have the biggest teeth," her teacher said, "So the giants with the biggest teeth will be able to eat a lot more food than the giants with small- and medium-size teeth."

○ Extend children's comments. For example, Josh was washing his hands at the sink when his teacher turned on the water in the next sink full blast. Josh said, "Mine is running slow." She turned down her water and said, "I made mine slow*er* like yours."

○ Call children's attention to cycles in nature with concrete examples. Point out the seasonal variations in schoolyard plants or the changing thickness of children's jackets from fall (lightweight) to winter (heavy) to spring (back to lightweight). Document changes with photographs.

Adult-guided experience is especially important for learnings such as:

Identifying and extending complex patterns

Simple patterning is something young children do spontaneously. With experience and adult input, they can learn to do more. For example, older preschoolers and kindergartners are able to analyze, replicate, and extend the core unit of a complex repeating pattern with three or more elements (A-B-C-A-B-C; 1-22-3-1-22-3), provided they see or hear it several times (Clements 2004). They can also begin to recognize what are called "growing" patterns—that is, patterns in which successive elements differ (rather than repeat) but still proceed according to an underlying principle, such as counting by ones or twos (2-4-6). The same principles apply to patterns in nature. Younger children may notice past and present seasons; older preschoolers are ready to grasp the cycling of four seasons in a year.

Teaching strategies. Young children recognize simple patterns on their own. Complex patterns are more dependent on someone pointing them out, particularly if the viewer is not looking for them in the first place. Therefore, teachers can play an especially active role in helping young children identify and create multipart repeating and growing patterns and sequences using strategies such as the following:

- Create complex patterns and then give children art and construction materials to copy them. Encourage them to create patterns and series on their own with three or more elements.

- Comment on the patterns children create, identifying repeating elements. For example, Leah showed a painting of "two rainbows" to her teacher. It was actually two sequences or patterns of color that were exactly the same. Her teacher pointed to each and commented that one rainbow had green, red, purple, and yellow, and so did the other.

- Introduce children to the books and catalogs with complex patterns used by ceramic tilers, landscape designers, (brick and paver patterns), and fiber artists (weaving, quilting, needlepoint, basketry). Decorating stores often give away books of discontinued wallpaper and rug samples. With these, engage children in describing the patterns and finding corresponding examples in their own environment that contain one or more comparable repeated elements, such as the walkway to the school or a knitted woolen hat.

- Call children's attention to complex patterns and sequences in their environment, such as markings on plants and animals or art and crafts in their community. Encourage children to duplicate and extend the patterns they see. For example, collect things with complex patterns on a nature walk and have children copy and extend the patterns (or create their own comparable ones) at small group or art time.

- Provide computer programs that allow children to recognize and create series and patterns.

- Use music to call attention to patterns. Play instrumental music with patterns in pitch, tempo, or loudness and encourage children to identify them. (This works best if the children are already familiar with the music.) Sing songs with repeating patterns (where verses and chorus alternate) or growing patterns (countdown songs such as "I Know an Old Lady Who Swallowed a Fly"). Comment on the patterns and encourage children to identify them.

- Use movement to focus on patterns, including traditional dances with simple repeating steps. Older preschoolers can sequence three movements. If children can master these, encourage them to be leaders and suggest three-step sequences.

Controlling change

Younger children spontaneously notice changes in themselves and their environment. Older preschoolers not only observe but can also begin to articulate the reasons for such changes. Moreover, they can deliberately manipulate variable(s) to produce a desired effect. For example, they may alter the choice of materials and their arrangement to better represent something in a collage, or alter the length and angle of a ramp to affect the speed of a toy car.

Teaching strategies. Teachers can promote awareness of and curiosity about change by fostering a spirit of inquiry in the classroom. An adult's investigative attitude is transmitted to the children. They will begin to pose the kinds of questions that scientists use when they want to know about the properties of materials and how they operate, and then predict and estimate or measure the results to satisfy their curiosity. Children are eager to try different things (manipulate variables) and see the outcomes. Here are some strategies to encourage their explorations:

- Make "I wonder what would happen if . . ." statements (for example, "I wonder what would happen if you made this end of the ramp higher").

- Ask "Suppose you wanted to . . ." questions (for example, "Suppose you wanted to make the car go slower. How do you think you could do that?").

- Encourage older preschoolers to anticipate the consequences of their proposed solutions to social problem-solving situations (see p. 60 in Chap. 4). If they foresee difficulties, have them consider how to change all or part of the solution to avoid them.

Data Analysis

In the preschool years, learning about data analysis focuses on three elements. *Classifying or organizing* involves collecting and categorizing data (for example, the favorite foods of children in the class). *Representing* is diagramming, graphing, or otherwise recording and displaying the data (for example, a list of different foods with check marks for every child who likes them). *Using information* involves asking questions, deciding what data is needed, and then interpreting the data gathered to answer the questions (for example, what to have for snack).

Of the key knowledge and skills in the area of data analysis, children seem most capable of making collections and sorting/classifying by quantitative attributes when they learn through child-guided experience; they seem most capable of representing and interpreting/applying gathered information when they learn through adult-guided experience.

Child-guided experience is especially important for learnings such as:

Making collections and sorting/classifying by quantitative attributes

Children love to collect and sort things. Sorting involves noticing, describing, and comparing the attributes of things (animals, people, objects) and events. Young children can classify according to one attribute (for example, shape) and when they are bit older by two attributes (such as shape and size). Examples of other quantitative (measurable) attributes that young children typically use to classify objects or phenomena include temperature, loudness, speed, duration, and weight. Classification is also an important skill in science. To differentiate these content areas, sorting that involves quantitative attributes is emphasized here in mathematics, while sorting based on qualitative attributes (such as color, texture, magnetism, or function) is the focus of classifying under science (see p. 163 in Chap. 8).

Teaching strategies. Because children are natural collectors, they will eagerly initiate and respond to suggestions in this area of mathematics. By showing interest in their collecting and arranging and by asking skillful questions that focus on the measurable attributes of the materials children gather, teachers can extend child-guided explorations. Consider using the following strategies:

- Encourage children to make collections of items in the classroom, natural objects gathered on field trips, and various objects they bring from home. Provide containers (bowls, boxes, baskets) for them to sort the items. Ask them to explain and describe their collections, especially attributes related to time and other characteristics that can be measured.

- Have children explain why things do *not* fit into the categories they have created. For example, pick up a feather and, gesturing to a pile of metal objects, ask, "Would this feather fit there?"

- Provide opportunities for children to experiment with materials whose attributes involve all the senses, such as shape, texture, size, color, pitch, loudness, taste, and aroma. While some of these attributes are not directly measurable, children can still compare them in quantitative terms, such as whether one piece of fabric is more or less smooth than another swatch of material.

- Acknowledge and repeat children's attribute labels, including invented ones ("This fruit feels *squishier* on my tongue" or "These pebbles are more *bumply* than those pebbles"). Use common words to build children's vocabulary ("You used lots more *blue* in the top part of your painting than on the bottom part") and introduce new language to expand their descriptive language ("This cloth feels *silkier*" or "You chose one of the *rectangular* crackers to eat first"). Encourage dual language learners to describe quantitative attributes in their home language, and simultaneously supply the comparable term in English ("Yes, this tree trunk is más amplio, wider, than this board").

Adult-guided experience is especially important for learnings such as:

Representing gathered information

Representing information for purposes of data analysis means documenting categories and quantities with numbers, diagrams, charts, graphs, counters (for example, one button for each occurrence), and other symbols. These activities involve knowledge of key mathematics concepts.

Teaching strategies. Children are naturally curious about their environment, but their investigations tend to be limited in scope and haphazard in procedure. Adult intervention can make children's explorations and conclusions more systematic and meaningful. The following strategies help them use mathematics to answer questions of interest to them:

- Provide materials children can use to record and represent data, such as clipboards, graph paper, and pencils, as well as simple computer programs.

- Pose questions in which finding the answers requires children to gather and analyze data, such as "How many bags of gerbil food do we need to feed Pinky for one month?" Focus on things of particular interest to children, such as their bodies (height, age, hair color), animals and nature (types of pets), the dimensions of things they build, and what they and their friends like and dislike (foods, favorite story characters). For example, chart the ingredients children like best in trail mix, and use the data to make snacks in proportion to their tastes.

- Put a question box in the classroom and help children write out and submit questions that arise. For questions that involve data collection, ask children to suggest ways to answer them.

- Be alert to situations that lend themselves to documentation, such as construction projects that involve multiples of materials. For example, if children build a train, help them chart the number of cars or units in the track. If the cars are of different sizes, create rows or columns and encourage children to record the number of each. If train building is a recurring activity, investigate whether trains made on different days are longer or shorter and by how many cars.

Interpreting and applying information

This component of data analysis refers to making and testing predictions, drawing conclusions, and using the results of an investigation to establish or clarify facts, make plans, or solve problems.

Teaching strategies. Without adult intervention, children's mathematical inquiries often end with just collecting information. They may need help to analyze the data to draw one or more conclusions. Further, children's learning is less likely to end there if teachers encourage them to apply their learning to related topics and to solving problems. Try strategies such as these:

- Encourage children to test out their hypotheses to resolve differences when they arise. For example, if children debate who in the group runs the fastest, you could help them select a beginning and endpoint for a racecourse, record and enter their running times with a stopwatch, and discuss the results to reach a conclusion.

- Make simple summaries and comment on the data the children have collected or displayed (for example, "So in our class we have two children who are 5 years old, eight who are 4, and six who are 3").

- Ask children for their ideas about what to do with the information they gather (for example, "Everyone likes pretzels, half of you like raisins, but there are only two check marks next to sesame sticks. So what does this mean we should put in the trail mix for our walk tomorrow?").

- Encourage children to predict the outcome of something, record their predictions, and then compare them with the results. For example, have each child guess the length of a wall and record their estimates. Measure the wall and then discuss whose guess was too long, too short, or just right.

In her book *The Young Child and Mathematics,* Copley (2010) asks rhetorically,

> Should we immediately correct young children's misconceptions about mathematics? Can we expect all children to solve problems in identical ways? Should we expect all the young children in a group to "get it" at the same time? . . . [T]he answer to all these questions is No! As teachers, we need to remember that young children construct mathematical understanding in different ways, at different times, and with different materials. Our job is to provide an environment in which all children can learn mathematics. (7)

This chapter demonstrates that young children are eager to enter the world of mathematics. If adults create an atmosphere that encourages investigation and engages children in reflection using English, their home languages, and nonverbal cues, they will experience the small and large pleasures of math in their daily lives. In addition, "positive experiences with using mathematics to solve problems [will] help children to develop dispositions such as curiosity, imagination, flexibility, inventiveness, and persistence that contribute to their future success in and out of school" (NAEYC & NCTM 2010, 4).

For Further Consideration

1. Why do some early childhood educators underestimate young children's mathematical abilities? What does this underestimation say about how practitioners define this subject area and their self-perceived knowledge and skills?

2. Would you describe yourself as someone who is comfortable with math or as someone with "math anxiety"? How does, or how will, your attitude toward math affect how you engage children with this subject?

3. How can early childhood educators change the public perception of early mathematics to encompass more than numbers and counting, for example, to include all five areas identified by mathematics educators (NCTM 2000)?

4. Do gender differences in mathematics (favoring the involvement of boys) emerge in the preschool years? If your answer is no, what lessons can we learn from early childhood practice to sustain girls' interest in this subject and prevent the emergence of a gender gap in later years? If your answer is yes, how can we alter our practices to instill and fortify lasting interest in this subject by girls?

5. How can (and should) we take advantage of emerging technologies to enhance early learning in mathematics? Is there such a thing as harmful technology, or do the (dis)advantages lie only in its application?

Chapter 8

Science

Annie, an older 4, plays with a magnetic board, sticking different objects (magnetic puzzle pieces, keys, and metal washers) to it. When she finds that a paper clip will not stick, she observes to her teacher, "This is metal, but it's not sticking." Petra, also an older 4, tries three other paper clips, and when they also do not stick she says something in Russian to Annie and the teacher that they do not understand. She takes Annie's clip, puts it in her own pile of clips, and shoves them all aside, shaking her head to indicate no.

❀   ❀   ❀

Karl, nearly 5, puts the painting he has just finished on the shelf under the window. He tells his teacher, "The sun will dry it faster so I can take it home today when my daddy comes to get me."

❀   ❀   ❀

Tyler, 4, and Uri, 3, are building a sand castle. "Don't add too much water," Tyler warns Uri, "or it will get muddy."

❀   ❀   ❀

While mixing watercolor paints to make a shade of orange that matches her shirt, 5-year-old Amelia tells her teacher, "I'm sciencing." When the teacher asks her what she means, Amelia explains, "Sciencing is when you figure something out. I'm sciencing how much yellow to add to the red."

According to science researchers Rochel Gelman and Kimberly Brenneman, "to do science is to predict, test, measure, count, record, date one's work, collaborate and communicate" (2004, 156). Based on this definition, young children are always "sciencing," just as Amelia describes her investigations with paint colors. For children like her, science is not about memorizing facts; rather, it is a lively process that involves observing, predicting, experimenting, verifying, and explaining (Brenneman 2009). This approach to science is consistent with the Next Generation Science Standards (2013) for kindergarten through grade 12, which, in addition to covering core content, now also address scientific practices and emphasize cross-cutting concepts. Teachers once questioned whether science was an appropriate topic for preschool education, but in fact science is "here, there, and everywhere" in the early childhood classroom (Neill 2008).

"Science is privileged as a content area in the preschool classroom because it fits so naturally with young children's natural way of processing experience and their inherent curiosity about the functioning of the everyday world" (French 2004, 140). As a result of this desire to engage in the investigative process, young children's fascination with science can be connected to virtually every other area of learning. They develop *critical thinking skills* as

"Doing Science" the Preschool Way: An Example

When young children encounter something they did not expect to happen, their scientific thinking progresses through three steps as, with adult support, they consider the following:

1. What's wrong here?

The children in Mrs. Takanishi's preschool class had washed all the doll clothes during morning group time and hung them outside on the line to dry. Before afternoon free play, they go to bring the doll clothes inside and are surprised that, while some are dry, others are still damp, and several are nearly as wet as when they'd been hung up that morning.

"Now I can't put the blue shirt on Sam [a doll]," says Manuel, clearly disappointed.

"You can use the red one," says Ivan to Manuel. "It's dry."

Manuel accepts the red shirt from Ivan but eyes the blue shirt longingly.

2. What is happening here?

"Why do you suppose some doll clothes are dry, others are still a little wet, and others are very wet?" asks Mrs. Takanishi.

Manuel looks up, his disappointment now converted to curiosity. He ventures an explanation, although his voice isn't certain. "The blue shirt is bigger? So it takes longer to dry?"

Soledad feels the yellow dress and shakes her head. "Uh, uh. The yellow dress is even bigger than the blue shirt, and it's all dry."

"Mmm," says Mrs. Takanishi. "The yellow dress and the red shirt were next to each other on the clothesline. I wonder if that has anything to do with it."

The children walk up and down the clothesline. At one point, Ivan says, "Hey, I can see my shadow!"

Jenna stands beside Ivan and says, "That's because we're in the sun."

"I know!" says Manuel, excited. "The clothes in the sun are dry, but the ones in the shade aren't."

3. Where's the proof?

"So you think the sun dried some of the doll clothes, but the ones we hung in the shade are still wet. How can you know for sure?" asks Mrs. Takanishi.

"Me and Ivan can feel the ones in the sun," offers Manuel, "and Jenna and Soledad can do the ones in the shade." The children divide into two groups and call out their observations.

Indeed, it initially appears that the doll clothes hanging in the sun are dry and those in the shade are wet, but the children make another discovery.

"Hey wait!" says Manuel, wrapping his hand around a thick brown-checked doll jacket in the sun. "This is still kind of wet."

"And this is almost dry," says Jenna, touching a thin white doll shirt on the shady end of the clothesline.

"So some clothes in the sun are still a little wet, and some clothes in the shade are dry," says the teacher and waits to see if the children agree with her summation.

"Did you move them?" Ivan asks Mrs. Takanishi.

"No," she answers, laughing. "I was inside the classroom with you all morning. Could there be another reason?"

The children offer different explanations. One child says he thinks it is the color ("White dries fastest, and brown dries slowest"). Another child, remembering an activity the class did the previous day with sponges and water, suggests that the clothes that were dry had been wrung out "really, really hard" before being hung up. Soledad, recalling a recent time when her family came home from swimming, says, "My bathing suit dried quick, but my towel took longer. It's thick like a blanket."

The preschoolers consider these ideas, and Mrs. Takanishi asks how they can find out which one(s) explains what they observe. The children decide to rewash two shirts that are about the same size and similar in color, and then they will hang one in the sun and one in the shade. They will check them again when they finish afternoon snack.

Manuel takes the small red shirt inside. "I sure hope it fits Sam," he says.

they attempt to understand the what, how, and why of the events they observe. Using all their senses to fully experience the world around them heightens children's *perceptual abilities.* The study of science promotes *language* learning as preschoolers share their observations and conclusions. Science learning also supports *mathematics,* as children count, measure, and look for patterns in the phenomena they observe. Representing their science-related actions and ideas engages children in *creative arts.* Finally, scientific inquiry involves *social collaboration.* In fact, trying to resolve the conflicting explanations of peers can motivate children to change their theories more than comments or questions from adults (Tudge & Caruso 1988; Vygotsky 1978).

Science learning in the early childhood curriculum should capitalize on children's "natural inclination to learn about their world" (Landry & Forman 1999, 133), expose them to the uses and benefits of scientific processes in everyday life, and involve them in scientific inquiry as they figure out how things work. While children are eager to explore their surroundings on their own, they nevertheless depend on adults to give them a rich environment for scientific inquiry and to develop their child-guided discoveries into a growing understanding of how the world works.

Young Children's Development in Science

"Doing science" involves three related strands of development (Gelman & Brenneman 2004). First is recognizing that something that was expected to happen did not occur. Very young children may simply accept what they see. However, as they accumulate knowledge and experience, children develop expectations and become aware of discrepancies. They ask themselves, "What's wrong here?"

Realizing they need to adjust their thinking, preschoolers next ask, "What is happening here?" They may repeat an action or look and listen again to double-check their observation. Next they may vary it slightly. If they still don't observe what they expect to happen, children construct an alternate theory. It may not be accurate, but they will be satisfied if it fits with their experience.

The final step is answering the question, "Where's the proof?" On their own, preschoolers are not likely to methodically test their theories. They use intuition and overgeneralize. However, with adult support, preschoolers can be more systematic and refine their ideas. The adult's role is *not* to tell children the answer but rather to provide materials and support "so children can test and find out on their own whether their ideas are correct or not" (DeVries & Sales 2011, 2).

This process of scientific inquiry is a natural subject of study for early childhood researchers because of young children's evident interest in observing and thinking about their world (Eshach & Fried 2005). Adults can see inquiry skills at work whenever preschoolers are doing the following:

1. Raising questions about objects and events around them
2. Exploring objects, materials, and events by acting upon them and noticing what happens
3. Making careful observation of objects, organisms, and events using all of their senses
4. Describing, comparing, sorting, classifying, and ordering in terms of observable characteristics and properties
5. Using a variety of simple tools to extend their observations

6. Engaging in simple investigations in which they make predictions, gather and interpret data, recognize simple patterns, and draw conclusions

7. Recording observations, explanations, and ideas through multiple forms of representation including drawings, simple graphs, writing, and movement

8. Working collaboratively with others

9. Sharing and discussing ideas and listening to new perspectives (Worth & Grollman 2003, 18)

Teaching and Learning in Science

To promote meaningful experiences in science, the intentional teacher takes care to design the physical setting, plan the areas of science children will focus on, design experiences that build on the materials and activities of interest to children, and establish overall goals for learning. Once children begin exploring, however, "what actually happens emerges from a dynamic interaction among the children's interests and questions, the materials, and the teacher's goals" (Worth & Grollman 2003, 158). To enhance this interchange, adults can do the following:

- Introduce children to the steps in the scientific method. While preschoolers are more random in their investigations than adults, they use many of the same procedures. To help children become familiar with each step in the process, adults can use science-related words to label their actions. Gelman and Brenneman (2004) suggest introducing preschoolers to "the vocabulary and methods of *observe, predict,* and *check*" (153). They offer an example in which children explore a whole apple and the teacher writes down what they say (it's red, round, smooth, and cold) because, as the teacher tells them, "scientists record their observations." Next, the children make a prediction—"something like a guess," the teacher says—about what's inside (it's white and has seeds). Finally, after cutting open their apples, children check their predictions against what they find (it's white and has seeds; it's also wet).

- Create opportunities for surprise and discrepancy. Young children's scientific ideas develop when they encounter *cognitive discrepancy* (that is, when they observe something they did not expect). "Unexpected events, when embedded in the child's own processes of exploration, provide rich opportunities for encouraging the flow of thinking" (Landry & Forman 1999, 147). Adults can create natural (not contrived) opportunities for them to have these experiences. For example, furnishing new materials that act differently from familiar ones will pique their interest (such as tree blocks that do not stack as neatly as unit ones). To help children reflect on the reason(s) behind the discrepancy, adults can provide related materials for children to test out their ideas and occasionally make "I wonder why . . ." statements and pose "What if . . . ?" questions to children.

- Encourage documentation. Because preschoolers focus on the here and now, they may forget what they observed earlier. This can limit their ability to make connections and draw conclusions. Fortunately, 3- and 4-year-olds are able to create and interpret representations of their experiences. This allows them, with adult assistance, to record data by drawing pictures, taking photos, and making and interpreting simple charts and graphs (Katz & Chard 2000). This documentation acts as a visual reminder as children construct their scientific explanations.

- Support collaborative investigation and problem solving. Social interaction doesn't just help children construct ideas; it actually deepens their understanding. As they attempt to describe what they see, children attend to more details and seek words to explain their reasoning.

Fitting the Learning Experience to the Learning Objective

As noted, early science learning is primarily about carrying out scientific procedures, not memorizing facts. Although children are not as systematic as adults, they engage in a version of the scientific method that lets them explore, discover, and draw conclusions (not necessarily correct ones) from their experiences. That said, there is a body of knowledge that is appropriate for preschoolers to learn in this content area. For example, they are uncovering basic laws of physics when they figure out how a mechanical device works or experiment with ramps and pathways, and they learn what sustains life when they plant a garden or take care of the class pet. Increasingly, in today's society, young children are also learning about technology and using interactive media to learn about other subjects. As children engage with their environment, the questions they ask inevitably lead them to acquire specific information about the natural and physical world around them. The following sections discuss two areas of children's science learning: scientific procedure and learning and sharing scientific ideas.

Scientific Procedure

Preschoolers carry out the scientific method in an age-appropriate fashion. On their own, they observe objects and events, and classify (sort) them according to their attributes. [*Note*: When children sort things by measurable attributes—such as length, weight, volume, or duration—they are primarily engaging in mathematics, which is covered in Chap. 7.] Because everything is new to young children, many tend to accept whatever they observe. Adult guidance is therefore needed to help them engage in those aspects of the scientific method that involve thinking and reasoning, such as experimenting, predicting, and drawing conclusions from their experiences.

Child-guided experience is especially important for learnings such as:

Observing

The ability to observe accurately is essential in science. "Observing is paying close attention to something to learn more about it" (Neill 2008, 10). Young children pay attention with all their senses to learn about the natural and physical world. Their observational skills increase over time as their awareness of details progresses from the few to the many, the simple to the complex, and the isolated to the connected. For example, a child's observations about leaves might progress from "the leaf is green, it sticks to the branch, and it feels smooth" to "the leaf also has veins and a stem, leaves grow on opposite sides all down the branch, and leaves on the ground crumble when I pick them up and squeeze them." Children also become increasingly verbal with their observations because they are motivated by a desire to share—and confirm—with others what their senses are experiencing (Gronlund 2006).

Teaching strategies. Children need objects and events to observe, a safe place to carry out their observations, and the descriptive language to share their observations. The following strategies will provide young children with these observational basics:

- Create a sensory-rich environment indoors and outdoors. Set up a sensory table (available through school supply companies) or use galvanized metal tubs or large plastic basins. Fill the table or basin with a rotating set of materials such as sand, water, dishwashing liquid, beads, cotton balls, pebbles, bark, acorns, or shredded paper. For children with sensory sensitivities, consider setting up separate containers for them with materials they are comfortable working with (neither over- nor under-stimulating). If appropriate, offer children thin latex gloves that allow them to feel wet or sticky substances without getting their hands dirty.

- Offer a variety of sensory materials for children to explore during choice time and small group activities—for example, things that
  - Create light and shadow (flashlights, cellophane taped to windows, scarves, wind spinners)
  - Offer distinctive textures (bark, straw, gourds, nubbly wool)
  - Have different aromas (spice jars, beeswax, herb garden)
  - Make noise (musical instruments, timers, hammers, pebbles, feeders that attract songbirds)
  - Have different tastes (fruits, vegetables, grains, condiments)

- Make the environment safe for children to carry out their observations. Reassure them that they are free to explore without either danger to themselves or sanctions from adults. Children should be allowed to make a mess and experiment to observe the effects of their actions. At the same time, children must also have the right to *not* taste, smell, touch, or otherwise use their senses. Grant them full autonomy over what and how they conduct their observations. Provide a way for children who are initially reluctant to approach new materials to do so gradually in their own way, such as using rubber gloves to finger-paint, smelling diluted solutions, or tasting small samples.

○ Provide the vocabulary to help children label, understand, and make use of their observations. "Adult language provides vocabulary to describe the concepts emerging from these investigations and provides models for discourse functions such as describing and explaining" (French 2004, 142). In addition to providing labels for objects (nouns) and actions (verbs), use descriptive words (adjectives, adverbs) to enhance children's observational skills. Repeat the words children use (including those they invent, such as *squinchy* or *flippery*) and match the new ones you introduce to their developmental level. Do the same for dual language learners, using words in English and in their home languages (spelled phonetically so you can pronounce them when talking with the children). Begin by labeling easily observed properties (such as color or loudness) and then mention less obvious ones (such as dampness and temperature). Finally, after focusing on sensory attributes, talk about how things change based on the children's actions or the interactions among the materials themselves (for example, "First the cup floated. Then you poured water in it, and it sank" or "When the sun came out, it melted the snow on the sidewalk").

Classifying

Children classify spontaneously during play (Langer et al. 2003). Early on, they separate objects that share an attribute (such as by taking all the red beads from the pile), although they may switch categories midstream. At the next level, children sort consistently and use the words *same* and *different*, followed by *some, none,* and *all.* They can also say when an object does *not* belong to a set (for example, beads that are not red do not belong in the set of red beads). Next children sort objects based on more than one attribute, such as color and shape. The highest level is when children describe the reason behind the classification, even when someone else has done the sorting. [*Note*: As explained previously, classifying in science refers to qualitative attributes. Sorting by quantitative or measurable attributes is covered on p. 146 in Chap. 7.]

Teaching strategies. Young children love to collect and sort things. In that sense, they are like the adult scientists of a previous era, who primarily concerned themselves with collecting, sorting, and describing species of plant and animal life. To promote and enhance children's spontaneous interest in classification, use the following strategies:

○ Encourage children to collect and sort objects. By labeling classroom areas and materials (using all the languages that the children use), you provide children with an initial basis for categorizing things. (For example, paints belong in the art area; hammers go in the woodworking area.) Nature provides many materials for sorting—shells of different shapes, things that fly or crawl. Neighborhood walks and field trips create added opportunities to make interesting collections. Give each child a container (a small bag or bucket) to gather items. Back in the classroom, encourage children to sort and label their collections and incorporate them in their play. For example, acorns can be placed in the house area for pretend cooking, used in the art area for gluing on paper, or buried in the sand table.

○ Call attention to the similarities and differences between objects. With young children, start with sets of objects that are clearly different (such as buttons and small cars). Then focus on a single attribute that is the same (such as all the red buttons), followed by objects that differ by one attribute (such as red buttons and blue buttons). Later, children can work with two attributes (such as large red buttons and small blue buttons). Last, call attention to things that are the same in some way but different in one or more other ways (such as by noting that all the buttons are red, but some have two holes and some have four holes). Use these types of materials to introduce the concepts of some, none, and all. Do the same with actions; for example, introduce movements at circle time that are the same and different, or a motion that some, none, or all the children do. Play I Spy and go on treasure hunts to look for objects that are the same and/or different. For snacks, serve a variety of foods so children can classify them by look, taste, smell, or texture. Invite parents to suggest or bring in foods that reflect diverse family tastes and cultures, and talk with the children about the similarities and differences they observe.

○ Use *no* and *not* language. For example, when children dress to go outside, note whose jacket has a hood and whose does not. At mealtime, comment on who does and does not want juice. When children make collections, encourage them to identify the attributes that items in a group do not have (for example, "These beads are shiny. Those are not shiny"). Introduce the universal symbol for no (a red circle with a diagonal line superimposed on an image of an object or action). An example is the work-in-progress sign for projects children haven't yet finished. A hand with a line through it means "Do not touch" and sets an object apart from items that are okay to handle. Other ideas for introducing the idea of no or not include these:

Children who are or are not in the program that day

Names that do or do not begin with a particular letter

Words that do or do not rhyme with one another

Things that do or do not make noise

Movements that do or do not use the feet

Adult-guided experience is especially important for learnings such as:

Experimenting

Children experiment for two reasons: out of curiosity (to see how something works) and to solve problems they encounter in play (to get something to work that is not working). Experimentation lets them observe cause-and-effect relationships. Their efforts are still largely trial and error early in preschool, but with adult scaffolding, they can become more systematic. Preschoolers are also increasingly aware that time plays a role in the natural and physical world (Van Scoy & Fairchild 1993). They pay attention to sequence and also observe how long an effect lasts (for example, the water stays slippery after you add dish detergent, but the bubbles dissolve). When children become aware of these factors (cause and effect, sequence, and timing), their questions and the experiments they carry out to answer them become more sophisticated and complex.

Teaching strategies. As with other aspects of science (as well as mathematics), young children sometimes accept things without questioning how or why, or without pursuing further investigation. It's not that they aren't curious; it just may not occur to them to wonder why or how, or they may wonder but not know how to carry out a simple experiment to answer their questions. Adults can help children extend their investigations with the following teaching strategies:

- Ask and answer "What if . . . ?" "Why?" and "How?" questions. For example, you might ask, "How did you get the ball to bounce so high?" "Why do you think it stopped bouncing and began to roll?" "How can we get the sled to slow down?" "What if we move the cups of seeds we planted over to this window?" or "Why do you think the screen changed when you pushed this button, but it didn't change when you pressed that one?" For dual language learners, learn to ask some of these basic questions in the children's home languages. Perhaps more important than the questions adults ask are the questions children ask themselves. If you show interest and surprise ("Wow! It bubbled over the top when we put vinegar in the baking soda!"), it inspires children to ask why or how something happened. You can then provide guidance and ask follow-up questions to help them test out their ideas.

- Encourage children to gradually replace trial and error with systematic experimentation. To promote critical thinking, talk with children about what they are doing and the results of their actions. Carry out simple hands-on experiments with easily observed results (for example, paint with water outdoors and watch the pavement dry or listen to the sounds of shakers filled with different materials). Suggest that children try new ways of using familiar materials, and comment on how changing an action changed an outcome. Offer challenges that suggest step-by-step investigation (for example, "How could you make the waterwheel turn a little bit faster? What about a medium amount faster? How could you make it go *really* fast?").

- Provide materials and experiences for investigating how things change with time. Make time concrete for preschoolers with materials such as tools to signal stopping and starting (timers, stop signs, instruments) and things they can set in motion (wheeled toys, metronomes, balls, tops, pinwheels). Draw children's attention to the role that time plays in nature—for example, kittens grow bigger, leaves turn brown, and sand compacts as it's walked on day after day. Ask questions that encourage them to test their theories about time (for example, "Do you think the little tomato seeds or the big squash seeds will germinate faster? How can we keep track?").

Predicting

Predicting is more than simply making a guess or saying what one hopes will happen. It involves using prior knowledge to anticipate what is likely to happen in the future. Preschoolers have enough experience to make an educated guess in many situations. They can be relatively objective, differentiating between what they *want* to happen and what they think is *likely* to happen. Prediction thus involves emotional maturity as well as intellectual capacity. As children become more systematic with their experiments, they also become better predictors. Their predictions may not be accurate, but they follow the children's logic. Predicting also helps preschoolers think in new ways. Instead of focusing on the here and now, they think about the there and then. The more opportunities children have to engage in this type of thinking, the better they get at reflecting on their experiences and observations, and using them to make predictions (Church 2003).

Children who are dual language learners are just as able as their monolingual English-speaking peers to anticipate and predict, but they may not be able to understand the questions teachers ask in English and they may not be able to communicate what they know. For this reason, it is best to focus initially on science explorations that involve the here and now and save prediction activities for later in the year as dual language learners gain a better understanding of the language the teachers use.

Teaching strategies. The following strategies will draw on preschoolers' knowledge and logical reasoning to help extend their capacity for making predictions:

- Help children reflect on the similarities between their past and present experiences. Scaffold their predictive abilities by using their skills in observing, classifying, and experimenting. For example, help children recall what they observed before asking them whether the same thing might happen again with similar objects; use classification to help children determine whether objects might behave the same way or differently; and encourage children to reflect on the information they gathered through experimentation. The adult's role is not to figure out the answer for children but to help them apply their knowledge and skills to make their own prediction.

- Encourage children to say what they think will happen (and why). This creates an opportunity for them to think about their knowledge and experience and how they might apply to the current situation. For example, when his teacher asked Rajiv why he predicted, "There's gonna be lots of leaves at outside time," Rajiv pointed out the window and replied, "It's really windy and the wind makes them fall down. When I help my auntie rake leaves, she lets me jump in them." Asking children to voice their predictions opens the door for you to ask about the reasoning behind them.

- Invite children to verify their predictions. Children are generally content with making a prediction, and they are not likely to test it on their own. Adult encouragement can make them curious about whether their expectations are accurate. Useful comments and questions include "Let's check it out" and "How can we be sure?" To encourage further reflection, discuss which observations did (or did not) match children's predictions and why they think this is so.

Drawing conclusions

Based on their observations and experiments, children may conclude that their current beliefs are correct or that they need to change their thinking. Piaget (1950) used the term *assimilation* to describe when children take in new information that matches their current thinking, and the term *accommodation* to describe when they alter their understanding to account for contradictory information. At first, preschoolers' conclusions are based on immediate experiences, but later they begin to generalize (Bruner, Olver, & Greenfield 1996). For example, if roses smell and roses are flowers, then other flowers must smell too. Children often overgeneralize, but additional experiences that contradict their initial conclusions eventually lead them to change their thinking. Being in a safe environment where they feel free to change their minds helps them think flexibly.

Teaching strategies. To encourage children to reflect on their experiences and draw conclusions with increasing flexibility and logic, try these ideas:

- Provide materials and experiences that work in similar but not identical ways (for example, playdough and clay change properties depending on the amount of water in them; only some bushes have berries). These opportunities allow children to make generalizations but also discover differences that can alter their thinking. To help preschoolers draw conclusions from several sources of evidence, encourage them to gather a wide range of data and explore different alternatives. For example, you might ask the following questions:

  - What else could you do (or look at) to find out?
  - Is there another way to check out your idea?
  - Is there something else that looks (or sounds or smells) the same? What about something that is different?

- Encourage children to reflect on the processes and outcomes they observe. Make comments ("I notice the water isn't going down the drain") and ask open-ended questions ("Why does the furnace make noise when it comes on?"). Call children's attention to things that contradict their expectations. They may not notice them on their own but may be intrigued if you point them out. The adult's role is not to impart a body of facts but to promote a spirit of scientific inquiry. Your sense of wonder and curiosity will be contagious. (For more on the value of reflecting, see p. 40 in Chap. 3.)

Learning and Sharing Scientific Ideas

Young children's curiosity propels their interest in science. With little outside inducement, they explore different types of tools and, in today's world, rapidly changing technology. Preschoolers are eager to find out how things work and how they can use them to carry out their play ideas. Excited by these discoveries, children readily communicate their findings with others. Learning about the natural and physical world is also of great interest to young children. However, as with other bodies of knowledge, children depend on adults to impart specific information about the natural and physical world and call their attention to scientific phenomena that children might miss or take for granted on their own.

Child-guided experience is especially important for learnings such as:

Learning about tools and technology

Children initially explore *tools* as materials in their own right, curious to discover how they work and eager to gain control over the tools. As they acquire competence with a particular tool (such as scissors), they think about how that tool can help them accomplish a goal or solve a problem (such as cutting strips of paper for pretend money). The ability to create a mental representation of the tool allows preschoolers to imagine how it can be applied in a new situation to produce a desired result (such as cutting different shapes to glue on a collage). Problem solving with tools builds young children's conceptual awareness because it involves "planning, sequential thinking, and predicting what specific actions with a tool might do" (Haugen 2010, 50).

Technology can play a useful role in early science learning (as well as mathematics) when used appropriately. First and foremost, technology should supplement rather than replace hands-on learning with real materials. Moreover, *interactive media* should be "designed to facilitate active and creative use by young children and to encourage social engagement with other children and adults" (NAEYC & Fred Rogers Center 2012, 1). While the American Academy of Pediatrics discourages screen time for children under the age of 2 (2011), preschoolers can benefit from developing digital literacy, such as becoming familiar with the mechanics of devices (turning a device on or off, using arrow keys or touchscreens) and using software that is interactive and open ended and that promotes discovery rather than emphasizing drill-and-practice. Watching brief video clips can support dual language learners with linguistically appropriate activities and help them understand science tools and concepts (Simon & Nemeth 2013). Computers can also serve as catalysts for social interaction. Preschoolers enjoy working together at the computer to solve problems, talk about what they are doing, help and teach friends, and create rules for turn taking and cooperation (Simon & Donohue 2011).

Teaching strategies. Using tools offers children many chances to discover how they work and fosters other types of science learning. Appropriate forms of technology can also support young children as they explore the world of science during play. The following strategies encourage children to learn about tools and technology in their environment:

○ Provide tools in all areas of the classroom. Don't limit these to typical science tools, such as magnifying glasses, magnets, scales, pulleys, or plastic thermometers. Many other items promote science learning—windup clocks, cell phones (with batteries removed), sticky tape, flashlights, and carpentry tools. Look for tools at garage sales and ask families to contribute mechanical gadgets from home.

○ Encourage children to use the same tool in different ways. For example, children might use hammers to pound various objects (nails, golf tees) into different surfaces (wood, clay) or to make different musical sounds (banging against metal or a wooden block). Create opportunities for children to use tools as they learn in other content areas—for example, using a variety of modeling tools with playdough (creative arts), measuring with conventional and unconventional tools (mathematics), or using a timer to take turns (social and emotional development). Take field trips to hardware or kitchen supply stores so children can discover a range of mechanical and electrical gadgets that perform one or more functions.

○ Choose appropriate computers, mobile devices, and interactive software. While computers and other electronic devices should not dominate the learning environment, technology is a fact of life today. Making it available in the classroom is important, especially for preschoolers with limited access at home. To provide appropriate experiences, model the safe and careful use of electronic equipment, choose child-friendly devices and interactive software, encourage social interaction by locating computers in a spot where two or more children can use them together, and talk to children about their problem-solving strategies as they use the computer and other devices.

Communicating ideas

Communicating their scientific discoveries encourages children to use if/then language and to think in terms of cause and effect. The very act of talking makes them more observant. Symbolic communication (such as drawing, writing, demonstrating, building, and role playing) helps preschoolers document their observations, find patterns, and recognize relationships (Chalufour & Worth 2004). When adults and peers show interest in these various forms of scientific communications, it affirms to children that what interests them is worth paying attention to.

Teaching strategies. Because each child has his own way of communicating, adults should provide a variety of opportunities for children to share their scientific discoveries. Try the following ideas to encourage verbal and symbolic expression about science learning:

- Use scientific language to talk with children about their actions, observations, and discoveries. As science researchers Landry and Forman (1999) note, "Science, for children as well as adults, is not done in a vacuum but in a social realm within which ideas are discussed, debated, and take shape" (137). Listen to what children say, especially their "how" and "why" questions, and answer them patiently. Share your own observations and introduce new vocabulary words ("I scraped *frost* off my windshield this morning"). Use new words repeatedly and in context to help children understand and eventually use these terms themselves.

- Provide opportunities for children to symbolically represent their scientific experiences. Nonverbal representations are especially valuable for children who are dual language learners because they allow the children to show which scientific inquiries are of interest to them; such representations also provide adults with the opportunity to introduce science vocabulary (in the home language and English) as they describe and discuss what the children have chosen to draw, build, or act out. Here are some examples:

  - **Artwork.** Provide drawing and modeling materials and ask children to describe elements of their art-making processes (for example, the materials they used, what they did with them, what happened as a result). Their descriptions will provide a window into their scientific thinking (for example, about how houses are built or where animals live).

    Josie puts shells and marbles on the balance scale, gets paper and markers, and says to her teacher, "I'm gonna draw a picture with two shells here (pointing to one side), a line down the middle, and six marbles here (pointing to the other side)." Her teacher comments, "You are going to draw a picture of how you got the shells and marbles to balance on the scale."

    Josie's friend, Mei-lin, is still learning English. When Mei-lin finishes her own drawing of the shells and marbles, the teacher gently takes her hand and walks her and her picture over to the science area. The teacher holds Mei-lin's picture next to the scale to show that she understands that was what Mei-lin's drawing showed.

  - **Pretend play.** Children show their understanding of how things work during role play. Provide time, props, and prop-making tools, and play as a partner in their scenarios. For example, while pretending to bake a cake with a child in the house area, a teacher asked for something to stir with. The child handed her an electric mixer (with the cord removed) and said, "You can't really plug it in. You have to pretend it works." To extend the child's idea, the teacher replied, "You need a cord so electricity can run the motor that turns the beaters."

  - **Writing.** Writing tools such as clipboards and markers encourage children to record their ideas during playtime as well as on field trips.

Computer Technology

Computers can play a valuable role in early science education if the technology is used appropriately. "Effective uses of technology and media are active, hands-on, engaging, and empowering; give the child control; provide adaptive scaffolds to ease the accomplishment of tasks; and are used as one of many options to support children's learning" (NAEYC & Fred Rogers Center 2012, 6). For young children, this involves becoming competent with the mechanics of the devices and learning different software programs and apps, which should be open ended and promote discovery. Good programs pose a problem, ask children to solve it, and provide feedback. Programs that pose problems that have "correct" answers can be productive if the feedback causes children to reflect on where their reasoning was off and solve the problem differently. If the program does not do this, then an adult working alongside the children can.

Technology has the added advantage of increasing children's flexibility with manipulatives; that is, they can often move on-screen objects more easily than real objects. On-screen objects don't pose the problems of size or awkwardness of handling that real-life objects might, and most children work well with a keyboard and mouse or touchscreen. This is *not* to say that computers should replace real objects, which also provide other sensory feedback and foster motor skills. Rather, computers can extend the range of materials children use and the possibilities for their transformation.

Finally, "contrary to initial fears, computers do not isolate children. Rather, they serve as potential catalysts for social interaction" (Clements 1999, 122). Children working at the computer solve problems together, talk about what they are doing, help and teach friends, and create rules for cooperation. In fact, they often prefer working on the computer with a friend to doing it alone (Simon & Donohue 2011).

Adults play a critical role in mediating children's exposure to and use of computers in early learning. The following are the responsibilities teachers must fulfill, and the opportunities they can create, while using technology with young children.

- Choose child-friendly hardware, such as oversized keyboards, colored keyboard keys, a small mouse, and touchscreens. Help children acquire basic mechanical skills through modeling and guided instruction. Arrange the environment so children are able to work together and, thus, learn from their peers.

- Select software or apps that emphasize open-ended discovery learning rather than drill-and-practice activities. Introduce the software to a few children at a time. For example, demonstrate what you can do with a program at small group time or at the beginning of choice time. Give every interested child the opportunity to try it. Then make the program available throughout the day.

- Use computers and mobile devices to facilitate social exchange. Allow enough space for more than one chair; an ideal setup is two in front of the screen for children and one to the side for an adult. If resources permit, have more than one computer or tablet so children can share ideas. Place computers where they are visible from other areas in the room so children can wander over and join in. Encourage children to work together. Be available to help to mediate social disputes (see p. 60 in Chap. 4 for more on this).

- Encourage children to verbalize their thinking and reasoning as they solve problems with the technology itself or with problems and puzzles posed by the program. Encourage them to reflect on their solutions if the program's feedback says their answer is wrong. It is especially important for adults to be present at these times so children do not get discouraged and walk away. Turn error messages into learning opportunities.

- Balance computer and tablet activities with lots of opportunities to manipulate real objects and solve comparable real-life situations.

Reading books written for preschoolers about science and scientists will also inspire children to communicate their own ideas by "writing" them down. Be sure to include scientists from different backgrounds (cultures, countries, and languages as well as those with physical disabilities, such as physicist Stephen Hawking) so children will feel pride and begin to see themselves as potential scientists, too.

○ **Lists, charts, and graphs.** Young children can apply their emerging ability to work with data (see p. 153 in Chap. 7) to share the results of their scientific investigations. Ask reflective questions to help them document and interpret their findings, such as "How should we label the columns?" "Should we make hatch marks or write numerals?" and "Why do you suppose there are more in this column than the other column?"

Adult-guided experience is especially important for learnings such as:

Learning about the natural world

The natural world includes topics typically covered under the life sciences (biology, botany, zoology) and covers the diversity and variation of the organisms in our environment. For young children, learning about the natural world means recognizing what is (or is not) alive, examining the characteristics and behaviors of plants and animals, learning where things live (habitats) and what they need to stay alive, and experiencing the process of growth and decay. Preschoolers become aware of what can change or transform different types of wildlife (for example, sun and water help plants grow; when the weather gets cold, the leaves turn colors and fall off the trees). Their emerging ability to hold in mind a mental image of what something was like before makes it possible for them to see how it is different now. Young children focus on the aspects of the life cycle that are meaningful to them. For example, if they plant a garden, children will be curious about how quickly the seeds germinate, the effect of their caretaking on the plants' growth, and the attributes that mean a flower is ready to bloom or a fruit or vegetable is ready to eat.

Young children have many ideas about how the natural world works. Although their concepts can seem naive to adults, they are often quite sophisticated when viewed within the child's system of logic (for example, trees grow big to keep us cool in the summer; worms live under rocks because it's dark there and they can sleep). Children hold on to their scientific theories because these theories make sense to them and help them organize their observations (Landry & Forman 1999). Only after repeated experiences—and discrepancies from their expectations—do they adjust their thinking. Preschoolers also begin to approach the natural world in a less egocentric fashion. Instead of considering only how phenomena affect them (whether an animal is friendly or scary, whether a vegetable tastes good or yucky), they begin to think more broadly about how living things relate to one another.

Children's questions reveal what aspects of the natural world interest them. For example, here are some questions overheard in one preschool classroom over the course of a year:

> What do plants eat?
>
> Why do bees buzz?
>
> Why did my dog die?
>
> Where does the food go after I swallow it?
>
> Why does medicine make us better?
>
> Why is your hair a different color than mine?
>
> Why does sand stick to my skin?
>
> Why do birds build nests?
>
> Why do turtles have shells?
>
> Why does dust make you sneeze?
>
> How come we can't fly?
>
> Why do only some flowers smell?

Teaching strategies. The plant and animal diversity in the environment is all new and exciting to young children. To support their curiosity and amazement about the natural world, try the following strategies in both the indoor and outdoor learning environment:

○ Provide materials and experiences for children to gather knowledge about the natural world. Assemble collections of living (or once living) things for them to examine and compare (plants, animals, shells, seeds). Supplement real objects with printed materials and realistic replicas. Encourage children to sort these collections, using all their senses, to identify similarities and differences. Call their attention to how the materials change over time or as a result of their actions (flowers decay and lose their smell; dry leaves crumble if you squeeze them). Use objects and experiences to build children's awareness of basic animal and plant needs (air, food, water, light, rest). Visit nearby rural and/or urban environments (bodies of water, forests, farmland, deserts, mountains, city parks). Go on field trips. Take pictures for a class album and bring back representative natural objects for the children to sort and use as props in their pretend play.

○ Encourage children to connect their observations about the natural world. Build on the objects and events that interest them in the indoor and outdoor environment. Ask "How?" and "Why?" questions that lead them to reflect on the physical characteristics or behavior of things in nature (for example, "How do birds fly?" "Why are berries sweet?" "Why do we grow bigger as we get older?"). You do not have to know the answers to these questions yourself. Generate theories and seek answers together with them. Listen to their explanations for a window into their understanding of nature.

Learning about the physical world

Studying the physical world (which in the context of this discussion includes physical science and earth science) allows young children to explore objects, materials, and events to understand how things work and what happens when they are acted upon in different ways. As young children investigate the physical world, they explore such phenomena as how a ramp's angle affects the speed of their toy cars, how water flows around barriers, what makes blocks balance or fall down, why objects of the same size have different weights, what the properties of solids and liquids are, how to make bubbles, what does or does not stick to a magnet, what makes a shadow, how to alter sounds by blowing through a tube or hitting a drum hard or soft, or how fast snow melts in sun and shade. As with phenomena in the natural world, preschoolers become aware of changes and cycles important to them. For example, weather in the abstract carries little meaning (hence, daily calendar time about the weather evokes little interest), but if the arrival of snow means they can go sledding, children will pay attention.

Similar to their experiences with the natural world, young children develop theories about the physical world that make sense to them (for example, the sun makes things warm, so if the sun is out, it must be warm, even in the winter). Cognitive discrepancies—

when their observations do not match their expectations—gradually spur them to rethink their reasoning. Likewise, as with their curiosity about the natural world, the questions children ask tell us the things about the physical world that interest them. Here are some of the questions a group of preschoolers asked about the physical world:

Why is the stick heavier than the feather even though they are the same size?

How does the sun light up the sky?

What makes a shadow?

Why do ice cubes melt?

Why can I slide on ice but not on wood chips?

How do scissors cut?

What makes gears go around?

Why did the bulb burn out?

Why does a magnet attract some things and not others?

Why do rocks come in different sizes?

Why does it snow when it's cold outside?

Where does the shadow go when you turn off the flashlight?

Teaching strategies. Adults can apply the same strategies to the study of the physical world that they use to support young children's investigation of the natural world. The particular materials and experiences will differ (handling pulleys instead of plants; observing speed instead of seeds), but adults play a crucial role in helping children reflect on the attributes and transformations they observe. To help preschoolers make sense of the physical world, try following the ideas.

- Provide materials and experiences to enable children to gather knowledge about the physical world. Encourage children to investigate objects such as soil, rocks, and hardware fasteners. Provide materials for them to make things such as different sounds, shadows, bubbles, ramps, and other structures. Encourage children to explore these objects and the things they create using all their senses, and to describe the similarities and differences they observe. Provide opportunities for them to explore how things work physically (such as mechanical devices, musical instruments) and how their actions change an object's attributes (for example, when they soak a towel in water, it gets heavier). Take field trips to safe building sites, hardware stores, and planetariums with age-appropriate exhibits and programs. As with field trips to explore the natural world, take pictures to put in a class album and bring back materials for the children to sort and use in construction or pretend play.

- Encourage children to connect their observations about the physical world. Ask "How?" and "Why?" questions that lead them to reflect on the appearance and function of familiar objects and actions (such as "Why does the door swing closed by itself?" and "Why does pumping your legs make you go higher on the swing?") Again, you need not know the answers yourself. The aim is to encourage children to reflect and seek answers. Refer them to one another to broaden their perspective and expand their thinking.

Ian announces that his family is making an ice rink in their backyard. "We're going to shovel snow, put water on it, and wait one minute for it to turn to ice." His teacher comments to the group, "I wonder how snow turns into ice." The children offer various theories: "When the water dries, the snow gets hard"; "The water makes the snow cold"; "It takes more than a minute. You gotta wait all night"; and "When the water freezes, it gets slippery."

"Because science is so engaging for children, it serves as an ideal content area for supporting children's learning and development. We, and many of the teachers we have worked with, have never seen anything—with the possible exception of being read aloud to—that consistently engages young children's interest and participation to the extent that science activities do. Why would this be the case?" (French 2004, 139). This chapter answers French's rhetorical question. Young children's natural curiosity about how the world works drives them to investigate what they perceive using all their senses. Despite their innate curiosity, however, preschoolers depend on adults to help them think about what they observe, become aware of and resolve discrepancies, and document and communicate their conclusions. For this deeper learning to occur, the intentional teacher must embark on a scientific journey of discovery alongside the children.

For Further Consideration

1. Why do some early childhood educators underestimate young children's scientific abilities? What does this underestimation say about how practitioners define this subject area and their self-perceived knowledge and skills?

2. Would you describe yourself as someone who is comfortable with science? How does, or how will, your attitude toward science affect how you engage children with this subject?

3. What scientific knowledge should we expect preschoolers to master? What areas of substantive knowledge are appropriate or necessary for young children to have?

4. Do gender differences in science (favoring the involvement of boys) emerge in the preschool years? If your answer is no, what lessons can we learn from early childhood practice to sustain girls' interest in this subject and prevent the emergence of a gender gap in later years? If your answer is yes, how can we alter our practices to instill and fortify in girls a lasting interest in science early on?

5. When and how are technology and interactive media appropriate for use with young children? How can we evaluate whether media are interactive and promote cognitive and social learning?

Chapter 9

Social Studies

The preschoolers in Ms. Sharif's class take a walk around the block at outside time. They pass the bodega, a fish store, the pharmacy, a produce stand, and a used clothing store. In front of the produce stand, Adam waves to Mr. and Mrs. Torricelli, the owners, who are piling fruit on the carts. "They live upstairs from me!" Adam announces. Concetta points to the fruit and says, "Manzanas and plátanos," and Ms. Sharif replies, "Yes, apples and bananas." "I know Mr. Franks," pipes up Adeela. "He owns the grocery store on my block." "My mommy and I go to the library," says Rajeev. The children continue talking about the neighborhood places they visit with their families and the people who work there (for example, "the man at the shoe store," "the money lady [cashier] at the corner store," "the popcorn guy at the movies").

Later that day, at choice time, Adam sets up a "fruit store," and the other children make purchases. Ms. Sharif asks for some of the fruits they saw at the produce stand (such as plantains, mangoes, rambutan), and the children talk about the vegetables and fruits they eat at home with their families.

Often young children's first sense of community outside the home comes from attending an early childhood setting. As children learn to get along, make friends, and participate in decision making, they are engaging in social studies learning. Typically, the social studies curriculum also expands children's horizons beyond the school into the neighborhood and the wider world.

The National Council for the Social Studies (NCSS) says that "the aim of social studies is the promotion of **civic competence**—the knowledge, intellectual processes, and democratic dispositions required of students to be active and engaged participants in public life" (2010, 1). Although state standards for social studies in early childhood vary, they address the following common themes: 1) membership in a democratic classroom community, 2) location and place relationships, 3) similarities and differences in personal and family characteristics, 4) basic economic principles as they relate to children's lives, and 5) appreciation of one's own and other cultures in a diverse society (Gronlund 2006). Early childhood teachers help children begin to understand these concepts so they can later generalize the ideas to school and eventually the larger society.

Social studies draws on several disciplines, including history, geography, economics, and ecology. Although these subjects sound abstract when applied to young children, preschoolers deal with them in concrete ways (Seefeldt, Castle, & Falconer 2013). For example, children between 4 and 7 years old become aware of personal time—that is, how past, present, and future are sequentially ordered in the history of their own lives. By age 6 or 7, they have rudimentary clock and calendar skills. Likewise, the components of geography include spatial relations and the places people occupy. An awareness of nature and the importance of taking care of animals and plants in one's immediate environment give real meaning to an appreciation of ecological diversity and interdependence. As Mindes (2005) notes,

> In the preschool and primary years, social studies offer a structure for broad, theme-based content—content organized around a topic [or project] and offering multiple entry points and significant opportunities for investigation. For children, such content serves as a training ground for acquiring problem-solving skills as well as a laboratory for the development and elaboration of interpersonal coping skills and strategies. (16)

While social studies learning is related to social and emotional development (see Chap. 4), these content areas are increasingly being differentiated in the early childhood curriculum. Social studies learning helps children connect to the larger society around them as they become aware of the practices, times, places, and values that associate them with and/or distinguish them from others. Social and emotional learning underlies this growing awareness—for example, children need to form a unique self-identity before they identify where they fit in a group. However, social studies leads children down a wider and more divergent set of paths as they gain knowledge of themselves and their immediate community. In social studies learning, young children lay a foundation for their later understanding of the principles and practices that guide the institutions of the society in which they live.

Young Children's Development in Social Studies

From the moment of birth, children are attuned to their social world. Preschoolers are already quite adept at observing and interpreting the behavior of others with respect to themselves. The early childhood setting helps them expand this capacity and develop the knowledge and skills they will need to live in a complex and increasingly diverse society. Beginning with their interactions with the individuals in their families, neighborhoods, and school, young children establish a foundation that will later enable them to branch out to encounter new people and settings when they become older and eventually take their place in the adult world. Aside from their families, early childhood settings are where young children typically first learn to become responsible citizens.

For example, preschoolers learn about human diversity—language and culture, beliefs and practices, living environments and relationships, abilities and needs—by interacting with a wide range of adults and peers. They take on different roles during pretend play, read stories and informational books about interesting people and situations, explore the arts of many lands, and go on field trips in their communities. When young children solve problems collaboratively in the classroom, it is a microcosm of the democratic process (Gartrell 2012). Caring for the indoor and outdoor learning environment prepares them for becoming stewards of the planet. These types of skills and understandings are evident in the following vignettes:

> When Sheena, the teacher, notices rice on floor of the house area, she says she is afraid that someone might slip and fall. Doyle, age 3, gets the broom, and 4-year-old Nadia offers to hold the dustpan while he sweeps up the spilled rice. "Now no one will get hurt," Nadia says, as she empties the dustpan into the trash.

❀　　❀　　❀

Since Marcus is absent when it is his turn to pass out the napkins at snack time, the preschoolers decide that Penny, who is next on the list, should do it that day. However, they agree that as soon as Marcus comes back, it will be his turn, even if another name is next on the list by then.

❀ ❀ ❀

At arrival time, Carl tells the other children, "Last night I went to the powwow and danced the bear dance with Grandpa John. That's how they did it in the old days, before I was born. A man told a story about Mistahi-maskwa. That's how you say 'Big Bear' in Cree."

❀ ❀ ❀

When Gabe's mom comes to pick him up, he tells his teacher, "Theo lives around the corner from me. I'm playing at his house after school today."

❀ ❀ ❀

During cleanup time, Kristen puts the torn newspapers she'd used to line her "doggie cage" into the paper recycling bin.

The development of social studies knowledge and skills parallels early learning in other areas. It progresses from the simple to the complex, shifts from a self-focus to taking the perspectives of others, and involves learning about social systems (such as how communities operate) and specific social concepts (in history, geography, and so on; Seefeldt, Castle, & Falconer 2013). Two cognitive components are especially important to social studies learning in the preschool years. One is the child's growing awareness of social norms and customs (at home, at school, and, through media exposure, to the wider culture), also known as socialization. The other is using classification skills. Preschoolers are increasingly adept at identifying things that are the same and things that are different. They also begin to realize that two or more things can be similar in some ways and dissimilar in others. These cognitive and social understandings help children engage with social studies in ways that are meaningful to them and connect them with others.

Teaching and Learning in Social Studies

Two general strategies are helpful in enabling young children to acquire an understanding of social studies and apply this learning in their daily experiences: starting with concrete experiences and moving to general principles, and helping children grow from self-awareness to more awareness of others.

Building From Concrete Experiences to General Principles

Because preschoolers are capable of forming mental representations, they can apply their concrete knowledge of the here and now to the there and then (Seefeldt, Castle, & Falconer 2013). This means they can picture situations they have not (yet) experienced themselves, such as real people living in times and places they have never seen or imaginary creatures doing things they have never done. Young children use concrete signs, such as clothing, facial features, furniture, plants, and transportation, as clues about the "when and where" of the situation depicted. They draw on their own experiences—for example, visiting a grandparent's house where things appear and are done differently than in their own homes—to understand the general idea that things can change with time and place.

Interactions with different people also help children become aware of the principles that shape and explain human relationships. For example, talking with one another about their home lives, preschoolers learn that families have different living arrangements, languages, jobs, celebrations, religious beliefs, evening routines, and food and music preferences. With adult support, they begin to form mental categories within which to classify this information. Thoughtful, well-timed adult comments can help children create these structures for appreciating similarities and differences (for example, "Juan's daddy is a teacher, un maestro, and Malcolm's daddy paints houses, un pintor de casas. People have different jobs").

Moving From Self-Awareness to Other Awareness

An important principle of social studies is that personal actions can affect others, beginning with the people one knows personally and extending to other people and systems around the world. This knowledge motivates people to act responsibly. So, for example,

when adults share appropriate classroom decisions with children, the children learn that their choices and actions matter. They can see the results themselves. This model of shared control helps preschoolers feel empowered and spurs them to take further responsibility.

It is especially important to focus on the positive outcomes of children's behavior. Too often when adults talk about "consequences," they are referring to the negative effects of unsocial actions (for example, "You took all the purple markers and crayons. Now there are no purple ones left for others to play with"). However, if we want children to feel empowered, we need to acknowledge their capacity for bringing about positive changes. You can do this by commenting when they assist others ("Ruby, you explained to the other children at the table that Alberto wanted a muffin when he called it a 'magdalena'"), recognizing collaborative problem solving ("You found a way to use the dump truck together"), and acknowledging voluntary attempts to help in the classroom ("You wiped up the water so no one would trip"). The simple gratification of knowing they have behaved in socially responsible ways will encourage children to do more of the same.

Fitting the Learning Experience to the Learning Objective

The terms *social studies, socialization,* and *society* all come from the Latin root word *socius,* which means companion, partner, sharing, fellowship, or union (*American Heritage Dictionary of the English Language*, 2011). Therefore any best practices (described in Chap. 2) that bring children and adults together to work and play for the common good of the group can promote social studies learning. For example, a shared daily routine creates a sense of community, cleaning up as a group distributes the responsibility for maintaining equipment and materials so everyone can use them, and greeting the children in English and in other languages spoken by children's families helps all children feel like they are part of the classroom community. The goal of such experiences is to help children act and think beyond their own self-interests to consider the principles that govern and affect the world around them.

Social studies learning in early childhood has two components, discussed in the remainder of this chapter. **Social systems** are the norms, values, and procedures that affect human relationships in our day-to-day lives. For preschoolers, they include experiencing the diversity of people and cultures, becoming aware of the roles people perform at home and in the community, understanding the need to have rules for group behavior, and beginning to participate in the democratic process. In the past, such topics were typically subsumed under "social skills," a topic discussed in Chapter 4. However, as researchers and educators discovered that early experiences in this area formed the foundation for later citizenship, these topics were defined, expanded, and moved to the emerging curriculum domain of social studies.

The second component is **social concepts**. Its subject matter is what we traditionally think of as social studies—the standard topics taught later in school. They include economics, which for preschoolers involves gaining a rudimentary understanding of how money works as the basis for human transactions and interdependence. History at this age focuses on the sequence of events, as young children are increasingly able to recall the past and anticipate the future. Preschool geography is about locations and their relationship to one another, especially direction and distance. Preschoolers are also interested in the lives of people from other parts of the world, provided these are made concrete and connected to their own lives (e.g., customs related to food, housing, games children enjoy, family relationships). In recent years, ecology has been added to the mix. As a social concept, it is not about how the natural and physical world operate (which is covered under science; see Chap. 8), but rather about how human behavior affects nature and the health of the planet. While mastering these subjects might seem like a tall order for preschoolers, meaningful early experiences can have a positive impact on the rest of their lives.

Social Systems

Because of their observant natures and their curiosity about people, children become aware of human diversity on their own, although they depend on adults to help them develop sensitivity in responding to the differences they encounter among people. Likewise, young children are very attuned to the roles performed in their own families and, as they venture out into the world, to roles in the community. When it comes to creating and following rules, however, children do not always see the wisdom or necessity behind them. Adults need to play a more active role in helping preschoolers see how and why rules might apply to them. Involving children in making reasonable decisions about how the classroom should be run (adults still decide matters related to health and physical and emotional safety) helps them appreciate and follow rules voluntarily. Related to this practice is encouraging children to help establish and participate in the democracy of the classroom. With adult guidance, they can learn to listen to others, contribute their own ideas, and accept majority decisions that affect the group as a whole.

Child-guided experience is especially important for learnings such as:

Valuing diversity

Diversity can take many forms, including gender, ethnicity, age, religion, family structure, ability levels, body shape, hair/eye color, culture, language, ideas, aesthetic preferences, and so on. Valuing diversity means accepting and appreciating the differences of ourselves and of others as normal and positive. It means treating people as individuals and not as stereotypes and recognizing that preferences are not always value judgments (for example, if Daiwik brings curried lentils for lunch and Ramon brings macaroni and cheese, it does not mean each child can refer to the food the other one likes as "yucky" or "bad").

Teaching strategies. We all may be uneasy with differences we encounter for the first time. If children's experiences with variety are positive, they may develop an appreciation for diversity on their own. Nevertheless, preschoolers are old enough to have encountered and possibly internalized harmful stereotypes from the culture that surrounds them. Intentional teachers can help them accept and even embrace diversity in the classroom and community (as well as other cultures they may encounter through the media) in ways such as these:

- Model respect for others by the way you listen to and accept children's ideas and feelings. Let them see you treat everyone equally and fairly, including children, families, and your coworkers.

- Avoid judgmental comparisons. Instead, comment on specific attributes and accomplishments without labeling one as better than the other. For example, if you say to Yolanda, "I like red hair," Nicole may infer there is something wrong with her brown hair. A better observation would be, "Yolanda has short, red hair, and Nicole has her brown hair in braids."

- Include diversity in every classroom area and activity.

    - In the dress-up area, provide a range of clothing representing the cultures and activities of the children and their families (and others that may be unfamiliar to the children), including everyday styles and clothing worn for celebrations.

    - The house area might contain work clothes and tools used in different types of jobs and equipment used by people with various disabilities, such as crutches and magnifiers.

    - Serve food from a variety of cultures and ethnicities (such as Ethiopian, American Southern, kosher or traditional Jewish dishes) on a regular basis at snack time, as well as special treats brought in by parents at holiday times.

    - Put empty food containers and the cooking utensils used to prepare a range of ethnic foods in the house center. Be sure to include those that are labeled in the children's home languages as well as in English.

    - In the reading area, feature books, magazines, and catalogs with illustrations and photographs of people performing nonstereotypical jobs, families of varying structures, and people of different ages and appearances. Include books written in the children's home languages. All children should see their languages and cultures represented in their classroom in ways that are relevant to them (for example, not all families with African names relate to tribal life; many may come from bustling cities). Getting to know the families and asking them about family traditions, foods, and activities will help you bring in elements that are truly recognizable to each child.

○ Diversity isn't only about differences in people. Hang reproductions of artwork in diverse media and representing different cultures at eye level throughout the room. At large group time, explore a variety of styles of music and dance, again being sure to include the many styles that children's families enjoy. Grow various vegetables and flowers in the school garden. Invite families to contribute plants and seeds. Go to places and events in the community that showcase local diversity, such as different kinds of shops, festivals, concerts, cars, animals, buildings, and the like.

○ Ensure that bias and prejudice are not part of your program. For example, preview materials and field trip sites before sharing them with children. Anticipate questions children might have about the individuals and groups portrayed; answer questions with simple, honest responses. For example, a child might ask, "Why is this man dark?" You don't need to give a complex answer about the science of skin color; you can simply say, "He has dark skin because his mother or father has dark skin. You have freckles just like your mother."

○ Ensure that bias and prejudice are not part of your larger setting—your school or center. Work with program administrators to enact nondiscriminatory recruitment and admissions policies, including reaching out to educators from diverse cultures, male educators, teachers with disabilities, and members of the early childhood lesbian, gay, bisexual, and transgender (LGBT) community. Make sure informational brochures and key features on your website are available in the languages spoken by the children's parents, and where feasible, provide translators. Families and visitors from different backgrounds will feel either welcomed or unwanted depending on factors such as where and how the program is promoted (for example, only in English, picturing only families of one race or ethnicity, depicting only two-parent families), as well as office furnishings, staff behavior, and the terms staff use when addressing family members. For example, displaying posters on the office wall from a local multiethnic fair, avoiding cultural taboos such as unrelated men and women shaking hands, and addressing parents formally or informally according to their preferences are all signs of recognition and respect that can enhance feelings of acceptance (Nemeth 2012).

Learning about community roles

The first roles preschoolers become aware of are those played by the people in their families. At first, they are concerned about the roles that affect them directly, such as who cooks their meals, provides comfort when they feel hurt or upset, or reads to them at bedtime. Provided they feel secure about having their basic needs met, young children next begin to pay attention to the roles family members perform outside the home, such as their jobs or the volunteer work they do. As their world expands, preschoolers also take an interest in the services performed by people outside the family, such as doctors, firefighters, police officers, teachers, bus drivers, zookeepers, performing artists, and barbers and hair stylists. These roles often appear in their pretend play (see p. 219 in Chap. 10). Over time, the number of roles and the details included in acting them out become more elaborate.

Teaching strategies. Materials and experiences inside and outside the classroom can support children's interest in learning about community roles. Here are some ideas:

- ○ Create opportunities for children to learn about and act out different community roles. Build on their initial interest in the relationships within their own families. Provide materials for pretend play (dress-up clothes, housewares, shop and garden tools, office equipment). Talk about what family members do at home (for example, "Sean's daddy made dinner last night" or "Mattie did the laundry with her mom. She helped sort los calcetines, the socks") and the roles they play outside the home (for example, "Jerome's uncle is a pilot" or "Charlotte's grandmother sings in the choir at church"). Make a class book with photos of children's families performing different roles (planting a garden, taking the bus to the library). Invite family members to come to the classroom and share their roles, especially if they can bring related materials for the children to use themselves (such as subway passes, wrenches, tuning forks, spools of thread, empty cartons clearly labeled with their former contents). Encourage parents to bring their children to work, if possible, and make time for children to share these experiences with the rest of the class. Use Skype to connect with children's relatives in their home country or to befriend children in a different part of the country.

- ○ Take field trips and invite visitors to the classroom so children can expand their awareness of people and roles in their community. On neighborhood walks point out people at work—for example, people who are driving trash and recycling trucks, selling produce at the farmers' market, or fixing cars at the corner garage. Visit various places of work, especially those that often show up in children's pretend play, such as the fire station or supermarket. Bring back materials (grocery bags, receipt pads) they can incorporate in their play scenarios. Invite members of the community to the classroom and ask them to bring the tools they use in their work. Talk with visitors ahead of time so the experience is hands-on and appropriate for young children.

Adult-guided experience is especially important for learnings such as:

Creating and following rules

A rule is an authoritative direction for how to act or what to do. Just as licensed programs must follow health and safety rules, programs and teachers have rules that children must concern themselves with, such as who will pass out snacks, feed Duke the hamster, sit next to the teacher, choose the song for circle time, use the computer, and so on. Children may create rules for games they invent, such as the start and finish line in a race or what constitutes inbounds in a beanbag toss. Sometimes the group feels the need to establish policies for preserving quiet areas, respecting block structures built by others, or protecting work in progress overnight. Setting rules also can be a way to deal with interpersonal conflicts, especially if they affect groups of children or the whole class. Have the children act out the rules, and use photos of them to serve as nonverbal rule reminders that everyone can understand.

Teaching strategies. Young children need explicit information and guidance from teachers to understand, establish, and follow rules governing classroom behavior. They also need help sorting out when rules may be fluid (for example, when players agree to change the rules mid-game) and when they must remain fixed (for example, when they deal with health or safety). Like a personal code of morality, competence in respecting and making rules begins in childhood and continues to develop into adolescence and early adulthood. Teachers can be instrumental in laying the foundation for this development by carrying out practices such as the following:

- Make children aware of basic health and safety rules that have everyday meaning to them. Be concrete and positive. Children relate mostly to the "what" of behavior (for example, "Always wash your hands after using the bathroom"), although they can also benefit from a simple explanation of "why" (for example, "Soap and water get rid of the germs so they don't make us sick"). Even if children don't yet fully understand the explanation, they get the idea that rules serve a useful function, and they may be more willing to accept and follow them. Avoid abstractions, however (for example, "It's inconsiderate to transmit germs that can cause disease"), as these will be meaningless to preschoolers. After discussing a few simple rules with children, write them out in short words and pictures, and post them at children's eye level. Be sure to demonstrate the important rules rather than assuming that all of the preschoolers understand them based simply on your discussion. For dual language learners, write them in their home language (for example, lávese las manos [wash your hands]), which will help them learn key words as well as the rules themselves.

- During small group time or a class meeting, describe a problem that affects everyone and invite children to suggest one or more rules to solve it. Typical examples include children running through the block area and knocking things down or cleanup taking so long that it shortens outside time. (Children may also use small group time or class meetings to allow the whole group to resolve problems that involve just a few children, provided those directly affected agree to using this strategy. See the Engaging in Conflict Resolution section on p. 80 in Chap. 4.) Encourage children to discuss the pros and cons of each suggestion. Write down and post the rules they decide to try, and refer to them when appropriate. Revisit the rules as a group in a few days to see whether or not they are working. Ask children to take turns announcing to the class the rules that work.

- Encourage children to share responsibility for taking care of the classroom (for example, cleaning up, passing out snacks or meals, weeding and watering the garden, feeding the class pet). Establish rules and procedures together with the children for carrying out these responsibilities and for deciding who will do which jobs.

Making Up Rules to Govern Play

When children's play becomes too rough or dangerous, adults need to step in to set limits. Often, however, children themselves can be involved in creating rules to ensure their own comfort or safety (see also Carlson 2011), as illustrated in the following example.

After Steven, age 4, goes to a wrestling match, he gets several classmates in his preschool interested in playing "wrestling" during choice time. They use an area rug as their mat, push up their sleeves, and thoroughly enjoy the rough-and-tumble play. The game goes on for several weeks, becoming progressively elaborate; for example, they give themselves wrestlers' names and develop a scoring system.

In the second week, however, a few children begin to feel that the play is *too* rough. The teachers do not want to stop a game that many children clearly enjoy and that promotes learning in many areas. So at the beginning of choice time, when the wrestlers are setting up their game, a teacher gathers them and voices her concern, "What rules can we make up so that no one will get hurt?" She writes down their ideas and posts them on the wall above the mat:

1. Take off your shoes (but not your socks).
2. No hitting.
3. No punching. (The children debated whether punching was the same as hitting, but decided it deserved its own rule.)
4. No pinching.
5. You can't call someone a bad name.
6. No spitting.
7. No head butts.
8. ~~Only boys can play.~~ (Several girls protested this rule, and it was dropped.)
9. At least three people have to play so one can be the referee and make sure the fight is fair.
10. The referee has to be able to count to 10. (After a count of 10, the match is declared over.)
11. You can't wrestle if you don't have a wrestler name.
12. You can't have the same wrestler name as someone else.
13. Everyone who wants to wrestle gets a turn. The referee decides who goes next.
14. People who want to watch have to stand behind the line. (After some debate, they decided the edge of the block shelf would mark the watching line.)

The children refer to the rules in subsequent weeks as their interest in wrestling continues. If one of them breaks a rule, the other children—rather than the teacher—are always quick to point out the infraction.

○ Model the use of rules by creating some for yourself and following them. Invite ideas from children when appropriate (for example, how to decide who gets to sit beside you at story time each day). Write down the rules to share with the children and point out when you are following them. Give children occasional opportunities to remind or correct you. Involve the children as responsible upholders of the rules—even those that apply to adults.

Creating and participating in democracy

Democracy in the early childhood classroom means conditions of equality and respect for the individual. "Education that teaches children the skills they need to be contributing members of a civil society begins with classroom communities that embrace inclusive—mutually respectful—communication" (Gartrell 2012, 5). Developing a sense of democracy grows out of experiences with rule making and social problem solving. For young children, it means learning that everyone has a voice, even those with minority opinions.

Democracy entails compromise and negotiation. We do not always get our way, but the democratic process does provide the satisfaction of being heard and knowing that solutions, policies, decisions, and the like can be reviewed and revised if needed.

Teaching strategies. Participating in a democratic society and in a democratic classroom require similar skills. They both call for "reflective problem solving and decision making, managing one's emotions, taking a variety of perspectives, and sustaining energy and attention toward focused goals" (Elias et al. 1997, 8). Preschoolers are not ready for abstract civics lessons, but fostering the development of skills in appropriate, concrete ways prepares them to become responsible and productive citizens. To bring about this understanding in ways that make sense to young children, teachers can use strategies such as these:

- Ask children to consider alternative ways to reach a goal; for example, "What do you think would happen if . . . ?" or "Can you think of another way to do that?" Encourage them to plan more than one way to accomplish a task. Pose questions to help them anticipate consequences and reflect on outcomes; for example, "What will you do if the children who are making the refrigerator box into an airplane don't follow the rules tomorrow that you came up with today?"

Preschool Democracy in Action

Here is an example in which 3- and 4-year-old children helped to solve a classroom safety problem. Some experienced the satisfaction of seeing their ideas or beliefs adopted; one had to deal with the disappointment of having a minority opinion. All ended up feeling good about contributing to the well-being or enjoyment of the group.

Many of the children enjoy carrying water from the sink to different areas in the classroom, such as the house area when they are "cooking spaghetti." The teachers support the idea but are concerned by the large amounts of water being spilled on the floor. Because virtually everyone is affected by the situation, the teachers decide to bring up their concerns at a class meeting and ask the children for ideas to solve the problem. They write down the children's suggestions, and after the group discusses each, they vote on which one to adopt.

Tamika: Tell the children they cannot carry water anymore.

Teacher: What if they want to fill pots for cooking? (Several children say they liked being able to cook "just like at home.")

Dominic: Turn off the water. My mommy did that when we had a flood in the kitchen.

Lisa: We can put a towel in the house area. Whenever someone spills water, they have to go back and wipe it up.

Leah: We can put a towel in every area! Then we can bring water there, as long we clean up.

Lisa: We can put two towels so children can wipe up together.

Teacher: (after reading back the list of ideas) Which idea should we try? (Dominic votes to turn off the water, but all the other children are in favor of the towels.)

Teacher: We have five areas in the room. If we put two towels in each area, we'll need ten towels. Where can we get that many towels?

Tamika: We can buy them at the store.

Teacher: We don't have enough money for that. Any other ideas? (The children cannot think of another way to get towels, so the teacher offers a suggestion.) Do you suppose if we asked parents, they could bring in some old towels your family doesn't use any more?

All the children agree this is a good idea. The teachers post a request on the Family Bulletin Board, and by the following week, families donate a dozen old towels. Water carrying (and probably some intentional spilling) actually increases for a while because children enjoy wiping up after themselves. They invent different wiping methods, including "skating" towels along the floor or having one child hold each end of the towel. Dominic, whose idea had been voted down, is one of the most avid spiller-wipers.

○ Help children develop perspective-taking and turn-taking skills. Remind children to listen before they add their ideas to the discussion. Ask them to repeat back what they hear and check it out with the speaker. Encourage children to use their imagination. Role-playing helps them adopt the behavior and viewpoint of another. Because preschoolers are not natural turn takers, use a tool to help them develop this skill so they will not have to fight for a turn to speak and be heard. For example, you can use a timer or a talking stick. Such tools are especially effective for encouraging children who tend to be shy or quiet to participate in group processes.

○ Comment when you see children working collectively. Observe aloud how much more can be accomplished as a team than as one or two individuals. Note when children spontaneously divide tasks according to their abilities (for example, "Liza is taller, so she put away the puzzles on the top shelf. Josef is shorter, so he stored the puzzles that go on the bottom shelf").

○ Deal even-handedly with children who use bullying behavior and those they target. Give them equal attention and respect the feelings of both parties. First, stop hurtful behaviors immediately, whether physical or verbal, and remind children of the classroom rule about keeping all children safe. Engage children in conflict-resolution strategies (see the Engaging in Conflict Resolution section on p. 60 in Chap. 4). Likewise, be sensitive to children who may be too timid or reluctant to speak up in social problem-solving situations, and provide safe and comfortable ways for them to become involved in generating and carrying out solutions. (See the box on p. 189 in this chapter.)

○ Introduce other ideas and vocabulary words that are at the core of democratic principles and actions. Carry out mathematics activities to help children develop the concepts of *more/greater* versus *less/fewer*, which are foundational to the principle of majority rule. For example, ask children to indicate their preferences (for instance, for a color or food) by a show of hands. Count and record the results on chart paper, using the appropriate vocabulary words. Many other terms we associate with early mathematics or scientific investigation also apply to social processes—for example, *is/is not*, *same/different*, *all/some*, *other/else*, *before/after*, *now/later*, and *when/where/with whom*. Apply these concepts to people and actions as well as concrete objects (for example, the languages children in the classroom speak; the composition of their families; whether they come to school by bus, subway, car, or walking). Help children develop an overall sense of the patterns in human interaction and the principles governing behavior.

○ Expand conversations children may initiate about their parents' voting at election time. If your location is a polling place, ask permission to visit the voting booths with children during off-hours. Keep your explanation of the voting process simple, such as "Everyone gets to say whom they think will do the job best. Whoever is picked by the most people wins the job."

Social Concepts

Some social concepts, such as economics and history, tend to emerge from children's own observations and experiences. For example, as they accompany family members on errands, they encounter people exchanging money for goods and services. Looking at photos of a family vacation or a trip to their home country, preschoolers begin to recall what happened at a time in the past, when they took their trip. They also begin to anticipate events, such as an upcoming birthday, although their sense of time is still shaky. Understanding other standard social studies topics, such as geography, requires more active adult intervention. Children are so used to being taken places, for example, that they may only become aware of where they are coming from or going to if adults call their attention to it. Likewise, preschoolers often take nature for granted. Being naturally egocentric, they may not consider how their actions, let alone those of others, affect the plants and animals around them. A child's appreciation of nature and awareness of simple ecological principles therefore depend upon guidance from adults.

Child-guided experience is especially important for learnings such as:

Understanding simple economics

While the field of economics can seem abstract, even for adults, preschoolers, in fact, know many things about this aspect of social studies. Observing the roles of family members and others in the community, they develop basic ideas about reciprocity, including the exchange of money (Seefeldt, Castle, & Falconer 2013). For example, young children can grasp that people work to earn money to buy food, medicine, and movie tickets. They know that money, or its equivalent, comes in various forms (paper and coins, checks, plastic cards), and preschoolers are able to make simple choices about how spend to money. Overhearing comments from adults or in the media, they gather that certain goods and services are more valuable than others. At this age, however, they are more likely to judge an item's worth by its importance to themselves rather than by its actual market value.

Teaching strategies. Money often assumes a prominent role in children's pretend play. For example, the daddy pays the doctor to give his sick baby a shot. Children pay for food at the restaurant; the more they order, the more it costs. While children carry out these exchanges, they are often just imitating what adults do. On their own, they are not likely to consider how money (or its equivalent) is the basis behind many complex social interactions. Adult guidance can help preschoolers begin to think about the connections that underlie a society's economic system. Try the following strategies:

○ Provide materials and props so children can incorporate money and the exchange of goods and services into their pretend play. Build on typical family experiences, such as going to the grocery store, paying the doctor or baby-sitter, or purchasing new shoes. Children enjoy using play money in these scenarios, but they also like to make their own. Provide strips of paper, rocks, beads, and other small items for preschoolers to use as pretend money.

In the house area, Jeremy, age 5, pretends he's a supermarket cashier. He sets out play food on the table, baskets in which the children who are customers can put their purchases, and a small block with squares of paper and pencils. When his teacher asks about the block, papers, and pencils, Jeremy explains it is a machine for charge cards and demonstrates how it works. "You rub it along the side and then you sign your name on the top."

○ As you partner with children in their play, make comments and pose occasional questions to help them consider simple economic principles, such as the relationship between work and money. For example, you might ask, "Doctor, *how much* do I have to pay you to give my baby a shot?" or "*How much more* will it cost if I order the large salad instead of the small one?" When you read books that include stories with people buying and selling things, briefly engage children in discussing the transactions. Older children might enjoy pondering "what if . . . ?" questions, such as "What if there were no grocery store to buy our food? Where would we get the food we need to eat?"

Understanding history

Children's understanding of history is closely tied to their ideas about time (Wyner & Farquhar 1991). At first, it is a highly personal understanding, associated with events in their daily lives. By late preschool, however, children begin to apply logic to understanding time. They know time moves forward, are able to look backward, and understand that the past and present can affect the future (for example, they can wear the jacket they bought yesterday to school today). Their growing ability to create mental representations allows children to picture events further in the past and future (Povinelli et al. 1999). They make use of visual cues, such as the style of dress or type of transportation, to judge whether an image is from a long time ago or closer to the present (Seefeldt, Castle, & Falconer 2013). A growing vocabulary (words such as *before* and *after*, *first* and *last*, *then* and *next*) enables preschoolers to understand and talk about time (Thornton & Vukelich 1988). They begin to grasp that a minute is shorter than an hour, and a day is shorter than a year.

Teaching strategies. With a consistent schedule, children become aware of the daily sequence of events in the classroom on their own. However, it helps if adults occasionally point out "what we just did" or "what comes next," especially to children who are new to the group. Materials and books also provide many opportunities to help children develop a sense of time. Try these strategies:

- Post and discuss your program's daily schedule to help children become aware of the present, recent past, and short-term future events. Use pictures, photos, cards, and objects to help children represent and sequence the parts of the day (for example, breakfast followed by free play followed by circle time). Some programs begin the day with a message board that reminds children of the recent past and near future. For example, you might include a photo of a new material you introduced yesterday so children know it's available to play with today. If an important event such as field trip is coming up, you can cross off (count down) the days until the event.

- Play sequencing games at group times. For example, at circle time, have the children do two movements in order (for example, "First tap your ears; next tap your shoulders"). Give children an opportunity to be leaders and to show and/or tell their idea to their classmates. Do the same thing with sounds. For example, sequence two animal sounds or sing two notes that vary in pitch or loudness. As children become adept at these activities, increase the sequence from two to three or more steps.

- Provide concrete representations, such as books, artwork, and music, to make children aware of the distant past and far future. Old family photos or movies set in other times often arouse their curiosity about how people used to dress, cook, travel, or build houses. (To see how one preschool classroom set up an old-fashioned general store inspired by adaptations of the *Little House* books, see Miles 2009). Media images might similarly encourage them to think about futuristic settings where people have superpowers, travel in unusual vehicles, and use fantastic equipment to accomplish their goals. Young children may assume these already exist, but older preschoolers are beginning to understand that people have yet to invent them. To support children's interest in time periods other than their own, read books whose illustrations are clearly set in another time. Sing folk songs that refer to life in the distant past. Talk about the characters, such as those featured in nursery rhymes, and how their lives compared to life today (for example, "Simple Simon wore short pants called *knickers,* but he liked pies the same way you do" or "Susannah traveled in a covered wagon instead of a car"). Do the same with stories set in the future that feature spaceships, robots, or odd-looking houses and vehicles.

- Use and encourage children to use an expanding vocabulary of time and sequence words. Begin with terms such as *before* and *after*, *first* and *last*, *yesterday* and *tomorrow*; include their home-language equivalents for dual language learners. Then introduce expressions such as *once upon a time, then and now, a long time ago*, and *when you grow up*. Hearing and using these words helps children think about the passage of time. You may even hear them use these expressions in their own pretend play or when they dictate stories.

○ For children recently arrived from another city, state, or country, encourage them to describe their lives "before" and "after" they moved to their new home. Encourage families to share photos of the places they have lived, and talk with children about what is the same and/or different in the locations.

Adult-guided experience is especially important for learnings such as:

Understanding geography

Geography is "a field of study that enables us to find answers to questions about the world around us—about where things are and how and why they got there" (Geography Education Standards Project 1994, 11). The challenge for early educators is to introduce young children to geography concepts that are meaningful to them. As early as 1934, Lucy Sprague Mitchell's influential book *Young Geographers* emphasized the need to build on the here-and-now world of preschoolers to expand their understanding of the near-and-far universe. Research shows that young children are capable of engaging with three areas of geography: reading simple maps (Liben & Downs 1993), identifying familiar locations and landmarks (Mayer 1995), and recognizing prominent features in the landscape (Seefeldt, Castle, & Falconer 2013).

Teaching strategies. The perspective taking that allows young children to solve problems with materials and peers can also help them acquire simple concepts in geography. As with any area of learning at this age, children begin with what is concrete and familiar to them. Teachers can thus help preschoolers engage with geography by beginning with their daily experiences—where they go, what they do there—and then branching out to a wider range of places and features. The following strategies will make learning about geography interesting and appropriate for young children:

○ Talk with children about the places in the community that are familiar to them and their families. These include their homes, the homes of friends and family members, schools, parks, libraries, stores, places of public transportation, restaurants, and movie theaters. Take walks around the school building to find locations that are important and meaningful to the children, such as the front door, office, other children's classrooms, and kitchen. Walk around the neighborhood and point out landmarks connected to the children's daily lives as well as to your own (for example, "Tomorrow is my daughter's birthday. I'm going to buy her cupcakes at this bakery").

○ Draw simple maps or diagrams of the classroom, school, and neighborhood. Include obvious features such as doors and windows, the playground and parking lot, benches, bus stops, and stores. Talk about the maps with the children, emphasizing how the various places are related (for example, the direction and distance one must travel when getting from one place to another). Provide the children with flags, stickers, or other symbols they can use to mark places on the map. Older preschoolers may begin to draw their own simple maps (for example, a diagram of the classroom showing the different interest areas and some of the materials located in each of them).

○ Display a map of the neighborhood near the block area and encourage children to use it to work together to re-create the neighborhood using blocks and other props (such as cars, people, animals, signs; Colker 2013).

○ Use concrete representations, such as books, photos, artwork, songs, and puzzles, to connect children to places beyond their own experience. Just as children are curious about other periods in time (see the Understanding History section on p. 190 in this chapter), they are interested in learning about the food, clothing, houses, toys, and animals in locations other than where they themselves live. Preschoolers also enjoy looking at road and contour maps, globes, aerial photographs, and compasses if they are connected to their personal experiences. Discuss familiar landscapes (the hill behind the school, the river that winds through town) as you look at photos of other locations with similar features.

Appreciating ecology

Learning about ecology involves understanding our roles as caretakers of the planet. For young children, this begins with regular and enjoyable encounters with the natural world. As stated by the World Forum Nature Action Collaborative for Children in its Universal Principles for Connecting Children With Nature (2010):

We believe that regular connections with the natural world encourage children to develop
- Respect for local cultures and climates and for themselves as part of nature
- Feelings of unity, peace, and well-being as global citizens (n.p.)

Children's ideas about ecology develop together with their emerging social and emotional skills. As members of the classroom community, preschoolers can take responsibility for its physical care, such as picking up litter, feeding pets, or planting a garden. Their growing capacity for empathy makes them capable of showing concern for wildlife. Children's emotions, attitudes, and values about nature are formed early in life (Kellert 2002). They must develop a love for nature before they can think about the environment abstractly and become its guardians (Sobel 2008). Therefore, "during early childhood, the main objective of environmental education should be the development of empathy between the child and the natural world" (White & Stoecklin 2008, n.p.). This includes opportunities to play in nature, take care of plants, and cultivate relationships with animals.

Teaching strategies. Connecting children to the environment can be as simple as getting out into nature. Because children may take these experiences for granted, however, it is important to help them become aware of the diversity of plants and animals around them. The indoors also presents many opportunities for helping children learn the importance of taking care of things if we want those things to remain available to ourselves and others. Use the following strategies to inspire young children to care about the environment and to make ecology a meaningful subject for them:

- Help children become aware of and appreciate nature. The more young children enjoy the sensations of the natural world, the more meaningful their concerns about ecology will become as they get older. Except during days of extreme weather conditions, include time in your daily routine to go outside each day. Call attention to the feel of the sun and wind on children's faces and examine the plants and animals native to your area. Involve the children in projects such as planting a garden or making and hanging a simple bird feeder. Walk around the neighborhood and go on field trips to experience different nearby environments (such as a park, farm, forest, beach, lake, waterfall, or rooftop garden).

- Help parents understand why it is important for their children to engage in less screen time and more outdoor time. While not all families are equally concerned about the environment, they can appreciate nature's benefits to their children's physical and mental health. If safety is an issue in the neighborhood, help parents form an advocacy group to encourage civic leaders to establish safe play zones or to network with one another to construct play yards on nonschool grounds.

- Encourage children to take care of the indoor classroom and outdoor learning environment. When children play a meaningful role in taking care of the settings where they play and interact every day, it supports the development of empathy and the sense of community that undergird ecological awareness. Be sure children have opportunities to take responsibility outdoors as well as indoors. Appropriate activities and opportunities for preschoolers include the following:
  - Taking care of materials and using them properly to avoid damage (putting tops on markers so they do not dry out, treating dress-up clothes carefully so they do not tear, handling mechanical tools [hammers, drills, scissors] or electronics safely and gently)
  - Putting away materials in their designated places so others can find them
  - Helping with simple repairs (taping the torn corner of the snack chart or a book cover)
  - Taking care of pets (feeding them, changing their water, shredding paper for their cages)
  - Planting, labeling, watering, and weeding the class garden
  - Picking up litter in the hallway and on the playground (under adult supervision and with appropriate safety measures to avoid broken glass, contamination, or other dangers)
  - Returning wheeled vehicles to the toolshed at the end of outside time
  - Being careful not to damage plants or animal habitat on the playground

✿   ✿   ✿

Social studies is the "new kid on the block" when it comes to content areas in the early childhood curriculum, yet it is also the oldest area of study in general. The preschool classroom is a microcosm of the larger society. As concerns mount about the unraveling of civil behavior in the fabric of our social world, early childhood educators, in partnership with families, can help to lay the foundation for a future that guarantees that all of us have an opportunity to fulfill our human potential while respecting the rights of others and the sustainability of our planet.

For Further Consideration

1. What role can early childhood programs play in counteracting the intolerance (based on race, ethnicity, culture, religion, social class, and so on) young children may observe and learn at home, in their communities, and in the media?

2. As the US population becomes more and more culturally and linguistically diverse, the potential grows for conflicting social values and beliefs between home and school. How can early childhood professionals anticipate and address this gap?

3. Examine your own prejudices and stereotypes. As an experienced or a novice teacher, how do (or will) you intentionally make sure these attitudes do not affect the fairness and respect with which you treat all the children and families in your program?

4. Is consumer education a necessary and appropriate new content area in early social studies? If so, what constitutes an appropriate consumer education curriculum and pedagogy?

5. What types of classroom rules are appropriate for preschoolers to help make and enforce? How can adults respond when children suggest a rule that could endanger their health or safety or that of others?

6. Because of heavy advertising in the media and other influences, preschool children may become aware of economic disparities between their families. How can teachers handle comments (positive or negative) the children might make about differences in family income or purchasing power?

7. What are some concrete ways teachers can represent the passage of time for preschoolers?

8. Ecology is an important topic and features prominently in the news at the time of this writing. How can early childhood educators make concerns about nature and the environment pertinent to young children?

Chapter 10

Creative Arts

Four-year-old Celia maneuvers her wheelchair behind the puppet stage, for which the platform has been adapted so she can slide the chair underneath it. She puts the witch puppet on her right hand and the dog puppet on her left hand. Then she tells the following story to her teacher, Ryan, and two other children, Lance and Valentina, sitting out front: "Once upon a time, there was a bad witch and she wanted to poison all the dogs." Celia makes the witch puppet fly around by waving her right hand in circles and swooping it up and down.

"You have to say, 'Heh, heh, heh,'" says 5-year-old Lance. "That's how you know it's a bad witch and not a good witch."

When Celia says, "Heh, heh, heh," Ryan imitates her and encourages the other children to do the same. Lance talks in his deepest "really, really bad witch" voice, while 3-year-old Valentina, whose English-language skills are just emerging, watches and listens at first. On the third repeat, however, she joins in, saying "Heh" and looking delighted to be part of the fun.

"I wonder how else you know it's a bad witch," muses Ryan.

"She has a big bump on her nose!" says Lance. "See!"

Celia looks at the puppet, which does indeed have a bump on its nose, and thrusts it forward for everyone to see. Then she continues with her story. "One day the bad witch tried to poison Wags. [Wags is the name of Celia's family dog.] But Wags ran away and she couldn't catch him." Celia thrusts the dog puppet under the stage and hides him in her lap. "Then all the other dogs came out and chased the witch away." Celia shakes the witch puppet off her hand and throws it backward over her head. Then she brings the dog puppet back up and bends her hand to make it bow. As she wheels herself back out front, Ryan leads the group in clapping.

The creative arts include visual art, music, movement and dance, and dramatic (or pretend) play, as well as appreciation of these art forms. Developing children's artistic knowledge and abilities has been a central feature of early childhood programs since their beginning. For example, attention to the role of the arts in perceptual, cognitive, and social development spans the pioneering work of preschool educator Rhoda Kellogg (Kellogg & O'Dell 1967), the constructivist theories of Vygotsky (1978), and the current worldwide interest in Reggio Emilia's use of representation to support learning (Gandini et al. 2005). The philosopher and educator John Dewey (1934) believed that learning about art should not be limited to the talented few but rather should be available to all children from an early age. He saw the arts as a great economic and social equalizer.

Although early art education has been supplanted somewhat by a focus on school readiness, most educators continue to believe that the arts are central to young children's development and merit a place in the early childhood curriculum:

> The arts invite children to imagine, solve problems, express ideas and emotions, and make sense of their experiences. Creative arts are a meaningful part of the early childhood curriculum for their own sake and because they can enhance children's development of skills in literacy, science, mathematics, social studies, and more. (Koralek 2005, 2)

Evidence for this claim comes from a study of graduates of science, technology, engineering, and mathematics (STEM) programs, which found that the graduates who were business entrepreneurs or owned patents were up to eight times more likely to have been involved in the arts as young children than the general population (LaMore et al. 2013). The researchers note that such experiences with the arts encourage nonconventional thinking.

The value of artistic learning for children is both emotional and intellectual, as illustrated by the story themes and interactions in the vignette that opened this chapter. Art is *intrinsically rewarding;* that is, engaging with art is important for its own sake. The arts provide a sense of competence and control when experienced in a judgment-free setting. For children whose language skills are just developing (due to age, dual language learning, special needs, and so on), the arts open up new avenues for expression and communication. Particularly for children of diverse linguistic and cultural backgrounds, visual art, songs, poetry, dance, storytelling, and so on help link home and school, and build connections between their inner and outer lives (Espinosa 2010). Because all cultures and most religions use art in their traditions and practices, art enables children to integrate their cultural background into the school's curriculum (Wardle & Cruz-Janzen 2004). For children who cannot express themselves in words, art lets them express who they are inside and what they are thinking, and it allows children with special needs to be included in educational experiences, often without the need for specialized equipment (West 2005). Here is a continuation of the vignette on page 197:

"My turn," says Lance. He chooses the bear and African American boy puppets. "There was a bear in a cage at the circus," his story goes, "and the boy freed him and then the bear went 'Grrr!' and chased the boy and he was scared but then they were friends and went to McDonald's until the boy's daddy called him home to bed." When he finishes, Lance lays the puppets on the stage, gets a blanket from the nearby doll carriage, and covers them up.

"The daddy let the bear inside to sleep with the boy?" asks Ryan.

"Yes," answers Lance. "The boy made the bear invisible so his daddy couldn't see it."

This time, Valentina is the first to clap. Ryan asks if she would like a turn with the puppets. Valentina shakes her head no, but she reaches out and picks up the bear puppet. Celia wheels back behind the stage and brings out the witch puppet, which she hands to Valentina. Sitting with the group rather than behind the stage, Valentina puts a puppet on each hand and tentatively waves them around. "Bruja, witch," Ryan says as he points to one, and "Oso, bear," he says as he points to the other. Valentina says, "Bruja, heh, heh" then tries the word *bear* in English.

"Grrr!" says Lance. "Grrr!" say Celia and Ryan. Valentina laughs. Grrr!" she says quietly, then louder. "Bear, grrr!"

The arts can be empowering for all children. The Task Force on Children's Learning and the Arts (1998) notes that "as they engage in the artistic process, children learn they can observe, organize, and interpret their experiences. They can make decisions, take actions, and monitor the effect of those actions" (2). Diversity is another important, intrinsically rewarding concept expressed through the arts:

> Humans have always used the arts to share and make sense of their deepest joys and fears. When we bring the shadows out of the caves and turn them into story, dance, song, or picture, we transform our emotions into something to share with others. And on those rare days when all the planets are perfectly aligned, we react in ways that lead to a greater understanding for all. (Matlock & Hornstein 2005, 7–8)

To help empower children, institutions such as Wolf Trap Institute for Early Learning Through the Arts provide arts-based teaching strategies to teachers, parents, and young children.

The arts are also *extrinsically valuable* in promoting other areas of development, as studies have shown. For example, the work of Eisner (2004) on the development of aesthetic intelligence applies critical thinking in the arts to educational practices across many disciplines. The Arts Education Partnership (Deasy & Stevenson 2002) also recognizes this correlation, summarizing research that shows arts teaching and learning can increase children's cognitive and social development, and concluding that the arts can be a critical link for children in developing the crucial thinking skills and motivations they need to achieve at higher levels.

Research confirms the role of the arts in promoting development from infancy through adolescence. For example, exposure to patterns is important for early brain development (Healy 1994).

> We know from research on the brain that the search for meaning is innate and this search occurs through patterning. The arts offer a direct path to seeking patterns, layering experiences, and making meaning. Meaningful learning engages feelings, experiences, relationships, and the ability to see clearly with our eyes, hands, and bodies. Children become problem posers in arts-rich environments. They call on their personal life of images and experiences to solve . . . word, number, or people problems. (Pinciotti 2006, 11–12)

For many years there has been an effort to include both self-expression and intellectual components in creative arts education for children of all ages. An influential movement in this regard has been discipline-based art education (DBAE), a concept introduced by Greer (1984) and field-tested with support from the Getty Center for Education in the Arts (later renamed the Getty Education Institute for the Arts, and eventually discontinued). This movement takes the position that the teaching of art should integrate art history, art criticism, aesthetics, and the creation of art. An earlier goals statement of the National Art Education Association (1982) also endorses a comprehensive approach, comparable to DBAE, that includes analyzing art as well as producing art. And the educational objectives of the National Endowment for the Arts (1988) list fostering creativity, promoting communication skills, making choices based on critical assessment, and learning about the significant achievements of the world's civilizations.

This broad focus was later reflected in *National Standards for Arts Education: What Every Young American Should Know and Be Able to Do in the Arts* (US Department of Education 1994). The arts were also included in the mandated reforms of the Goals 2000: Educate America Act passed by Congress (National Education Goals Panel 1994), which established the Task Force on Children's Learning and the Arts: Birth to Age Eight (Arts Education Partnership 1998). The Task Force explicitly recognized the role of the arts in promoting language and literacy and thereby concluded that they contribute to Education Goal 1 that "all children will start school ready to learn" (vi). Many state standards now reflect the importance of the creative arts in early learning (Gronlund 2006), and Common Core State Standards (CCSS) developers and Arts Education Partnership have teamed to eventually incorporate the arts into the CCSS for kindergarten through grade 12 (Riley & Munson 2013).

Young Children's Development in the Creative Arts

Developmental changes during the preschool years enable children to benefit in many ways from art experiences. Because of young children's growing language skills, the arts open up new avenues for expression and communication. The ability to form mental images is also significant for creative arts development, as it allows preschoolers to represent their experiences in different media. They can paint a picture of their family (visual art), make up a song about a puppy (music), stomp like a monster (movement), or act out a favorite story (dramatic or pretend play).

> [Children's] ability to use various modes and media to convey their meaning increases in range and scope. By the preschool years, these modes may include oral language, gestures and body movement, visual arts (drawing, painting, sculpting), construction, dramatic play, and writing. Their efforts to represent their ideas and concepts in any of these modes enhance the knowledge itself. (Copple & Bredekamp 2009, 13)

While children's artistic skills develop noticeably in the early years, the stages of growth are not clearly marked by beginnings and endings (Fox & Schirrmacher 2012). Children tend to move back and forth between levels, much as adult artists do when they work with a new medium. Art appreciation also waxes and wanes, depending on children's cognitive and social experiences. Despite these fluctuations, theory and research can identify general progressions in making and appreciating art that relate to children's growing abilities in language, representation, abstraction, and complexity (Epstein 2012b; see the box on p. 201 in this chapter).

Four general principles define the development of the creative arts in the early years:

- **Representation emerges from young children's experiences.** To form mental images and represent them using the arts, young children first need real, hands-on experiences with objects, people, and events. They then portray these concrete experiences by making drawings and models, copying and creating songs and movements, and inventing stories and pretend-play scenarios.

- **Children's artistic representations develop together with their perceptual, cognitive, and social-emotional abilities.** Representations begin simply and become more complex over time and with practice. Children gradually observe and portray more detail (perception), sequence and connect artistic elements (cognition), use art to express feelings and ideas (emotional growth), and involve others in their artistic endeavors (social development).

- **Each child's representations are unique.** Children use the arts to express themselves in ways that make sense to them. Their artistic creations and reactions reflect their individual interests, experiences, and personalities, including their home language and culture. Artistic development thrives when children have the

Stages in Making and Appreciating Art

Stages in Making Art

- **From accidental to intentional representation.** Younger children accidentally create a form or movement and then decide it's like something; for example, they might pat clay into a rectangle and call it a car or roll on the floor and say they are a ball. This order is later reversed; children start with specific characteristics in mind and then search out materials or perform an action to match their mental image.

- **From simple to elaborated models.** Initially, children hold one or two characteristics in mind when they draw, sing, move, or pretend. Later, their representations become more detailed. For example, a younger child might pretend to be a baby by saying, "Waa! Waa!" An older child might wriggle and make faces, crawl, suck on a bottle, or reach out to be picked up.

- **From randomness to deliberation.** When children are introduced to an artistic medium, they explore its possibilities without regard to the effects they create. As they gain more control over materials and tools, their actions become more deliberate. For example, after moving all over the musical scale with their voices, children will later try to reproduce a specific pitch (note).

- **From unrelated elements to relationships.** Children become more aware of how marks, sounds, movements, and play themes relate to one another. For example, initially they make marks wherever their hand lands, but later they consider how marks or colors look next to one another. Movements are combined into a sequence, or one play scenario leads logically to the next one.

Stages in Appreciating Art

- **Sensorial.** Toddlers and young preschoolers like artwork that appeals to their senses. They respond to bright colors and bold patterns, music with a strong beat, movements with a dominant action, and characters with clear features and personalities. They engage with art emotionally and focus on one aspect of the artwork (an image, sound, movement, or behavior) to the exclusion of others. They do not differentiate between artistic forms such as a painting and a photograph.

- **Concrete.** As older preschoolers begin to work with symbols, their preferences depend more on subject matter or theme. They like art that is realistic and whose ideas relate to their own experiences. Children in this middle stage develop a concept of beauty based on whether the subject matter appeals to them. They see the purpose of art as telling a "story" about real people and events through images, sounds, or actions. Children at this stage can sort art by its medium.

- **Expressive.** By late preschool or early kindergarten, children think about the artist's point of view ("What is the artist trying to show or say?"). They still prefer realism but also pay attention to how artists use the features of a medium (color and composition, sound and speed, large and small movements, character and plot) to express an idea or a feeling. Children in this stage become aware of different artistic styles and begin to understand how culture affects artwork.

Adapted, by permission, from A.S. Epstein, *The HighScope Preschool Curriculum: Creative Arts* (Ypsilanti, MI: HighScope Press, 2012b), 6–7.

freedom to explore without being pressured to demonstrate a specific skill or make a particular product.

- **Young children are capable of appreciating as well as making art.** Young children's powers of observation and their finely tuned senses make them capable of appreciating and sharing ideas about art. Adults can support these abilities by talking about those aspects of art that interest the children, asking open-ended questions, introducing new vocabulary words, and talking about the concept of creativity itself—that is, the process of experimenting without fear of failure (Burton 2000).

Teaching and Learning in the Creative Arts

Developing knowledge and skills in the arts, like mastering any other content area, requires time, materials, and encouragement. Adults must value the lessons to be learned from art and make a conscious decision to feature an arts program in the curriculum. Without this commitment from administrators and teachers, young children's artistic development will not extend beyond the conventional and unsophisticated. Attitudes as well as behaviors will be affected; children will have lost an early opportunity to view art as a legitimate field of study.

Art educators agree that the intention to teach and respect art is vital to create a climate in which art learning can thrive, but they do hold differing views on how to best establish an artistic foundation in young children. Followers of *expressive* theories of art believe that children's everyday lives provide them with inspiration, and they often support mostly child-guided teaching strategies. These theorists conclude that the more teachers help children explore everyday experiences in-depth—through discussion, small group activities, field trips—the more elaborate the creative arts expressing those experiences will be.

Theorists and practitioners who believe artistic growth is tied to *perceptual development* tend to advocate more direct, adult-guided teaching strategies. These involve focusing children's attention on specific attributes of any number of things in their environment to improve their visual and auditory discrimination. Research suggests such training does help children see more details in and relationships among objects and sounds, although highly directive methods, such as teaching drawing by copying or music by duplicating notes, are not effective with young children. These methods may help children advance through the stages of representation more quickly (for example, including more details or rendering proportions more accurately; matching pitch more closely), but there is no evidence that their learning generalizes beyond the immediate task or leads to more sophisticated artistic production or appreciation overall.

These two views of art education may pose a false dichotomy, however:

> When we view art as a distinct discipline, with a distinct body of knowledge that must be taught and mastered, we are not frightened to teach skills and techniques, as well as appreciation and art history. . . . Based on the children's ideas, we can prepare a structured art program that allows for the sharing of the power and responsibility and positions the children as artists and all that this view of children, art, and art teaching entails. (Wright 2003, 154 & 156)

General teaching strategies that acknowledge both positions and support the development of the creative arts in young children include the following:

- **Provide open-ended art materials and tools.** Include materials throughout the classroom to support the arts, such as paints, crayons, clay, beeswax, blocks, natural materials such as shells and leaves, computer drawing programs, and recycled paper and plastics (visual art); simple percussion instruments and other sound makers (music); scarves and streamers (movement); and dress-up clothes, props, and puppets (dramatic play). Encourage children to use them in a variety of expressive ways. Help children make connections between materials as they explore them in open-ended ways (Drew & Rankin 2005).

- **Establish a climate that supports creative risk taking.** The arts thrive when children know they will not be judged for what they do and say. Instead of feeling as if they must create in a certain, teacher-approved way, young children who feel supported are willing to try new materials and forms of expression. They are also more apt to offer their opinion on what others create (art appreciation).

- **Create alongside children.** Research shows that children who are left on their own tend to use art materials in repetitive or stereotypical ways. However, when adults work and create alongside them, provided they are not directive, children engage with the arts longer and are more likely to experiment with materials, tools, and ideas (Kindler 2005).

- **Emphasize process over product.** Allow time for experimentation, repetition, and reflection so children can discover the properties of materials and practice using them. Cutting this process short or introducing too many materials at once may stunt their creativity (Wright 2003).

- **Encourage artistic collaboration.** Do not be concerned that children will copy each other's work. Creativity is often social (Matlock & Hornstein 2005), and research shows that when children work together, their art increases in originality because they share and build on one another's ideas (Taunton & Colbert 2000).

- **Talk with children about the arts.** Encourage children to describe and discuss the visual art, music, movement, or dramatic play scenarios they invent. Use these conversations to increase their arts vocabulary. Never presume to know what children have created or how they feel about their own or others' creations. Ask them about their creations and show your genuine interest in their answers to your questions. The words used by teachers during an art activity "have the tremendous power to awaken the child to imagination, observation, investigation, exploration, planning, utilization, contemplation, and reflection with the art materials" (Burton 2000, 330).

- **Incorporate art from the culture of children's families and communities.** Intentionally include representative art from every medium in the everyday furnishings, materials, and activities in the classroom. Invite artists (including family members) to the program to share their work, and take field trips where children can observe and have hands-on experience with the arts. Be sure these experiences highlight the art forms and content of many cultures, such as fiber arts from East Asia and Latin America; music and dance from Africa and the Caribbean; Middle Eastern architecture and mosaics; and Native American storytelling.

Fitting the Learning Experience to the Learning Objective

Both expressive and perceptual theories about teaching art have validity, but again, it is best to balance child-guided and adult-guided experiences in this curriculum area. Effective art teachers "blur the boundaries between natural unfolding and guided learning and between creativity and the training of skills and techniques" (Wright 2003, 156). Across the areas of the creative arts—visual art, music, movement, dramatic play, and art appreciation—children are most likely to explore materials, tools, and forms of expression on their own. They don't need prodding to squeeze clay, bang on a drum, bounce to music, pretend to be a character in a favorite book, or say whether they like a picture or song. However, to understand the multiple possibilities of each artistic medium, and to move into more complex forms of representation, children generally depend upon adult guidance to advance their artistic development.

Visual Art

Of the key knowledge and skills in the area of visual art, child-guided experience seems particularly important for manipulating two- and three-dimensional art materials and tools, making representations from experience, making accidental representations, and making simple representations. Adult-guided experience seems to be especially significant for naming art materials, tools, and actions; becoming adept at using two- and three-dimensional art materials and tools; making representations using imagination; making intentional representations; and making complex representations.

Child-guided experience is especially important for learnings such as:

Manipulating two- and three-dimensional art materials and tools

Handling two-dimensional media requires having the manual dexterity to draw, paint, and print with appropriate materials and tools. Manipulating three-dimensional media requires the manual dexterity and strength to mold, sculpt, or build with materials using one's hands or tools.

Teaching strategies. The primary role of teachers in encouraging young children to make visual art is providing abundant and diverse materials, along with the time and space to explore them. Try out the following strategies:

○ Set up a spacious, attractive, and permanent art area. A permanent art area that is labeled and inviting tells children that what happens there is important. Make sure there is ample room to work individually and collaboratively and to store easily accessible materials. Locate the art area near water (an indoor sink or outdoor spigot). Make sure the floor is easy to clean (tile, linoleum, large sheets of plastic) and that cleanup materials are nearby. The art area should have both vertical and horizontal work spaces (easels, walls, tables, pavement) and provide natural as well as artificial light (if possible, use warm rather than cool fluorescent bulbs to mimic incandescent lighting). There should be drying areas for finished work (clotheslines, flat surfaces, cubbies) and safe areas to protect unfinished work (including work-in-progress signs). Finally, make sure there is ample display space at children's eye level, including walls, bulletin boards, shelves, pedestals, boxes, and frames.

○ Provide a wide and abundant variety of tools and materials. Children need more variety than the crayons, paints, playdough, and modeling clay typically provided in early childhood settings. Many inexpensive materials—recycled items, carpet scraps, items gathered from nature—offer opportunities to create. For children with perceptual or physical disabilities, provide aids such as adaptive scissors, large paintbrushes and handgrips, spotlights, magnifying lenses, and so on. Teachers should be careful not to overwhelm children with too many materials at once and to introduce new materials gradually. Give children easy access to the materials so they can retrieve and use them independently and return unused supplies where they belong. Also provide additional materials and experiences that develop children's fine motor and eye–hand coordination, such as scissors, puzzles, and small manipulative toys. For more specific ideas on two- and three-dimensional art materials and tools for the early childhood classroom, see Althouse, Johnson, and Mitchell

(2003, 25–40) and Epstein and Trimis (2002, 67–69). For information on adaptations for children with special needs, see Mitchell (2005, 41–42). Also, look for creative reusable resource centers or scrap stores in your local area or online (for example, Reusable Resources Association 2014).

○ Incorporate art activities throughout the daily routine. The visual arts should not be limited only to choice or small group time. For example, children can move with scarves and banners during large group time, seeing how color and shape are altered by light and wind. Outdoor time in general is a wonderful opportunity to explore visual variety in nature. At snack and mealtime, make comments about the color, shape, and textural appearance of food. Also, when culturally appropriate, take advantage of special occasions, such as holidays and birthdays, to showcase the role of art. Invite families to share the ways that the arts feature into their celebrations of these events.

○ Encourage in-depth exploration. Enlist children's interest by making comments and observations about what they are doing and by manipulating the art materials yourself. Encourage them to sort and classify the materials to discover their basic properties. Let children work with their hands before introducing tools so they get a feel for each type of medium, its properties, and how their actions transform it. Limit what you introduce at any one time; for example, let children explore one color with black or white before they mix two or more colors together.

○ Encourage collaboration. Ask children to share their discoveries about materials and tools. Their insights will inspire further innovation in their peers. Remember that art can be a wonderful means of self-expression, which is especially helpful for dual language learners who face many obstacles to communication all day long.

○ Stress process over product. Children need to work with the same materials over and over again to discover their properties and gain mastery over their use. Only by letting children freely explore can they eventually produce original and unique art. "Product-centered craft activities that use adult-designed templates will not allow children to develop and use symbolic representations" (Wright 2003, 157). Explain to parents and school administrators why pressuring children to make a certain product a certain way is actually counterproductive to artistic development. Resist pressure to showcase "polished" work.

○ Challenge children to use materials in creative ways. For example, a group of preschoolers were cutting paper into squares and strips. Their teacher said, "I wonder what we could do with the paper so it doesn't lie flat." The children made loops, coils, and accordion folds with the paper. One boy, whose family was from Japan, made an origami boat. The teacher later invited this child's grandfather to the classroom to teach the children how to make other simple origami shapes.

Making representations from experience

This area of learning refers to young children representing familiar objects, people, places, and events through all forms of visual media. Children might create representations of family members, pets, home and school settings, foods, birthday parties, or anything else present in their lives.

Teaching strategies. Just being aware of children's experiences and interests will suggest numerous possibilities for the things they can represent in their visual art. An observant teacher can build on and expand these possibilities using the following ideas:

- Suggest that children represent specific objects, places, people, and experiences that are familiar to them and reflect their home language and culture. Drawing familiar places (such as the family's kitchen or the classroom) also helps children develop map-making skills. (See also the Understanding Geography section on p. 192 in Chap. 9.)

- When children's experiences arise naturally in the course of conversation, say, "I wonder if we could draw (or paint or construct) that at small group time?" Ask the children to suggest materials for representing the object or idea. For example, while getting ready for outside time, a discussion of new winter clothing led one group of preschoolers to represent their jackets, mittens, and boots with fabric, carpet samples, and recycled cardboard.

- Draw on other imagery and experiences as subjects for visual representations. For example, take photographs of the objects children play with and construct, and post them in the art area as inspiration for things children might represent in their artwork. Use the natural environment to motivate art expression. For example, take a walk in a garden or bring cut flowers to class. Hang art reproductions showing familiar experiences (for example, a Mary Cassatt painting of a mother bathing a child). Encourage children to represent comparable experiences in their own lives, as well as others important to their families (for example, going to a powwow; decorating an ancestor's gravesite on Día de Los Muertos, the Day of the Dead). After a field trip, give children a variety of art materials to use in representing what they remember.

Making accidental representations

An accidental representation means making something that becomes recognizable *after* it is created. For example, a child exploring clay might flatten it and then declare, "Hey, look what I made. It's a pancake."

Teaching strategies. Because something cannot be purposely accidental, the role of the intentional teacher here is to create an environment in which such discoveries are likely to occur using strategies such as the following:

- Provide a wide variety of materials and tools children can use to represent things. Be sure to include adaptive tools for children with special needs (see the preceding strategies in this chapter).

○ Accept what children say when they announce they made something. Encourage them to describe the attributes they see in their creation ("It's round and floppy like a pancake") that led to their conclusion about what it is.

○ Encourage children to observe the attributes of things even when they are not making art. Their improved observational skills will generalize to art-making activities. Attach descriptive labels to these attributes, using both English and home-language words for dual language learners.

Making simple representations

Young children begin making art with only one or two details. In these creations, they are not concerned with spatial or other representational accuracy. For example, a mouth may be the only feature drawn in a face, or a rectangular shape may represent a house.

Teaching strategies. In supporting children's earliest representations, the most important thing teachers can do is accept and take an interest in their initiatives, no matter how simple they are. With appropriate support, children will gradually elaborate on their art ideas. If we pressure children to include more, we imply that what is there is inadequate. Children may then become discouraged and stop making art. Here are some ideas to support children where they are:

○ Accept what children create. Do not request or require them to add more details. They may interpret such requests as negative judgments on their work and lose interest or motivation, or come to depend on adults to tell them how to make something in the future.

○ Acknowledge the details children do include in their art. Show interest as a means of encouraging the child to elaborate on the image or the process of creating it. For example, when a teacher commented, "You drew a big circle with a smaller one inside it," the child said, "That's our fish tank and the new baby fish. There were more, but the big fish ate them all up." Keep a recording device handy to record what children tell you about their art so you don't miss key interpretations that some dual language learners may be telling you. Later you can ask a colleague, parent, or other person who speaks the children's language to translate what was said.

○ Do not presume to know what a child is representing. It is easy to misinterpret, especially when the details are minimal. Instead, invite the child to tell you about it. As a caution, Althouse, Johnson, and Mitchell (2003) relate this embarrassing incident:

> A first grade teacher said to Maria, "I see a dog in your picture." Maria answered in a frustrated tone, "That's not a dog; that's my mama." Realizing his mistake, Mr. Allen responded, "Tell me more about your mother." This gave the child the opportunity to give more details about the picture. (55)

Adult-guided experience is especially important for learnings such as:

Naming art materials, tools, and actions

Learning the names of objects and operations in the visual arts is no different than it is in other domains. That is, children need to hear these names explicitly from adults—whether the words are *the letter A*, *subtraction*, or *sculpting*. With teacher input, young children learn labels and are able to differentiate identifying attributes of materials (crayons, paints, pastels, clay, wood, yarn), tools (cameras, paintbrushes, loom, potter's wheel, canvas, frame), and creative actions (painting, dripping, drawing, spinning, weaving, molding, framing).

Teaching strategies. Strategies to develop children's vocabulary in the visual arts are comparable to those in other content areas. If teachers supply these terms while children are actively engaged with art rather than at unrelated times, the terms will be more meaningful to them. Try the following strategies:

- Provide the names of art materials, tools, and actions in context and when they are introduced to children (in English and in children's home languages). Tie the names to concrete objects and actions as children experience them. Keep the statements simple and factual.

- Accept the language children use to describe tools, materials, and actions. Then add words to expand their vocabulary. For example, when Marissa said, "I squished my paper," her teacher said, "Yes, I see you squished the paper. I'm going to crumple mine, too." And when Estefan, holding the scissors, exclaimed "Tijeras! Puntiagudos!" his teacher commented, "The scissors are pointy and sharp!" Write down what children say about their artwork, in the same way that you would take dictation about other ideas children want you to record (see p. 118 in Chap. 6). For example, label how they describe areas, techniques, or subject matter in their artwork. Be sure to include key words in a child's home language to encourage parents to discuss the artwork with the child. If children do not want you to write directly on their pictures, write on the back, use sticky notes, or make labels such as those found in museums to clip on the side or attach underneath.

- Ask children open-ended questions about materials, actions, and effects to encourage their use of art language. For example, ask, "What happened when you added a big squirt of red paint to your cup?" Or, if a child is comparing dry and wet balls of clay, wonder, "How do they feel? What happens when you try to roll them flat?" For children with limited language or English, simply sitting beside them with a look of interest may encourage them to describe, with the words available to them, their artwork and how they created it.

Becoming adept at using two- and three-dimensional art materials and tools

As they get older and have more practice with art materials, young children develop more control. They can use materials on a smaller scale and tools that require greater dexterity, such as beads, sequins, and yarn, as well as glue, staplers, hole punches, and scissors.

Teaching strategies. Children need time and practice to enhance their art-making skills. However, left on their own, their level of expertise may not increase. Adults are essential to model techniques, make suggestions, and help children solve problems. As with the mastery of any challenge, adults should be sensitive to children's frustration levels. Sometimes a hint is all that's needed to get a child over a hurdle; other situations call for more explicit instruction. Here are some strategies:

- Show children that they can use increasingly complex art materials, tools, and techniques. Make them available throughout the day so children have many opportunities to practice and refine their skills. For example, ask children to draw the day's upcoming events at greeting circle, chalk a class mural at large group time, weave yarn and twigs through a fence at outside time, or create a mosaic with tiles (made of paper, vinyl, or ceramic). Introduce diverse tools (for example, chisel, frame loom) after children have had ample time to explore with their hands and simple implements. Once children are familiar with the raw medium, they can explore more complex transformations with conventional and unconventional tools and techniques. Provide some sophisticated art materials. Narrower paintbrushes enable children to incorporate significantly more detail in their paintings, as do pencils instead of markers in their drawings. Don't change tools every day or two for the sake of novelty or variety. Leave artistic media out for a long time so children can experiment and become adept with them before moving on to something else.

- Challenge children to combine art materials and use tools in unconventional ways. Bring back art materials they used earlier in the year. Encourage them to apply new techniques to old, familiar materials as in the following example:

> The children in one preschool class began the year experimenting with paper. They tried tearing, twisting, crumbling, rolling, and other manipulations. Then they used scissors and hole punches, and finally glue and paint. Later in the year, the teacher introduced the class to yarn and fabric. Again the children began working with their hands and then using tools such as scissors, crimpers, and large tapestry needles. They looked at books on weaving and quilting. Finally, they experimented with dyeing. After a few weeks, the teacher brought out the paper again. Children were excited to see an "old friend," but now they applied the stitching and dyeing techniques they had used with fiber to paper. Some tore or cut strips and wove "paper tapestries." Others painted squares of paper and arranged them in "paper quilts."

- Experiment with the materials yourself to encourage children's exploration. Do not direct them to copy what you are doing; rather, model curiosity and an investigative attitude.

Making representations using imagination

This creative activity involves portraying things that are not present or that children have never experienced. It includes depicting make-believe (fantastical) objects, people, and events, as well as making representations of real things in fanciful ways that distort proportions, colors, spatial relations, and so on, to emphasize an attribute or idea.

Teaching strategies. Imagination is vital to all artistic pursuits. Teachers can employ many techniques to inspire creative representation by incorporating materials and activities from literacy, dramatic arts, mathematics, science, movement and music, or virtually any other domain. In fact, using artistic representation to integrate learning across disciplines is a hallmark of many curricula. Try the following strategies:

○ Read books, make up stories, and engage in other activities that inspire children to use their imaginations and represent their fantasies. Dramatic play often involves the creation of artwork (props and scenery) to further children's role-playing. Ask children to draw things or experiences they would like to have or people they would like to befriend. Their ideas may range from exotic pets to trips to the moon to cartoon characters.

○ Encourage children to talk in their own terms about the process of creating their representations. Do not ask children to name or tell you what they have made. Sometimes there is no "what"—only an idea or a feeling. You might say, "Tell me how you made this" or note, "I saw you carrying lots of paint cups and brushes to the table." Such statements invite the child to talk about the different colors, brush widths, and so on he used to create the artwork, as in the following example:

When Mrs. Shaw comments to Tony, "You're mixing a big tray of blue and black paint," he responds, "I'm making a sad color because my grandma is in the hospital." Tony fills his paper with swirls of dark color and Mrs. Shaw acknowledges, "You made your painting sad because you are sad about your grandmother."

○ Bring in reproductions of nonrepresentational or abstract artwork (for example, Jackson Pollock drip paintings, Joan Miró mobiles, Middle Eastern geometric patterns, Appalachian quilts, or Japanese ikat cloth). Encourage children to talk about what they see or feel in the imagery. Provide comparable materials and tools for them to create artwork of unreal or imaginary ideas, images, and events.

Making intentional representations

In exercising this skill, children decide beforehand what they intend to depict and then assemble the materials and tools needed to make it. To accomplish this end, children must have a mental image of their final product. They may then alter or refine the artwork to achieve greater representational accuracy, sometimes with remarkable persistence. For example, a child might spend a long time gluing strips of yarn to create the hair on a sculpture.

Teaching strategies. Intentionality in children indicates that they are using mental representations to recall prior experiences, make plans, and anticipate problems and outcomes. These cognitive behaviors are important tools that not only enrich the resulting artwork but also can generalize to learning in other content domains as well. Artistic intentionality is enhanced when teachers encourage children's forethought and reflection using strategies like these:

○ Encourage children to plan art projects. Ask them what they will make and how, including what materials, tools, and techniques they will employ; whether they will do it alone or with others; how long it will take; how big it will be; and whether and where they will display it.

○ Engage children in discussing their artwork, including their conscious (intentional) decisions about use of materials and imagery.

○ Encourage the deliberate use of inspiration from other sources, including nature and the artwork from children's home cultures. Provide materials and examples of artwork for children to observe and incorporate elements of in their own work, similar to how adult artists may use models for inspiration. The emphasis should be not on making an exact duplication of the model but rather on each child observing the attributes of the model and then representing it in her own way. Encourage children to talk to each other about what they draw or sculpt. Children build on each other's ideas, not to copy but to interpret similar experiences in their own way.

Making complex representations

Just as children's language becomes more complex with development, so do their visual representations. As they get older, children's art increasingly includes details such as facial features (eyes, eyebrows, nose, mouth, ears, hair, jewelry, freckles), architectural components (doors, windows, stairs, sidewalk, curtains, bricks, plants), and natural elements (leaf veins, seed pods, patterns on a butterfly's wings). Children strive for factual accuracy in their artwork with regard to size, spatial relations, social relationships, time, feelings, and so on. They may work on a single project over several days or even weeks to include the desired level of detail and complexity.

Teaching strategies. Any activity that encourages children to be observant will translate into their art activities. In addition, children need time and space to elaborate their artwork without feeling rushed or confined. The following are some recommended strategies:

○ Encourage children to observe and describe things in detail, even when they are not making art. Provide opportunities to observe objects and activities from different perspectives. Photograph an art or construction project in progress and encourage the children to talk about each stage—materials and tools used, what they did with them, how the project's appearance or function changed as a result. Observing and describing will heighten children's attention to details, which will be reflected in their artwork. It can also generalize to other content areas, such as recalling more elements in a story (literacy) or analyzing a problem with complex data from various viewpoints (mathematics and science).

○ Encourage children to share observations with one another as they make representations. Children's awareness is enhanced by the details that others call their attention to. They will then add their own. For example, Taunton and Colbert (2000) found that when working together to depict a potted plant, children shared observations about the plant's structure and discussed differences in their artistic approaches to representing the plant. With another method—the Project Approach—Helm and Katz suggest questions teachers can ask in a "motivational dialogue" to encourage children to focus and elaborate on the details in their observational drawings, for example, "Do you know what this is called? Do you know what it is used for?" and "Which part will you draw first? How will you connect this part?" (2011, 47). By learning a few multipurpose questions in children's home languages, teachers can start conversations about any number of activities.

- Encourage teamwork and collaboration on art projects. As each child contributes something, it opens the others' eyes to more possibilities. Their ideas will build on one another. Pair dual language learners with children whose home language is English to provide the opportunity and motivation for them to find ways to communicate with each other as they share the materials, actions, and outcomes of their enterprise.

- Label and store projects in a safe place so children can continue to elaborate on them on subsequent days. Works-in-progress can also become focal points for children to share details about their endeavors with peers, teachers, and parents.

- Display and discuss children's artwork with their permission. Seeing their own and others' artwork encourages children to think about the images and process, and to use more detail when creating future art.

Music

Young children enthusiastically explore many aspects of music on their own. They investigate and experiment with sounds in general, and with the qualities and capabilities of their voices in particular. They also enjoy playing simple musical instruments. Adult guidance furthers the preschool child's singing ability and understanding of music's rhythmic and tonal qualities.

Child-guided experience is especially important for learnings such as:

Exploring sounds

The exploration of sounds begins in infancy. Babies are alert to the sounds around them, beginning with the voices of their primary caregivers and other environmental noises at home, in their early childhood settings, and in their communities. Gradually children differentiate the sounds made by people, animals, actions, and machines and tools. Preschoolers connect sounds to their sources and begin to use sound as the basis for classification (such as loud and soft, fast and slow, thumping and tinkly).

Teaching strategies. To help young children become more aware of sounds in the environment and to encourage them to experiment by creating their own sounds, try these strategies:

- Listen to and identify sounds with children. Call their attention to indoor and outdoor sounds, such as birdsong, rain, traffic, school bells, or fans. Help children anticipate sounds (for example, before going outside, say, "I wonder what we'll hear if we're quiet"). For children with hearing disabilities, use assistive devices to amplify sound and incorporate sounds whose vibrations they can feel with their hands, feet, and whole bodies (for example, a rumbling subway car or a thrumming cello string).

- Provide noisemaking materials, such as instruments, music players, timers, wind-up clocks, or talking computer programs. Name and describe the sounds children hear with these materials and encourage them to do the same.

- Create sounds with children. Preschoolers use their voices during pretend play, whether acting out roles (reproducing a baby's "waa") or accompanying actions (going "jing, jing" like a bell). In addition, young children simply enjoy exploring the range of sounds their voices can produce. Listen to and imitate their sounds, and encourage children to experiment with more variations: "What are some other sounds that cars make?" "What sounds do you hear on the playground?"

Exploring the voice

Young children explore different qualities in their voices, including pitch (the range of notes), volume (from soft to loud), and emotion (using the voice to convey feelings). Preschoolers enjoy humming and sliding their voices from low notes to high ones and then back again. While they clearly enjoy seeing how loud they can make their voices, they also respond to challenges to talk or sing as softly as possible. Young children are particularly responsive to the affective components of the voice. As their social skills grow, they listen intently to capture the emotions behind words or sounds. They use their voices to express their own feelings, and they inflect their voices to imitate and portray the feelings of animals and people during pretend play.

Teaching strategies. To encourage young children to explore the sound-making potential of their voices, try the following ideas:

- Use your own voice in different ways. Experiment with your voice as you read books and tell stories with children, and assume different roles in dramatic play. For example, invent stories in which characters have to talk loudly to be heard over a noisy engine or must talk softly so as not to awaken a sleeping monster. Make the sounds of machines, animals, and people of different ages as you act out different scenarios (for example, a baby whose crying gets softer as it falls asleep, a car engine that sputters when it runs out of gas, a giant with a deep voice, a bird with a high-pitched voice, or a bear who whispers so as not to wake up Goldilocks).

- Imitate and comment on the many ways children use their voices. Children vocalize to express enthusiasm and displeasure, imitate human and mechanical sounds, converse, and hum and sing. They create different sound effects and patterns by moving their lips and tongues and varying their breathing, often unconsciously. However, if you comment on the sounds children make during play, they are likely to experiment even more and pay attention to the different effects their voices create.

Playing simple musical instruments

Playing musical instruments requires the manual dexterity and breath control that young children are just beginning to develop. For that reason, simple percussion, wind, and string instruments work best at this age. Children enjoy playing these instruments on their own, with others (in a "band"), and to accompany live or recorded music. It does not matter whether they are on pitch or in rhythm; the fun is in creating musical sounds.

Teaching strategies. Use the following strategies to encourage young children to explore simple musical instruments and enjoy the sounds they produce:

○ Provide children with simple instruments, both commercial and homemade. Instruments that allow preschoolers to actively use their hands and bodies include wooden blocks, rhythm sticks, drums (played with hands or drumsticks), bells, xylophones, tambourines, triangles, maracas, washboards, pots and spoons, kazoos (or other woodwinds without finger holes), and child-size guitars (such as those with four strings). Reflect the children's cultures, for example, with simple stringed instruments, gourds, or flutes. Children can also create noisemakers by filling containers (made of metal, wood, cardboard, or cloth) with beads, pebbles, sand, metal washers, or wood chips; be sure the lids are securely closed. Use these instruments at choice time, to signal transitions, and to play stop-and-start games at group times.

○ Offer recordings of different musical instruments. Play selections that feature one instrument at a time, so children can focus on the sound that each one makes. Provide pictures to accompany the recordings so children can see what the instruments look like, preferably as they are being played by a musician. Use the sounds of instruments at transition times or give children choices about which instrument(s) to play. For example, say, "When you hear the drum, it's time to move to the rug for circle time" and then play two or three other instruments before playing the drum. Encourage children to ask for recordings of specific instruments, for example, as they settle down for rest time or to accompany cleanup time.

Adult-guided experience is especially important for learnings such as:

Singing

Singing abilities develop gradually. Infants as young as 3 or 4 months try to match the pitch of their voices to a range of sounds, for example, in back-and-forth games with caregivers. Toddlers can reproduce melodic intervals, match-singing one note and then another higher or lower note. By age 3, children sing with lyrical quality, capturing the essential melody and/or rhythm of a familiar song. The tonal and rhythmic qualities of singing are well established by kindergarten age.

Teaching strategies. Singing is a universal pleasure shared by children and adults alike. To help children develop their singing abilities, use the following strategies:

- Sing with children at different times of the day. Young children enjoy singing many types of music, including sing-song nursery rhymes ("Rain, Rain, Go Away"), traditional children's songs ("The Farmer in the Dell"), simple folk songs ("She'll Be Comin' 'Round the Mountain"), and songs for special occasions ("Happy Birthday" or "Feliz Cumpleaños"). Be sure to include songs that represent the children's cultures (for example, lullabies from different lands) and that include words in their home languages, or substitute the home language for English words (for example, animal names in "Old MacDonald Had a Farm"). Use songs to heighten children's attention (for example, chant "Five minutes 'til cleanup time") or describe what they're doing (sing "Blue, blue, blue square here. Red square over there" to the tune of "Row, Row, Row Your Boat" as a child sorts blocks). Read books that illustrate familiar songs. Play singing games at group time, such as matching pitches or singing a note that is higher or lower than the last note. Playing recorded music for children to sing along with may be difficult or distracting, but if the song is already familiar to them, children may enjoy accompanying the recording with their own voices and gestures.

- Encourage children to invent their own songs. Children can make up simple tunes and words as they role-play (such as a lullaby to rock a baby to sleep), to accompany a game (such as a line to sing when they touch the tree), or to describe their actions (such as when they pour water into a big hole in the sand to create mud).

Understanding rhythmic and tonal qualities

Rhythmic qualities include beat (underlying pulse), rhythm (sound duration), and tempo (speed). An awareness of these qualities begins in toddlerhood, but a sense of rhythmic structure is more firmly set by preschool, especially when children have been frequently exposed to music with a prominent and steady beat (Geist, Geist, & Kuznik 2012; Weikart 2000). Tonal qualities include pitch (the highness or lowness of a note), melody (tune), and harmony (the interval between pitches). Children understand music's tonal qualities later than they understand rhythmic qualities (Kim & Robinson 2010), and this understanding can be helped by simple melodies with a limited number and range of pitches (such as "Row, Row Row Your Boat"). By late preschool, most children can hum or sing a recognizable melody (of a very familiar song), and might even make up a simple tune to accompany their play.

Teaching strategies. To help children's understanding of the properties of music become gradually more sophisticated, try the ideas suggested here:

- Play recorded music in which the rhythmic and tonal qualities vary. Children benefit from hearing a wide range of styles, such as folk music from around the world (e.g., Eastern European polkas, Tuvan throat singing, or South African mbaqanga—featured by Ladysmith Black Mambazo on Paul Simon's *Graceland* album), classical music, jazz, merengue, ballet, marches, waltzes, or tangos. Play music from different cultures and traditions (for example, Indian raga, Tibetan chants, mariachi, flamenco, and gospel and spirituals), with different types of instrumentation (for example, Native American flute, West African kora [harp], Indian sitar and tabla [hand drum], Australian didgeridoo]. Play primarily instrumental rather than vocal music so children are not distracted by the words. Their brains attend to language first, which can prevent them from hearing other aspects of the music, such as tempo or instrumentation. Also, do not play music as a background during play or other activities. The distraction makes it hard for children to focus on their own thoughts and actions, and it can interfere with conversation. Instead, play music at times when you can encourage children to actively listen to the music itself (Kemple, Batey, & Hartle 2004).

○ Sing and play live music in which the rhythmic and tonal qualities vary. Live music is a treat for everyone. Choose a wide selection of songs and musical genres with different instrumentation to teach, sing, and play with children. Invite staff members, parents, and local musicians to share their music in the classroom. Arrange field trips to a local middle or high school to listen to their band, jazz quartet, or orchestra. Go to local street fairs and cultural festivals where musical entertainment fills the air.

Movement

While movement depends in part on large motor development (see p. 69 in Chap. 5), creative movement emphasizes expressiveness rather than physical development. On their own, children enjoy moving their bodies in different ways to represent their observations and experiences. They spontaneously imitate the simple movements (with one or two components) performed by others. With adult guidance, preschoolers can copy more complex movements. Eventually, they can create movement sequences, or dances, for their own pleasure and for others to imitate and extend.

Child-guided experience is especially important for learnings such as:

Moving the body in different ways

As young children gain greater motor control, they use their bodies in ways that are not merely functional. For example, instead of simply moving from point A to point B, they investigate *how* they can do so (by crawling, slithering, rolling, walking backward, hopping, and so on). In fact, the fun of experimenting with creative movement may take precedence over the child's original goal of getting someplace! Children delight in spontaneously testing the boundaries of what their bodies can do, a pleasure that supportive adults can share in.

Teaching strategies. To reinforce the joy young children experience in moving their bodies, try the following ideas:

○ Provide time and space for children to move their bodies, both indoors and outdoors. Include open spaces where they can move freely and tighter spaces so they can practice more controlled movements. Offer simple equipment (such as low beams, steps and ladders, inner tubes and Hula-Hoops) and provide different types of materials (such as scarves and streamers) to encourage children to vary their creative movements.

- Offer simple challenges that inspire children to experiment with movement. Focusing on movement alone (that is, without music), ask children questions such as "How can we move to our cubbies without our toes touching the floor?" or "How could you move around a really big puddle?" or "What are all the ways you can move in and out of the hoop?"

- Encourage simple ways of moving creatively to instrumental music. Play music of different styles, such as fast and slow, smooth and staccato, or intense and relaxed. Capture the rhythms and moods of different cultures, from bouncy Cajun zydeco to plaintive Japanese koto music to resonant South African mbanqanga. Adjust the volume or use special headphone so children with auditory disabilities can hear or feel the vibrations of the music with their bodies. Comment on how the children's movements are connected to the quality of the music (for example, "Miguel is swinging his arms back and forth in time to the lively beat" or "Leah is sliding her walker back and forth in time to the gentle waltz music").

- Include props such as scarves, streamers, paper plates, rhythm sticks, and other percussion instruments to further encourage the children to move creatively as they listen to music that varies in tempo, pitch, and volume.

Imitating simple movements

Young children frequently copy the simple movements of people, animals, or mechanical devices. They may do this as part of a pretend-play scenario, in response to music, or simply for its own sake. Typical examples in preschool include galloping like a horse, driving a car, or spraying a hose back and forth to put out a fire. The ability to represent enables preschoolers to use movement, along with the other creative arts, as a kind of language. Imitating simple movements can also be a form of social participation. For example, when children copy the actions of an adult or peer at large group time, movement becomes a way of saying, "I am part of the classroom community."

Teaching strategies. To take advantage of children's spontaneous inclination to imitate many types of movement, try the following strategies:

- Sing songs and recite chants that incorporate simple movements. Use songs that already include movements (such as "If You're Happy and You Know It") or create simple movement sequences for other songs. For example, take a song with two parts (such as "Yankee Doodle") and ask children to suggest a different movement for each part (march to the verse and wave their arms to the chorus). Introduce simple movements at transitions and when beginning new activities (for example, as the children gather for circle time). Encourage children to copy your movements as they settle into the activity and then to create their own simple movements. Call attention to each child's movements so the other children can observe, imitate, and suggest their own ideas.

- Describe and encourage children to describe their creative use of movement throughout the day. For example, during free play, you might say, "You're stepping slowly so the scarf doesn't fall off your head." At cleanup time, note how children carry objects as they put them away ("Justin is walking tippy-toe to the puzzle shelf"). At large group time, label and encourage others to imitate children's movements ("Josie and Luke are flapping their arms like birds. I'm going to try that too"). Talking with children about their creative movements also helps them become more conscious of what they are doing and lets them be more deliberate in their actions.

At large group time, Jules (a teacher) plays the guitar, stops, and then plays again. While he plays, the children move their arms to the music. When he stops playing, they stop moving. When he resumes playing, the children move their arms a different way. During the "stop" time Jules comments, "You moved your arms in all kinds of ways!" The children respond with comments such as these: "I waved mine around." "I bounced mine up and down like you played the guitar." "My arms bended like a straw." "I made mine go faster than anything!" "I waved to you!"

Adult-guided experience is especially important for learnings such as:

Imitating complex movements

Although children move their bodies in different ways, the amount of variety in their movements can actually be quite limited. For example, while listening to music, 3-year-olds are likely to move in place (bending their knees or waving their arms), while 4- and 5-year-olds repeat a limited number of movement patterns (going up and down, side to side, or in a circle). However, if adults intentionally introduce new ideas—such as different body postures, actions, and hand gestures—children will themselves try a wider range of movements in response to music and as a general mode of creative expression (Dow 2010).

Teaching strategies. To expand the range of creative movements that young children imitate and create, try these strategies:

- Introduce new postures, movements, and gestures gradually throughout the day. Be sure to include movements that children with physical disabilities can perform with different parts of their bodies (for example, upper-body movements for those in wheelchairs; movements done in a sitting position for children with balance problems; head movements for children who have difficulty moving their arms and legs). Once children have mastered a basic movement, demonstrate variations for them to try out on their own. For example, alternate big steps and small steps; bend your body at different angles or in different directions; or hold one hand against your side and move only the other hand. Move your arms, legs, and entire body from different positions (for example, lying on your side). Encourage the children to copy these increasingly varied movements and then to invent their own. Introduce new vocabulary words to accompany their new and complex movements (for example, "We're holding the fingers on one hand stiff and wiggling the fingers on the other hand"). For dual language learners, label body parts and actions in their home languages and English (for example, "Stretch your arm in the air. Rale bra ou nan lè a [Haitian Creole].").

- Provide opportunities for children to represent their experiences using movement. Encourage children to use their bodies to express emotions, such as sad, mad, frightened, brave, friendly, shy, and silly ("How do you move when you feel happy?" or "Let's move to the snack table as though we're tired and sleepy"). Ask children to move in ways that match how characters feel at key points in a story— for example, how Max (in *Where the Wild Things Are* by Maurice Sendak) might move when he comes home and finds his dinner is still warm, or how Sophie (in *Sophie's Squash* by Pat Zietlow Miller) might react when her mother tries to make Sophie's beloved pet squash into dinner. Have children represent a field trip with movement, including the journey there and back and their experiences at the site.

Creating movement sequences

Once children have mastered simple one- and two-step movements, they can copy and create sequences of three or more steps. Preschoolers enjoy this more creative aspect of movement expression—that is, "taking a familiar movement and changing it in some way" (Sawyers, Colley, & Icaza 2010, 32). Adult guidance and encouragement can help children consider multiple possibilities to expand on familiar actions. For example, after a child creates a two-step sequence, the teacher might ask, "Is there another place we can tap our bodies with our hands?" and then use the children's suggestions to create a three-step tapping sequence. Furthermore, by introducing complex creative movements during group times, adults indirectly encourage children to incorporate elaborated movement sequences during choice time and at outside time.

Teaching strategies. To build on preschoolers' growing capacity to create movement sequences, use the following ideas:

- Invite children to do three or more movements in a row. For example, at circle time, after repeating a two-step movement several times (to be sure all the children can do it), say, "Let's add one more movement." Solicit the children's ideas. Slowly demonstrate the three steps and give children time to practice them. It is best to first introduce complex movement sequences *without* music, so children are not overwhelmed by too many factors at once. Later, after children are familiar with a music-movement combination, add one or more movements to the sequence.

- Encourage children to solve movement problems at different times of the day. The ideas can come from anywhere, including from observations of how children move spontaneously, unusual movements in books and nursery rhymes, or observations of how mechanical objects and things in nature move. For example, ask children to put away the blocks using just their elbows, encourage them to move to the next activity like a certain type of animal (for example, a snake or rabbit), or wonder how many ways children can move "in, out, over, and around" a row of tires. Movement problems are especially appropriate at group times, outside time, and transitions. Children may then incorporate the ideas into their play.

Dramatic (Pretend) Play

Dramatic play (also called pretend or sociodramatic play) is a hallmark of early childhood that involves both imitation and imagination. Children express their understanding of the world by reenacting their experiences with people, objects, and events. Pretend play strengthens skills in attention, memory, reasoning, language, and emotional understanding (Tomlinson & Hyson 2009). Preschoolers' social interactions are more advanced during pretend play than other forms of play, such as construction projects not tied to acting out scenarios or puzzles (Chafel 1984).

The motivation behind dramatic play appears to be universal and spontaneous. Young children independently imitate gestures, sounds, and words. They use simple props and create scenarios alone or with one other person. Inspired by the stories they hear and read with parents and teachers, they tell and act out their own narratives, using themselves, dolls and other figures, and puppets. Dramatic play becomes more complex, however, when scaffolded by an adult (Bodrova & Leong 2007). Adult guidance encourages children to imagine characters and events outside their own immediate experience, to create more complex props to support their play scenarios and storytelling, and to engage in dramatic play with two or more other people.

Child-guided experience is especially important for learnings such as:

Imitating gestures, sounds, and words

The first step in dramatic play involves simple imitation of the people, objects, and actions in the environment. Young children use their bodies (gestures, facial expressions), copy sounds (human, animal, or mechanical), and repeat words (such as "Go to sleep, baby") to represent the world they know. Pretend play begins at about 18 months and becomes more sophisticated throughout toddlerhood and preschool as the child's ability to observe and reproduce details increases.

Teaching strategies. To support young children's early imitation of gestures, sounds, and words in their dramatic play experiences, try these strategies:

- Foster children's spontaneous imitations. Copy children as they, in turn, attempt to reproduce the actions and sounds around them. For example, if a child flattens a piece of playdough and pretends to "flip pizzas," flatten some playdough and flip pizzas alongside the child using the same motions. Imitating children's actions may lead to an "action dialogue" in which the adult and the child communicate with gestures instead of words.

- Encourage children's imitation throughout the day. For example, after you read a book, ask children to imitate the actions of the characters (themselves or with figures and puppets). They can also imitate the movements in the words of a song. Use imitation to make cleanup fun (for example, walking backward like a crab to put away the carpet squares). Go on field trips so children will see and hear new things to imitate. Observe the movements and sounds in nature (pattering raindrops, dried stalks rustling in the breeze; swarming insects). Re-creating actions and sounds is also a meaningful way for children to remember and process their observations and experiences.

Using simple props

The earliest use of props in pretend play is with ready-made objects, such as a real or child-size version of a tool or utensil (for example, stirring "soup" with a wooden spoon; driving the multiseat "bus" on the playground). Once children begin to form simple mental representations, they use one thing (such as a block) to stand for something else (such as a telephone). At first, children tend to employ an object in their vision or close at hand. Later, they may seek out something whose properties (such as size or shape) bear a similarity to the object they want to incorporate in their play scenario (for example, a small wooden dowel may stand in for a birthday candle).

Teaching strategies. Use the following ideas to support children in their use of simple props:

○ Provide materials that children can easily incorporate as simple props in their play. Generally, young children will use anything they can easily handle and that doesn't need to be transformed in some way. This includes blocks and other construction toys, items from the house area (such as a cutting board or dish cloth), and individual art materials (such as a marker or piece of yarn).

○ Use simple props yourself. Incorporate props in your interactions with children (for example, use a block as a telephone and say, "Calling all children to snack time"). During small group time, introduce children to new items they can use as props so they can explore these materials and later use them in dramatic play. As you play as a partner alongside children, use simple props to carry out the roles they assign you (for example, use a marker as a "needle" to give the baby a shot).

Pretending alone or with one other person

Very young children engage in sociodramatic play alone. For example, they may "drive" a block along the table. Parallel play (playing *alongside* others) begins in the second year, and social play (playing *with* others) emerges around age 3. In the early years of preschool, however, social play is generally limited to pretending with one other person. Juggling the play scenario and negotiating roles with more partners is cognitively and socially too complex for most 3-year-olds.

Teaching strategies. To support children's earliest attempts at pretend play, the following strategies are effective:

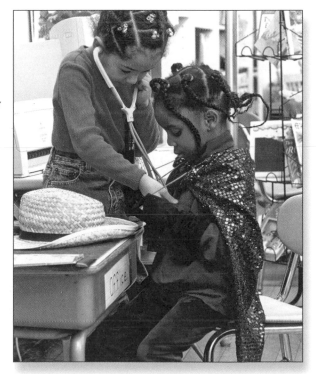

○ Participate as a partner in children's pretend play. Child development and storytelling expert Vivian Paley (2004) says adults who act as partners in children's play are better observers, understand children more, and communicate with them more effectively. However, partnering must be done with sensitivity. Observe first to understand children's intentions before you join in. Wait until you are invited or look for cues that you are welcome. Continue with the play theme established by the children. Match the level of your play to theirs.

Occasionally suggest an extension (for example, "Does the dough need more water *and* salt?"), but respect the child's right to reject it.

O Ask a question now and then or offer a slight modification to accustom children to explaining their own thoughts and (eventually) incorporating the ideas of others into their play. In this way, you are acting as a model of how to play cooperatively with others. It is easier for children to begin playing with an adult than another child because the adult is more flexible and willing to go along with the child's ideas. However, by gently raising other possibilities, you can help young children learn to accommodate and extend their ideas in the context of a partnership.

Adult-guided experience is especially important for learnings such as:

Imagining characters and events

Children imitate familiar people, animals, and actions on their own, but using their imaginations to create pretend-play scenarios requires more active adult intervention. Imaginative play is about the world of "Suppose . . . " and "What if . . . ?" When adults partner with children, they can gently raise such questions, provided they still let the children take the lead in the evolving scenario. As children become better able to remember stories and songs, adults can also prompt them to re-create and expand on characters and events as they carry out their own imaginary play themes.

Teaching strategies. The following strategies will encourage young children to use their imaginations as they engage in dramatic play:

O Support imaginative role play in the classroom. Provide space and materials for pretending and role-playing. Arrange the room with open areas that can become jungles, spaceships, or shopping malls. Allow dramatic play to overlap from one area of the room into another. For example, children in the house area may "build" a backyard barbecue in the block area. By locating these areas next to one another, you facilitate this type of creative play. Fill the room with materials that support imaginative play. For example, equipment and dress-up clothes in the house area might inspire children to act out a family dinner table scene, open a restaurant, or set up a doctor's office. Small human and animal figures in the manipulatives area and puppets in the book area lend themselves to making up and acting out stories.

O Support imaginative role-playing outdoors. Wheeled toys (bicycles, wagons) can serve as buses, trains, airplanes, spaceships, or boats, while climbing structures become houses, forts, tents, and igloos. Small items from nature, such as pebbles and leaves, are a feast for a banquet. Bringing indoor materials (scarves, dolls, cooking utensils) outside further extends children's imaginative play ideas.

O Visit places in the community to expand the experiences children can draw on, and bring back materials (cash register receipts, hardware) to add authenticity to their dramatic play. Attend storytelling events at the library and/or local festivals that are geared for preschoolers. Invite storytellers to the classroom, including those who specialize in folktales from different countries, cultures, and traditions.

Creating complex props

Preschoolers create increasingly complex props to support their sociodramatic play. Instead of relying on ready-made objects with similar characteristics, they seek out and combine materials in unique ways (for example, instead of using an unadorned doll blanket as a magic carpet, they might attach streamers so it can fly through the air). Sometimes these props are needed to simply represent an object or creature in the play scenario (for example, the firefighter needs a hose with a nozzle taped to the end; the dragon needs a tail). Other times, the prop solves a problem (two pet owners need a car to transport four dogs—more than they can carry—to the vet). You may find that children can get so involved creating props that the dramatic play takes a backseat! If children are occasionally stymied by a problem during pretend play ("We can't all fit on the bus"), adults can encourage them to consider a wider range of materials and tools to solve it.

Teaching strategies. Children will expand the number and type of props they create with the following types of adult support:

○ Provide materials that children can combine into complex props in their play. As children gain manual dexterity and are able to think in terms of multipart representations, they are more likely to combine and transform materials to support their play scenarios. A well-organized art area, block area, or other part of the room helps them survey the possibilities and see how they might create something new to fit the needs of a scenario or even suggest a new direction for their play (for example, a roll of blue paper may suggest a scuba dive to look at creatures on the bottom of the ocean).

○ Use complex props yourself. Incorporate props that combine or transform materials in your interactions with children. For example, signal transitions with a flashlight that you have decorated with streamers and sequins and that you call your magic timer. As you play as a partner alongside children, model making complex props to carry out pretend-play roles. For example, if a child invites you to work in her "office," ask what you need to have at your desk, and invite the child to help you make the props using a variety of materials.

Pretending with two or more other people

Social conflicts often arise during sociodramatic play. The more children there are, the greater the opportunity for problems to arise. Children disagree over who gets to play which role, how the scenario (story) should evolve, and what props are needed. In these instances, adults can teach children conflict-resolution techniques (see p. 60 in Chap. 4) to help them work through their social problems and continue their play. The ability to carry out a pretend scenario with two or more peers generally does not appear until 4 or 5 years of age. By then, with adult guidance, children can invent more elaborate story lines that involve multiple roles for themselves, human and animal figures, and/or puppets. Moreover, their interactions last longer and illustrate more cooperation than in other social situations (Nicolopoulou & Richner 2007).

Teaching strategies. To expand the number of partners children can include in their pretend-play scenarios, try the following ideas:

○ Provide materials and equipment that encourage children to collaborate. This might include rocking boats or wheeled toys (such as a bus) that accommodate several children. Also have on hand large boards, boxes, blankets, or other equipment that require three or more children to carry, move, or arrange. The very act of working together can inspire children to develop play scenarios with multiple roles.

○ Facilitate social problem solving. Encourage children to think of alternate roles or scenarios that will let them all participate in the play. For example, you might say, "So Bethany, Soo-yi, and Marta all want to be the mother. How can we solve this problem?" or "You both want to use the firefighter puppet and play the good guy. I wonder if any other puppets can be good guys too." Not only will you facilitate a resolution to the conflict, the children may come up with creative ideas that expand the dramatic play theme. For example, they may decide that Bethany will be the mother, Soo-yi the aunt, and Marta the fairy godmother who grants them wishes and bakes a birthday cake, or that it might be more fun to make the doctor puppet into a bad character and have the firefighter take away her "needle machine."

Art Appreciation

Of the key knowledge and skills involved in appreciating the creative arts, child-guided experience seems particularly important for focusing on one aspect of a work of art, making simple aesthetic choices, and recognizing and understanding the feelings expressed through art. Adult-guided experience seems to be especially significant for naming artistic media, elements, and techniques; focusing on multiple aspects of a work of art; articulating the reasons for aesthetic choices; describing and articulating the feelings expressed through art; and recognizing cultural and temporal influences on art.

Child-guided experience is especially important for learnings such as:

Focusing on one aspect of a work of art

Young preschoolers pay attention to one dominant or salient feature in a work of art, such as color or line in visual art or tempo in music. Even with a complex image, musical composition, movement, or story scenario, they may focus on just one aspect rather than the work as a whole.

Teaching strategies. Children's keen interest in a particular feature or section of a piece of a work of art provides teachers with an opening to explore that subject matter in depth. Build on the children's specific interest rather than forcing attention or interest elsewhere. A broader focus will come with time if adults allow young children's detailed focus to thrive. Try the following strategies:

○ Provide works of art that have a limited number of features, such as a painting with bold colors, recorded music with a strong beat, a single movement imitating an animal, or a story with a repeated action. Encourage children to describe what they observe ("What did you notice about how he got to the top of the hill?") and how it relates to them ("Do you ever move like that?").

○ Accept children's fascination with one aspect of a more complex piece of art. Encourage them to talk about the first or main element they notice. Ask what drew their eye or ear to this feature. For example, if a child focuses on the lower right corner of a painting, learn why it is interesting to her. Imitate the movement that the child picks up on, or repeat the child's favorite words in a song. When children are ready, they will switch their attention to another artistic feature.

○ Plan activities where children can focus on a single art element in depth, such as color or line, tempo, or a pretend-play role. For example, look at reproductions of sculptures by Japanese American artist Isamu Noguchi, whose works focus on abstract shapes rather than color or recognizable imagery. Consider African American artist Romare Bearden's collages. Play recordings of two string instruments, such as a West African kora (harp) and an Indian sitar, so children can compare the sounds and move their bodies expressively to the music. If the children have been pretending they are kitties, tell or read folktales that feature cats and add bowls and empty milk cartons to the house area to extend their pretend play.

Making simple aesthetic choices

Children express aesthetic choices in verbal and nonverbal ways. They may look at one picture longer than another, pick their favorite song every time it's their turn to choose, demonstrate a particular movement for others to copy at circle time, or choose the same role day after day in a dramatic play scenario. However, even when their choices are quite definite, young children are often unable to explain the reasoning behind their preferences.

Teaching strategies. Young children need opportunities to make choices and to express their preferences and desires. By providing many options and acknowledging children's right to choose, teachers support aesthetic development and encourage decision making in general. Here are some strategies to try:

○ Offer a wide variety of art and artistic materials so that children with diverse preferences will find at least one medium, style, or technique they like to experience and create.

○ Provide materials that foster art appreciation, being culturally inclusive. For example, offer objects and images depicting ink drawings, collages, pottery, weaving, mosaics, calligraphy, landscape architecture, and photography (visual art). Play instrumental selections in many styles from many countries, such as Indian raga, African drums, Indonesian gamelan, Native American flute, and Mexican mariachi (music). Watch short videos or invite dancers and acrobats who perform in different genres, such as ballet, salsa, flamenco, hip-hop, Balinese, and belly dancing (movement); and read illustrated folktales from many cultures and act them out together with the children (dramatic play).

○ Encourage, rather than compliment or praise, children's aesthetic choices (see the box on p. 226 in this chapter). For example, say, "I see you used lots of blue in your painting" instead of "Blue is my favorite color." Or, rather than make a comment such as "I like the way you're moving to the music," imitate the child's actions or encourage others to copy or extend the movement themselves. When we praise one child, children not praised may think their work is inferior or unworthy. Children who receive praise one day but not another may think their work is no longer any good.

○ Create a warm and supportive atmosphere for all activities and choices in the classroom, and for children of all backgrounds and ability levels. An emotionally safe environment will generalize to making and appreciating the creative arts.

○ Share your own aesthetic preferences (without downgrading those of others), and express pleasure in experiencing different types of art. In this way, the intentional teacher communicates the joy that art can bring to life.

○ Observe art as it occurs in nature, using all the senses. The formal properties of art—such as light, color, form, and texture; pitch and tempo; range and speed of movement; and plot, theme, and characters—have counterparts in the natural world. For example, flowers come in many colors, birds sing different songs,

Encouragement Versus Compliments

Encouragement communicates your interest as you take the time to observe and comment on what the creative artist is doing, even joining in the experience. Compliments are well meaning, but they can actually discourage the child artist, as well as other children who see and overhear the exchange. The likely reward of encouragement is an authentic conversation about art.

Many teachers wonder, as this teacher does, how best to respond to children's art making:

Martin is painting at the easel. His painting is an array of colors and unrecognizable forms. As the teacher approaches Martin, she pauses, unsure of what to do or say. Should she praise his effort by saying something like, "Very beautiful, Martin. You've worked hard on your painting"? Should she ask questions about the colors and shapes she sees in his painting? Should she ask Martin if he wants to talk to her, or should she wait for him to initiate a discussion about his work?

Probably the most common approach adults take to communicating with children about art is to compliment, or praise, their work: "I really liked the way you used the chalk" or "That's a beautiful painting." Though such statements are intended to be supportive and encouraging, they can actually have a negative impact. Praise, though positive, is still judgmental, giving the message that it is the adult's role to evaluate the child's artwork. As a result, the child may grow inhibited, afraid to explore or be creative. This can create a climate in which children become "praise junkies," who feel good about their work only when adults tell them it is good, beautiful, or nice.

The alternative to mechanical compliments is to engage in a dialogue with children that encourages them to reflect on and discuss their work. Such a dialogue develops naturally when adults interact as *partners* with children. In a partnership approach, adults participate in art activities—they truly become part of the children's art experience. This can lead to a sustained dialogue with children.

To become a partner in children's art, a good first step is to **stop talking so much or thinking so much about what to say.** Instead, observe children closely when they are busy with the process of art. Sit or kneel next to children and simply watch what they are doing. Many times, observation is the best way to start a conversation—the child will begin talking to you about what he is doing. The dialogue that grows out of this approach is natural, and the questions the adult asks are related to the child's actions and how the child sees and thinks about his artwork.

Using art materials the same way the children do is another effective strategy for helping you form a partnership with children. Because of the abundance of materials in the art area, it is often easiest to use this strategy. If the child is making holes in clay, get another piece of clay and do the same. By imitating, you are telling the child nonverbally that you accept and value what she is doing. This type of encouragement often prompts the child to start a conversation.

The conversations that occur during art partnerships are free flowing and offer the adult many opportunities to talk with children not only about the *process* of making something—the materials, how the child uses them, and the sequence of activities—but also the *elements of art*—color, line, pattern, shape, space, and texture. Because the adult discusses these concepts in the context of the child's project, they are more meaningful than they would be if taught directly.

Adapted, by permission, from M. Tompkins, "A Partnership With Young Artists," in *Supporting Young Learners 2: Ideas for Child Care Providers and Teachers,* ed. N.A. Brickman, (Ypsilanti, MI: HighScope Press, 1996a), 187, 189–90.

clouds move at different speeds, and animals live and play in different habitats. Helping children consider nature from an aesthetic perspective not only broadens their appreciation of the creative arts but also heightens their sensitivity to the environment (see also the Appreciating Ecology section on p. 193 in Chap. 9). Also, simply being in nature encourages children to use all their senses, which is vital to developing a broad artistic appreciation of the world.

Recognizing and understanding the feelings expressed through art

Young children can be aware of and comprehend the underlying feeling an artist is trying to express in a work of art. For example, they may recognize whether a line drawing expresses joy or sadness, a piece of music sounds busy, a movement conveys being tired, or a dramatic incident is scary. They may not be able to label or explain this feeling to someone else, but they can convey their emotional understanding through body and facial gestures (a slump or frown to communicate sadness), a dance movement (hopping with glee), or a comparable representation in their own artwork (tight circles of energy drawn in red crayon).

Teaching strategies. Children, like adults, need emotional outlets, whether they are socializing, solving an intellectual problem, or making art. In fact, art is an excellent way for children who are preverbal, nonverbal, or learning more than one language to identify and express feelings and to begin to understand the emotions of others. Teachers can use the natural affinity between art and expression with the following strategies:

- Share storybook illustrations and art reproductions with children, then provide art materials and ask children to create something that shows how those works make them feel or how they think the artist was feeling when she made the work. Give children simple instruments or encourage them to move in ways that represent their own or the artist's emotions. Have them act out a story, using gestures, facial expressions, and words to convey the underlying feelings. Children who may not feel comfortable acting out emotions themselves, whether for personal and/or cultural reasons, may find it easier to do so with figures or puppets.

- Combine artistic media so children can explore the feelings they evoke. For example, play different types of music at large group time and give the children scarves to move in different ways inspired by the music's tempo, pitch, or mood. At small group time, provide different types of food for the children to smell, and ask them to pick a crayon whose color is like the smell.

- Let the feelings in a work of art speak for themselves. Allow time during the day for children to engage in quiet, peaceful contemplation.

Adult-guided experience is especially important for learnings such as:

Naming artistic media, elements, and techniques

Children learn from adults specifics about art such as

- The vocabulary words to describe and differentiate forms of representation (for example, *painting*, *sculpting*, and *collage*; *melody* and *lyrics*; arm and leg *extensions* and dance *steps*; *stories*, *poems*, and *plays*)

- The formal properties or elements of the creative arts (for example, line, color, and texture; rhythm and tone; movement and stillness; plot, setting, and character)

- The techniques used by artists to create aesthetic effects (for example, molding, layering, and stitching; solo performances and orchestral or ensemble works; free-flowing versus mechanical movements; humor and conflict)

Teaching strategies. Mastering the language of art often takes repeated exposure before children fully grasp the words and concepts and feel confident employing them in their own conversations. Teachers have many options available to introduce this rich vocabulary and give children multiple opportunities to understand and use it in producing and analyzing art. Try the following strategies:

- Develop a language to talk about art with children (see the box below). Look at and talk about what the product is made of, what the children see (lines,

Talking With Children About the Creative Arts

Thoughtful comments and occasional open-ended questions in which adults invite children's ideas can lead to genuine discussions about making and appreciating art. Here are some conversational openers that encourage children to share and reflect on their art experiences.

"How does the (material) feel (or smell, sound, or other appropriate sense)?"

For example, "How do the beads feel?" or "How does the clay smell?" or "How does the tambourine sound?"

"What does the (sound, image) remind you of?"

For example, "What does this slow music make you think of?" or "I wonder if this jagged shape reminds you of anything on the playground?"

"How can we move to this (sound or music)?"

For example, "Here's a quiet and slow song. How could we move to it?"

"This (image, sound, movement) makes me think of _____."

For example, "This dark red reminds me of the lipstick your mommy wears" or "That noise sounds like the fire truck that just went by."

"I'm curious about how you made that. What did you use?"

For example, "How did you build the boat?" or "Tell me what you used to make your boat."

"How will you be the (pretend role)? What will you use?"

For example, "You're going to be the guy who puts out the fires. I wonder what you will use to do that."

"How did you use the (material or tool)?"

For example, "I wonder how you used the chisel to make your bookends" or "I wonder how you made your scarves fly to the windy music."

"Tell us what you found out about the (material or tool)."

For example, "Jason used the tapestry hook today. Jason, what did you learn about using the tapestry hook?"

"How did you do that (movement)?"

For example, "Show (or tell) us how you jumped so we can all try to do it that way."

"What did you do so the (material or action) looks like (describe effect)?"

For example, "What did you do to make the paint so thick in this corner?" or "What did you do to make your arms spin around?"

"Tell me (or us or another child) about the (materials) you used or (action) you did."

shapes, colors), what it represents, how it is organized, what it is about, and where the ideas came from. Several publications include glossaries of art terms to use with young children (e.g., Althouse, Johnson, & Mitchell 2003, 130–37; Epstein & Trimis 2002, 259–61). Add to these published glossaries the vocabulary words, phrases, and definitions that you and the children use while discussing their art interests, including those for the art prevalent in their cultures and community. Provide words in children's home languages as well as in English.

○ Expose children to the works of different artists from many traditions and cultures, including their own and those of their classmates. Children often encounter visual images and music but may be unaware of the artistry contained in them. Moreover, there are art experiences (such as live performances) that children are unlikely to have without a conscious effort on the part of

For example, "Liza, Alicia wants to know how you painted your cup yesterday so she can paint her bowl today" or "Max, how can I slide slowly from the chair to the door like you just did?"

"What made you think of making/doing that?"

For example, "Chris, what made you decide to make a doghouse?" or "Elena and Cherise, I wonder why you decided to both be the mommies."

"What are some other ways to (use the material or tool) or (move to that sound)?"

For example, "I wonder how else we can fold the paper" or "Let's see how else we can move to this bouncy music."

"What do you think would happen if (suggest a way to manipulate a material or move in a unique way)?"

For example, "What do you suppose would happen if we dipped the yarn in water first?" or "What would happen if we didn't use our hands to move the balloons?"

"I wonder how you could get the (material or your body) to (act or move a certain way)."

For example, "I wonder how you could get the paper to stand up" or "How do you think you could make your arms go high and then low?"

"I'd like to hear more about (material, tool, or action)."

For example, "I'd like to hear more about the way you used these brushes on the wood" or "Tell me more about the rules you made up for your speedboat race."

"I wonder what's the same (or different) about these (materials, sounds, or actions)."

For example, "I wonder what's the same about the watercolor and tempera paints" or "What's different about these two notes?" or "Garth stretched his arms this way (demonstrate) and Keira stretched her this way (demonstrate). How do you think they're the same? different?"

"These (images, sounds, actions) look (sound) different. I wonder why."

For example, "I wonder why your pictures look so different even though you both used blue paper and red markers" or "We all moved differently to the same fast music. I wonder why."

"Why do you suppose the artist (painter, composer, dancer) made (or did) it that way?"

For example, "I wonder why this artist paints big pictures and this one makes small pictures?" or "The first composer wrote fast notes and the second one wrote slow notes. Why do you suppose they each wrote their music a different way?"

Adapted, by permission, from A.S. Epstein, *The HighScope Preschool Curriculum: Creative Arts* (Ypsilanti, MI: HighScope Press, 2012b), 22–23.

adults. To expand preschoolers' experiences with various artistic media, try the following:

- ○ *Art*—Offer illustrated storybooks with artwork in different styles and reproductions of art, such as postcards and posters, depicting a range of media and subject matter

- ○ *Music*—Play musical selections featuring classical, jazz, opera, folk songs, world music, and other genres; show pictures (album covers, posters) depicting music being performed by individuals, small groups, choirs, and orchestras; provide a variety of simple percussion, string, and wind instruments for children to play

- ○ *Movement*—Use music that inspires children to move in response to tonal quality, tempo, or pitch; show photos that illustrate dance styles and performance settings from around the world

- ○ *Dramatic play*—Provide props, figures, and puppets for children to develop play themes and reenactments based on familiar stories and folktales; encourage children to expand the complexity of the play beyond scripted lines

- ◉ Provide children with materials and tools similar to those used by the artists they study. As they draw and sculpt, make up songs and dances, or invent play scenarios, comment on the similarities between their techniques and styles and those of the artists that interest them.

- ◉ Point out when the background of an artist is the same as the children and their families. For example, talk about popular hip-hop artists who grew up in the inner city or country singers who are from the same area of the South. For children from other countries, mention that Wyclef Jean is from Haiti, El Anatsui is a Nigerian artist, Amadou and Mariam are both blind and were born in Mali, and Iraqi architect Zaha Hadid is a woman who designs buildings all over the world.

Focusing on multiple aspects of a work of art

As children mature in their cognitive and artistic abilities, they can pay attention to the overall work of art and how its components are interconnected. For example, they might notice how the colors in a painting contrast with one another, how tempos shift in a piece of music, the way arm and leg movements are coordinated in a simple dance, or how an event in a story changes the way a character solves a problem.

Teaching strategies. Teachers can develop children's ability to attend to aesthetic relationships by exposing them to increasingly complex and evocative works of art. Because their growing awareness depends on analytical abilities, any teaching strategies that encourage children to reflect on and articulate their observations will help them apply these skills to appreciating the arts, such as the following:

- ◉ Gradually increase the complexity of artwork depicted in the reproductions displayed in the classroom, the music or movements explored at group times, and the stories you read or act out with the children. Be sure they portray a variety of subjects (themes), feelings, and techniques.

- ◉ As you engage children in conversations about art, comment on how one aspect relates to another. For example, say, "The red hat next to the green tree makes both colors really stand out" or "When the music slowed down, the mood changed from happy to sad."

○ Encourage children to view artwork from various perspectives or positions (for example, up close, far away, from the side, squinting) and to see whether things look different in relation to one another. This observational exercise works well with paintings that feature pointillism (as in the work of Georges Seurat), multiple layers (as in the works of Mark Rothko and Josef Albers), primitivism (as in the work of Jean-Michel Basquiat), squares of color (as in the work of Chuck Close as well as Middle Eastern tile mosaics), and different elevations (as in the work of I.M. Pei). Do the same with music (for example, does the mood change when we turn out the lights to listen to jazz musician Django Reinhardt?), movements (how do the arm gestures of the Balinese dancers look when seen from below or above, in front or behind?), and dramatic narratives (does one character perceive a problem situation differently than another in a Russian or Brazilian folktale?).

Articulating the reasons for aesthetic choices

As children's growing self-awareness is accompanied by an expanding vocabulary, they are increasingly able to give voice to their own and others' aesthetic preferences. They can explain artistic decisions and choices in the formal language of art, such as by describing a work's color and line, tempo, mood, or character. If asked open-ended questions, preschoolers can say what they think an artist is trying to represent or communicate. In fact, when given opportunities and a variety of experiences, young children enjoy talking about art and identifying the characteristics of artists and their work.

Teaching strategies. Teachers enable children to talk about aesthetics when they provide language specific to art. Strategies such as the following help children observe and express the rationale behind aesthetic decisions:

○ Anchor art in children's lives to help them express personal ideas, as illustrated in the following summary of a project related by Kolodziej (1995):

> During a project in which preschoolers created their own picture museum before visiting the International Museum of Photography in Rochester, New York, the children brought in their favorite photographs of themselves. They then titled the pictures, which encouraged reflection and discussion about where and when the pictures were taken and why they were important to each child. The children also labeled the photographs and made an exhibit catalog with their comments about the images. Creating the picture museum involved children in many participatory ways. In choosing a photograph, they expressed an aesthetic preference. By describing the image, they engaged in art criticism. While creating titles, labels, and an exhibit catalog, the children acquired a sense of how museums are organized and operated. As a result, when the children later visited the museum, they had a firsthand basis for understanding the value of museums and such concepts as "art collection," as well as an appreciation of photography as an art form.

○ Accept children's explanations of their aesthetic preferences. Display their visual art, sing the songs and copy the movements they invent, and take on the roles they assign you in dramatic play. Encourage them to talk about what, how, and why they made something—a painting, tune, dance, or prop. Ask open-ended questions to elicit reasons for their choice of materials, images, and techniques. Express your own aesthetic preferences (though not in judging children's work) and state why a work of art or other aesthetic item does or does not appeal to you.

○ Provide works of art in different media and styles, from many cultures, including those represented in the classroom community. Encourage children to talk about what they see and hear and what they think is behind the artist's choice of medium, subject matter, and style. For example, say, "Why do you think this artist makes little pictures but that one makes big pictures?" or "I wonder why the author named the squirrel Crunchy." Help children connect the artist's expressive choices to their own experiences and the backgrounds of their families (for example, "The bright colors in Frida Kahlo's paintings are like the colors in her house. When I visited you at home, I saw bright colors like these too").

Describing the feelings expressed through art

This ability involves explaining what the artist may have been thinking or feeling in creating a work of art. As children's social-emotional skills and vocabulary expand, together with their understanding of the arts in general, they have at their disposal the words to describe the emotions that go into creating art and the feelings that works of art evoke in the viewer.

Teaching strategies. When we jointly support children's aesthetic and social-emotional growth, we enable them to become more articulate about the expressive qualities of the creative arts. Teaching strategies. such as the following can simultaneously build linguistic skills, personal confidence, and artistic understanding:

○ Model descriptive and metaphoric language when talking about art, using comparisons children will recognize from daily life. For example, make statements such as "Moving up and down like this reminds me of bending and digging in the garden." Use descriptive art terms in daily conversations. Instead of focusing only on *functional* traits ("Please pass me the red cup"), comment on features that also evoke an *aesthetic* or *emotional* response ("Wearing this bright red shirt makes me feel like dancing!"). When speaking with dual language learners, include descriptive words in their home language and English. While teachers often introduce the terms for objects (nouns) and actions (verbs), talking about art also helps dual language learners acquire the broader descriptive vocabulary of adjectives, adverbs, and interjections.

○ Incorporate and integrate all the senses into the study of art. For example, play music with varying attributes or moods (tempo, loudness, pitch, major and minor keys) and provide art materials for children to represent the feelings evoked from each. Let them listen to each selection for a while before they begin to create a corresponding work of visual art, and give them sufficient time with each piece before changing to one with a different mood. Have children smell different fruits or spices (including those from their native cuisines) with their eyes closed and think of a color that goes with that aroma. Beginning with a movement, ask children to think of a familiar song they could sing to accompany that action.

○ Provide suggestions for parents to talk to their children about what they were thinking or how they were feeling as they created the art when you send children's visual artwork home or share children's song, dance, or story creations by email or on your program's blog, e-newsletter, or website. Holding a workshop for parents in which they practice talking about the feelings represented in and evoked by a work of art can make it easier for them to do this at home with their children.

Recognizing cultural and temporal influences on art

This area of art appreciation entails being aware of how context influences the creation and interpretation of a work of art. Such influences include the personal background, community, cultural beliefs, and geographic setting of the artist or viewer, and also the time in which the art was created or seen. Because children are increasingly aware of their own circumstances and those of their families, older preschoolers are able to recognize similarities and differences in time, place, and community represented through art.

Teaching strategies. Activities that support multicultural awareness in general are also effective in sensitizing young children to the ways in which background influences artistic creation. As long as we draw on familiar experiences to find a point of contact or relevance for young children, they can reflect on the factors that affect how art is created and perceived. Try the following strategies:

- Provide examples of art in various media types from other cultures and times, particularly those that reflect the diversity in the classroom or community now. For example, include pottery from Asia, music from the Middle East, dances from South America, and folktales from Africa. Talk about similarities and differences with the children's lives and how these are reflected in the works of art.

- Encourage families to share art from home that reflects their culture or background in its media (for example, woodworking and calligraphy, drums and flutes, ballet and folk dance, mime and poetry) and subject matter (for example, architecture, agriculture, urban living, daily family life, holiday rituals).

- Connect with artists in the community and invite them to visit the classroom. Take a field trip to their studios or performances designed for young children. Ask them to demonstrate how they work and to explain where their ideas come from. If possible, arrange for the children to use materials and tools in the studio, concert hall, or theater, or bring them back to the classroom, or both. This encourages children to think of themselves as artists.

- Take children to outdoor art fairs; landscaped parks and gardens; and public music, dance, and theater performances. On your excursions, describe what you see and hear, and ask children to share their observations. Take photos, and in the classroom mount them where children and parents can see and talk about them. Provide materials for children to represent the experience. Encourage families to visit similar locations in the community with their children.

- Visit museums, galleries, and performance spaces to view art from other times and cultures. Plan ahead with docents and artistic directors. To help children heed the "look, don't touch" prohibition, give them something to hold. For example, in advance of your trip to the art museum, obtain four or five postcards showing art the children will see. Make duplicates so each child has a small reproduction to hold and compare with the works hanging on the walls. Children will enjoy making the matches. Back in the classroom, follow up on the experience by providing props to reenact the trip and materials for children to use in exploring the images and techniques they saw and/or heard at the museum, theater, concert, or dance hall.

❋　　❋　　❋

The creative arts can be a vital component in an integrated preschool curriculum if teachers intentionally give the subject matter the respect and attention to diversity it deserves. This position is summed up by Taunton and Colbert (2000):

> To have a significant role in early childhood education, art experiences must be authentic in approach and content and include opportunities for children's reflection through extended classroom dialogues. Authentic art experiences in the classroom are organized through a teacher's knowledge of patterns of artistic and aesthetic development, consideration of the intentions of children as they make art, and recognition of the significant content in the subject of art and art's relationship to other disciplines. (68)

Making and appreciating the creative arts has the potential to enrich young children's aesthetic and emotional lives, as well as to enhance their perceptual, intellectual, and social development. Diversity in the arts can also offer children from different cultural and linguistic backgrounds opportunities to learn about and value their heritages. For these promises to be fulfilled, teachers must treat art as a legitimate discipline. Intentional teachers take it upon themselves to acquire knowledge about early artistic development, provide the resources necessary to advance art exploration and awareness, and hone the active teaching skills that support mastery of this content domain in young children.

For Further Consideration

1. What arguments can early childhood advocates use to preserve the arts in the face of budget allocations favoring academic disciplines at the expense of other content areas?

2. How do we cut through the media hype that alternately overstates or debunks the promise of early art experiences to contribute to young children's later intellectual success?

3. Why, after so many years of discussion of "process, not product," do some early childhood teachers continue to plan and carry out art activities in which young children all make or do the same thing, and aim toward a finished product that can be displayed or performed for the benefit of adults?

4. What are the barriers to accepting the idea that preschoolers are capable of engaging in art appreciation? How can practitioners overcome the anxieties and inhibitions about teaching art appreciation to young children?

5. Why is it important to become more knowledgeable about art from a variety of cultures and traditions, including those represented by the children and families in your program? How can you acquire this knowledge?

Chapter 11

Reflections on Intentional Teaching

Three preschoolers—Marcus, Asia, and Zeke—have asked their teacher, Jolene, to help them make playdough. From the house area, Asia fetches a big bowl, and Marcus gets the recipe page from the class cookbook. As Jolene reads aloud the ingredients and their amounts, the children take them out of the grocery bag Jolene has brought and set them on the table: one cup of flour, one-half cup of salt, one package of unsweetened fruit juice powder, two teaspoons cream of tartar, one cup of water, and one tablespoon of vegetable oil. "What else do we need?" asks Jolene. "Measuring cups and spoons!" says Asia, and she returns to the house area to get them. "Anything else?" asks Jolene. The children look at the recipe page, ingredients, and cooking utensils and decide they have everything they need.

These young children are about to engage in scientific discoveries during an everyday activity. As you read the rest of the vignette, note how Jolene takes advantage of a cooking situation to help the children become aware of scientific properties (dry and wet, shiny and not shiny) and the transformation of materials, while simultaneously introducing concepts in mathematics (numerals, measuring) and literacy (reading, vocabulary, the alphabet).

Jolene: (points to the words in the recipe) The recipe says to mix all the dry ingredients first.

Marcus: I want to put in the flour. (He scoops out a heaping cupful and dumps it in the bowl.)

Asia: I want to do the salt. Which spoon do I use?

Jolene: (hands her the measuring spoons) See if you can find the spoon with the numerals 1 and 2 on the handle.

Asia: (She looks and shakes her head.)

Jolene: It looks like this. (She writes ½ on a piece of paper and hands it to Asia.)

Asia: I found it! (She scoops salt out of the salt dish and adds it to the bowl.)

Jolene: There are still two more dry ingredients.

Zeke: (picks up the oil) Not this!

Jolene: How do you know the oil isn't dry?

Zeke: 'Cause it's gloopy.

Jolene: The oil is gloopy and wet.

Marcus: This is dry! (He holds up the package of juice powder. Jolene nods, and he adds it to the other dry ingredients). And this. (He holds up the dish of cream of tartar.)

Jolene: (helps Asia find the teaspoon by writing out the letters for her to match) Now we have to stir the dry ingredients together. (She looks expectantly at the children.)

Zeke: Hey! We forgot the big wooden spoon! (He gets it from the house area and each child takes a turn stirring the mixture.)

Marcus: (peers into the bowl and points to the juice powder) The red dots are shiny!

Jolene: Sometimes dots like that are called crystals. The pieces of salt are called crystals, too. (The children look at the mixture, commenting that they can't tell the difference between the flour and cream of tartar once they are mixed together because both are white and *not* shiny.)

Zeke: Can we add the water and oil now?

Jolene: (She hands Zeke the cup to get very hot water with the help of her coteacher. Then she helps Asia measure the oil. The children carefully mix the ingredients in.)

Zeke: (watches playdough drip off the wooden spoon) It's too gloopy!

Asia: Yeah, it's way too wet!

Jolene: How can we make the playdough drier?

Asia: Add more crystals!

Jolene: We only had one package. What else could we do?

Marcus: Add more flour. (He adds another heaping cup.)

Zeke: Now it's too dry! (He refills the water cup.)

Jolene: How do you know that's the right amount of water to add?

Zeke: (hesitates) Maybe a little less? (He pours off half and then pours off a little more.)

The children again take turns stirring the mixture. They decide to add another half of a cup of flour and a "teensy, weensy bit" of cream of tartar. Then they announce that the playdough is "just right!" and ready for them and the other children to use.

In the next vignette, Abdel uses trial and error to sort objects he has collected into piles labeled "sticky" (lifted by the magnet) and "not sticky" (not lifted by the magnet). When he discovers an object that falls under both categories, he solves the problem by replacing it with a clear-cut choice.

Four-year-old Abdel sits in the toy area with a magnet and a basket filled with small objects he has gathered: plastic counting bears, nails and screws, wooden puzzle pieces, cardboard cubes, a jeweler's screwdriver, an assortment of cooking utensils, and pieces of twine. He tries to lift each item with the magnet, and then sorts them into two piles, which he labels "sticky" and "not sticky." When Abdel gets to a can opener with a plastic handle and a metal tip, he goes back and forth between the two ends several times before finally putting the can opener back in the basket. He finishes sorting the other items and looks at the can opener again. Then, he returns it to the house area and finds a different all-metal can opener, which he checks with the magnet and adds to the pile of other "sticky" objects. Abdel sits back, surveys the two piles, and smiles with satisfaction.

The children in both scenarios initiated the activity and were clearly involved in pursuing their interests. But in Abdel's case, the teacher provided materials and time, while in the playdough example, the teacher also offered thoughtful comments and questions to further the children's understanding of scientific concepts.

The teaching and learning principles illustrated in these examples apply to every area of learning addressed in this book—whether it is approaches to learning, social and emotional learning, physical development and health, language and literacy, mathematics, science, social studies, or the creative arts. In every domain, the most meaningful and lasting learning occurs when children are interested in the topic and actively engaged in mastering its specific knowledge and skills. Children can explore and understand some of this body of content through child-guided learning experience, either on their own or through interactions with peers and older children. For children to acquire other information, concepts, and skills, adult-guided learning experience is essential. Intentional teachers know they have a role to play in both child-guided and adult-guided modes, and they do so using their own knowledge and skills.

Guiding Principles of Intentional Teaching

It is my hope that teachers can use the framework and examples in this book as a starting point in choosing teaching strategies. While there will still be many instances where teachers have to make their own decisions about whether child- or adult-guided learning experience is more suited to a particular topic, setting, individual child, or group of children, the guiding principles that follow can be used to help intentional teachers decide which strategies to use across a range of learnings and situations.

The first set of principles describes the basic characteristics of all intentional *teachers*— that is, what they know and do. The remaining two sets list the conditions, respectively, under which intentional teachers either encourage child-guided experience or engage in instruction that is more adult guided. The focus of all these principles is on *children* because it is in observing and being sensitive to those they teach that adults can best determine the most effective instructional strategy to use.

While these guiding principles are derived from the theory, research, and practices presented in this book, they are offered here as hypotheses rather than proven facts. You are invited to view them critically and think about how these principles can be tested through further study and application. Although the idea of the intentional teacher is based on long-held beliefs, the term itself is relatively new. We still have much to learn from additional research and reflection as we strive to make intentionality a standard part of our professional development and daily work with children.

To teach with intention, teachers . . .

- Create a learning environment rich in materials, experiences, and interactions
- Encourage children to explore materials, experiences, relationships, and ideas
- Talk respectfully, reciprocally, and frequently with children
- Consciously promote all areas of learning and development
- Know the content (concepts, vocabulary, facts, skills) that make up each area of learning
- Know and use general teaching strategies that are effective with most young children
- Know and use specific teaching strategies that are effective in different content areas

- Match content with children's developmental levels and emerging abilities and interests
- Are sensitive to the needs of dual language learners, children from diverse cultures and traditions, children who are gifted, and children with special needs
- Are planful, purposeful, and thoughtful
- Take advantage of spontaneous, unexpected teaching and learning opportunities
- Carefully observe children to determine their interests and level of understanding and to plan next steps
- Adjust their teaching strategies to work with different individuals and groups
- Neither underestimate nor overestimate what children can do and learn
- Challenge children to question their own thinking and conclusions
- Scaffold learning, with careful consideration of introducing new materials and ideas
- Reflect on and change teaching strategies based on children's responses

Intentional teachers support child-guided learning experiences when children are...

- Exploring materials, actions, and ideas actively and making connections on their own
- Establishing interpersonal relationships and learning from one another
- Turning to one another for assistance
- Considering and investigating their own questions about materials, events, and ideas
- Motivated to solve problems on their own
- So focused on their enterprise that adult intervention would be an interruption
- Challenging themselves and one another to master new skills
- Applying and extending existing knowledge and skills in new ways

Although these behaviors and attitudes signal to teachers that child-guided experience will be particularly fruitful, this does not exclude using other teaching strategies and planned activities. Even when teachers pick up on cues like these, they will likely want to make strategic use of adult-guided experience to optimize children's learning.

Intentional teachers employ adult-guided learning experiences when children . . .

- Have not yet encountered the material or experience at home or in other settings
- Cannot create established systems of knowledge (such as letter names) on their own
- Do not see, hear, or otherwise attend to something likely to interest them
- Have not reflected on how or why something has happened, or considered what might happen "if ..."
- Do not engage with something teachers know they will need for further learning
- Ask for information or help explicitly

- Are bored or distracted and need help focusing
- Appear stalled, discouraged, or frustrated
- Appear ready for the next level of mastery but are not likely to attain it on their own
- Are not aware of the potentially unsafe or hurtful consequences of their actions
- Appear to use materials or actions very repetitively over time
- Are conscious of and upset about something they cannot yet do but wish to

For knowledgeable teachers, although these behaviors and attitudes suggest that children will benefit from adult-guided learning experience, this does not mean that child-guided experience will not also be an important part of the full learning picture.

Final Thoughts

I would like to leave you with some final thoughts and beliefs, some already expressed implicitly or explicitly in the foregoing pages. Just as this book has attempted to present a balanced approach to teaching and learning, so too are the following thoughts offered in the form of "on-the-one-hand" and "on-the-other-hand" propositions. You may agree fully, partially, or not at all. The important thing, from my perspective, is that you consider the ideas and reflect on how they apply to you in your capacity as an early childhood practitioner, administrator, researcher, and advocate.

Respecting Teachers

- There is much wisdom in early childhood educators. If teachers have the proper training, mentoring, and experience in a supportive work atmosphere (admittedly a big "if"), they can be creative and thoughtful in the classroom. Teachers do not need prescriptive lesson plans to work effectively with young children.

- On the other hand, meaningful learning cannot be left to chance or instinct. There is a body of knowledge that teachers should know regarding how children learn and how best to teach them. Moreover, each content area has a set of knowledge and skills that teachers should study and be familiar with in order to assess what children know and determine how to scaffold further learning.

Respecting Content

- The knowledge and skills children need to acquire are not limited to language and literacy, mathematics, and science. School readiness also includes social skills and dispositions. Physical education is essential to maintain good health and develop respect for one's body. And the arts not only are integral to other areas of learning but also are inherently gratifying and basic to our sense of community.

- However, because early childhood educators have traditionally emphasized the social-emotional domain, we need to explain our approach to teaching and learning to the public at large. When we say that "learning happens through play" and that "play is a child's work," we must be prepared to explain how and why play can be worthwhile. The best play is purposeful and engages children's minds, bodies, and emotions. Random activity is ultimately not satisfying, nor does it enhance learning in a meaningful way.

Respecting Children

- Preschoolers are still young children, not little adults or even scaled-down elementary school students. They come to us as individuals with their own personalities, their own languages and cultures, and their own prior knowledge. We should ease up on the pressures for testing and achievement that can label children, parents, teachers, and schools as failures. Teachers need to follow the developmentally based and research-based recommendations we call best practices. In that way, we can stop pushing the early elementary curriculum down into preschool and kindergarten and restore early childhood, ensuring that children maintain their eagerness for learning and carry that eagerness with them throughout their childhood and adult lives.

- Nevertheless, teachers should respect young children's curiosity and eagerness to learn and not be afraid to introduce information, model and coach specific skills, use unusual vocabulary words, or challenge children to solve complex problems. If teachers observe children's thinking and actions, the attempts to scaffold their learning are likely to be on target. And if teachers occasionally introduce something that is over the children's heads, the children themselves will be quick to let the teachers know. Teachers can then back up a step or two, but they shouldn't go back to leaving the children on their own.

From the research on child development and real classroom examples in this book, it is clear that teachers can help children learn—and enjoy learning—in all the content areas they will need to be ready for school and succeed in later life. We already know a great deal about what it means to teach with intention and the kinds of knowledge and skills we can help young children acquire. There is still more that we as professionals can explore about how to foster child- and adult-guided experiences in the early years. Advancing the concept of the intentional teacher will require further theoretical work, research, curriculum development, staff training and mentoring, program evaluation, child observation, administrative leadership, and reflective practice.

We each have one or more roles to play in this research and development process. I hope this revised edition of *The Intentional Teacher* continues to inspire you to take advantage of all we know to further your own professional growth and to contribute to the wisdom and practice of the field.

Glossary

academic domains: Important knowledge and skills that young children want and need to master in the content areas of literacy, mathematics, science, and social studies.

adult-guided learning: Experience that proceeds primarily along the lines of the teacher's goals, although that experience may also be shaped by children's active engagement.

alphabet knowledge: Understanding that there is a systematic relationship between letters and sounds. Whole words have a structure made up of individual sounds and of sound patterns or groupings. Also known as the alphabetic principle.

approaches to learning: Styles of learning or dispositions toward responding to educational experiences in varying degrees of curiosity, creativity, confidence, independence, initiative, and persistence. Approaches to learning also involve breaking down a task into its components, organizing a plan of work, and reflecting on the success of one's endeavors.

best practices: Educational practices based in child development theory, educational research, and the reflections of generations of teachers that reflect common ideals and beliefs about human development.

child-guided learning: Experience that proceeds primarily along the lines of children's interests and actions, although teachers often provide materials and other support.

coaching: Dividing a positive behavior into its component parts, providing children with explicit instruction on how to perform and sequence the parts, creating opportunities for them to practice the behavior, and offering feedback on their efforts.

comparing and ordering: Determining which of two groups has more or less of some attribute, and seriating or ordering objects according to some attribute.

composing and decomposing: Mentally or physically putting small groups of objects together, and then breaking a group into two or more parts.

comprehension: Understanding the meaning of spoken and written language.

conflict resolution: Using appropriate, nonaggressive strategies to discuss and develop solutions to interpersonal differences; also known as social problem solving or guidance.

content: The substance or subject matter that is the object of children's learning and the knowledge (certain vocabulary and concepts) and skills in an area of learning.

counting: Learning the sequence of number words, identifying the quantity of items in a collection, and recognizing counting patterns.

dramatic play: Pretend-play scenarios that children invent and act out.

early learning domains: Important knowledge and skills that young children want and need to master in the areas traditionally associated with early childhood education: social and emotional, cognitive, physical, and creative development.

effort awareness: Awareness of how the body moves in space. These are awareness of the components of time (speeds, rhythms), force (degree, creation, absorption), and flow/control (dimensions).

emergent literacy: A gradual progression of literacy learning that begins in infancy and continues through formal reading and writing instruction in school.

emotional awareness: Understanding that one has feelings as distinct from thoughts, being able to identify and name those feelings, and recognizing that others have feelings that may be the same or different from one's own.

emotional self-regulation: Responding to experiences with an appropriate range of immediate or delayed emotions.

equal partitioning: Dividing a collection into equal parts.

equivalence: Recognition that different collections have the same number of objects without actually enumerating items, or that equal collections in different arrangements still have the same number of objects.

executive functioning: The command-and-control ability that allows one to manage and execute tasks.

fine motor development: Development of fine motor muscles that enable the body to manipulate materials and tools. Common preschool actions that require these types of movements include molding, squeezing, poking, smoothing, positioning, writing, stacking, pouring, and cutting.

grouping: Creating sets of objects so that each has the same quantity. Grouping in sets of 10 is the basis for later understanding of place value.

intentional teaching: Planful, thoughtful, and purposeful acts teachers implement to ensure that young children acquire the knowledge and skills (content) they need to succeed in school and in life. Intentional teachers use their knowledge, judgment, and expertise to act with specific outcomes or goals in mind for children's development and learning, and they integrate and promote meaningful learning in *all* domains.

intentionality: Interactions between children and teachers in which teachers purposefully challenge, scaffold, and extend children's skills and have an understanding of the expected outcomes of instruction.

locomotor: Physical movement in which the body is transported in a horizontal or vertical direction from one point in space to another. Children's locomotor skills are walking, running, hopping, skipping, galloping, sliding, leaping, climbing, crawling, chasing, and fleeing.

manipulative: Physical movement in which the body moves to apply force to or receive force from objects. For young children, these movements are throwing, catching/collecting, kicking, punting, dribbling, volleying, striking with a racket, and striking with a long-handled instrument.

modeling: Teaching by example.

movement concepts: The movement knowledge component of the early childhood curriculum relating to *where, how, and in relationship to what* the body moves.

movement skills: Physical/motor skills that young children need to develop and refine.

number sense: Intuition about numbers and their magnitude, their relationship to real quantities, and the kinds of operations that can be performed on them.

numeration: Reading, writing, and naming numbers.

openness to experiences: A child's initial willingness to explore materials, ideas, people, and events.

pacing: Responsiveness to a child's need to try new things, solve problems, practice skills, or think about what she is learning.

phonemic awareness: A subset of phonological awareness that involves the understanding that individual sounds make up words (blending) and that words can be separated into sounds (segmentation).

phonological awareness: The general ability to attend to the sounds of language as distinct from its meaning. Initial awareness of speech sounds and rhythms, rhyme awareness, recognition of sound similarities, and phonemic awareness are all elements of this ability.

place value: Value of the location of a digit in a number.

planning *(child)*: Choosing with intentionality one's own course of action; an important component of executive functioning.

print awareness: Understanding how print is organized and used in reading and writing. Children learn that speech and written language carry messages and that words convey ideas.

processing experiences: How children deal with the physical and interpersonal environment both during and after a learning experience.

reading readiness: A point, generally age 6, at which children have historically been assumed ready for the formal reading and writing instruction of elementary school; children's literacy learning is now considered to be a more gradual progression starting in infancy; *see* emergent literacy

scaffolding: Finding the right balance within a child's approach to learning and developmental level by first supporting the child's current level of understanding and then gently extending his learning.

self-awareness: The understanding that one exists as an individual, separate from other people, with private thoughts and feelings.

sensory mode: Avenues of processing information, such as visual, aural, and tactile/kinesthetic.

social and emotional learning: One of the primary domains of early childhood education; development of social and emotional competence that includes emotional self-regulation, social knowledge and understanding, social skills, and social dispositions.

social concepts: Subject matter that forms the standard topics taught in school as social studies, including economics, history, geography, and ecology.

social context: The social environment for learning, whether solitary or with other individuals.

social skills: The range of appropriate strategies for interacting with others.

social systems: The norms, values, and procedures that affect human relationships in our day-to-day lives.

socialization: The acquisition of knowledge of social norms and customs.

space awareness: Awareness of where the body moves in space. Space awareness concepts are space, directions, levels, and pathways.

stability: Physical movement in which the body remains in place but moves around its horizontal or vertical axis, or it balances against the force of gravity. For young children, these movements include turning, twisting, bending, stopping, rolling, balancing, transferring weight, jumping/landing, stretching/extending, curling, swinging, swaying, and dodging.

teaching: The knowledge, beliefs, attitudes, and especially the behaviors and skills teachers employ in their work with learners.

Resources

Best Practices

Assessment

Dichtelmiller, M.L. 2011. *The Power of Assessment: Transforming Teaching and Learning.* Bethesda, MD: Teaching Strategies.

Gronlund, G., & M. James. 2013. *Focused Observations: How to Observe Young Children for Assessment and Curriculum Planning.* 2nd ed. St. Paul, MN: Redleaf Press.

Jablon, J.R., A.L. Dombro, & M.O. Dichtelmiller. 2007. *The Power of Observation: Birth to Age 8.* 2nd ed. Washington, DC: Teaching Strategies and Washington, DC: NAEYC.

Koralek, D., ed. 2004. *Spotlight on Young Children and Assessment.* Washington, DC: NAEYC. Available in Spanish.

McAfee, O., D. Leong, & E. Bodrova. 2004. *Basics of Assessment: A Primer for Early Childhood Educators.* Washington, DC: NAEYC.

McLean, M., M. Wolery, D.B. Bailey, Jr. 2004. *Assessing Infants and Preschoolers With Special Needs.* 3rd ed. New York: Pearson.

NAEYC. 2005. "Screening and Assessment of Young English Language Learners: Supplement to the NAEYC and NAECS/SDE Position Statement on Early Childhood Curriculum, Assessment, and Program Evaluation." Available in Spanish and English. www.naeyc.org/files/naeyc.file/positions/ELL_Supplement_Shorter_Version.

NAEYC. 2013. *Classroom-Based Assessment of Preschoolers: An Introduction to What Teachers Need to Know.* Trainer's Manual. Book With DVD-ROM. Washington, DC: NAEYC.

NAEYC. 2013. *NAEYC Early Childhood Program Standards and Accreditation Criteria and Guidance for Assessment.* www.naeyc.org/academy/files/academy/file/AllCriteriaDocument.pdf.

NAEYC & National Association of Early Childhood Specialists in State Departments of Education (NAECS/SDE). 2003. "Early Childhood Curriculum, Assessment, and Program Evaluation: Building an Effective, Accountable System in Programs for Children Birth Through Age 8." Joint position statement.www.naeyc.org/filesl/naeyc/file/positions/pscape.pdf.

Parnell, W., & J. Bartlett. 2012. "iDocument: How Smartphones and Tablets Are Changing Documentation in Preschool and Primary Classrooms." *Young Children* 67 (3): 50–57.

"Using Documentation and Assessment to Support Children's Learning." 2013. Cluster theme. *Young Children* 68 (3).

Websites

Council for Exceptional Children (CEC)—www.cec.sped.org. An authoritative source for information about assessment of children with special needs.

The Early Childhood Technical Assistance (ECTA) Center— http://ectacenter.org/topics/earlyid/screeneval.asp. Provides information on screening, evaluation, and assessment of young children.

Developmentally Appropriate Practice

Bouhebent, E.A. 2008. "Providing the Best for Families: Developmentally Appropriate Home Visitation Services." *Young Children* 63 (2): 82–87.

Chen, D.W., & P. Battin-Sacks, With R. Prieto & C. Prieto. 2008. "When Will I Be Special? Rethinking Developmentally Appropriate Practice in a Classroom Routine." *Young Children* 63 (3): 44–51.

Copple, C., & S. Bredekamp. 2006. *Basics of Developmentally Appropriate Practice: An Introduction for Teachers of Children 3 to 6*. Washington, DC: NAEYC.

Copple, C., & S. Bredekamp, eds. 2009. *Developmentally Appropriate Practice for Early Childhood Programs Serving Children From Birth Through Age 8*. 3rd ed. Washington, DC: NAEYC.

Copple, C., S. Bredekamp, D. Koralek, & K. Charner, eds. 2014. *Developmentally Appropriate Practice: Focus on Kindergartners*. Washington, DC: NAEYC.

Copple, C., S. Bredekamp, D. Koralek, & K. Charner, eds. 2013. *Developmentally Appropriate Practice: Focus on Preschoolers*. Washington, DC: NAEYC.

Division for Early Childhood (DEC)& NAEYC. 2009. "Early Childhood Inclusion." A joint position statement of DEC and NAEYC. www.naeyc.org/files/naeyc/files/positions/DEC_NAEYC_EC_updatedKS.pdf.

Dowling, J.L., & T.C. Mitchell. 2007. *I Belong: Active Learning for Children With Special Needs*. Ypsilanti, MI: HighScope Educational Research Foundation.

Dombro, A.L., J.R. Jablon, & C. Stetson. 2011. *Powerful Interactions: How to Connect With Children to Extend Their Learning*. Washington, DC: NAEYC.

"Environments That Engage and Inspire Young Learners." 2012. Cluster topic. *Young Children* 68 (4): 6–45.

Gronlund, G. 2006. *Make Early Learning Standards Come Alive: Connecting Your Practice and Curriculum to State Guidelines*. St. Paul, MN: Redleaf Press; Washington, DC: NAEYC.

Gronlund, G. 2010. *Developmentally Appropriate Play: Guiding Young Children to a Higher Level*. St. Paul, MN: Redleaf Press.

"Individualizing in Early Childhood: The What, Why, and How of Differentiated Approaches." 2013. Cluster topic. *Young Children* 68 (2): 6–49.

NAEYC. 2009. *Developmentally Appropriate Practice: A Focus on Intentionality and Play*. DVD-ROM. Washington, DC: NAEYC.

NAEYC. 2009. "Developmentally Appropriate Practices in Early Childhood Programs Serving Children From Birth Through Age 8." Position statement, in Spanish and English. www.naeyc.org/files/naeyc/file/positions/PSDAP.pdf.

Phillips, E.C., & A. Scrinzi. 2013. *Basics of Developmentally Appropriate Practice: An Introduction for Teachers of Kindergartners*. Washington, DC: NAEYC.

Wien, C.A. 2014. *The Power of Emergent Curriculum: Stories From Early Childhood Settings*. Washington, DC: NAEYC.

Websites

Embracing the Child—www.embracingthechild.org/prek.html. Recommends books on a wide range of topics organized by subject and age. Topics include counting, geometry and shape, estimation, science, alphabet, self-esteem, and more.

Exchange—www.childcareexchange.com. Promotes the exchange of ideas among leaders in early childhood programs worldwide. Offers books, a magazine, training resources, and daily emails with news, excerpts and quotes, reviews, and other useful information for practitioners and policy makers.

National Association for the Education of Young Children (NAEYC)—www.naeyc.org. Offers a wide variety of information for the early childhood field, including position statements on critical issues.

Families

Bang, Y.-S. 2009. "Family Ties: Helping All Families Participate in School Life." *Young Children* 64 (6): 97 –99.

Cheatham, G.A., & R.M. Santos. 2011. "Collaborating With Families From Diverse Cultural and Linguistic Backgrounds: Considering Time and Communication Orientations." *Young Children* 66 (5): 76–83.

Dodge, D.T., & J. Pinney. 2006. *A Parent's Guide to Preschool.* Washington, DC: Teaching Strategies.

Gestwicki, C. 2013. *Home, School, and Community Relations.* 8th ed. Belmont, CA: Cengage.

Kersey, K.C., & M.L. Masterson. 2009. "Teachers Connecting With Families—In the Best Interest of Children." *Young Children* 64 (5): 34–38.

Keyser. J. 2006. *From Parents to Partners: Building A Family-Centered Early Childhood Program.* St. Paul, MN: Redleaf Press; Washington, DC: NAEYC.

Koralek, D., ed. 2007. *Spotlight on Young Children and Families.* Washington, DC: NAEYC.

Mitchell, S., T.S. Foulger, & K. Wetzel. 2009. "Ten Tips for Involving Families Through Internet-Based Communication." *Young Children* 64 (5): 46–49.

Ray, J.A., J. Pweitt-Kinder, & S. George. 2009. "Partnering With Families of Children With Special Needs." *Young Children* 64 (5): 16–22.

Souto-Manning, M. 2010. "Family Involvement: Challenges to Consider, Strengths to Build On." *Young Children* 65 (2): 82–88.

Websites

Harvard Family Research Project—www.hfrp.org. Evaluates and supports effective ways for families to become involved in children's schools, homes, and communities. Offers research, publications with practical applications, and a network of parents, educators, researchers, and community members—Family Involvement Network of Educators (FINE).

For Families (from NAEYC)—http://families.naeyc.org. Offers resources and information to support families in their early childhood education and parenting needs.

Parent Services Project—www.parentservices.org. National nonprofit organization dedicated to integrating family support into early childhood programs and schools through training, technical assistance, community outreach, and education.

Learning Domains

Approaches to Learning

Bodrova, E., & D.J. Leong. 2007. *Tools of the Mind: The Vygotskian Approach to Early Childhood Education.* 2nd ed. Upper Saddle River, NJ: Pearson.

Copple, C., ed. 2012. *Growing Minds: Building Strong Cognitive Foundations in Early Childhood.* Washington, DC: NAEYC.

Epstein, A.S. 2012. "How Planning and Reflection Develop Young Children's Thinking Skills." In *Growing Minds: Building Strong Cognitive Foundations in Early Childhood,* ed. C. Copple, 111–18. Washington, DC: NAEYC.

Florez, I.L. 2011. "Developing Young Children's Self-Regulation Through Everyday Experiences." *Young Children* 66 (4): 46–51.

Galinksy, E. 2010. *Mind in the Making: The Seven Essential Life Skills Every Child Needs.* New York: HarperCollins.

Helm, J.H., & L. Katz. 2011. *Young Investigators: The Project Approach in the Early Years.* 2nd ed. New York: Teachers College Press; Washington, DC: NAEYC.

Hyson, M. 2008. *Enthusiastic and Engaged Learners: Approaches to Learning in the Early Childhood Classroom.* New York: Teachers College Press; Washington, DC: NAEYC.

Katz, L.G. 2014. "Standards of Experience." *Teaching Young Children* 7 (3): 6–7.

Pawlina, S., & C. Stanford. 2011. "Preschoolers Grow Their Brains: Shifting Mindsets for Greater Resiliency and Better Problem Solving." *Young Children* 66 (5): 30–35.

Ricci, M.C. 2013. *Mindsets in the Classroom: Building a Culture of Success and Student Achievement in Schools.* Waco, TX: Prufrock.

Da Ros-Voseles, D., & S. Fowler-Haughey. 2007. "Why Children's Dispositions Should Matter to *All* Teachers." *Young Children* 62 (5): 90–98. www.naeyc.org/files/yc/file/200709/DaRos-Voseles.pdf.

Salmon, A.K. 2010. "Tools to Enhance Young Children's Thinking." *Young Children* 65 (5): 26–31.

Thompson, S.D., & J.M. Raisor. 2013. "Meeting the Sensory Needs of Young Children." *Young Children* 68 (2): 34–43.

Websites

Project Zero—http://www.pz.harvard.edu/. Provides information on a multitude of research projects on the development of the learning process, lists conferences and other resources, and shares ideas on how to use Project Zero frameworks in various settings.

Creative Arts

Dow, C.B. 2010. "Young Children and Movement: The Power of Creative Dance." *Young Children* 65 (2): 30–35.

Eckhoff, A. 2010. "Using Games to Explore Visual Art With Young Children." *Young Children* 65 (1): 18–22.

Edwards, C., L. Gandini, & G. Forman. eds. 2012. *The Hundred Languages of Children: The Reggio Emilia Experience in Transformation.* 3rd ed. Santa Barbara, CA: Praeger.

Friedman. S. 2010. "Theater, Live Music, and Dance: Conversations About Young Audiences."*Young Children* 65 (2): 36–41.

Gandini, L., L. Hill, L. Cadwell, & C. Schwall. 2005. *In the Spirit of the Studio: Learning From the* Atelier *of Reggio Emilia.* St. Paul, MN: Redleaf Press.

Koralek, D., ed. 2005. *Spotlight on Young Children and the Creative Arts.* Washington, DC: NAEYC.

Paley, V.G. 1990. *The Boy Who Would Be a Helicopter: The Uses of Storytelling in the Classroom.* Cambridge, MA: Harvard University Press.

Pelo, A. 2007. *The Language of Art: Inquiry-Based Studio Practices in Early Childhood Settings.* St. Paul, MN: Redleaf Press.

Pica, R. 2009. "Make A Little Music." Learning By Leaps and Bounds. *Young Children* 64 (6): 74–75.

Prairie, A.P. 2013. "Supporting Sociodramatic Play in Ways That Enhance Academic Learning." *Young Children* 68 (2): 62–67.

Thompson, S.C. 2005. *Children as Illustrators: Making Meaning Through Art and Language.* Washington, DC: NAEYC.

Websites

Arts Education Partnership—www.aep-arts.org. Provides art education advocacy resources and information on arts research, policy, and best practices.

International Child Art Foundation (ICAF)—www.icaf.org. Offers educators information on the benefits of creative arts in the classroom and on art programs sponsored by ICAF, including international art festivals.

Reusable Resources Association—www.reuseresources.org. Informal community of centers providing recycled, open-ended materials at low cost to support creative, hands-on teaching and learning. Maintains list of centers nationwide.

Wolf Trap Institute for Early Learning Through the Arts—www.wolftrap.org/Education/Institute_for_Early_Learning_Through_the_Arts.aspx. Provides arts-based teaching strategies and services through drama, music, and movement to early childhood teachers, caregivers, parents, and their children from 0 to 5.

Language and Literacy

Christ, T., & X.C. Wang. 2010. "Bridging the Vocabulary Gap: What the Research Tells Us About Vocabulary Instruction in Early Childhood." Research in Review. *Young Children* 65 (4): 84–91.

Gadzikowski, A. 2007. *Story Dictation: A Guide for Early Childhood Professionals.* St. Paul, MN: Redleaf Press.

Gaffney, J.S., M.M. Ostrosky, & M.L. Hemmeter. 2008. "Books as Natural Support for Young Children's Literacy Learning." *Young Children* 63 (4): 87–93.

Nemeth, K. 2013. *Basics of Supporting Dual Language Learners: An Introduction for Educators of Children From Birth Through Age 8.* Washington, DC: NAEYC.

NGA (National Governors Association Center for Best Practices) & CCSSO (Council of Chief State School Officers). 2010. "Common Core State Standard—English Language Arts Standards." www.corestandards.org/ELA-Literacy.

Pica, R. 2007. *Jump Into Literacy: Active Learning for Preschool Children.* Beltsville, MD: Gryphon House.

Roskos, K.A., P. Tabors, & L. Lenhart. 2009. *Oral Language and Early Literacy in Preschool: Talking, Reading, and Writing.* 2nd ed. Newark, DE: International Reading Association.

Schickedanz, J.A., & R.M. Casbergue. 2009. *Writing in Preschool: Learning to Orchestrate Meaning and Marks.* 2nd ed. Newark, DE: International Reading Association.

Schickedanz, J.A., & M.F. Collins. 2013. *So Much More Than the ABCs: The Early Phases of Reading and Writing.* Washington, DC: NAEYC.

Shedd, M.K., & N.K. Duke. 2008. "The Power of Planning: Developing Effective Read-Alouds." *Young Children* 63 (6): 22–27.

Shidler, L. 2012. "Teaching Vocabulary in Preschool: Teachers, Children, Families." *Teaching Young Children* 5 (3): 13–15.

Shillady, A., ed. Forthcoming. *Spotlight on Young Children: Exploring Language and Literacy.* Washington, DC: NAEYC.

Strickland, D.S., & J.A. Schickedanz. 2009. *Learning About Print in Preschool: Working With Letters, Words, and Beginning Links With Phonemic Awareness.* 2nd ed. Newark, DE: International Reading Association.

"Supporting Dual Language Learners and Their Families." 2013. Cluster theme. *Young Children* 68 (1).

Tabors, P.O. 2008. *One Child, Two Languages: A Guide for Early Childhood Educators of Children Learning English as a Second Language.* 2nd ed. Baltimore, MD: Brookes.

Vukelich, C., & J. Christie. 2009. *Building a Foundation for Preschool Literacy: Effective Instruction for Children's Reading and Writing Development.* 2nd ed. Newark, DE: International Reading Association.

Zambo, D., & W.G. Brozo. 2009. *Bright Beginnings for Boys: Engaging Young Boys in Active Literacy.* Newark, DE: International Reading Association.

Websites

BookPALS—www.bookpals.net. Program of the Screen Actors Guild Foundation; places actors and oth9er performers in schools to read stories to young children and let books come alive through acting. A related program, Storyline Online, offers videos of actors reading books and provides activity ideas for each book.

Colorín Colorado!— www.colorincolorado.org. Bilingual site for families and educators of dual language learners; provides guides, tool kits, resource lists, podcasts, video, and e-newsletters.

Language Castle—www.languagecastle.com. Provides information, research, news, and tips about teaching dual language learners.

Reading Is Fundamental—www.rif.org. Offers literacy news, resources, and activities/programs to spark children's and families' interest in reading.

Reading Rockets—www.readingrockets.org. Gives information and activities to families and educators.

Mathematics

Beneke, S.J., Ostrosky, M.M., & L.G. Katz. 2008. "Calendar Time for Young Children: Good Intentions Gone Awry." *Young Children* 63 (3): 12–16.

Chalufour, I., & K. Worth. 2004. *Building Structures With Young Children.* St. Paul, MN: Redleaf Press.

Charlesworth, R. 2011. *Experiences in Math for Young Children.* 6th ed. Boston: Wadsworth.

Copley, J.V. 2010. *The Young Child and Mathematics.* 2nd ed. Washington, DC: NAEYC; Reston, VA: National Council of Teachers of Mathematics.

Epstein, A.S., & S. Gainsley. 2005. *I'm Older Than You, I'm Five! Math in the Preschool Classroom: The Teacher's Idea Book 6.* 2nd ed. Ypsilanti, MI: High/Scope Press.

Moomaw, S. 2011. *Teaching Mathematics in Early Childhood.* Baltimore, MD: Brookes.

National Council of Teachers of Mathematics (NCTM). 2000. *Principles and Standards for School Mathematics.* Reston, VA: NCTM. Also see http://standards.nctm.org/document/index.htm.

NCTM. 2006. *Curriculum Focal Points for Prekindergarten Through Grade 8 Mathematics: A Quest for Coherence.* Reston, VA: NCTM. Also see www.nctm.org/focalpoints.

Nelson, G. 2007. *Math at Their Own Pace: Child-Directed Activities for Developing Early Number Sense.* St. Paul, MN: Redleaf Press.

Notari-Syverson, A., & F.H. Sadler. 2008. "Math Is for Everyone: Strategies for Supporting Early Mathematical Competencies in Young Children." *Young Exceptional Children* 11 (3): 3–16.

Shillady, A., ed. 2012. *Spotlight on Young Children: Exploring Math.* Washington, DC: NAEYC.

Witzel, B.S., Ferguson, C.J., & D.V. Mink. 2012. "Number Sense: Strategies for Helping Pre-school Through Grade 3 Children Develop Math Skills." *Young Children* 67 (3): 89–94.

Websites

Illuminations: Resources for Teaching Math (from the National Council of Teachers of Mathematics [NCTM])—http://illuminations.nctm.org/. Provides resources for pre-K through grade 12 based on NCTM's *Principles and Standards for School Mathematics* and the Common Core State Standards. Offers online lesson plans and activities searchable by grade level, keyword, and both sets of standards.

Math at Play—www.mathatplay.org. Offers math resources for children from birth to age 5, including PDFs of math games and activities, tip sheets, math book lists, links to articles, and a blog. The site is also available in Spanish.

Mathematical Perspectives Teacher Center—www.mathperspectives.com/tcenter.html. Provides pre-K to grade 5 educators with tools, strategies, and assessments.

Physical Movement and Health

American Academy of Pediatrics, American Public Health Association, & National Resource Center for Health and Safety in Child Care and Early Education. 2012. *Preventing Childhood Obesity in Early Care and Education Programs: Selected Standards From Caring for Our Children: National Health and Safety Performance Standards, 3rd ed.* 2nd ed. AAP, APHA, & NRC.

Aronson, S.S., ed. 2012. *Healthy Young Children: A Manual for Programs.* 5th ed. Washington, DC: NAEYC.

Carlson, F.M. 2011. *Big Body Play: Why Boisterous, Vigorous, and Very Physical Play Is Essential to Children's Development and Learning.* Washington, DC: NAEYC.

Eliassen, E.K. 2011. "The Impact of Teachers and Families on Young Children's Eating Behaviors." *Young Children* 66 (2): 84–89.

Kalich, K., D. Bauer, & D. McPartlin. 2009. *Early Sprouts: Cultivating Healthy Food Choices in Young Children.* St. Paul, MN. Redleaf Press.

Marigliano, M.L., & M.J. Russo. 2011. "Moving Bodies, Building Minds: Foster Children's Critical Thinking and Problem Solving Through Movement." *Young Children* 66 (5): 44–49.

National Association for Sport and Physical Education (NASPE). 2009. *Active Start: A Statement of Physical Activity Guidelines for Children Birth to Five Years.* 2nd ed. Reston, VA: NASPE.

Pica, R. 2010. *Experiences in Movement: Birth to Age 8.* 4th ed. Belmont, CA: Wadsworth, Cengage Learning.

Pica, R. 2006. *Moving and Learning Across the Curriculum: More Than 300 Activities and Games to Make Learning Fun.* 2nd ed. Clifton Park, NY: Thomson Delmar Learning.

Rivkin, M.S. Forthcoming. *The Great Outdoors: Advocating for Natural Spaces for Young Children.* Rev. ed. Washington, DC: NAEYC.

Sanders, S.W. 2006. "Physically Active For Life: Eight Essential Motor Skills for All Children." In *Dimensions of Early Childhood* 34 (1): 3–10. Little Rock, AR: Southern Early Childhood Association.

Vagovic, J.C. 2008. "Transformers: Movement Experiences for Early Childhood Classrooms." *Young Children* 63 (3): 26–32.

Websites

Achievement Products for Special Needs—www.achievement-products.com. Offers therapy, exercise, and special education products.

Discount School Supply—www.discountschoolsupply.com. Carries products for educators and families, organized by type(s) of needs.

eSpecial Needs—www.especialneeds.com. Features adaptive equipment, rehabilitation equipment, and therapy solutions.

National Association for Sport and Physical Education (NASPE)—www.naspeinfo.org. Includes national standards and physical activity guidelines and a monthly "teachers toolbox" with activities.

US Department of Agriculture (USDA)—www.choosemyplate.gov/kids/. Offers resources to help children make healthier food choices.

Science

Achieve, Inc. 2013. *Next Generation Science Standards.* Washington, DC: Achieve Inc. www.nextgenscience.org.

Anderson, S. 2012. *Math and Science Investigations: Helping Young Learners Make Big Discoveries.* Lewisville, NC: Gryphon House.

Ansberry, K., & E. Morgan. 2010. *More Picture-Perfect Science Lessons: Using Children's Books to Guide Inquiry, K–4.* 2nd. ed. Arlington, VA: National Science Teachers Association Press.

Bosse, S., G. Jacobs, & T.L. Anderson. 2009. "Science in the Air." *Young Children* 64 (6): 10–15. www.naeyc.org/files/yc/file/200911/BosseWeb1109.pdf.

Brenneman, K. 2009. "Let's Find Out! Preschoolers as Scientific Explorers." *Young Children* 64 (6): 54–60.

Brooks, J.G. 2011. *Big Science for Growing Minds: Constructivist Classrooms for Young Thinkers.* New York: Teachers College Press.

Constable, K. 2012. *The Outdoor Classroom Ages 3 –7: Using Ideas From Forest Schools to Enrich Learning.* New York: Routledge.

DeVries, R., & C. Sales, 2011. *Ramps & Pathways: A Constructivist Approach to Physics With Young Children.* Washington, DC: NAEYC.

Edson, M.T. 2013. *Starting With Science: Strategies for Introducing Young Children to Inquiry.* Portland, ME: Stenhouse.

Ingram, M. 2014. "Preschoolers as Engineers." *Teaching Young Children* 7 (3): 30–31.

Gelman, R., K. Brenneman, G. Macdonald, & M. Roman. 2009. *Preschool Pathways to Science: Facilitating Scientific Ways of Thinking, Talking, Doing, and Understanding.* Baltimore, MD: Brookes.

Lisenbee, P. 2009. "Whiteboards and Websites: Digital Tools for the Early Childhood Curriculum." *Young Children* 64 (6): 92–95.

Louv, R. 2008. *Last Child in the Woods: Saving Our Children From Nature Deficit Disorder.* Rev. ed. Chapel Hill, NC: Algonquin.

Moomaw, S. 2013. *Teaching STEM in the Early Years: Activities for Integrating Science, Technology, Engineering, and Mathematics.* St. Paul, MN: Redleaf Press.

NAEYC & Fred Rogers Center for Early Learning and Children's Media. 2012. "Technology and Interactive Media as Tools in Early Childhood Programs Serving Children From Birth Through Age 8." Joint position statement. Washington, DC: NAEYC. www.naeyc.org/files/naeyc/file/positions/PS_technology_WEB2.pdf.

Pancheri-Ambrose, B., & J. Tritschler-Scali. 2013. "Beyond Green: Developing Social and Environmental Awareness in Early Childhood." *Young Children* 68 (4): 54–61.

Shillady, A., ed. 2011. *Spotlight on Young Children and Nature.* Washington, DC: NAEYC.

Shillady, A., ed. 2013. *Spotlight on Young Children: Exploring Science.* Washington, DC: NAEYC.

Shillady, A., & L.S. Muccio, eds. 2012. *Spotlight on Young Children and Technology.* Washington, DC: NAEYC.

Ward, J. 2011. *It's a Jungle Out There! 52 Nature Adventures for City Kids.* Boston: Trumpeter.

Websites

Council for Environmental Education (CEE)—www.councilforee.org and www. Projectwild.org/GrowingUPWild.htm. Provides programs and services to promote environmental education for young children and educators.

National Geographic Kids—www.kids.nationalgeographic.com. Offers magazine for preschool children *(National Geographic Little Kids)* that includes beautiful photography and animal stories, science activities, puzzles, and games. The website offers a special section for parents.

National Science Teachers Association—www.nsta.org. Offers a wealth of online information and teaching ideas.

Natural Start Alliance—www.naturalstart.org. Provides tools to help children connect with nature and care for the environment.

The Smithsonian Institution—www.si.edu/Educators and http://smithsonianeducation.org/educators/index.html. Offers numerous science resources for educators of children from preschool through grade 3. Users can search for science activities and lesson plans for different age groups.

Technology in Early Childhood [TEC] Center at Erikson Institute—www.teccenter.erikson.edu. Seeks to promote appropriate use of technology in early childhood settings with news links, listing of center events, free webinar series, and other resources.

Social and Emotional Learning

Baumgartner, J.J., & T. Buchanan. 2010. "Supporting Each Child's Spirit." *Young Children* 65 (2): 90–95.

Brinamen, C., & F. Page. 2012. "Using Relationships to Heal Trauma: Reflective Practice Creates a Therapeutic Preschool." *Young Children* 67 (5): 40–48.

Carlson, F. 2006. *Essential Touch: Meeting the Needs of Young Children.* Washington, DC: NAEYC.

Doucet, F., & J.K. Adair. 2013. "Addressing Race and Inequity in the Classroom." Research in Review. *Young Children* 68 (5): 88–97.

De-Souza, D., & J. Radell. 2011. "Superheroes: An Opportunity for Prosocial Play." *Young Children* 66 (4): 26–31.

Epstein, A.S. 2009. *Me, You, Us: Social-Emotional Learning in Preschool.* Ypsilanti, MI: HighScope Press; Washington, DC: NAEYC.

Gartrell, D. 2005–2008, 2011–2014. Guidance Matters. Column on Positive Approaches to Guiding Young Children's Behavior. *Young Children.* www.naeyc.org/yc/columns/guidance.

Hyson, M., & J.L. Taylor. 2011. "Caring About Caring: What Adults Can Do to Promote Young Children's Prosocial Skills." Research in Review. *Young Children* 66 (4): 74–83.

Kennedy, A.S. 2013. "Supporting Peer Relationships and Social Competence in Inclusive Preschool Programs." *Young Children* 68 (5): 18–25.

Levin, D.E. 2013. *Beyond Remote-Controlled Childhood: Teaching Young Children in the Media Age.* Washington, DC: NAEYC.

Manaster, H., & M. Jobe. 2012. "Bringing Boys and Girls Together: Supporting Preschoolers' Positive Peer Relationships." *Young Children* 67 (5): 12–17.

Mankiw, S., & J. Strasser. 2013. "Tender Topics: Exploring Sensitive Issues with Pre-K Through First Grade Children Through Read-Alouds." *Young Children* 68 (1): 70–75. www.naeyc.org/yc/pastissues/2013/march.

Pierce, J., & C.L. Johnson. 2010. "Problem Solving With Young Children Using Persona Dolls." *Young Children* 65 (6): 106–108.

Prothers, J. 2013. "Third Culture Children: Identification and Support in Early Childhood Education." Young Children 68 (3): 56-61.

Willis, C.A., & P. Schiller. 2011. "Preschoolers' Social Skills Steer Life Success." *Young Children* 66 (1): 42–49.

Websites

Center on the Social and Emotional Foundations for Early Learning (CSEFEL)—http://csefel.vanderbilt.edu/. Promotes children's social-emotional development and school readiness. Offers scripted stories for social settings, tools for relationship building and creating behavior support plans, and ideas for teaching social-emotional skills.

Technical Assistance Center on Social Emotional Intervention for Young Children (TAC-SEI)—www.challengingbehavior.org/. Offers research-based products and resources to help educators, parents, and others improve the social-emotional outcomes for young children with, or at risk for, delays or disabilities.

Zero to Three—www.zerotothree.org. Provides resources for parents, professionals, and policymakers to help nurture children's early development.

Social Studies

D'Addesio, J.A., B. Grob, L. Furman, K. Hayes, & J. David. 2005. "Social Studies: Learning About the World Around Us." *Young Children* 60 (5): 50–57.

Delpit, L. 2006. *Other People's Children: Cultural Conflict in the Classroom.* 2nd ed. New York: The New Press.

Derman-Sparks, L., & J. Olsen Edwards. 2010. *Anti-Bias Education for Young Children and Ourselves.* Washington, DC: NAEYC.

Gartrell, D. 2012. *Education for a Civil Society: How Guidance Teaches Young Children Democratic Life Skills.* Washington, DC: NAEYC.

Koralek, D., ed., With G. Mindes. 2006. *Spotlight on Young Children and Social Studies.* Washington, DC: NAEYC.

Seefeldt, C., S. Castle, & R.C. Falconer. 2013. *Social Studies for the Preschool/Primary Child.* 9th ed. Upper Saddle River, NJ: Pearson.

Seefeldt, C., & A. Galper. 2006. *Active Experiences for Active Children: Social Studies.* 2nd ed. New Jersey: Prentice Hall.

Vance, E. 2014. *Class Meetings: Young Children Solving Problems Together.* Rev. ed. Washington, DC: NAEYC.

Websites

KaBOOM!—www.kaboom.org. Works with communities to provide safe, appealing play-spaces for children.

References

Administration for Children and Families, Head Start Bureau. 2002, October. *Program Performance Standards and Other Regulations*. Washington, DC: US Government Printing Office.

Althouse, R., M.H. Johnson, & S.T. Mitchell. 2003. *The Colors of Learning: Integrating the Visual Arts Into the Early Childhood Curriculum*. New York: Teachers College Press; Washington, DC: NAEYC.

American Academy of Pediatrics. 2011. "Policy Statement: Media Use by Children Younger Than 2 Years." *Pediatrics* 128 (5): 1–7.

Aronson, S.S., ed. 2012. *Healthy Young Children: A Manual for Programs*. 5th ed. Washington, DC: NAEYC.

Arts Education Partnership. 1998. *Young Children and the Arts: Making Creative Connections— A Report of the Task Force on Children's Learning and the Arts: Birth to Age Eight*. Washington, DC: Arts Education Partnership.

Baroody, A.J. 2000. "Does Mathematics Instruction for Three- to Five-Year-olds Really Make Sense?" *Young Children* 55 (4): 61–67.

Baroody, A.J. 2004a. "The Developmental Bases for Early Childhood Number and Operations Standards." In *Engaging Young Children in Mathematics*, eds. D.H. Clements, J. Sarama, & A-M. DiBiase, 173–219. Mahwah, NJ: Lawrence Erlbaum Associates.

Baroody, A.J. 2004b. "The Role of Psychological Research in the Development of Early Childhood Mathematics Standards." In *Engaging Young Children in Mathematics*, eds. D.H. Clements, J. Sarama, & A-M. DiBiase, 149–72. Mahwah, NJ: Lawrence Erlbaum Associates.

Berk, L.E. 2008. *Infants and Children: Prenatal Through Middle Childhood*. 6th ed. Boston: Pearson/Allyn & Bacon.

Berliner, D.C. 1987. "Simple Views of Effective Teaching and a Simple Theory of Classroom Instruction." In *Talks to Teachers,* eds. D.C. Berliner & B.V. Rosenshine, 99–110. New York: Random House.

Berliner, D.C. 1992. "The Nature of Expertise in Teaching." In *Effective and Responsible Teaching: The New Synthesis*, eds. F.K. Oser, A. Dick, & J.L. Patry, 227–48. San Francisco: Jossey-Bass.

Bialystok, E. 2001. *Bilingualism in Development: Language, Literacy, and Cognition*. Cambridge, UK: Cambridge University Press.

Bodrova, E., & D. Leong. 2007. *Tools of the Mind: The Vygotskian Approach to Early Childhood Education*. 2nd ed. New York: Prentice Hall.

Bredekamp, S., & T. Rosegrant. 1992. "Reaching Potentials: Introduction." In *Reaching Potentials. Vol. 1: Appropriate Curriculum and Assessment for Young Children,* eds. S. Bredekamp & T. Rosegrant, 2–8. Washington, DC: NAEYC.

Brenneman, K. 2009. "Let's Find Out! Preschoolers as Explorers." *Young Children* 64 (6): 54–60.

Bruner, J.S. 1986. *Actual Minds, Possible Worlds*. Cambridge, MA: Harvard University Press.

Bruner, J.S., R.R. Olver, & P.M. Greenfield. 1996. *Studies in Cognitive Growth*. New York: Wiley.

Brussoni, M., L.L. Olsen, I. Pike, & D.A. Sleet. 2012. "Risky Play and Children's Safety: Balancing Priorities for Optimal Child Development." *International Journal of Environmental Research and Public Health* 9: 3134–48. doi:10.3390/ijerph9093134

Buckleitner, W., & C. Hohmann. 1991. "Blocks, Sand, Paint . . . and Computers." In *Supporting Young Learners: Ideas for Preschool and Day Care Providers*, eds. N.A. Brickman & L.S. Taylor, 174–83. Ypsilanti, MI: HighScope Press.

Burton, J. 2000. "The Configuration of Meaning: Learner-Centered Art Education Revisited." *Studies in Art Education* 41 (4): 330–42.

Campbell, P.F. 1999. "Fostering Each Child's Understanding of Mathematics." In *The Early Childhood Curriculum: Current Findings in Theory and Practice*, 3d ed., ed. C. Seefeldt, 106–32. New York: Teachers College Press.

Carlson, F.M. 2011. *Big Body Play: Why Boisterous, Vigorous, and Very Physical Play Is Essential to Children's Development and Learning*. Washington, DC: NAEYC.

Center on the Social and Emotional Foundations for Early Learning (CSEFEL). 2003. *What Works Briefs*. Champaign, IL: University of Illinois at Urbana-Champaign.

Centers for Disease Control and Prevention (CDC). 2009. "Overweight Children Ages 6–17: Percentage Has Increased From 6% in 1976 to 17% in 2006." Atlanta, GA: Centers for Disease Control and Prevention. www.cdc.gov/features/dsoverweightchildren/.

Centers for Disease Control and Prevention (CDC). 2013. "Progress on Childhood Obesity: Many States Show Decline." Atlanta, GA: Centers for Disease Control and Prevention. www.cdc.gov/VitalSigns/ChildhoodObesity/.

Chafel, J.A. 1984. "'Call the Police, Okay?' Social Comparison by Young Children During Play in Preschool." *Early Child Development and Care* 14: 201–216.

Chalufour, I., & K. Worth. 2004. *Building Structures With Young Children* (The Young Scientist Series). St. Paul, MN: Redleaf Press; Washington, DC: NAEYC.

Cheatham, G.A., & Y.E. Ro. 2010. "Young English Learners' Interlanguage as a Context for Language and Early Literacy Development." *Young Children* 65 (4): 18–23.

Chess, S., & A. Thomas. 1996. "Temperament." In *Child and Adolescent Psychiatry: A Comprehensive Textbook*, 2nd ed., ed. M. Lewis, 170–81. Baltimore: Williams & Wilkins.

Christ, T., & X.C. Wang. 2012. "Supporting Preschoolers' Vocabulary Learning: Using a Decision-Making Model to Select Appropriate Words and Methods." *Young Children* 67 (2): 74–80.

Church, E.L. 2003. "Scientific Thinking: Step-by-Step." *Scholastic Early Childhood Today* 17 (6): 35–41.

Clements, D.H. 1999. "The Effective Use of Computers With Young Children." In *Mathematics in the Early Years,* ed. J.V. Copley, 119–28. Reston, VA: National Council of Teachers of Mathematics; Washington, DC: NAEYC.

Clements, D.H. 2001. "Mathematics in the Preschool." *Teaching Children Mathematics* 7 (5): 270–75.

Clements, D.H. 2004. "Major Themes and Recommendations." In *Engaging Young Children in Mathematics: Standards for Early Childhood Mathematics Education*, eds. D.H. Clements, J. Sarama, & A.-M. DiBiase, 7–72. Mahwah, NJ: Erlbaum.

Clements, D.H., & J. Sarama. 2009. *Learning and Teaching Early Math: The Learning Trajectories Approach*. New York: Routledge.

Colker, L.J. 2005. *The Cooking Book: Fostering Young Children's Learning and Delight*. Washington, DC: NAEYC.

Colker, L.J. 2013. "A Place for Building Your Community." *Teaching Young Children* 7 (1): 18–19.

Collaborative for Academic, Social, and Emotional Learning (CASEL). 2013. *2013 CASEL Guide: Effective Social and Emotional Learning Programs: Preschool and Elementary School Edition.* Chicago: Collaborative for Academic, Social, and Emotional Learning. www.casel.org/guide/.

Collins, M.F. 2012. "Sagacious, Sophisticated, and Sedulous: The Importance of Using 50-Cent Words With Preschoolers." *Young Children* 67 (5): 66–71.

Copley, J.V., ed. 2004. *Showcasing Mathematics for the Young Child: Activities for Three-, Four-, and Five-Year-Olds.* Reston, VA: National Council of Teachers of Mathematics.

Copley, J.V. 2010. *The Young Child and Mathematics,* 2nd ed. Washington, DC: NAEYC; Reston, VA: National Council for Teachers of Mathematics.

Copple, C., & S. Bredekamp. 2006. *Basics of Developmentally Appropriate Practice: An Introduction for Teachers of Children 3 to 6.* Washington, DC: NAEYC.

Copple, C., & S. Bredekamp, eds. 2009. *Developmentally Appropriate Practice in Early Childhood Programs Serving Children From Birth Through Age 8.* 3rd ed. Washington, DC: NAEYC.

Corsaro, W., & L. Molinari. 2005. *I Compagni: Understanding Children's Transition From Preschool to Elementary School.* New York: Teachers College Press.

Creasey, G.L., P.A. Jarvis, & L.E. Berk. 1998. "Play and Social Competence." In *Multiple Perspectives on Play in Early Childhood Education,* eds. O.N. Saracho & B. Spodek, 116–143. Albany: State University of New York.

Deasy, R., & L. Stevenson. 2002. *The Arts: Critical Links to Student Success.* Washington, DC: Arts Education Partnership, Council of Chief State School Officers.

De Houwer, A., M.H. Bornstein, & D.L. Putnick. 2013. "A Bilingual–Monolingual Comparison of Young Children's Vocabulary Size: Evidence From Comprehension and Production." *Applied Psycholinguistics:* 1–23. doi: 10.1017/50142716412000744

DeBruin-Parecki, A., & M. Hohmann. 2003. *Letter Links: Alphabet Learning With Children's Names.* Ypsilanti, MI: HighScope Press.

Denham, S. 2006. "The Emotional Basis of Learning and Development in Early Childhood Education." In *Handbook of Research on the Education of Young Children,* eds. B. Spodek & O.N. Saracho, 85–104. Mahwah, NJ: Erlbaum.

Derman-Sparks, L., & J.O. Edwards. 2010. *Anti-Bias Education for Young Children and Ourselves.* Washington, DC: NAEYC.

DeVries, R., & C. Sales. 2011. *Ramps & Pathways: A Constructivist Approach to Physics With Young Children.* Washington, DC: NAEYC.

Dewey, J. 1934. *Art as Experience.* New York: Perigee Books.

Dombro, A.L., J. Jablon, & C. Stetson. 2011. *Powerful Interactions: How to Connect With Children to Extend Their Learning.* Washington, DC: NAEYC.

Dow, C.B. 2010. "Young Children and Movement: The Power of Creative Dance." *Young Children* 65 (2): 30–35.

Drew, W.F., & B. Rankin. 2005. "Promoting Creativity for Life Using Open-Ended Materials." In *Spotlight on Young Children and the Creative Arts,* ed. D. Koralek, 32–39. Washington, DC: NAEYC.

Driscoll, K.C., A.J. Mashburn, L. Wang, & R.C. Pianta. 2011. "Fostering Supportive Teacher–Child Relationships: Intervention Implementation in a State-Funded Preschool Program." *Early Education and Development* 22 (4): 593–619. doi:10.1080/10409289.2010.502015

Dweck, C.S. 2002. "The Development of Ability Conceptions." In *Development of Achievement Motivation,* eds. A. Wigfield & J.S. Eccles, 57–90. San Diego, CA: Academic Press.

Eisner, E.W. 2004. *The Arts and the Creation of Mind*. New Haven, CT: Yale University Press.

Elias, M.J., J.E. Zins, R.P. Weissberg, K.S. Frey, M.T. Greenberg, N.M. Haynes, R. Kessler, M.E. Schwab-Stone, & T.P. Shriver. 1997. *Promoting Social and Emotional Learning: Guidelines for Educators*. Alexandria, VA: ASCD.

Epstein, A.S. 1993. *Training for Quality: Improving Early Childhood Programs Through Systematic Inservice Training*. Ypsilanti, MI: HighScope Press.

Epstein, A.S. 2003. "How Planning and Reflection Develop Young Children's Thinking Skills." *Young Children* 58 (5): 28–36.

Epstein, A.S. 2009a. *Me, You, Us: Social-Emotional Learning in Preschool*. Ypsilanti, MI: HighScope Press; Washington, DC: NAEYC.

Epstein, A.S. 2009b. *Numbers Plus Preschool Mathematics Curriculum*. Ypsilanti, MI: HighScope Press.

Epstein, A.S. 2012a. *The HighScope Preschool Curriculum: Approaches to Learning*. Ypsilanti, MI: HighScope Press.

Epstein, A.S. 2012b. *The HighScope Preschool Curriculum: Creative Arts*. Ypsilanti, MI: HighScope Press.

Epstein, A.S. 2012c. *The HighScope Preschool Curriculum: Physical Development and Health*. Ypsilanti, MI: HighScope Press.

Epstein, A.S. & M. Hohmann. 2012. *The HighScope Preschool Curriculum*. Ypsilanti, MI: HighScope Press.

Epstein, A.S., & E. Trimis. 2002. *Supporting Young Artists: The Development of the Visual Arts in Young Children*. Ypsilanti, MI: HighScope Press.

Eshach, H., & M.N. Fried. 2005. "Should Science Be Taught in Early Childhood?" *Journal of Science Education and Technology* 14 (3): 315–36.

Espinosa, L. 1992. "The Process of Change: The Redwood City Story." In *Reaching Potentials (Volume 1): Appropriate Curriculum and Assessment for Young Children,* eds. S. Bredekamp & T. Rosegrant, 159–66. Washington, DC: NAEYC.

Espinosa, L. 2010. *Getting It RIGHT for Young Children From Diverse Backgrounds: Applying Research to Improve Practice*. Boston: Pearson Learning Solutions; Washington, DC: NAEYC.

Espinosa, L. 2013. *PreK-3rd: Challenging Common Myths About Dual Language Learners (PreK-3rd Policy to Action Brief No. 10)*. New York: Foundation for Child Development. http://fcd-us.org/sites/default/files/Challenging%20Common%20Myths%20Update.pdf.

Evans, B. 2002. *You Can't Come to My Birthday Party! Conflict Resolution With Young Children*. Ypsilanti, MI: HighScope Press.

Evans, B. 2005. "'Bye Mommy! Bye Daddy!' Easing Separations for Preschoolers." In *Supporting Young Learners 4: Ideas for Child Care Providers and Teachers*, eds. N.A. Brickman, H. Barton, & J. Burd, 49–57. Ypsilanti, MI: HighScope Press.

Fantuzzo, J.W., M.A. Perry, & P. McDermott. 2004. "Preschool Approaches to Learning and Their Relationship to Other Relevant Classroom Competencies for Low-Income Children." *School Psychology Quarterly* 19 (3): 212–230. doi:10.1521/scpq.19.3.212.40276

Fernald, A., V.A. Marchman, & A. Weisleder. 2012. "SES Differences in Language Processing Skill and Vocabulary Are Evident at 18 Months." *Developmental Science* 16 (2): 234–48. doi: 10.1111/desc.12019

Fight Crime: Invest in Kids. 2000. *America's Child Care Crisis: A Crime Prevention Tragedy*. Washington, DC: Fight Crime: Invest in Kids.

Fight Crime: Invest in Kids. 2013. *From America's Front Line Against Crime: Proven Investments in Kids Will Prevent Crime and Violence*. Washington, DC: Fight Crime: Invest in Kids. www.fightcrime.org/wp-content/uploads/sites/default/files/violence_reports/Our%20Plan%20to%20Reduce%20Crime%20and%20Violence.pdf.

Flavell, J.H., P.H. Miller, & S.A. Miller. 2001. *Cognitive Development.* 4th ed. New York: Prentice Hall.

Fox, J.E., & R. Schirrmacher. 2012. *Art and Creative Development for Young Children.* 7th ed. Belmont, CA: Wadsworth.

Fox, L., & R.H. Lentini. 2006. "'You Got It!' Teaching Social and Emotional Skills." *Young Children* 61 (6): 36–42.

French, L. 2004. "Science as the Center of a Coherent, Integrated Early Childhood Curriculum." *Early Childhood Research Quarterly* 19 (1): 138–49. doi: 10.1016/j.ecresq.2004.01.004

Gallahue, D.L. 1995. "Transforming Physical Education Curriculum." In *Reaching Potentials (Volume 2): Transforming Early Childhood Curriculum and Assessment*, eds. S. Bredekamp & T. Rosegrant, 125–44. Washington, DC: NAEYC.

Gambrell, L.B., & S.A. Mazzoni. 1999. "Emergent Literacy: What Research Reveals About Learning to Read." In *The Early Childhood Curriculum: Current Findings in Theory and Practice,* 3rd ed., ed. C. Seefeldt, 80–105. New York: Teachers College Press.

Gandini, L., L. Hill, L. Cadwell, & C. Schwall. 2005. *In the Spirit of the Studio: Learning From the Atelier of Reggio Emilia.* New York: Teachers College Press.

Gardner, H. 1991. *The Unschooled Mind: How Children Think and How Schools Should Teach.* New York: Basic Books.

Gartrell, D. 2012. *Education for a Civil Society: How Guidance Teaches Young Children Democratic Life Skills.* Washington, DC: NAEYC.

Geist, K., & E.A. Geist 2008. "Do-Re-Mi, 1, 2, 3—That's How Easy Math Can Be: Using Music to Support Emergent Mathematics." *Young Children* 63 (2): 20–25.

Geist, K., E.A. Geist, & K. Kuznik. 2012. "The Patterns of Music: Young Children Learning Mathematics Through Beat, Rhythm, and Melody." *Young Children* 67 (1): 74–79.

Gelman, R., & K. Brenneman. 2004. "Science Learning Pathways for Young Children." *Early Childhood Research Quarterly* 19 (1): 150–58.

Gelman, R., & C.R. Gallistel. 1978. *The Child's Understanding of Number.* Cambridge, MA: Harvard University Press.

Genishi, C., & A.H. Dyson. 2009. *Children, Language, and Literacy: Diverse Learners in Diverse Times.* New York: Teachers College Press; Washington, DC: NAEYC.

Genishi, C., & R. Fassler. 1999. "Oral Language in the Early Childhood Classroom: Building on Diverse Foundations." In *The Early Childhood Curriculum: Current Findings in Theory and Practice,* 3rd ed., ed. C. Seefeldt, 54–79. New York: Teachers College Press.

Geography Education Standards Project (GESP). 1994. *Geography for Life: National Education Standards—1994.* Washington, DC: Geography Education Standards Project.

Gerecke, K., & P. Weatherby. 2001. "HighScope Strategies for Specific Disabilities." In *Supporting Young Learners 3: Ideas for Child Care Providers and Teachers*, ed. N.A. Brickman, 255–66. Ypsilanti, MI: HighScope Press.

Ginsburg, H.P., J. Cannon, J. Eisenband, & S. Pappas. 2006. "Mathematical Thinking and Learning." In *The Blackwell Handbook of Early Childhood Development*, eds. K. McCartney & D. Phillips, 208–20. Malden, MA: Blackwell Publishing.

Ginsburg, H.P., & S.L. Golbeck. 2004. "Thoughts on the Future of Research on Mathematics and Science Learning and Education." *Early Childhood Research Quarterly* 19 (1): 190–200. doi: 10.1016/jeqresq.2004.01.013

Ginsburg, H.P., N. Inoue, & K.-H. Seo. 1999. "Young Children Doing Mathematics: Observations of Everyday Activities." In *Mathematics in the Early Years*, ed. J.V. Copley, 88–99. Reston, VA: National Council of Teachers of Mathematics; Washington, DC: NAEYC.

Goleman, D. 1995. *Emotional Intelligence.* New York: Random House.

Graham, G., S. Holt/Hale, & M. Parker. 2004. *Children Moving: A Reflective Approach to Teaching Physical Education*. St. Louis, MO: McGraw-Hill.

Graves, M. 1996. "Classification: Collecting, Sorting, and Organizing." In *Supporting Young Learners 2: Ideas for Child Care Providers and Teachers*, ed. N.A. Brickman, 207–214. Ypsilanti, MI: HighScope Press.

Greenes, C. 1999. "Ready to Learn: Developing Young Children's Mathematical Powers." In *Mathematics in the Early Years*, ed. J.V. Copley, 39–47. Reston, VA: National Council of Teachers of Mathematics; Washington, DC: NAEYC.

Greenes, C., H.P. Ginsburg, & R. Balfanz. 2004. "Big Math for Little Kids." *Early Childhood Research Quarterly* 19 (1): 159–166. doi: 10.1016/j.ecresq.2004.01/010

Greer, W.D. 1984. "Discipline-Based Art Education: Approaching Art as a Subject of Study." *Studies in Art Education* 25 (4): 212–18.

Gronlund, G. 2006. *Make Early Learning Standards Come Alive: Connecting Your Practice and Curriculum to State Guidelines*. St. Paul, MN: Redleaf Press; Washington, DC: NAEYC.

Guernsey, L. 2012. *Screen Time: How Electronic Media—From Baby Videos to Educational Software—Affects Your Young Child*. New York: Basic Books.

Harris, V. 1991. "The Playground: An Outdoor Setting for Learning." In *Supporting Young Learners: Ideas for Preschool and Day Care Providers*, eds. N.A. Brickman & L.S. Taylor, 167–73. Ypsilanti, MI: HighScope Press.

Hart, B., & T. Risley. 1995. *Meaningful Differences in the Everyday Experience of Young American Children*. Baltimore: Brookes.

Haugen, K. 2010. "Learning to Use Tools and Learning Through Tools: Brain Development and Tool Use." *Exchange* 32 (5), 50–52.

Healy, J.M. 1994. *Your Child's Growing Mind: A Practical Guide to Brain Development and Learning From Birth to Adolescence*. New York: Doubleday.

Heckman, J.J., & D.V. Masterov. 2007. "The Productivity Argument for Investing in Young Children." *Review of Agricultural Economics* 29 (3): 446–93.

Helm, J.H., & L. Katz. 2011. *Young Investigators: The Project Approach in the Early Years*. 2nd ed. New York: Teachers College Press; Washington, DC: NAEYC.

HighScope Educational Research Foundation. 2004. *Growing Readers Early Literacy Curriculum*. Ypsilanti, MI: HighScope Press.

Hildreth, G. 1936. "Developmental Sequences in Name Writing." *Child Development* 7: 291–303.

Hoffman, M. 2000. *Empathy and Moral Development: Implications for Caring and Justice*. New York: Cambridge University Press.

Hohmann, M. 2005. "Vocabulary-Building Strategies." In *Supporting Young Learners 4: Ideas for Child Care Providers and Teachers*, eds. N.A. Brickman, H. Barton, & J. Burd, 245–52. Ypsilanti, MI: HighScope Press.

Howes, C. 1988. "Peer Interaction of Young Children." *Monographs of the Society for Research in Child Development*, 53 (1): 1–92.

Huffman, J.M., & C. Fortenberry. 2011. "Helping Preschoolers Prepare for Writing: Developing Fine Motor Skills." *Young Children* 66 (5): 100–103.

Hyson, M. 2000. "Is It Okay to Have Calendar Time? Look Up to the Star . . . Look Within Yourself." *Young Children* 55 (6): 60–61.

Hyson, M., ed. 2003. *Preparing Early Childhood Professionals: NAEYC's Standards for Programs*. Washington, DC: NAEYC.

Hyson, M. 2004. *The Emotional Development of Young Children: Building an Emotion-Centered Curriculum*. 2nd ed. New York: Teachers College Press.

Hyson, M. 2008. *Enthusiastic and Engaged Learners: Approaches to Learning in the Early Child-hood Classroom*. New York: Teachers College Press; Washington, DC: NAEYC.

International Reading Association (IRA). 2005. "Literacy Development in the Preschool Years." Position statement. Newark, DE: International Reading Association. www.reading. org/Libraries/position-statements-and-resolutions/ps1066_preschool.pdf.

International Reading Association (IRA) & NAEYC. 1998. "Learning to Read and Write: Devel-opmentally Appropriate Practices for Young Children." Joint position statement. Wash-ington, DC: NAEYC. www.naeyc.org/files/naeyc/file/positions/PSREAD98.PDF.

Iruka, I.U., & P.R. Carver. 2006. *Initial Results From the 2005 NHES Early Childhood Program Par-ticipation Survey (NCES 2006-075)*. Washington, DC: US Department of Education, National Center for Education Statistics.

Jantz, R.K., & C. Seefeldt. 1999. "Early Childhood Social Studies." In *The Early Childhood Curriculum: Current Findings in Theory and Practice*, 3rd ed., ed. C. Seefeldt, 159–78. New York: Teachers College Press.

Kagan, J. 2005. "Temperament and the Reactions to Unfamiliarity." In *Readings on the De-velopment of Children*, 4th ed., eds. M. Gauvain & M. Cole, 73–78. New York: Worth Publishers.

Kagan, S.L., E. Moore, & S. Bredekamp, eds. 1995, June. *Reconsidering Children's Early Devel-opment and Learning: Toward Common Views and Vocabulary*. Goal 1 Technical Planning Group Report 95-03. Washington, DC: National Education Goals Panel.

Kaiser, B., & J.S. Rasminsky. 1999. *Meeting the Challenge: Effective Strategies for Challeng-ing Behaviours in Early Childhood Environments*. Ottawa, Ontario: Canadian Child Care Federation.

Kamii, C. 2000. *Young Children Reinvent Arithmetic*. 2nd ed. New York: Teachers College Press.

Katz, L. 1993. *Dispositions, Definitions, and Implications for Early Childhood Practice*. Cham-paign, IL: ERIC Clearinghouse on Elementary and Early Childhood Education.

Katz, L.G., & S.C. Chard. 2000. *Engaging Children's Minds: The Project Approach*. 2nd ed. Green-wich, CT: Ablex.

Katz, L.G., & D.E. McClellan. 1997. *Fostering Children's Social Competence: The Teacher's Role*. Washington, DC: NAEYC.

Kellert, S.R. 2002. *Children and Nature: Psychological, Sociocultural, and Evolutionary Investiga-tions*. Cambridge, MA: MIT Press.

Kellogg, R., & S. O'Dell. 1967. *The Psychology of Children's Art*. New York: Psychology Today/ CRM-Random House.

Kemple, K.M., J.J. Batey, & L.C. Hartle. 2004. "Music Play: Creating Centers for Musical Play and Exploration." In *Spotlight on Young Children and the Creative Arts*, ed. D. Koralek, 24–31. Washington, DC: NAEYC.

Kim, J., & Robinson, H.M. 2010. "Four Steps for Becoming Familiar With Early Music Stan-dards." *Young Children* 65 (2): 42–47.

Kindler, A.M. 2005. "Art and Art in Early Childhood: What Can Young Children Learn From 'a/ Art Activities?'" *International Art in Early Childhood Research Journal*, 2 (1): 1–14.

Kolodziej, S. 1995. "The Picture Museum: Creating a Photography Museum With Children." In *The Visual Arts and Early Childhood Learning*, ed. C.M. Thompson, 52–55. Reston, VA: National Art Education Association.

Kontos, S., C. Howes, B. Shinn, & E. Galinsky. 1994. *Quality in Family Child Care and Relative Care*. New York: Teachers College Press.

Koralek, D. 2005. "Introduction." In *Spotlight on Young Children and the Creative Arts*, ed. D. Koralek, 2–3. Washington, DC: NAEYC.

Ladd, G.W., Herald, S.L., & Andrews, R.K. 2006. "Young Children's Peer Relations and Social Competence." In *Handbook of Research on the Education of Young Children*, 2nd ed., eds. B. Spodek & O.N. Saracho, 23–54. Mahwah, NJ: Lawrence Erlbaum.

LaMore, R., R. Root-Bernstein, M. Root-Bernstein, J.H. Schweitzer, J.L. Lawton, E. Roraback, A. Peruski, M. VanDyke, & L. Fernandez. 2013. "Arts and Crafts: Critical to Economic Innovation." *Economic Development Quarterly* 27 (3): 221–29. doi:10.1177/0891242413486186

Landry, C.E., & G.E. Forman. 1999. "Research on Early Science Education." In *The Early Childhood Curriculum: Current Findings in Theory and Practice*, 3rd ed., ed. C. Seefeldt, 133–57. New York: Teachers College Press.

Langer, J., S. Rivera, M. Schlesinger, & A. Wakeley. 2003. "Early Cognitive Development: Ontogeny and Phylogeny." In *Handbook of Developmental Psychology*, eds. J. Valsiner & K. Connolly, 141–71. London: Sage.

Levin, D.E. 2003. *Teaching Young Children in Violent Times: Building a Peaceable Classroom.* Washington, DC: Educators for Social Responsibility & NAEYC.

Levin, D.E. 2013. *Beyond Remote-Controlled Childhood: Teaching Young Children in the Media Age.* Washington, DC: NAEYC.

Liben, L.S., & R.M. Downs. 1993. "Understanding Person-Space-Map Relations: Cartographic and Developmental Perspectives." *Developmental Psychology* 29 (4): 739–52. doi:10.1037/0012-1649.29.4.739

Li-Grining, C., C. Maldonado-Carreno, E. Votruba-Drzal, & K. Haas. 2010. "Children's Early Approaches to Learning and Academic Trajectories Through Fifth Grade." *Developmental Psychology* 46 (5): 1062–77.

Manross, M.A. 2000. "Learning to Throw in Physical Education Class: Part 3." *Teaching Elementary Physical Education* 11 (3): 26–29.

Matlock, R. & J. Hornstein. 2005. "Saber-Toothed Tiger: Learning and the Arts Through the Ages." In *Spotlight on Young Children and the Creative Arts*, ed. D. Koralek, 6–11. Washington, DC: NAEYC.

Mayer, R.H. 1995. "Inquiry Into Place as an Introduction to World Geography—Starting With Ourselves." *Social Studies* 86: 74–77.

McMullen, M.B., J.M. Addleman, A.M. Fulford, S.L. Moore, S.J. Mooney, S.S. Sisk, & J. Zachariah. 2009. "Learning to Be *Me* While Coming to Understand *We*." *Young Children* 64 (4): 20–27.

Medina, J. 2008. *Brain Rules: 12 Principles for Surviving and Thriving at Work, Home, and School.* Seattle, WA: Pear Press.

Miles, L.R. 2009. "The General Store: Reflections on Children at Play." *Young Children* 64 (4): 36–41.

Mindes, G. 2005. "Social Studies in Today's Early Childhood Curricula." *Young Children* 60 (5): 12–18.

Mitchell, L.C. 2005. "Making the MOST of Creativity in Activities for Young Children With Disabilities." In *Spotlight on Young Children and the Creative Arts*, ed. D. Koralek, 40–43. Washington, DC: NAEYC.

Mitchell, L.S. 1934. *Young Geographers*. New York: Bank Street College.

Mix, K.S., S.C. Levine, & J. Huttenlocher. 1999. "Early Fraction Calculation Ability." *Developmental Psychology* 35 (1): 164–74.

Montie, J.E., Z. Xiang, & L.J. Schweinhart. 2006. "Preschool Experience in 10 Countries: Cognitive and Language Performance at Age 7." *Early Childhood Research Quarterly* 21 (3), 313–331. doi:10.1016/j.ecresq.2006.07.007

NAEYC. 2001. "NAEYC Standards for Early Childhood Professional Preparation: Initial Licensure Programs." Washington, DC: NAEYC. www.naeyc.org/files/ncate/file/faculty/initalLicensureProg.pdf.

NAEYC. 2007. "NAEYC Early Childhood Program Standards and Accreditation Criteria: The Mark of Quality in Early Childhood Education." Washington, DC: NAEYC.

NAEYC & Fred Rogers Center for Early Learning and Children's Media. 2012. "Technology and Interactive Media as Tools in Early Childhood Programs Serving Children From Birth Through Age 8." Joint position statement. Washington, DC: NAEYC.

NAEYC & National Association of Early Childhood Specialists in State Departments of Education (NAECS/SDE). 1991. "Guidelines for Appropriate Curriculum Content and Assessment in Programs Serving Children Ages 3 Through 8." Joint position statement. Washington, DC: NAEYC. www.naeyc.org/files/naeyc/file/positions/PSCAG98.PDF.

NAEYC & National Association of Early Childhood Specialists in State Departments of Education (NAECS/SDE). 2003. "Early Childhood Curriculum, Assessment, and Program Evaluation: Building an Effective, Accountable System in Programs for Children Birth Through Age 8." Joint position statement. Washington, DC: NAEYC. www.naeyc.org/files/naeyc/file/positions/CAPEexpand.pdf.

NAEYC & National Council of Teachers of Mathematics (NCTM). 2010. "Early Childhood Mathematics: Promoting Good Beginnings." Joint position statement. Washington, DC: NAEYC. www.naeyc.org/files/naeyc/file/positions/psmath.pdf.

National Art Education Association. 1982. *Quality Goals Statement*. Washington, DC: National Art Education Association.

National Association for Sport and Physical Education (NASPE). 2002. *Active Start: A Statement of Physical Activity Guidelines for Children Birth to Five Years*. Reston, VA: National Association for Sport and Physical Education.

National Association for Sport and Physical Education (NASPE). 2009a. *Active Start: A Statement of Physical Activity Guidelines for Children Birth to Five Years*. 2nd ed. Reston, VA: National Association for Sport and Physical Education.

National Association for Sport and Physical Education (NASPE). 2009b. *Appropriate Practices in Movement Programs for Children Ages 3–5*. 3rd ed. Reston, VA: National Association for Sport and Physical Education.

National Center for Health Statistics. 2004. *Health, United States, 2004*. Hyattsville, MD: National Center for Health Statistics.

National Committee on Science Education Standards and Assessment (NCSESA), National Research Council. 1996. *National Science Education Standards*. Washington, DC: The National Academies Press. www.csun.edu/science/ref/curriculum/reforms/nses/nses-complete.pdf.

National Council for the Social Studies (NCSS). 1984. "Social Studies for Young Children." Position statement. Silver Spring, MD: National Council for the Social Studies.

National Council for the Social Studies (NCSS). 2010. *National Curriculum Standards for the Social Studies: A Framework for Teaching, Learning, and Assessment*. Silver Spring, MD: National Council for the Social Studies.

National Council of Teachers of Mathematics (NCTM). 2000. *Principles and Standards for School Mathematics*. Reston, VA: National Council of Teachers of Mathematics. www.nctm.org/standards/.

National Council of Teachers of Mathematics (NCTM). 2006. *Curriculum Focal Points for Prekindergarten Through Grade 8 Mathematics: A Quest for Coherence*. Reston, VA: National Council of Teachers of Mathematics.

National Education Goals Panel. 1994. *Goals 2000: Educate America Act*. Washington, DC: US Government Printing Office.

National Endowment for the Arts. 1988. *Toward Civilization: A Report on Arts Education*. Washington, DC: US Government Printing Office.

National Governors Association. 2013. *A Governor's Guide to Early Literacy: Getting All Students Reading by Third Grade.* Washington, DC: National Governors Association. www. nga.org/files/live/sites/NGA/files/pdf/2013/1310NGAEarlyLiteracyReportWeb.pdf.

National Governors Association Center for Best Practices & Council of Chief State School Officers. 2010. *Common Core State Standards for English Language Arts and Literacy in History/Social Studies, Science, and Technical Subjects.* Washington, DC: National Governors Association Center for Best Practices & Council of Chief State School Officers. www. corestandards.org/assets/CCSSI_ELA%20Standards.pdf.

National Mathematics Advisory Panel. 2008. *Foundations for Success: The Final Report of the National Mathematics Advisory Panel.* Washington, DC: US Department of Education.

National Reading Panel (NRP). 2000. *Teaching Children to Read: An Evidence-Based Assessment of the Scientific Research Literature on Reading and Its Implications for Reading Instruction.* Washington, DC: National Institute of Child Health and Human Development, National Institutes of Health.

National Research Council. 2000a. *Eager to Learn: Educating Our Preschoolers.* Washington, DC: The National Academies Press.

National Research Council. 2000b. *From Neurons to Neighborhoods: The Science of Early Childhood Development.* Washington, DC: The National Academies Press.

National Research Council. 2009. *Mathematics Learning in Early Childhood: Paths Toward Excellence and Equity.* Washington, DC: The National Academies Press.

Neill, P. 2008. *Real Science in Preschool: Here, There, and Everywhere.* Ypsilanti, MI: HighScope Press.

Neill, P. 2013. "Open-Ended Materials Belong Outside Too." *HighScope Extensions Newsletter* 27 (2): 1–8.

Nemeth, K.N. 2012. *Basics of Supporting Dual Language Learners: An Introduction for Educators of Children From Birth Through Age 8.* Washington, DC: NAEYC.

Neuman, S.B., C. Copple, & S. Bredekamp. 2000. *Learning to Read and Write: Developmentally Appropriate Practices for Young Children.* Washington, DC: NAEYC.

Next Generation Science Standards (NGSS) Lead States. 2013. *Next Generation Science Standards: For States, By States.* Washington, DC: The National Academies Press.

Nicolopoulou, A. & E.S. Richner. 2007. "From Actors to Agents to Persons: The Development of Character Representation in Young Children's Narratives." *Child Development* 78 (2): 412–429.

No Child Left Behind Act of 2001. Pub. L. 107-110, 115 Stat. 1425 (Jan. 8, 2002).

Paley, V.G. 2004. *A Child's Work: The Importance of Fantasy Play.* Chicago: University of Chicago Press.

Perrett, B. 1996. "Group Times: What Makes Them Work?" In *Supporting Young Learners 2: Ideas for Child Care Providers and Teachers,* ed. N.A. Brickman, 71–76. Ypsilanti, MI: HighScope Press.

Phillips, E.C., & A. Scrinzi. 2013. *Basics of Developmentally Appropriate Practice: An Introduction for Teachers of Kindergartners.* Washington, DC: NAEYC.

Piaget, J. [1932] 1965. *The Moral Judgment of the Child.* New York: The Free Press.

Piaget, J. 1950. *The Psychology of Intelligence.* London: Routledge.

Pianta, R.C. 2003. *Standardized Classroom Observations From Pre-K to 3rd Grade: A Mechanism for Improving Access to Consistently High Quality Classroom Experiences and Practices During the P–3 Years.* New York: Foundation for Child Development.

Pica, R. 1997. "Beyond Physical Development: Why Young Children Need to Move." *Young Children* 52 (6): 4–11.

Pica, R. 2009. "Can Movement Promote Creativity?" *Young Children* 64 (4): 60–61.

Pinciotti, P. 2006. "Changing Lenses: It's All About Art!" In *Curriculum—Art, Music, Movement, Drama: A Beginnings Workshop Book*, ed. B. Neugebauer, 11–14. Redmond, WA: Exchange.

Post, J., M. Hohmann, & A.S. Epstein.2011. *Tender Care and Early Learning: Supporting Infants and Toddlers in Child Care Settings*. 2nd ed. Ypsilanti, MI: HighScope Press.

Povinelli, D.J., A.M. Landry, L.A. Theall, B.R. Clark, & C.M. Castille. 1999. "Development of Young Children's Understanding That the Recent Past Is Causally Bound to the Present." *Developmental Psychology* 35 (6): 1426–1439.

Quann, V., & C.A. Wien. 2014. "The Visible Empathy of Infants and Toddlers." In *The Power of Emergent Curriculum: Stories From Early Childhood Settings,* ed. C.A. Wien, 65–77. Washington, DC: NAEYC.

Ranweiler, L. 2004. *Preschool Readers and Writers: Early Literacy Strategies for Teachers*. Ypsilanti, MI: HighScope Press.

Raver, C.C., C. Izard, & C.B. Kopp. 2002. "Emotions Matter: Making the Case for the Role of Young Children's Emotional Development for Early School Readiness." *Society for Research in Child Development Social Policy Report* 16 (3): 1–19.

Reusable Resources Association. 2014. "List of Resource Centers." http://www.reuseresources. org/find-a-center.html.

Reuse Alliance. 2011. "An Overview of Creative Reuse Centers." http://www.reusealliance.org/ wp-content/uploads/RA-Creative-Reuse-Centers-Overview-8-11.pdf.

Reynolds, A.J., J.A. Temple, D.L. Robertson, & E.A. Mann. 2001. "Long-Term Effects of an Early Childhood Intervention on Educational Achievement and Juvenile Arrest: A 15-Year Follow-Up of Low-Income Children in Public Schools." *Journal of the American Medical Association* 285 (18): 2339–46.

Riley, S.M. & L. Munson. 2013, February. *Art and the Common Core (Education Week Webinar)*. http://www.aep-arts.org/wp-content/uploads/2013/02/Education-Week-Webinar-Slides.pdf.

Rogoff, B. 2003. *The Cultural Nature of Human Development*. New York: Oxford University Press.

Rothbart, M.K., & J.E. Bates. 2006. "Temperament." In *Handbook of Child Psychology (Volume 3): Social, Emotional, and Personality Development*, ed. N. Eisenberg, 99–166. New York: Wiley.

Rowe, D. 1994. *Preschoolers as Authors: Literacy Learning in the Social World*. Cresskill, NJ: Hampton Press.

Sanders, S.W. 1992. *Designing Preschool Movement Programs*. Champaign, IL: Human Kinetics.

Sanders, S.W. 2002. *Active for Life: Developmentally Appropriate Movement Programs for Young Children*. Washington, DC: NAEYC.

Sanders, S.W. 2006. "Physical Education In Kindergarten." In *K Today: Teaching and Learning in the Kindergarten Year*, ed. D. Gullo, 127–37. Washington, DC: NAEYC

Sawyers, K.S. (With E. Colley & L. Icaza). 2010. *Moving With Purpose: 54 Activities for Learning, Fitness, and Fun*. Ypsilanti, MI: HighScope Press.

Schickendanz, J.A., & M.F. Collins. 2013. *So Much More Than the ABCs: The Early Phases of Reading and Writing*. Washington DC: NAEYC.

Schunk, D.H., & F. Pajares. 2005. "Competence Perceptions and Academic Functioning." In *Handbook of Competence and Motivation*, eds. A.J. Elliott & C.S. Dweck, 85–104. New York: Guilford.

Schweinhart, L.J., J. Montie, Z. Xiang, W.S. Barnett, C.R. Belfield, & M. Nores. 2005. *Lifetime Effects: The HighScope Perry Preschool Study Through Age 40*. Ypsilanti, MI: HighScope Press.

Scott-Kassner, C. 1992. "Research on Music in Early Childhood." In *Handbook of Research on Music Teaching and Learning*, ed. R. Colwell, 633–50. Reston, VA: Music Educators National Conference.

Seefeldt, C., Castle, S., & Falconer, R. 2013. *Social Studies for the Preschool/Primary Child.* 9th ed. Upper Saddle River, NJ: Pearson.

Seo, K.-H. 2003. "What Children's Play Tells Us About Teaching Mathematics." *Young Children* 58 (1): 28–34.

Shillady, A., ed. 2012. *Spotlight on Young Children: Exploring Math.* Washington, DC: NAEYC.

Shore, R. 2003. *Rethinking the Brain: New Insights Into Early Development.* Rev. ed. New York: Families and Work Institute.

Simon, F. & C. Donohue. 2011. "Tools of Engagement: Status Report on Technology in Early Childhood Education." *Exchange* 199: 16–22.

Simon, F.S., & K.N. Nemeth. 2013."Using Technology as a Teaching Tool: Dual Language Learners in Preschool Through Grade 3." *Young Children* 68 (1): 48 –52.

Sims, W. L. (1985). "Young Children's Creative Movement to Music: Categories of Movement, Rhythmic Characteristics, and Reactions to Change." *Contributions to Music Education, 12,* 42–50.

Snow, C.E., M.S. Burns, & P. Griffin, eds. 1998. *Preventing Reading Difficulties in Young Children.* Washington, DC: National Academy of Sciences.

Sobel, D. 2008. *Children and Nature: Design Principles for Educators.* Portland, ME: Stenhouse.

Spinrad, T.L., & C.A. Stifter. 2006. "Toddlers' Empathy-Related Responding to Distress: Predictions From Negative Emotionality and Maternal Behavior in Infancy." *Infancy* 10 (2): 97–121.

Stellaccio, C.K., & M. McCarthy. 1999. "Research in Early Childhood Music and Movement Education." In *The Early Childhood Curriculum: Current Findings in Theory and Practice*, 3rd ed., ed. C. Seefeldt, 179–200. New York: Teachers College Press.

Stipek, D. 2002. *Motivation to Learn: Integrating Theory and Practice.* 4th ed. Boston: Allyn & Bacon.

Stipek, D., A. Shoenfeld, & D. Gomby. 2012. "Math Matters, Even for Little Kids." *Education Week*, March 28.

Strauss, V. 2013. "Literacy Experts Say Reformers Reviving 'Reading Wars.'" *The Washington Post*, August 13. www.washingtonpost.com/blogs/answer-sheet/wp/2013/08/13/are-reformers-reviving-reading-wars/.

Strickland, D.S., & T. Shanahan. 2004. "Laying the Groundwork for Literacy." *Educational Leadership* 6 (6), 74–77.

Strubank, R. 1991. "Movement and Music Throughout the Daily Routine." In *Supporting Young Learners: Ideas for Preschool and Day Care Providers*, eds. N.A. Brickman & L.S. Taylor, 104–11. Ypsilanti, MI: HighScope Press.

Tabors, P.O. 2008. *One Child, Two Languages: A Guide for Early Childhood Educators of Children Learning English as a Second Language.* 2nd ed. Baltimore: Brookes.

The Task Force on Children's Learning and the Arts & S. Goldhawk. 1998. *Young Children and the Arts: Making Creative Connections.* Washington, DC: Arts Education Partnership. www.artsdel.org/ArtsEducation/YoungChildren.pdf.

Taunton, M., & M. Colbert. 2000. "Art in the Early Childhood Classroom: Authentic Experiences and Extended Dialogues." In *Promoting Meaningful Learning: Innovations in Educating Early Childhood Professionals*, ed. N.J. Yelland, 67–76. Washington, DC: NAEYC.

Tegano, D., J. Moran, A. DeLong, J. Brickley, & K. Ramanssini. 1996. "Designing Classroom Spaces: Making the Most of Time." *Early Childhood Education Journal* 23 (3): 135–41.

Thompson, R.A. 2002. "The Roots of School Readiness in Social and Emotional Development." *The Kauffman Early Education Exchange* 1, 8–29.

Thornton, S., & R. Vukelich. 1988. "Effects of Children's Understanding of Time Concepts on Historical Understanding." *Theory and Research in Social Education, 16,* 69–82.

Tomlinson, H.B., & M. Hyson. 2009. "Developmentally Appropriate Practice in the Preschool Years—Ages 3–5: An Overview." In *Developmentally Appropriate Practice in Early Childhood Programs Serving Children From Birth Through Age 8*, 3rd ed., eds. C. Copple & S. Bredekamp, 111–48. Washington, DC: NAEYC.

Tompkins, M. 1996a. "A Partnership With Young Artists." In *Supporting Young Learners 2: Ideas for Child Care Providers and Teachers*, ed. N.A. Brickman, 187–92. Ypsilanti, MI: HighScope Press.

Tompkins, M. 1996b. "Spatial Learning: Beyond Circles, Squares, and Triangles." In *Supporting Young Learners 2: Ideas for Child Care Providers and Teachers*, ed. N.A. Brickman, 215–22. Ypsilanti, MI: HighScope Press.

Tudge, J., & D. Caruso. 1988. "Cooperative Problem-Solving in the Classroom: Enhancing Young Children's Cognitive Development. *Young Children* 44 (1): 46–52.

Tudge, J., & F. Doucet. 2004. "Early Mathematical Experiences: Observing Young Black and White Children's Everyday Activities. *Early Childhood Research Quarterly* 19 (1), 21–39. doi: 10.1016/j.ecresq.2004.01.007

US Department of Agriculture Center for Nutrition Policy and Promotion. 2011. "Health and Nutrition Information for Preschoolers: ChooseMyPlate." Washington, DC: US Department of Agriculture. www.choosemyplate.gov/preschoolers.html.

US Department of Education. 1994. *National Standards for Arts Education: What Every Young American Should Know and Be Able to Do in the Arts*. Washington, DC: US Government Printing Office.

US Department of Health and Human Services. 2013. "The Head Start Child Development and Early Learning Framework: How Do Preschool Programs Support School Readiness?" http://eclkc.ohs.acf.hhs.gov/hslc/sr/approach/cdelf.

Van Scoy, I.J., & S.H. Fairchild. 1993. "It's About Time! Helping Preschool and Primary Children Understand Time Concepts." *Young Children* 48 (2): 21–24.

Vance, E. 2014. *Class Meetings: Young Children Solving Problems Together*. Rev. ed. Washington, DC: NAEYC.

Vygotsky, L. 1978. *Mind and Society: The Development of Higher Psychological Processes*. Cambridge, MA: Harvard University Press.

Wardle, F., & M.I. Cruz-Janzen. 2004. *Meeting the Needs of Multiethnic and Multiracial Children in Schools*. Boston: Allyn and Bacon.

Weikart, P.S. 2000. *Round the Circle: Key Experiences in Movement for Young Children*. 2nd ed. Ypsilanti, MI: HighScope Press.

West, N.T. 2005. "Art for All Children: A Conversation About Inclusion." *Exchange* 27 (5): 47–51.

White House Task Force on Childhood Obesity. 2010. *Solving the Problem of Childhood Obesity Within a Generation: Report to the President*. Washington, DC: White House Task Force on Childhood Obesity. www.letsmove.gov/sites/letsmove.gov/files/TaskForce_on_Childhood_Obesity_May2010_FullReport.pdf.

White, R., & V.L. Stoecklin. 2008, November. "Nurturing Children's Biophilia: Developmentally Appropriate Environmental Education for Young Children." *Collage: Resources for Early Childhood Educators*. www.communityplaythings.com/resources/articles/2008/nurturing-childrens-biophilia-environmental-education-for-young-children.

Whitebook, M., C. Howes, & D. Phillips. 1989. *The National Child Care Staffing Study: Who Cares? Child Care Teachers and the Quality of Care in America*. Oakland, CA: Child Care Employee Project.

World-Class Instructional Design and Assessment. 2014. "Early Language Development Standards." www.wida.us/standards/eeld.aspx#standards.

World Forum Nature Action Collaborative for Children. 2010. *Connecting the World's Children With Nature Environmental Action Kit.* World Forum Foundation. www.worldforumfoundation.org.

Worth, K., & S. Grollman. 2003. *Worms, Shadows, and Whirlpools: Science in the Early Childhood Classroom.* Portsmouth, NH: Heinemann; Washington, DC: NAEYC.

Wright, S. 2003. *The Arts, Young Children, and Learning.* Boston: Pearson.

Wyner, N., & E. Farquhar. 1991. "Cognitive, Emotional, and Social Development: Early Childhood Social Studies." In *Handbook of Research on Social Studies Teaching and Learning,* ed. J. Shaver, 101–146. New York: Macmillan.

Yoshikawa, H. 1995. "Long-Term Effects of Early Childhood Programs on Social Outcomes and Delinquency." *The Future of Children* 5 (3): 51–75.

Zelazo, P.D., & U. Mueller. 2002. "Executive Function in Typical and Atypical Development." In *Blackwell Handbook of Childhood Cognitive Development,* ed. U. Goswami, 445–69. Malden, MA: Blackwell.

Index

Number sense, 26, 132, 134–35, 138–41, 235
  defined, 243
Numeration, 138–40
  teaching strategies, 139–40
  defined, 243
Nursery rhymes, 104, 108–9, 191, 215
Nutrition, xv, 18, 65, 70, 75, 95–96, 98
  teaching strategies, 95–96

O

Obesity, 66, 98
Observing, 160, 162–63, 207, 211–12
  teaching strategies, 162–63
Obstacle courses, 89
One-to-one correspondence, 5, 26, 118–19, 132, 135–36, 138
Openness to experiences, 30–37
  adult-guided experiences, 35–37
  child-guided experiences, 33–35
  defined, 243
  engaging with ideas, 36–37
  engaging with materials, 34–35
  planning, 35–36
  taking initiative, 33–34
Opportunities for practice, 46
Order irrelevance, 138
Ordering. See Comparing and ordering
Organizing information, 153
Orthopedic impairments, 21
Other awareness, 180
Outdoor environment, 13–15, 169
Outdoor play, 16, 42, 52, 72, 78–79, 93, 103, 173, 194–95, 205, 219, 222

P

Pacing, 30, 42
  accommodating, 31
  defined, 243
Partitioning, 137, 139
Part-part-whole concept, 136
Patience, 23, 24, 31
Patterns, 2, 26, 66, 89, 127–28, 130–31, 133, 150–53, 169, 199, 210, 218, 241
  adult-guided experiences, 152–53
  child-guided experiences, 150–51
  complex, 152–53
  controlling change, 153
  creating, 150–51
  materials, 133
  naturally occurring change, 151
  simple, 150–51, 160
  teaching strategies, 150–53
Pedagogy, 7

Peer interactions, 20–21, 50, 59, 97, 105, 122, 131–32
  supporting, 22–23
Peg-Boards, 84, 92, 132
Perceptual abilities, 159
Perceptual development, 202
Persistence, 29–30, 34, 38
Personal care
  adult-guided experiences, 94–97
  child-guided experiences, 92–93
  exercising, 93
  feeding and dressing, 92–93
  healthy behaviors, 92–97
  interpersonal hygiene, 94–95
  movement concepts, 84–91
  movement skills, 76–84
  nutrition, 95–96
  physical education, 70–75
  promoting, 75–91
  safety procedures, 96–97
  washing hands and brushing teeth, 94
Perspective taking, 143, 187–88
  activities, 50
Pets, 194
Phonemic awareness, 108–9, 163
  defined, 243
Phonological awareness, 101, 103–4, 106, 108–10, 119
  defined, 243
  teaching strategies, 103–4, 108–10
Photographs, 41
Physical development, xiii, xv, 1, 46, 65–98, 237, 242, 244
  fine motor, 69–70
  gross motor, 69
  healthy behavior, 75–97
  movement concepts, 84–91
  movement skills, 76–84
  personal care routines, 70–71
  physical education environment, 71–74
  physical education interaction strategies, 74–75
  teaching and learning, 70–71
  young children's development, 67–68
Physical disabilities, 218
Physical education, 70, 98
  class size, 71–72
  equipment and materials, 72–73
  interaction strategies, 74–75
  learning environment, 71–74
  scheduling, 71
Physical environment, 12, 51
  children's play, 13